A BLUE SEA OF BLOOD

A BLUE SEA OF BLOOD

DECIPHERING THE MYSTERIOUS
FATE OF THE USS *EDSALL*

DONALD M. KEHN JR.

ZENITH PRESS

First published in 2008 by Zenith Press, an imprint of MBI Publishing Company, 400 First Avenue North, Suite 300, Minneapolis, MN 55401 USA.

Zenith Press titles are also available at discounts in bulk quantity for industrial or sales-promotional use. For details write to Special Sales Manager at MBI Publishing Company, 400 First Avenue North, Suite 300, Minneapolis, MN 55401 USA.

To find out more about our books, visit us online at www.zenithpress.com.

Designer: Chris Fayers

Printed in the United States of America

Library of Congress Cataloging-in-Publication Data

Kehn, Donald M., 1953–
  A blue sea of blood : deciphering the mysterious fate of the USS Edsall / Donald M. Kehn Jr.
     p. cm.
  Includes bibliographical references and index.
  ISBN 978-0-7603-3353-2 (hbk.)
  1. Edsall (Ship) 2. World War, 1939–1945—Naval operations, American. 3. World War, 1939–1945—Regimental histories—United States. 4. World War, 1939–1945—Campaigns—Pacific Ocean. 5. World War, 1939–1945—Campaigns—Indian Ocean. 6. Shipwrecks--Indian Ocean. I. Title.
  D774.E37K45 2008
  940.54'5973—dc22

                     2008034957

On the cover:
Top: Naval Historical Center Collections
Bottom: USS *Edsall* 1939 crew photo, taken at Shanghai. The skipper was Lt. Cmdr. A. C. J. Sabalot (second row center). His XO (on his left) was Lt. Cecil Caufield. *The Nimitz Foundation*
Spine: Detail of 1940 crew photo; at left is S2c Loren Stanford Myers, who survived the sinking of the *Edsall. Jim Nix*
On the back cover: *Naval Historical Center Collections*

In Loving Memory of Dortha Lou Wilson Kehn: *"A brave vessel"*

Contents

Prologue

A Ship's Horn Sounds Farewell

Excitement of departure: sharp whistles, a hustle of stewards and passengers, the great gasps of the ship's horn. Father would put Mother and me into our stateroom with my portable grammophone, our luggage and steamer rugs. At the last gong he would leave us on deck and stand on the pier waving us off to the brassy strains of "Over the Bounding Main." Then, with the final blasts of the horn, the hawsers were released and I could feel the great ship pull free.

—Robin Prising, *Manila, Goodbye*

A young, blond boy named Walter, his eyes crinkled against the fierce equatorial sun, sits perched upon brass railings that ring the liner's upper deck. He looks out across the flat, glassy waters of an enormous bay crowded with shipping traffic. His sharp eyes drink in the bustling activity and the multitude of vessels: squat, powerful yard tugs; rust-flecked coastal boats; low, dark ammunition and stores lighters tied up alongside the warships; several four-stack destroyers and two big cruisers whose liberty boats carry clusters of white-clad sailors to and from the port's waterfront with its seven great piers. (Sometimes the sailors hold ice cream parties for the local youngsters aboard the cruiser *Houston*.)

A colorful miscellany of small craft putter amid stout oilers, tankers, and the dozen or so stranded ships from "Dan Mark"—or so it sounded to young Walter—that couldn't go home because the "Germ-men" had taken their country from them. In the blue distance, at Sangley Point off Cavite's welter of cranes, masts, and smokestacks, beyond the break-water, is the boxy silhouette of a submarine tender. Present also are gray military transports as well as gleaming commercial steamships and pas-senger liners, some with white eagles painted on their yellow funnels. And in addition to the little harbor ferry with its funny name, *Dap-Dap*, a pair of interisland vessels from the Dela Rama line shuttle back and forth from Manila to Iloilo with students, *provincianos*, coming to the capital to attend high school. Scattered among all of these are several U.S. submarines, as sleek and plump as steel porpoises. Vessels of many shapes and sizes are ablaze under a cloud-speckled sky.

One of them is Walter's father's ship, but the boy, no more and no less recalcitrant than any ten-year-old, has deliberately disobeyed his father's strict military instructions: "*No* sitting on the fence." And when his father catches him doing precisely what he has been told not to do, a brisk spanking is administered as punishment, after which he is ban-ished to his room. Young Walter is furious, and with his pride as injured as his backside, he sulks in the family's cabin, refusing to come out again in spite of his mother's pleading. He may or may not have wondered at the length of time his mother spent talking to his father that afternoon, or the brevity of his dad's temper. Or he may have resented the attention that his younger sibling, Robert, was getting that day.

They all seemed to have done more talking than usual, but the tow-headed youngster was busy with the preoccupations of childhood. And even if he did notice anything unusual, it didn't seem serious enough to keep him from provoking his father's anger, though this, too, may have been a child's way of gaining the attention he felt he was otherwise miss-ing. It would not have been the first time a child had chosen a paddling over no attention at all from a father preoccupied by his job.

Later, when his father relents and comes at last to say goodbye, Walter obstinately refuses to see him. After the ship's whistle had blown three times announcing its departure, the father could not come back. The youngster does not see or speak with his father again that day or, for that matter, any other day. This final parting would haunt Walter Nix for the remainder of his life.

Walter's father was indeed a professional military man, a career naval officer, bound by duty. And though the family had grown used to such separations, they did not want to believe that this one would be any different. Still, they must have known otherwise. A new admiral was sending home all navy dependents without exception. A brief rebellion by resentful wives and family members was quashed by threatening to indefinitely confine their spouses to their ships without leave.

Yes, it was very different, and Walter's father, Joshua James Nix, would soon be ordered to serve in the most mortal of circumstances in one of the world's deadliest theaters. He was a lieutenant then assigned to the veteran Asiatic Fleet destroyer USS *Edsall* (DD-219). He would serve as executive officer for almost a year before being given command of that venerable flushdecker some eight weeks prior to the attacks on Pearl Harbor. Less than ninety days later, the old destroyer would vanish completely, with Joshua James Nix and his entire crew passing into oblivion; for decades they would be little more than a confused footnote.

Although Walter Nix, then a U.S. Navy captain and the assistant defense attaché in Tokyo, would himself be introduced to *Showa Tenno* (Hirohito) four decades later, he passed away in 1999 knowing far less about his father's death than he should have. Through his Japanese contacts, Walter had attempted to learn more about the mysterious end of *Edsall*, but the results were fragmentary and suspect. Any author of the fantastic would be hard-pressed to conjure a scenario as unlikely or as replete with such weighty ironies as this, yet it is but one of the many astonishing facts surrounding the history of *Edsall*, and the mystery of her fate.

Foreword

Our family never really knew what happened to its patriarch, Joshua James Nix. He was born in 1908 in Fort Worth, Texas, and raised in Memphis, Tennessee. J. J., as his wife and sons called him, was an Eagle Scout and Naval Academy graduate (Class of 1930) who went on to become the youngest destroyer skipper in the U.S. Asiatic Fleet in October 1941.

J. J. and his son Walt were close, and this shows in the 8mm home movies we were blessed to have rediscovered in 2001. This footage, which dates from 1930 through the 1950s, had been stored away by our grandmother and then by our uncle until it was found in his basement after his passing. Part of the footage, of the Asiatic Fleet ships and personnel, has recently been converted to DVD.

After my father's last duty station in Tokyo as chief of the Military Assistance Advisory Group, Japan (MAAG), from 1983 to 1985—when he retired after a thirty-one-year career—Walt brought back information from sketchy and recently translated Japanese archives that dryly recorded the *Edsall*'s last battle. He'd also had the opportunity to meet with a deck officer of one of the Japanese battleships involved in the action who recalled the battle and was happy to relay what he knew. But it was not enough to answer many questions about the fate of the crew and other details of the action. That would come later.

With the Asiatic Fleet footage of 1939 and 1940 and the information my father had brought back from Tokyo, I set up a website on the Internet about the ship and crew with more information than had ever been known before. I invited relatives of this crew to contact me and exchange information. I felt that making this available would bring closure to the many families who never received word from the navy on how their men were lost. I considered this effort a last duty that should have fallen to the commanding officer. Because he was not able to complete this obligation, I would. It was the least I could do for the men who had done their duty in the face of overwhelming odds but had the memory of their courage and accomplishments censored into oblivion.

That was 1998, and I am sorry to see that after ten years barely fifty families have responded to the website. I wonder whether the missing one hundred of these men were the last in the bloodlines of their families. I was happy to learn that there were surviving family members related to two pairs of brothers lost on that fateful day in 1942, the Parsons brothers, serving separately on the *Edsall* and the *Houston*; and the Himmelmann brothers, who both served on the *Edsall*. I was also happy to learn that several survivors found relatives through the website whom they previously didn't know they had.

I started this journey to solve the mystery of the loss of the *Edsall* almost ten years ago. A few years later, Don Kehn Jr. started a similar journey. He tried to contact me early on, but my life at the time became chaotic with the loss of the core of the Nix clan. My grandmother, father, and uncle all passed away in the span of just two years, and my mother had a stroke not long thereafter. I had to put my research on hold. Later, Don and I finally connected and started exchanging material.

Don's work was painstaking, and his dedication to the search was above and beyond the call of duty. This wasn't one of those stories for which you could march down to the national archives, copy it out of war documents, and present it as a book. This journey entailed interviewing many hard-to-find persons and digging among a worldwide group of World War II naval history enthusiasts and amateur historians. Some of the material my father brought back from Tokyo was rare, and I was happy to pass it on to Don. In my efforts, I was stunned to be able to locate one of the last men to leave *Edsall* just hours before she was lost, an Army Air Forces (AAF) pilot still living in South Carolina. His wartime exploits are enough for another book, or at least he is eligible for the title of the luckiest unlucky man alive.

Don Kehn Jr. is a member of the USS *Houston* Survivors Association, an organization that meets every year in Houston, Texas, to honor the survivors of the heavy cruiser USS *Houston* (CA-30), which was lost the same day as *Edsall*. These men, despite being incarcerated, forced into labor, given less than subsistence rations, and brutalized physically and mentally by the enemy for three years, came home and moved on with their lives (without much thanks from their countrymen).

Their group, which was started by Otto Schwarz, raises scholarship money for the descendants of *Houston*'s crew with auctions and other community activities. Without that brave group of men who, in my opinion, endured more hardship at the hands of the enemy than any other U.S. servicemen in World War II, Don would not have been able to accomplish what he did in unraveling the mystery of *Edsall*. His fifteen-year association with the group, in addition to a lifetime of interest in the Asiatic Fleet, gave him the background to accomplish this work.

Regarding the USS *Houston* survivors, anyone in the presence of these men can sense the strength of character that sustained them through their ordeal. That strength is matched only by the courage displayed by other U.S. naval heroes such as John Sydney McCain and the men he was confined with, who suffered similarly while in captivity in North Vietnam. They kept themselves going in much the same way the men of the USS *Houston* kept one another going.

My sister and I helped look after the McCain children from time to time in those dark days of the late 1960s because we shared the same community of navy families based at Cecil Field outside Jacksonville, Florida. I recall a sense of connectedness in the families, one which revered honor and duty and is rarely seen in the civilian world. The last time I saw this was at my father's funeral, when the men of his squadron, VA 36, who had fought together over the skies of Vietnam and still meet every year, came to support us as my father was laid to rest at Arlington National Cemetery.

I was greatly inspired to see the collective support among families of the survivors of the USS *Houston*. My thanks to Val Poss, Otto Schwarz, and others for bringing along Don's education, so to speak. Other *Edsall* next of kin and I were welcomed by the group several years ago. Many of these USS *Houston* survivors remembered looking over the side of the USS *Houston* while on wartime patrol and seeing the *Edsall* on antisubmarine escort. The extra protection provided by the *Edsall* and her crew was a measure of comfort on these wartime voyages, and the *Houston* survivors haven't forgotten it.

Finally, a little more than a year ago, Don found what we were looking for. A bridge officer from one of the Japanese ships involved in the *Edsall*'s last action who recalled what happened from a more informed viewpoint than [the officer] whom my father had met. He remembered an amazing ship-to-ship engagement that was historic in many ways. This officer honors the men of *Edsall* as Samurai by virtue of their Bushido-like conduct in the battle.

The action of *Edsall*'s crew that first day of March 1942 is the very definition of the type of achievement that has earned many sailors the Navy Cross. The engagement carried out by the crew of the *Edsall* was in the best tradition of the U.S. Navy. It is a story that needs to be told.

Don, well done.

"Go tell the Spartans . . ."

James T. Nix
Dallas, Texas
January 2008

Preface

For the essence of a riddle is to express true facts under impossible combinations.

—Aristotle, *Poetics*

This work confronts many paradoxes and exhumes a number of explanations that are often as profoundly troubling as they were deeply buried. It is a mystery that has been deciphered only after almost seven decades in a series of riddles, as in a nest of Chinese boxes, which after all seems entirely appropriate to a ship that saw the bulk of her service in the Far East.

I did not set out to write a maritime *Heart of Darkness* or a nautical version of *The Manuscript Found in Saragossa*, yet there have been many oblique pathways radiating from this tale so strange that it seemed to have written itself, and there have been several darkened cul-de-sacs in which my search was thwarted. Nonetheless, as so many disparate elements essential to deciphering the *Edsall* mystery seemed to fall into my lap, I felt both an irresistible attraction to unraveling the paradoxes and a deep responsibility to inform the crew's descendants.

"Too muchee long time no home see, Old flend acloss the sea," reads the mock-Oriental doggerel from a Christmas card sent from the *Edsall* in the Asiatic Fleet off China in the 1930s. Yet even this Tsingtao sing-song bears witness to the remote and otherworldly station in which the little vessel lived out her life. It seems to ask that we do not forget those young men so far from home, but that is just the fate to which the ship and crew were left. For almost seven decades, no devoted voice spoke or sang of these men or their ship. We must now return, by degrees, to that abandonment and, seeing that it was undeserved and unjust, fashion the story anew.

Introduction

Somewhere off Christmas Island—an anomalous little fillet of land, with a steep crown and a narrow fringe of reefs, rising up through the blue-black swells of the Indian Ocean some two hundred miles south of Java—the seabed abruptly drops to unimaginable depths: twenty, twenty-two, twenty-four thousand feet. The ocean's very surface sags by several meters along the great Java Trench. And within another two hundred miles or so south of Christmas Island, lost amid submarine canyons, contorted basins, and imbricated sediment, wedged in a deep shelf, or perhaps lying on a frigid abyssal plain, is a slowly disintegrating hulk of blasted metal.

It is not likely that Dr. Robert Ballard, or, for that matter, any other specialized, well-funded oceanographer, will ever probe those waters in search of this crumpled wreck. The seas are too dangerous, and the Malay Barrier (as it was once known) to the north is ringed by volcanic islands with a history of geologic violence. It is bounded as if by sinister guardian deities at both extremes: volatile, slumbering Anak Krakatau, astride Sunda Strait to the west; and very much farther east, on Sumbawa Island, Tambora's awe-inspiring caldera, remnant of the greatest volcanic eruption known to human memory.

Java's southern coast is notoriously inhospitable; it was characterized in U.S. Naval Intelligence geographical surveys before World War II as "treacherous." Its heavy, pounding surf crashing against rocky limestone headlands creates lethal riptides along the barren beaches of dark-yellow and iron-colored sand, with but a few small, cramped bays and fewer good anchorages.

Many towns and fishing villages along that angry coast—from Pelabuhanratu on the western end across to Parangtritis, south of

Jogjakarta, in the east—preserve an ancient tradition of appeasing the maleficent sea goddess Raden Loro Kidul, Queen of the Southern Seas. Each spring, the time of year our subjects mysteriously vanished, local fishermen sacrifice heads of slaughtered oxen to the sea during a Labuhan ceremony, scattering flowers upon the waters as they do so. (*Pelabuhanratu* means "harbor of the queen.")

It is easy to imagine the crumpled wreckage, covered with rusticles and wrapped in cerements of silt, thousands of feet beneath the slate-gray Indian Ocean four hundred miles off the green Javanese shores, far from those spring flowers. She was, *is*, a half-forgotten American warship, already elderly in World War II, a veteran of the Atlantic and Pacific oceans and the Mediterranean, Aegean, and Black seas, and finally a member of the U.S. Asiatic Fleet's Destroyer Squadron 29: USS *Edsall* (DD-219). Her remains reposed in utter darkness for more than sixty-five years.

As well as historical narrative, this text is an attempt to reclaim her story from that black chasm, to draw up into the daylight from her deep grave a number of facts and truths that have been lost through negligence, error, and deceit.

Like many other students of World War II in general, and of the naval war against Japan in particular, I stumbled across the bizarre tale of the old Asiatic Fleet destroyer USS *Edsall* in Theodore Roscoe's *United States Destroyer Operations in World War II*:

> After parting company with Pecos and Whipple on the morning of March 1, *Edsall* headed in a northeasterly direction. Lieutenant Joshua J. Nix and his brave company went over the horizon—and into oblivion. . . . A somber cloud of mystery veiled the destroyer's final hour.

Although the ship is mentioned in passing by Samuel Eliot Morison in volume 3 of his magisterial fifteen-volume *History of United States Naval Operations in World War II (1947–62)*, it was in Roscoe's large book, beautifully illustrated by Fred Freeman, that I first encountered *Edsall*'s story in its basic outline as it was then understood. I became more than a little intrigued by this sad, baffling episode from the war's earliest, darkest months.

In contrast with Morison, who appeared to accept at face value the information found by post-conflict U.S. Navy analysts in the War Diary of the Imperial Navy's Third Battleship Division, Theodore Roscoe—no stranger to popular writing, with his extensive background in magazines—incorporated elements from early 1952 discoveries. Specifically, he incorporated a brief scrap of captured Japanese propaganda newsreel depicting the shelling and sinking of a four-funneled vessel of *Edsall*'s type at brutally close range. It was this discovery, with its attendant revelation concerning the identity of the Imperial Japanese Navy (IJN) warship that did the filming and the shelling (the heavy cruiser *Ashigara*), that caught my attention.

A striking series of images and ideas immediately sprang to life in my imagination: the doomed little ship overhauled by a superior force of Japanese vessels that had apparently toyed with it for some time before filming the coup de grâce. Decade after decade, next to nothing was known (or, rather, fully accepted) until the gruesome concluding note in Roscoe's account that hints indirectly of a pitifully small number of survivors' remains found after the war in "a forgotten South Pacific cemetery." That Roscoe somehow equated the "*Ashigara* clue" with the discovery of these bodies made no impression on me at all; I didn't have enough facts to know any better, and believed for several years that this cruiser was in fact the *Edsall*'s executioner.[1]

Theodore Roscoe also interpreted mention of dive-bombers from the carrier *Sōryu* being involved in *Edsall*'s end as somehow "contradictory" to the testimony of officers of the Imperial Navy's Third Battleship Division, who themselves had been doubted by U.S. investigators during postwar interrogations. Both of the battleships—*Hiei* and *Kirishima*—claimed to have sunk the destroyer. To American researchers, this made no sense. And the putative involvement of *Sōryu*'s dive-bombers applied another skin of misinterpretation that would last for decades.[2]

"Some truth and much error," wrote that singularly robust Victorian encyclopedist of the East Indies, the Scotsman John Crawfurd, speaking of what was then known of the mysterious, orchid-shaped island of Celebes. A century later, his remarks might apply to the published accounts of *Edsall*'s entire career, as well as her final action.

It is worth noting that Roscoe's *United States Destroyer Operations in World War II* was published at the height of cold war paranoia (1953), during an era that saw—with the grimmest irony—America's often justified fears of Soviet ambitions in Asia abruptly pushing the U.S. conquerors of Japan into bed with their former enemies. This *realpolitik* approach originated late in the war years with the behind-the-scenes machinations of ardent anti-Communists such as ex-president Herbert Hoover and the MacArthurite Bonner Fellers.

For Gen. Douglas MacArthur, SCAP (Supreme Commander Allied Powers), the occupation of Japan was another opportunity for self-aggrandizement, something the general had always excelled at; following the exoneration of *Tenno Heika* (Hirohito), MacArthur and staff made *this* their holy mission. Japan was occupied peacefully, and the efficient transition from a semi-feudal state controlled by the "military-industrial complex" to a faux Western-style democracy began. It mattered little enough to MacArthur that his petty machinations and egoistic opportunism left the Japanese economy moribund for several years after the war. Nor did SCAP feel any hesitation about glossing over fifty years of Japanese military aggression in Asia, or the swath of mass destruction and death left in its wake. MacArthur simply stated that Japan had only erred in "reach[ing] out to get resources," while praising the nation's "advanced spirituality."[3] By this, he naturally meant the spirituality which *he*, Japan's single-handed conqueror, had helped foster as her Supreme Commander. And as that figure of elevated spirituality it would be MacArthur's right—and his alone—to control the punishment of transgressions committed by the Japanese armed forces against Americans during the war.

Although Lord Louis Mountbatten at South East Asia Command (SEAC) controlled the areas into which the captives of the old Asiatic Fleet's sunken warships had disappeared after the fall of Java, American investigators were dispatched to those remote locales soon after the war's end. But Allied intelligence regarding the East Indies was dreadfully inadequate, and nowhere more so than in the outlying islands of what were once Dutch colonies, such as Celebes. Mountbatten broke away only once from his daily round of parties, formal dinners, and "peace celebrations" to make a very brief stopover at Makassar in December 1945, "amazed" to find "such a lovely town in the Celebes" and noting that "the Dutch are running civil affairs quite peaceably." Certainly this is the picture the Dutch wanted to paint for Lord Louis.[4]

At that time Celebes (now Sulawesi) was part of a newly designated geopolitical body—along with Borneo and the Lesser Sunda islands—called at first "the Great East" and later "East Indonesia." Most Allied war-crime cases in the Great East were joint affairs, with research by British, Dutch, Australian, and American investigators. The investigators were to work under some of the most severe, adversarial conditions in the vast Malay Archipelago. Internecine fighting exploded among homegrown (though often foreign-educated) revolutionaries—often with arms and training supplied by their former Japanese occupiers—as Dutch-Colonial troops; British, Indian, and Australian peacekeepers; and infuriated Dutch counterinsurgency units were thrown pell-mell into the unholy contest for the exploitation of the profits of Southeast Asian resources.

In Tokyo, at the hurried, tightly controlled but far-from-homogenous International Military Tribunal for the Far East (IMTFE), a large number of powerful, high-ranking, well-connected (and culpable) Japanese were set free or given much-reduced sentences. Original medical reports on human experiments, if not ignored, were silently and gratefully absorbed into America's burgeoning counterintelligence and "scientific" programs.* Mean political necessity, however "unpalatable," won out over the pursuit of justice. MacArthur's G-2, the autocratic Maj. Gen. Charles Willoughby, when he wasn't engaging in partisan witch-hunts within his own command, helped pay off former scientists and officials to obtain Japanese research data on bacteriological warfare experiments conducted on live test cases in Pingfan, Manchuria. But by then, in July 1947, SCAP had thoroughly hoodwinked the men presiding over the IMTFE trials, as was later realized with regret by one of the court's most vocal dissenters, the Dutch justice B. V. A. Roling, who

---

* Regarding the infamous Manchurian germ warfare experiments on human subjects, in Unit 731, under Lt. Gen. Ishii Shiro, and regarding MacArthur's complacency: "Although Washington refused to approve any deal with Ishii or his subordinates, it was evident that SCAP officials and the International Prosecution Section were willing to help the Japanese avoid war crimes charges in return for what the technical experts thought was useful information on bacteriological warfare. . . . Some Japanese were punished as a result of the Soviet trial, but the ringleaders in Japan got off scot-free. Both the United States and the USSR considered cold war politics more important than impartial justice." Richard B. Finn, *Winners in Peace*, pp. 186–87. See also Wakamiya Yoshibumi's *The Postwar Conservative View of Asia*, Chapter 5, "Scant Awareness of Having Been Defeated by Asia" and Yuki Tanaka, *Hidden Horrors*.

wrote in 1981, "It is a bitter experience for me to be informed now that centrally ordered Japanese war criminality of the most disgusting kind was kept secret from the court by the U.S. government."[5]

Those who knew anything of—let alone were actually responsible for—Allied personnel taken prisoner in obscure East Indies backwaters and subsequently murdered were much too small and obscure catches for the slipshod trials held in Tokyo, Yokohama, and Manila, where far bigger Japanese fish were not fried but freed. Complaints by British delegates of the IMTFE to the tribunal regarding "U.S. inefficiency and delay in obtaining evidence" were commonplace, as were Admiralty complaints of the "laxity of United States authorities in dealing with [the] Japanese bureau responsible for demobilization of naval officers"[6] that interfered, for example, with war-crime trials concerning British merchant shipping. Later, downward pressure from SCAP during the Class "B" and "C" trials would play a more direct role in excusing war crimes. However, Washington had always had its hands full with MacArthur's duplicity, political ambitions, and egregious disregard of instructions; his handling of the IMTFE was no exception.

In any event, this fundamental U.S. strategy—Japan as Western proxy in Asia stemming the monstrous "Red Tide" of Soviet Russia and Maoist China—would define relations between America and Japan for more than half a century, and pardon an immense web of lies and abuses involving everything from war crimes to economic scandals. The occupation of Japan went smoothly enough, but governing the conquered nation was another matter. And while the men of SCAP lived as comfortable bureacrats, the average Japanese suffered terrible deprivations. The ravaged Japanese economy wallowed in near-depression conditions for almost five years before a "gift from the gods" finally arrived in June 1950 with the outbreak of the Korean conflict.[7]

Not for nothing is it recorded in the gangster Kodama's charming memoir, *Sugamo Diary*, that even the incarcerated Japanese admirals, generals, and bureaucrats in prison were ready to "volunteer" once more in the looming war they saw coming against the hated Communists.* Kodama himself even wrote to Shogun MacArthur on July 20,

---

* "One of the convicted war criminals, Shigemitsu Mamoru, was released in November 1950 and became foreign minister in 1954. . . . Among those released were Kishi Nobusuke, a skillful bureaucrat who was minister of commerce and industry in the Tōjō cabinet at the time of Pearl Harbor and became prime minister in 1957, and two accomplished behind-the-scenes operators who had been active rightist agitators and later made

1950, offering his "services" in the fight against North Korea. His loyalty employing that logic was peculiar to patriotic criminals throughout human history: "The ones who ably understand the orientals," Kodama wrote, "are the orientals themselves and the ones who can successfully oppose an oriental must himself be an oriental." This indicates that Kodama's business acumen had not suffered during his imprisonment, even if his perception of exactly who had just defeated Japan was rather muddled. Still, it seems that he had a clear grasp of the illicit money to be made in this new war. Kodama, Saskawa, and others were shrewd individuals, craftier by far than the fatuous "American Caesar" crowned SCAP in Tokyo. And as John R. Dower wrote in his Pulitzer Prize–winning study *Embracing Defeat*, "It was all part of the challenge of conquering the conqueror."* As the United States strove to counter the specter of global Communism in the 1950s, the need to project an image of strength and resolve superseded the pursuit of justice in a half-remembered episode from a war that most then wanted to forget.

However, U.S. history books tend to leap from December 7, 1941, directly to the Battle of the Coral Sea in May 1942, with perhaps at most a terse sentence or two devoted to General MacArthur and the Philippines somewhere in between. Little or no attention was (or is) accorded the sacrificial role played by the aging, outnumbered vessels of the U.S. Asiatic Fleet. This symbolic force, a vestige of the nineteenth-century station fleet system and never intended to serve as a bulwark

a lot of money in dubious activities: Kodama Yoshiō and Saskawa Ryōichi." (See Notes, Introduction, number 6.) Actually, Kodama and Saskawa were cellmates at Sugamo; the former had an extensive prewar criminal background, including exploitation of Chinese resources for the Imperial Navy, and the latter was fond of referring to himself as "the world's most wealthy fascist." They both became even richer and more powerful after the war, with Kodama acquiring legendary status as *yakuza* godfather.

*These views are challenged by one of the finest books on the Occupation of Japan, *Sheathing the Sword*, by Meirion and Susie Harries, but even they conclude that no greater mystery remains concerning the demilitarization and reconstruction than the failure to prosecute Hirohito as a war criminal. In Chapter 14 of that book, "The Shadow of the Emperor," is the following: "Whatever the ultimate reason for Hirohito's non-indictment, the question remains—did MacArthur leave a war criminal on the throne of Japan? Again, this is difficult to answer. The question turns in part on the interpretation of 'war criminal.'" Whether or not one agrees with their evaluations, this book remains essential reading for anyone intrigued by this paradoxical strategic adventure in modern U.S. geopolitics. For a judicious counterargument to those most critical of Hirohito, as in Bergamini, see Charles D. Sheldon, "Japanese Aggression and the Emperor," in *Modern Asian Studies*, Vol. 10, Part 1, in which the emperor's advisor apologizes for "the whirlpool of tyrannies perpetrated by the so-called governing class in league with the *zaibatsu*."

against Japanese aggression, was snubbed by MacArthur himself—a charismatic leader fond of saying that "man's noblest quality" was sacrifice. The general smirked in Adm. Thomas Hart's face in the fall of 1941, taunting him, "Get yourself a real fleet, Tommy, then you will belong." One wonders how much contemptuous humor MacArthur had left to spew at the Asiatic Fleet's "combat inferiority" in March 1942, when he and his family were evacuated by Bulkley's PT boats, or "delivered from the Jaws of Death," as the general phrased his escape with characteristic bombast.[8]

It was just such self-serving bombast that kept him at the forefront of public perception, turning Gen. Douglas "Move over, God!" MacArthur into a symbol of resistance, courage, and fortitude to millions during the war, whereas the men who served and sacrificed in the Asiatic Fleet were all but forgotten. This remains a bitter pill to swallow (many are still choked by it) for men who lived through the war's cruel early months, to say nothing of former POWs who endured experiences worthy of Dante's *Inferno* in godforsaken compounds throughout the East Indies, Malaya, Burma, Siam, Manchuria, and Japan itself. And it's all the more painful to recognize the psychological value extracted by Japanese propagandists at the time—which brings us back to the somber chronicle of the *Edsall*.

Let us retrace the broken steps and uncertain stages of the tale of the so-called "destroyer that vanished": a decades-long story of confusion and misconceptions in which visual clues were misread, Japanese explanations were gullibly accepted, and the U.S. government and military were often willing to settle for half-truths at best. Of course, one cannot lay all blame directly on MacArthur, even though he had always been a master tactician when it came to evading responsibility. Yet, had MacArthur been evacuated from the Philippines at the eleventh hour by *Edsall*, this ship's posthumous history would likely have been altogether different.

One would imagine that the disappearance of a U.S. Navy warship carrying at least 185 officers and crew and additional military passengers should have prompted a thorough investigation. And it is bewildering that perhaps the largest number of U.S. prisoners of war captured from a single warship and executed by the Japanese was never acknowledged or closely scrutinized. This is all the more mysterious in view of the remarkable final engagement of the ship, which, despite a dearth of firsthand information, seemed to merit a fresh perspective and, hopefully, greater recognition; the attention given this action in the official Japanese records in *Senshi Sōsho* convinced me of this. And these events apply only to the *Edsall*'s wartime activities; her peacetime career was no less remarkable.

Chapter One

Flushdeckers

The best practical school the Navy has ever had . . . the good old "4-pipe" destroyer.
—Rear Adm. Robert W. Copeland, U.S. Naval Reserve

World War I brought harsh lessons for the world's navies, not the least of which was the vulnerability of all classes of ships to that insidious new weapon, the submarine. Consequently, the U.S. Navy, realizing the importance logistics would play in future conflicts, understood that its merchant shipping and battle fleets required greater numbers of protective escort vessels. This recognition—and the consideration of the vast, vulnerable distances in the Pacific to America's far-flung outposts such as Hawaii, Guam, and the Philippines—gave birth to that prolific class of destroyers known for three ensuing decades as "flushdeckers." The equally well-used term *four-pipers* is slightly less precise, as noted by Cmdr. John D. Alden in his seminal chronicle, because a small number of these ships actually had only three funnels, whereas all had the distinctive flush weather deck.[1]

Mammoth dreadnought battleships were still built, but a great many more destroyers of the flushdecker type emerged between 1917 and 1921 from the shipyards of Norfolk, Charleston, Mare Island, Bath Iron Works, Newport News, and New York Shipbuilding Corporation of Camden, New Jersey. The majority were built at a number of different Bethlehem Steel yards; another four dozen were constructed by William Cramp & Sons of Philadelphia. By 1922, about 270 new flush-deck destroyers had been commissioned.

The "mass production" of so many vessels in such a brief period of time, although flattering to American notions of industrial efficiency, had drawbacks as well: Eventually, some fifty-seven of the old flushdeckers were scrapped prior to World War II, in large part due to deterioration problems with their Yarrow-pattern boilers,[2] and most of the ships in this batch (all built by Bethlehem Steel) were faulted for shoddy construction.

These ships were nothing if not paradoxes. Small and spartan, yet beloved by almost all U.S. sailors and officers who served in them; equipped with temperamental powerplants, many were still quite serviceable well into their third decade; considered formidable "sea-hornets" when new, they were obsolete by the mid-1930s (in contrast with Continental and Japanese designs), yet still gave good accounts of themselves in combat; workmanlike in appearance, the appreciation for these cookie-cutter ships, once acquired, was quite stubborn and not easily lost.

Despite a reputation for rolling, the flushdeckers rarely exceeded 15 degrees in high seas. Although 35-degree rolls were experienced—and in an exceptionally terrifying gale, one of 52 degrees was registered—it was written that "this roll was the exception, for usually the motion of the ship was easy and gentle."[3] British recollections of the four-pipers turned over to the Royal Navy in the 1940 Lend-Lease exchange were less charitable.

The principal contributing factor to excessive rolling was lightness, especially at high speeds, and flushdeckers were advised to always have at least forty-five thousand gallons of fuel aboard before high-speed runs.

The flushdeckers' fine lines, both fore and aft, led to some difficulties in docking because the propellers were exposed and liable to damage from even relatively small objects. The ship's primitive steering design was prone to malfunctions, with a large number of collisions recorded, and steering gear breakdowns were commonplace. Yet, paradoxically, when handled with skill, the vesssels were nimble and known for their maneuverability: they "could almost leap from a standstill into flank speed without a moment's waste of time, turn on the proverbial dime and by reversing screws come to a halt for all the world like a cowboy's horse."[4]

This class had a large turning radius at high speed, greater than a battleship, but the small single rudders made them clumsy at low speeds. Admiral William F. Halsey, a great fan of flushdeckers, wrote years later in his autobiography, "They straggle at slower speeds and don't handle properly," and claimed to prefer docking while the ship was still making as much as ten knots.[5] Notwithstanding such design anomalies, for the next decade these robust and distinctive, if somewhat idiosyncratic, vessels formed the backbone of America's destroyer forces, serving in waters from Constantinople to Chefoo, and Malta to Manila. No other class of destroyers before the wartime "Fletchers" (and following classes) endured as long in active service with the U.S. Navy, which says much for their construction, strength, and versatility.

Although there were differences within the various "classes" of *Sampson* (DD-63–DD-68), *Caldwell* (DD-69–DD-75), *Wickes* (DD-75–DD-185), and *Clemson* (DD-186–DD-347), the latter three types shared enough characteristics, apart from fuel oil bunkerage and thus range,* to fall within the following general specifications:

Length 314 feet (waterline); beam 30 feet 10 inches; draft 9 feet 10 inches; standard displacement 1,090 to 1,190 tons; full load about 1,310 tons; bunkerage in the *Clemson*-class increased from 300 to 375 tons of fuel oil, expanding range to 5,000 nautical miles at 14 knots ("with machinery in good shape and a clean bottom")[6] or 2,500 nautical miles at 20 knots. Four White-Foster boilers provided steam to two Westinghouse geared turbines, producing roughly 27,000 shaft horsepower (shp), which translated to a maximum designed speed of 35 knots. No vessel exceeded 37 knots on trials. All had widely differing endurance properties.

With a handful of minor variations, weaponry consisted of four Mk. 9/5 4-inch (101.6mm) 50-caliber guns in Mk. 12/2 mounts; all were hand operated, firing a 33-pound projectile to a distance of 15,920 yards at 20-degree elevation. These guns were located on the fo'c'sle (No. 1), with two more (Nos. 2 and 3) above the galley deckhouse, and the last (No. 4) atop the after deckhouse. Some ships had the foremost gun in a Mk. 12 "P" mounting, which provided minimal protection with its thin 5mm shield. The original fire-control outfit included a Dotter director-scope and a Ford Range Keeper Mk. II, a small and primitive gunnery computer that could be installed on the bridge itself or on the signal deck behind a 1.5m rangefinder. Two torpedo directors were standard on the flushdeckers.

---

* These differences would be characterized by the men who served on them as "short hull" and "long hull," with the latter having an extra fuel-oil tank forward of the number one fire room. *Edsall* was a "long hull" ship.

Generally there was also a single 3-inch/23-caliber Mk. 14 AA gun, either forward of the bridge structure (in the early four-pipers) or more commonly aft on the fantail. This weapon was often referred to as the "pea-shooter"; its value was recognized as debatable against modern airplanes. Smaller light weapons, such as machine guns, and even Browning automatic rifles (BARs), were later used to augment these vessels' limited antiaircraft capacities, although the weapons were originally intended for landing parties. In *Edsall*'s case, the ship had been outfitted initially with three .30-caliber Model 1917 Lewis guns; three .30-caliber BARs, Model 1918; and twenty-five .45-caliber Colt Model 1911 pistols and .30-caliber Springfield Model 1903 rifles each. Sometime before World War II, .50-caliber antiaircraft machine guns were installed, usually above the deckhouses.

But the flushdeckers' true punch came with their heavy complement of four triple banks of tubes carrying twelve 21-inch Mk. VIII/3B torpedoes, which gave them a powerful broadside. But unlike their Japanese counterparts, they lacked reloads; once the torpedoes were expended, so might be the four-pipers, as most of their offensive value was lost. Only nimbleness and the high speeds for which they had been designed could then preserve them. During World War II, their advanced age, their degraded upkeep, and the inevitable wear and tear of combat operations left them incapable of speeds much above thirty knots. Extant records and reports show that they had to be driven to bolt-shaking, bone-jarring extremes to achieve twenty-seven to twenty-eight knots in the Netherlands East Indies (NEI) campaign. At no time does *Edsall*'s log in World War II, for example, record her speed as exceeding twenty-nine knots.

Unfortunately, the torpedo tubes were arranged so as to cause serious problems if the ships were attacking at anything above relatively slow speeds in calm waters, particularly during a turn. Such maneuvers could lead to the "spoon" end of the tubes plunging into the water, as well as risking wave damage to the mounts and/or torpedoes themselves.[7]

Interwar tactical doctrine, although understanding the roles for which these aging ships were best suited (escort duties and antisubmarine warfare [ASW] operations), still required large numbers of destroyers to screen the U.S. Fleet's battle line, as well as to act offensively against the enemy in attritional attacks. Overproduction of the class brought with it a degree of complacency, and budgetary restrictions further limited new designs. (Between 1923 and 1930 the average number of flushdeckers in commission at any given time was between 101 and 106 ships.[8])

A good example of the flushdeckers' self-reliance occurred in the late 1920s, when President Calvin Coolidge's thrifty administration decided that the cost of upgrading the fleet's radio systems was too high: operating costs for a four-piper in this period were somewhere in the vicinity of $300,000 per month. Frustrated, the Navy Department decided to do the job themselves. After much backbreaking labor and trial and error, the four-pipers' crews stripped out their radio rooms' antiquated spark transmitters with their "shiny coils," the AC intermediate transmitters, and the U.S. Navy Type 1420 reflex radio receivers. In went new equipment such as the "modern" two-kilowatt GE Model TD-2 transmitter, an intermediate frequency transmitter, and a shortwave transmitter.

The destroyers' men and repair gangs from squadron tenders installed three new superheterodyne miniature tube receivers and new motor generator sets on each ship. These were mounted opposite the gyro room aft of the forward crew's compartment. Edison-type storage batteries in banks were installed in well-deck cabinets with charging panels modified to the ship's 130-volt DC return electric power.

Despite minor problems, the new equipment functioned properly. As a veteran radioman of these self-controlled projects later wrote, "The extent of training was excellent, though exhausting, but the navy ended up with radiomen, artificers, electricians, and other ratings with experience far in excess of that gained in ordinary routine work."[9]

During the interwar years, the men of the peacetime navy took pride in maintaining these spartan little vessels, with the high morale and team atmosphere they fostered. The large red "E" painted on the stack, or elsewhere, justifiably symbolized excellence; Admiral Hart, however, felt that they simply rewarded slackers for doing what they were supposed to be doing anyway. Nevertheless, such displays did help promote fierce competition with other division mates.

By the early 1930s, more realistic attention was being paid to the probability of a conflict against Japan, and with it the need for more "long-legged" screening vessels. A series of war plans against Orange (Japan) required the Pacific Fleet to journey thousands of miles across open ocean to relieve the Philippines before a U.S. stranglehold on the Japanese mainland could be effected. It had become painfully clear that the *Clemson*-class ships were outdated, and following a decade-long hiatus, the U.S. Navy finally resumed new destroyer construction with the *Farragut*-class ships (or "gold-platers," as they were derisively termed at the time).

The Squadron Built by Cramp & Sons

Because this book addresses the fate of a single vessel—one of four ships making up the 57th Division within the Asiatic Fleet's Destroyer Squadron 29—and with all the ships being virtually identical, it is necessary at this point to look deeper into the past, two decades before the Pacific war, for basic background information and historical context. In the case of at least one destroyer, this "context" is truly extraordinary, from its inception until its final convulsive shudder twenty-two years later in the Indian Ocean. She would act as a cruising microcosm, embodying America's ambitions and dreams in addition to its failed aspirations, until, after many years and many hard times, she became at last a sacrificial victim herself.

All thirteen of the flushdeckers that would later make up Destroyer Squadron 29 of the U.S. Asiatic Fleet, from USS *Alden* (DD-211) to USS *Paul Jones* (DD-230), were constructed by William Cramp & Sons of Philadelphia. Authorized by the First Session of the 65th Congress in 1917 as "Torpedo-boat destroyers," they, too, were built rapidly, often in less than a year.[10] But Cramp ships were strongly framed, even if not designed with enough ventilation for service in the torrid East Asian climate.

And for those who may put stock in the portents of numerology in preference to the workmanship, the welded plates, rivets, and bolts of Cramp & Sons DDs 224, 225, and 226 (*Stewart, Pope*, and *Peary*) were all laid down on the same day: the ninth day of the ninth month of 1919. All three were lost in the Java campaign as members of the ill-fated Destroyer Squadron 29. Their hull numbers at Cramp & Sons were respectively 490, 491, and 492.

A fourth destroyer of that heroic, unlucky baker's dozen, hull number 485, was laid down six days after the previously mentioned three, on September 15, 1919, and she would be launched on July 29, 1920. The USS *Edsall* (DD-219) was named for a seaman serving aboard the USS *Philadelphia*, Norman Eckley Edsall, of Columbia, Kentucky. He was born in 1873 and died in 1899, slain in fighting on Samoa.

Built at a cost of just over $1.5 million (hull and machinery), *Edsall* was sponsored at her launching by Mrs. Bessie Edsall Bracey, a surviving sister of the seaman for whom the ship was named. In photos taken that summer day at Cramp's Philadelphia yard, Mrs. Bracey is shown standing at the bow fiercely clutching the bottle of ceremonial champagne, an expression of righteous, Old Testament pride on her face. Other photographs from Cramps reveal *Edsall*'s fitting out in the autumn of 1920 next to her soon-to-be Asiatic Fleet sibling, USS *Pillsbury* (DD-227), another ship lost under equally mysterious and fateful circumstances in the Java campaign.

Virtually all of these tough little ships had careers charged with momentous events. Nevertheless, the mystery of the *Edsall*'s sinking and the fate of her crew should not cloud or eclipse the singular fact of her long, varied service over a twenty-one-year period, or the symbolic significance of the vessel.

Shores of the Forsaken: From Smyrna to Shanghai

It was all a pleasant business. My word yes a most pleasant business.
—Ernest Hemingway, "On the Quai at Smyrna,"
from *In Our Time*

More than once, the *Edsall* was a pawn in the service of interests that likely involved neither real national security nor humanitarian concerns; yet it is also worth understanding something of her peacetime service in saving lives, which, despite official indifference or political machinations, may be said to have outweighed the highlights of her brief and tragic combat career.

Commissioned on November 26, 1920, *Edsall* departed Philadelphia in early December 1920 for her shakedown cruise. This journey took her to San Diego, where she remained throughout 1921, engaged in combat training with Pacific Fleet units. She then returned to the East Coast, arriving at Charleston, South Carolina, on December 28, 1921. *Edsall* was next ordered to the Mediterranean, leaving for the U.S. Naval Detachment in Turkish Waters* on May 26, 1922. *Edsall* arrived at Constantinople (Istanbul) on June 28. During this period of

---

* This force came into existence on January 28, 1919, when Rear Adm. Mark L. Bristol raised his flag in the old Spanish-American War–era converted yacht USS *Scorpion* at Constantinople.

international turmoil, *Edsall* served protecting U.S. interests—meaning business interests—in the midst of not only Anglo-Soviet schemes in famine-plagued Russia but a disastrous and bloody regional war, fomented by Allied political follies of both commission and omission between Greece and the Turkish Nationalist forces of Mustafa Kemal.

Although the U.S. Congress had responded in December 1921 with a vote of $20 million in funds for Russian relief, there were other motives behind the apparent altruism. Capitalism was playing on an all-too-human ability and willingness to exploit tragedy: "Farm groups saw in famine relief an outlet for their crop surpluses; shipping interests saw cargoes in the holds of their idle ships; [Secretary of State] Hughes saw the American Relief Administration [A.R.A.] as a fact-finding agency; and Hoover [head of the A.R.A.] saw it as an opportunity for American economic penetration."[11]

The U.S. Navy was authorized to ferry agents of American commercial companies seeking a foothold in these newly opened territories throughout the Near East for the small charge of one dollar a day. Additionally, the commanders of U.S. ships were permitted by regulation to receive a "small commission" for the service of transporting the gold used to pay for export products to the States.[12] The United States wanted desperately to introduce commercial operatives of the rail-steel-bank nexus into what was once the Ottoman Empire. The motive is not hard to apprehend: U.S. oil men wanted more oil.

In the spring of 1922, as the humanitarian calamity of the Anatolian littoral began to unfold, oil executives from the United States and the Netherlands met in New York for preliminary talks regarding negotiations with the state oil corporations of Great Britain, Mexico, and Russia. All were eager to obtain valid oil concessions in the newly dismembered corpus of what was once the Ottoman Empire. In February 1922, the British had struck a 50-50 deal with Walter Teagle's Near East Development Corporation (NED) for the "*Khostaria concession*" in northern Iran. In late 1921, Teagle, head of Standard Oil, had been advised by Secretary of State Charles Evans Hughes, a former lawyer for Standard, that the U.S. State Department could not promote a single company; Hughes suggested that a consortium be formed. Teagle produced NED, made up of the seven largest oil companies in America at that time. It is therefore no exaggeration to say that the foreign policy of the United States at this critical juncture, oil-fueled as it were, favored the nationalists of Mustafa Kemal, and therefore most excesses committed by Kemalist forces might thus be overlooked.

On August 10, 1922, *Edsall*, a member of Destroyer Division 39, could be found at Varna, Bulgaria, promoting American commercial ventures and coordinating relief efforts. The ship was allotted 112 men and 6 officers: Cmdr. Halsey (Harry) Powell in command; executive officer and navigator Lt. E. W. Morris; engineering officer Lt. (j.g.) E. B. Perry; first lieutenant and supply officer Ensign T. A. Gaylord; torpedo and communications officer Ensign Charles T. Maguire; and commissary and gunnery officer Ensign K. C. Caldwell.

Two weeks later, *Edsall* steamed east to Novorossik, Russia, where she remained until Tuesday, August 29, before beginning a clockwise circuit of other Black Sea ports. Novorossik had been a center of the White Russian conflict against the Bolsheviks and was also significant to the Russian oil industry, and thus an area of economic and political sensitivity. That afternoon, following the embarkation of J. H. Lange* of the American Relief Administration (A.R.A.) and a "Mr. Miller,"†the ship prepared to leave. By four o'clock in the afternoon, *Edsall* was under way, moving southeast, and had passed Cape Kadash Light and Sacha Island within several hours.

A little past noon on Wednesday, August 30, the destroyer anchored in Batoum (Batumi) Harbor, on the jagged Georgian coast, with dispatches for the Near East Relief. This, too, was an oil port of considerable relevance for the region, connected to the Baku fields by six hundred miles of railway and pipeline built in 1907. Baku had come under the nominal control of a British military governor, Maj. Gen. William Thompson. The British Oil Administration conducted a short-lived "experiment in democracy" in late 1918, following another bloody Turkish-Armenian conflict. Batoum, on the other side of the Caucasus, had also been the principal base for British troops in the region. This British attempt to exploit the Russian Revolution's power

---

* As a member of Herbert Hoover's A.R.A., Lange would certainly have been involved in dealing with the Russian famine of 1921 to 1923, in which millions starved to death, and through which late-nineteenth-century Marxist-Leninist delusions of "scientific" and "progressive" social engineering were exposed as grotesque frauds.

† Most of *Edsall*'s activities during the interwar years are taken from the ship's deck logs, which are on 35mm microfilm and held in Record Group 24 at the National Archives in Washington, D.C. Unattributed quotes throughout the text that detail such activities are from the ship's logs.

vacuum in order to access and control oil ended in the summer of 1919, when Allied forces were withdrawn. Later, in the spring of 1920, Red Army forces seized Baku's golden fountains of petroleum, which sharply lowered oil production figures. During *Edsall*'s brief layover, a group of local, and undoubtedly suspicious, Soviet officials visited the ship, coming from shore in a motor launch.

At this time, the destroyers were being utilized to transfer important dispatches, mail, provisions, and relief workers to the site of a looming humanitarian disaster on the western coast of Anatolia. Having disregarded the advice and warnings of experienced men on the scene, Western politicians were swayed by British Prime Minister David Lloyd George's heated anti-Turkish rhetoric and by their own eagerness to dismember ("partition") the Ottoman Empire at the war's end, commonly called the "sick man of Europe" during its period of decline. Although clear perceptions of this folly were seen and voiced by many, Britain's fears of losing oil-producing regions to Germany, France, Russia, or Italy, as well as concerns for destabilizing influences upon India, led them into a Middle Eastern quagmire that culminated in the catastrophe at Smyrna. When Kemalist troops routed the Greeks in late August 1922 after two years of fighting in Anatolia, a headlong retreat ensued. Over the next month, several hundred thousand Ottoman Greeks and Armenians abandoned their homes and fled to the coast. This exodus was followed by "the holocaust at Smyrna," in which "the U.S. Navy's contingents . . . helped greatly in the rescue work."[13]

Should These Endeavours Fail

On September 1, *Edsall* pushed on again, this time to the southwest for Trebizond (Trabzon), Anatolia. After anchoring there that morning, Cmdr. Halsey Powell left the ship at nine o'clock.* and tried to land for "an official visit." Thirty minutes later, the skipper of *Edsall* was back aboard the destroyer, "having been refused permission to land." No explanation is offered for this discourtesy, although at that period, Kemalist forces may have been engaged in another chapter of ethnic cleansing by forcibly expelling Armenians and Pontic Greeks from the region, and as such were disinclined to allow unsympathetic Westerners any opportunity to witness these persecutions (least of all a factotum of Western oil

---

* In 1922, the U.S. Navy still kept its deck logs according to civilian time rather than military time.

imperialists).* They would be far less concerned with secrecy at Smyrna, where Greek arrogance and smouldering ethnic and religious resentment had long since sown the seeds of the most horrific retribution.

"One cannot help remarking that the Greeks are doing their level best to make themselves obnoxious, unpopular, and hated by the Turks," wrote a chagrined British official from Smyrna in the autumn of 1919 after that port had been occupied by the Greek army. He noted that the Greeks' "provocative behaviour . . . cannot but create ill-feeling, and a wider breach between these two races." British diplomats understood from the beginning of the occupation of Smyrna that the Greeks were "breaking open an ant's nest—[resulting in] temporary stupefaction, much running about, and a few hardy souls spitting acid at the invaders."[14] "Incidents," "disorder and rioting," and "atrocities" committed against Turkish Muslims were noted as soon as the Greek troops landed. A more foolish, more perfect stimulus for the Nationalists, and for Islamic vengeance, would be difficult to imagine.[15] The Harbord Mission to Asia Minor (Armenia) and the Transcaucasus, far from Anatolia, wrote of its 1919 visit, "The events at Smyrna have undoubtedly cheapened every Christian life in Turkey, the landing of the Greeks there being looked upon by the Turks as deliberate violation by the Allies of the terms of their Armistice and the probable forerunner of further unwarranted aggression. The moral responsibility for present unrest throughout Turkey is very heavy on foreign powers."[16]

Three years later, the situation had deteriorated into open military conflict: a war between the Greeks and Turkish Nationalist armies of Mustafa Kemal broke out in late 1920. By the end of the summer of 1922, the dispirited Greek armies had expended their last strength unsuccessfully in the stony uplands of Anatolia. In the last week of August, the northernmost Greek forces collapsed under a powerful Turkish counteroffensive, and what was initially a measured retreat became a rout. In the first days of September, the British military rep-

---

* These persecutions would in all likelihood have been residual actions in the wake of the Turkish-Armenian War of late 1920, which resulted from territorial concessions given to the Armenian republic under provisions in the ill-fated Treaty of Sèvres. Turkish Nationalists under Gen. Kazim Karabekir quickly pushed back the Armenian forces, and a subsequent incursion by opportunistic Soviet military units from the Azerbaijan region compelled the Armenians to sign the Treaty of Alexandropol in December 1920. The treaty removed half of the prewar territory given to the Armenians as well as all of the lands they had received at Sèvres. Again, a mass exodus of refugees flooded the region, and large-scale outbreaks of "ethnic-cleansing" by Turkish forces were recorded.

resentative at Smyrna visited the front, hoping to find that the Greek army had rallied along an interior line. What he found was "15,000 men fleeing in disorder."[17] The next day came the devastating news that the Greek commanding general, Tricoupis, had been surrounded and taken prisoner by the Turks. British and American officials in Constantinople and Smyrna immediately began drawing up plans, and consulting their Italian and French counterparts as well, for approaching the Kemalist government in Angora (Ankara) with an armistice proposal in order to avert a gigantic disaster in Smyrna. Caught up within this kaleidoscopic political and military chaos were the flushdeck U.S. destroyers of the U.S. Naval Detachment.

Before seven in the evening on September 1, *Edsall* was once more under way from Trebizond, charting a westward course past Kalnik, Vona, and Tashkhana Point for Samsoun, Turkey, another important tobacco exporting center, where a U.S. destroyer was usually stationed. In Samsoun on September 2, Mr. Miller and Mr. Lange left the ship, boarding USS *Parrott* (DD-218) "for transportation to Constantinople." A Mr. Murphy of Near East Relief came aboard from *Parrott* "for quarters awaiting permission from Anatolian authorities to land."

It is not hard to perceive the deteriorating state of affairs across this region as the ship made her winding voyage around the Black Sea. One crisis follows hard upon another: drought, famine, war, and the exploitation of these doleful presences for commercial gain hang over the late summer weeks like flames fanning the apocalyptic pall that would soon envelop a beautiful ancient port city.

There, too, on the Aegean side of the continent, vast clouds of limestone powder and smoke were approaching from the interior steppes and plateaus of up-country Anatolia. "Our eyes smarted from the white, burning dust; the dreary landscape made one depressed," wrote Aleksandr Pushkin, covering an earlier Russo-Turkish war a century before in his "Journey to Arzrum," a colorful travelog with a dour colonialist subtext. The sharp, incisive bite of Pushkin's pen would not have been lost upon Ernest Hemingway, writing one hundred years later.

Two more days passed, then *Edsall* received six persons from a local sailing vessel that had suffered a gasoline fire on board. Two of them were treated on the destroyer for burns received in the fire. In the afternoon of September 6, *Edsall*'s officers were finally granted permission to go ashore. On Thursday, September 7, a "Mr. Prins of the Near East

Relief Agency" arrived and went aboard the destroyer "for transportation to Constantinople." That evening at 8:40, the ship got under way, steaming west at high speed (22.5 knots) to the Bosporus.

True to type, *Edsall*'s vulnerable steering gear broke down along the way when the clutch came out on the steering engine. The treacherous currents always prevalent in the straits would have made this no laughing matter, but the destroyer continued on one engine, passing Kelia (Kilyos) Point and Anatoli (Anadolu) lighthouses before she "stood into the Bosporus" at five the next afternoon.

Within the hour, the ship had secured at Selvi Bournu opposite Büyükdere, about midway down the strait, and an hour later began receiving fuel from the Standard Oil Company's dock. The destroyer must have been steaming with little reserves in her fuel compartments, for she then spent the next couple of hours taking on just over 104,000 gallons—about 340 tons—of bunker oil.

Never one to miss a chance to reinforce American business "interests" in the region, Rear Adm. Mark Lambert Bristol, commander of the U.S. Naval Detachment, had already stationed U.S. naval guards at the refinery, where a suspicious fire had broken out earlier. They helped fight the blaze and then remained there in order to provide security. Then as now, the navy was always concerned about security at fuel centers.

The following morning, Saturday, September 9, *Edsall* once more got under way for an hour and moved on to Dolma-Bagtché, near the site of the fabled palace, where she secured to a buoy there. This ostentatious locale was in stark contrast to the tremendous poverty and disease then ravaging postwar Turkey. *Edsall* was soon visited by the commanding officer of her sister four-piper USS *Parrott* (DD-218).

Under the direction of Rear Admiral Bristol, preliminary emergency relief efforts for Smyrna were established in the first week of September. Numerous telegrams of increasing urgency had been received from U.S. and British officials there warning of another imminent catastrophe. From Constantinople, Bristol sent the following telegram to Washington, D.C., on September 9:

> Smyrna situation most alarming. Greek troops in panic and pouring into city. Population fears violence between time Greek troops ordered to evacuate and temporary arrangements of Turks. On September 6th, American, English, French, and

Italian consuls telegraphed Greek Minister of War, Theotakis, asking for assurances Smyrna would not be burned or pillaged. Theotakis replied he could give no such assurances. Greek fleet left Smyrna Friday afternoon. . . . Greek High Commissioner Sterghiades taken on board Iron Duke. . . . British withdrawing women and children. Three United States destroyers now at Smyrna. My chief of staff, Captain Hepburn, in charge.[18]

The U.S. destroyers were *Simpson, Litchfield,* and *Lawrence.* One or more was usually moored at the Standard Oil dock. *Edsall* would be sent next, arriving at the climax of the catastrophe. What this handful of small U.S. Navy vessels was supposed to achieve at a scene of such chaos, and with such numbers—estimated by Near East Relief and Red Cross representatives at seven hundred thousand human beings—facing starvation, and worse, is not clear.

Perhaps foremost in a multitude of problems during the year and a half preceding the catastrophe, U.S. and Greek authorities in Smyrna had also been struggling with what the former considered "illegal taxes which the Greek government here has been attempting to levy upon certain American imported articles, notably petroleum, alcohol, sugar, etc."[19]

At the center of these travails was a "consumptive tax amounting to 125,000 pounds (Turkish)," demanded by the Greek government from Standard Oil Company, whose failure to pay led to the newly appointed Greek director of customs at Smyrna shutting down Standard's distribution of oil.[20] For some time, the Greek government had sought to bolster their threadbare treasury, sapped by years of war, through additional taxes upon American imports, which naturally led to ever greater tensions. Although rectified soon enough, such quarrels did nothing to endear Greece to her allies.

After the collapse of the Greek army's Anatolian campaign late that summer of 1922, the Hellenist dream devolved into nightmare. Grim military defeat and even grimmer political failures were compounded by the influx of half-starved, terrified refugees streaming into Smyrna and other coastal areas, driven before the advancing Turkish troops.

Glowing entries in the *Dictionary of American Naval Fighting Ships* (DANFS) notwithstanding, the massacre of Armenians and Greek Christians at Smyrna, which took place as Allied warships stood idly by in many instances, was not a moral high point for the Allied military, or for Western foreign policy and diplomacy (and has a chilling resemblance to postmodern genocides in Bosnia and Darfur, which also feature Western complicity and impotence).

DANFS records:

> [*Edsall*] did much for international relations by helping nations to alleviate postwar famine in eastern Europe, evacuating refugees, furnishing a center of communications for the Near East, and all the while standing by for emergencies. When the Turks set fire to Smyrna (Izmir), *Edsall* was one of the American destroyers who [*sic*] evacuated thousands of Greeks. On September 14, 1922[,] she took 607 refugees off USS *Litchfield* (DD-336) in Smyrna and transported them to Salonika, returning to Smyrna on September 16 to act as a flagship for the naval forces there. In October she carried refugees from Smyrna to Mytilene on Lesvosis. She made repeated visits to ports in Turkey, Bulgaria, Russia, Greece, Egypt, Palestine, Syria, Tunisia, Dalmatia, and Italy.[21]

This little-known episode from *Edsall*'s chronology is a glimpse into an event of too much significance in twentieth-century history to be glossed over by a few trite phrases. Its very occurrence, like the U.S. Navy's oblique part in the Bay of Pigs blunder, was spoken of with marked reluctance decades later by the officers and sailors who had been present at the debacle.* Official reports by the commanding U.S. naval officer in Constantinople, Rear Admiral Bristol—who held the diplomatic post of high commissioner concurrently—in the aftermath of this witches' brew of duplicity and cant, contained what appeared to be fantastic reversals of the facts, when any were dealt with at all. British officials later remarked that they felt that Bristol and his intelligence officer, Lt. A. S. Merrill, were naïve and were being "spoon-fed" by the Turks. (The British would have known something about such double-dealing.

---

* The standard text, and an exceptional, if gut-wrenching, work of scholarship, is Marjorie Housepian Dobkin's *Smyrna 1922: The Destruction of a City*. Dobkin's extensive research led her to contact and meet a small handful of surviving U.S. enlisted men from the American warships present at Smyrna. Those harrowing events of so many years past continued to haunt some of these elderly men, yet most were still wary—forty-five years later—of speaking too freely about their experiences.

In the postwar period of 1919–20, the British "prevented American companies from operating or exploring in Palestine or Mesopotamia on the grounds that no arrangements could [be] made until new governments were established."[22] Representatives of British firms such as Shell and the Anglo-Persian Oil Company, however, were active in the region at the same time, the lack of new goverments notwithstanding. This does not begin to capture the duplicity of Prime Minister Lloyd George, or the viper's brood of charlatans, arms dealers, and politicos, along with their clandestine "agreements" over oil, after World War I.)

Bristol was also encouraging American business "interests" at the time of his service as high commissioner, although his repeated protestations of impartiality may be questioned. Stationing the navy's ships in the Near East was not cheap; at the time it cost roughly "$4,000,000 a year to maintain them on this particular duty, which does not train the crews for use in battle."[23] It is difficult to reconcile the stated official U.S. motives behind our "selfless," "disinterested" commitments to protect "purely American" lives and property in Smyrna while at the same time thousands of Anatolian Christians were left to their fates at the hands of Muslim Turks.

Only one industry had such power, to so cynically value the lives of tens of thousands of helpless women, children, elderly, and infirm less than its own commercial interests—the one industry that was said to have "positively oozed" out of the U.S. cabinet in those years. Companies such as Gulf were entrenched in the Treasury Department, Standard in the Navy Department, and Mammoth-Sinclair in the Department of the Interior during a period when serious concern for the nation's oil supply encouraged penetrating and exploiting foreign fields.

One must bear in mind that these events took place during the presidency of the duncical Warren Harding, of whose administration it was said that "the proved evidence is enough to warrant the statement that [it] was responsible in its short two years and five months for more concentrated robbery and rascality than any other in the whole history of the federal government."[24] And as every high school student once knew, the central scandal of the Harding administration was the Teapot Dome affair, which involved U.S. Navy oil reserves, and an appropriately slimy black trail of uncomplicated greed among various cabinet members and government functionaries. After all, Harding had been selected and elected with oil money:

To the victor go the spoils, and having heavily financed the Harding campaign, the oil companies claimed the key cabinet positions. . . . Harding's Cabinet—the "Oil Cabinet" as it came to be called—put the highest levels of government under the control of the petroleum industry, not only for purposes of policy, but . . . also for purposes of plunder.[25]

"The Great Stonehead of Marion, Ohio," as Harding was called with genuine affection by H. L. Mencken, appears to have been as gullible as he was well intentioned, and easy meat for the good fellows of America's oil companies, who penetrated the Navy Department and the Department of the Interior and corrupted his own attorney general. The secretary of the treasury post was given to industrialist and banker Andrew W. Mellon of Gulf Oil; the assistant secretary of the navy job went to Theodore Roosevelt Jr., a director of Sinclair Oil; postmaster general went to Harry Sinclair's lawyer, Will Hays; secretary of the interior was given to Albert B. Fall, a crony of Edward Doheny, one of America's wealthiest, most ambitious, and most unscrupulous oil men.[26]

Pennsylvania Avenue was more than several worlds away from the Near East and Far East for Harding, whose amiable intellectual befuddlement was a boon to the petrochemical industry and its assorted hangers-on, all hungrily eyeing the remote Ottoman oilfields. A retired rear admiral named Colby Chester, for example, had been scheming for years to construct a vast rail system with generous associated mineral rights. It appears this grandiose project had the blessing of High Commissioner Bristol, but far more powerful forces—in the corporate form of Standard Oil—were not as eager to see Chester get his concession.

If Rear Admiral Bristol was naïve, it was in his unsound belief that an underdog venture such as the Chester Concession—with morality and legality on its side—could ever triumph against a predatory megalosaur like Standard. Within another eighteen months the under-funded Chester group had been brushed aside once and for all, and the big eaters moved in to glut themselves on the carcass. There is also some evidence that Walter C. Teagle of Standard may have been proactive in seeing that the Chesters were denied further credit on Wall Street. It must be understood that "the sanctified Open Door was a means of egress only to those with a favored position in Washington and Wall Street."[27]

Even a personality as durable and blithe as Ernest Hemingway, covering the Greco-Turkish War as a young reporter for the *Toronto Daily Star*, and who had forgotten more at age twenty-three than Harding ever learned, was reduced to shaded, ironic commentary when it came to Smyrna's destruction.* More poignant are the cautious memories of U.S. sailors serving with the Naval Detachment's destroyers, who took part in "peacekeeping" actions that made no sense to them and, worse still, were compelled to passively witness the atrocities committed by Kemalist troops against helpless refugees throughout Smyrna.

Holocaust at Smyrna

Wretched Christians! European greed, jealousy, competition, and twentieth century politics sacrifice you in cunning piety! I regret that America too has a silent part and says nothing because of oil interests!
—Abraham H. Hartunian, *Neither to Laugh Nor to Weep*

[State] Department is not inclined to do more than send destroyers to Smyrna to assist in the protection of American lives and property. The situation would not appear to justify this Government assuming the role of voluntary mediator.
—Acting Secretary of State William Phillips to High Commissioner at Constantinople Rear Adm. M. L. Bristol, September 5, 1922

On the evening of Sunday, September 10, *Edsall* got under way from buoy No. 2 at Dolma-Bagtché in the Bosporus and worked up to twenty knots on a southeasterly course. In an hour, she reached Prinkipo, located on the idyllic Prince's Islands (today Büyükada in the Adalar islands), that "little suburban archipelago,"[28] where she anchored in company with the detachment's station ship, USS *Scorpion* (AY-3).

It is unknown whether *Edsall*'s men and officers—like the British sailor who later remembered this merely as "an island called Prinky-

---

* The 1930 edition of *In Our Time* included "On the Quai at Smyrna" as an introductory vignette. Hemingway was not present at the events described in the little tale, but he had traveled by train from Paris through Germany and on to Constantinople over a three-week period to cover the Greco-Turkish conflict in the autumn of 1922.

poo"—were able to enjoy the spectacular view of the dark slopes wooded with pines, or the hilltop monastery of St. George, where the monks made an excellent white wine from local grapes. The nineteenth-century traveler Gustave Schlumberger had written, "These radiant islands [are] one of the most tragic sites of the ancient world. No corner of the earth is more fertile in stories of lamentable catastrophies." And he noted their "poignant lessons in the vanity of human grandeur."[29] Three hours later *Edsall* sent a boat ashore with a "confidential letter" for Rear Admiral Bristol, a man who would come to embody just such poignant lessons.

Since January 1919, Mark L. Bristol had been on duty as senior representative and high commissioner for the United States. According to his own words, Bristol had advocated a policy of "the non-partition of the old Turkish Empire as it existed in 1914," and the "abolition of the old Turkish administration over this Empire," along with placing "one strong power . . . over the whole of the old Ottoman Empire to establish good government."[30] He understood that the Turks would *never* consent to be ruled by Hellenic Greeks, and that any attempts at such an arrangement were unnatural, incendiary, and doomed. He also recognized the chicanery of British oil policy in the Near and Middle East during this period and their deceptive rhetoric when it came to political support for the Greeks in Anatolia.

The next day at 7:37 a.m., the energetic commanding officer of the Naval Detachment came aboard *Edsall* with his staff. The ship once more got under way and ferried Bristol and staff to Constantinople in a fifty-one-minute trip, the admiral and his men leaving for shore at 8:30 a.m. on a base motor sailer. Two minutes later, *Edsall* reversed course and began returning to her Dolma-Bagtché buoy.

That afternoon between 4:30 and 6:00, the destroyer received Near East Relief stores "for transportation to Smyrna." She also took aboard thirty-three bags of mail from HMS *Marlborough* for British naval authorities at Smyrna. This day the *Edsall* appears to have remained at the Near East Relief dock, during which time several more passengers arrived bound for Greece or Anatolia. After Misters Joblin, L. I. Thomas, F. Crane, and J. Agginan reported aboard early Wednesday morning, the destroyer cast off, and "in accordance with Detachment Cdr.'s Movement Order # 351 got under way for Smyrna."

By eight o'clock that evening she was steaming at just over twenty-five knots into the Aegean Sea, heading west, past the city of Antigonia, which "appeared to be entirely on fire," and at last into Salonika Bay. She moored dockside at Salonika and her passengers disembarked, although no specifics are given as to their number or identities. The log of *Edsall* notes, "Greek Naval officials gave excellent co-operation while Standard Oil Co. furnished a truck. All refugees were quickly taken off." The ship and her crew did not linger, though; they had yet to reach their destination at Smyrna.

Before daylight on Thursday, September 14, 1922, *Edsall* steamed into Smyrna's bay, and at 6:00 anchored off the seawall in five fathoms, astern of fellow four-piper USS *Litchfield* (DD-336). The doomed city was already an infernal spectacle: "Harbor full of various warships each loaded with refugees, town in flames . . . aided by high winds rapidly approaching. Numerous refugees parading on various docks and sea walls, each group carrying a flag of some nationality. No landing was made, but captain reported to Litchfield for instructions." These bland official remarks in her log should be weighed against those of Lieutenant Merrill, the intelligence officer who was also traveling aboard *Edsall* and whose descriptions are worth quoting at some length:

> The entire city was ablaze and the harbor light as day. Thousands of homeless were surging back and forth along the blistering quay, panic-stricken to the point of insanity. The shrieks of the women and children were painful to hear. In a frenzy they would throw themselves into the water, and some of them would reach the ship. The crowds along the quay were so thick and tried so desperately to close in abreast of the men-of-war anchorage, that the masses in the stifling center had nowhere to go but into the sea.[31]

"What a hellish scene!" wrote an Armenian evangelical pastor, Abraham Hartunian, attempting frantically to secure transportation for his family out of Smyrna's escalating violence.

> The quay was bulging with humanity from end to end. Exhausted! Defeated! Pale! Terrified! Hopeless! The sea on one side, the flames on the other. The fire had spread so rapidly and become so intense that it devoured all before it and advanced with a roar. In a little while the magnificent buildings on the quay would go up. And what about the people then? . . .

And those mighty battleships and brave European and American soldiers observed and took motion pictures of this hideous crime of their own contriving.[32]

One may still find these grim films taken at Smyrna.* Perhaps they were shot from the deck of *Edsall* herself; if so, the irony would be staggering. And the Reverend Hartunian was correct in the sense that the Allied nations were guilty beyond any reasonable doubt of creating the maelstrom of ethnic hatred, commercial greed, human vanity, and political folly that led to the holocaust at Smyrna. Although a recapitulation of the events leading up to the city's destruction is far too complex a subject for this text, there is no question that the British had played a major role in enabling Greece's occupation of Anatolia, and that Russian, French, Italian, and U.S. "interests" contributed to the disaster. And the Greeks themselves—as embodied by the high commissioner of Smyrna, Aristidis Sterghiades—did little to manage the situation sensibly and much to antagonize their ancient enemies, the Turks. Great Britain's prime minister, Lloyd George, is reported to have gloated that he "humiliated the Turks" at the Treaty of Sèvres. Yet it would be the hapless Christians of Anatolia from whom repayment was to be exacted for such foolish insults.[33]

The flushdecker then moved up, securing next to her sister ship, and sent off thirty-three bags of mail to HMS *Iron Duke*. *Edsall* transferred all of her passengers, plus 200 bags of flour and 1,400 loaves of bread, to *Litchfield*. Simultaneously *Edsall* began receiving refugees from *Litchfield* at eight that morning. She took aboard a baffling number of people; yet this, too, somehow seems fitting in view of the many mistakes and errors with which her history is riddled. DD-219's log says that she received "662 refugees: 420 Greeks, 140 Armenians, 1 Italian, and 1 Jew." Whatever the correct total—either 562 or 662—the four-piper, overloaded with grateful refugees (legend suggests that future shipping tycoon Aristotle Onassis, a Greek native of Smyrna, may have escaped as a youth aboard *Edsall*), was again under way at 8:55 a.m. She steamed out of the clogged harbor at fifteen knots before increas-

---

* As of this writing, a grainy strip of black-and-white film, shot from a ship in Smyrna's harbor as the city burned, may be found on the video-sharing site YouTube. It is no more than twenty seconds long.

ing speed to twenty-five knots at 3:45 p.m. as she crossed the Aegean, bound for Greece.

Sometime after 4:00 the next morning, which was Friday, September 15, *Edsall* moored at the East Mole in Salonika Bay, where her refugees were taken off. It is recorded that *Edsall*'s skipper, Commander Powell, was "pleasantly startled" when the port of Salonika's captain, a man who could speak but a little English, came aboard the destroyer and, in the name of Greece, thanked the Americans for their kindness in helping his stricken countrymen. "It is not surprising this is done by America, the best friend if not the only real friend the Greeks have," he stated to Powell with tears in his eyes.[34]

At Smyrna, Consul-General George Horton, having been manhandled "through the frantic crowds" by U.S. bluejackets to safety aboard USS *Simpson* (DD-221), witnessed the chaos and terror firsthand.

The last view of the ill-fated town by daylight was one of vast enveloping clouds rolling up to heaven, a narrow water-front covered with a great throng of people—an ever-increasing throng, with the fire behind and the sea before, and a powerful fleet of inter-allied battle-ships, among which were two American destroyers, moored a short distance from the quay and looking on. . . . As the destroyer moved away from the fearful scene and darkness descended, the flames, raging now over a vast area, grew brighter and brighter, presenting a scene of awful and sinister beauty.[35]

Aboard *Simpson*, the following radio message was received by the U.S. consul: "Direct for Horton. 0114 ref my 0114 dash 1136 Winona will have about 1000 refugees destroyer *Odsall* [*sic*] left 7 a.m. For Salonica [*sic*] with 600 all she could carry. Please announce and assist evacuation if possible Hepburn 1900."[36]

Within six hours on the other side of the Aegean, after *Edsall*'s refugees had disembarked, the destroyer set out from Salonika once again for Anatolia. Nineteen hours later, the ship re-entered Smyrna's harbor, her log noting, "city of Smyrna still burning a little and smoking much." The ship anchored a mile and a half north of the breakwater; yet even that far out, "two male bodies [were found] floating near the ship." Such situations were far from unusual. Dobkin records that one Allied admiral being ferried to a colleague's warship for dinner during this period was delayed due to a woman's corpse fouling the propeller of his launch. Another Royal Navy officer provided his own firsthand description of human destiny at Smyrna:

> What of an old Greek woman who from sheer weaknesss had fallen over the edge of the quay into the water. A decrepit old fellow, probably her husband, was kneeling and throwing towards the floating body a piece of string that he might succour her. Several attempts he made to reach her but failed each time. The body ceased to move, so the old man finished his efforts and turned away from the water side with a young boy who had stood by him watching the pitiful scene.[37]

Such dispassionate observation and the Allied officer's own moral inertia form the factual basis for accounts such as Hemingway's black-humored vignette.

On the afternoon of September 16, *Edsall* sent a landing party to Smyrna "as patrol for American interests." A little later she shipped "all N.E.R. flour ashore to be stored in Relief Organization storehouse." Most, if not all, of these supplies would have to be relocated or were lost in the conflagration as building after building succumbed to the wind-driven flames.

After September 16, Cmdr. Halsey "Harry" Powell aboard *Edsall* became the senior naval officer present at Smyrna, but it had taken precious time for relief efforts by the Americans, British, Italians, and French to coalesce and begin helping evacuate upward of a quarter of a million starving, brutalized refugees. For untold numbers, help came too late. Numerous civilians were rounded up and "deported" to the interior of Anatolia, and Turkish authorities made no attempt to conceal the severe fate that would befall them.

At eight o'clock on the morning of Sunday, September 17, *Edsall* landed a patrol "of eight men and one CPO" to guard the U.S. consulate. The ship's log additionally records "various officials of State and Relief Societies messing on board." Among these would have been one of Smyrna's unlikeliest heroes: an ex–Methodist minister from upstate New York turned YMCA official named E. C. "Asa" Jennings. Scarcely five feet tall, Jennings proved to be a biblical David after the city fell, championing relief efforts against the Goliath of bureaucratic indifference and hostility. He worked tirelessly, saving innumerable lives and organizing mass evacuations throughout the fiasco. He managed to ingratiate himself with Captain Powell aboard *Edsall* and was even permitted to give orders to U.S. sailors from the ship, which saved many more refugees' lives. Powell felt constrained by Bristol's orders and told Jennings to "do your darnedest." Jennings did just that.[38]

However, on September 17, Commander Halsey reported to Bristol from Smyrna aboard *Edsall* that the Turks had issued an "official proclamation" that declared all refugee males between the ages of eighteen and forty-five prisoners of war, and that they would be deported. He also noted, "Disorder still prevalent . . . fifty thousand [refugees] in readiness for evacuation north end of city. Relief again organized. Turks furnishing hard-tack to a certain extent; fire still burning but not considered dangerous."[39]

Almost all refugee females between the ages of fifteen and thirty-five had already been separated and taken away by the Turks. A British diplomat on the destroyer HMS *Serapis* (which was carrying *Edsall*'s mail back to Constantinople) saw fewer than a dozen women of this age among the nine hundred evacuees rescued by that vessel.[40]

Attempts to find adequate shipping to remove the tens of thousands of displaced, starving Armenians, Greeks, and miscellaneous Christians over the next days were painfully slow. At times plain bribery worked, as when Asa Jennings paid six thousand lire to the reluctant captain of a large, empty Italian cargo vessel called the *Constantinopoli*. Through Jennings' efforts, this ship managed to evacuate two thousand persons to Mytilene, on Lesbos. There Jennings found more than a dozen big transports lying idle; these ships had withdrawn most of the Greek army from certain destruction in Turkey.

After discharging the thankful mass of refugees, Jennings returned to Smyrna in three hours aboard another four-piper with a pledge from the Greek commander at Mytilene harbor, General Frankos, for six more transport ships to follow, provided that Frankos received a written guarantee of their protection. Mustafa Kemal had relented and finally granted the Allies permission to send Greek ships into the harbor at Smyrna. Asa Jennings immediately began organizing more evacuations.[41]

On the morning of September 24, *Edsall* "landed an additional patrol of 15 men to help embarkation of refugees." At two o'clock that afternoon, escorted by *Lawrence*, "Greek merchant ships went along-side dock at the Point and approximately 15,000 refugees embarked under direction of N.E.R. with assistance of American sailors and Turkish troops. Ships then stood out to sea under escort of USS *Lawrence*."

Ultimately, the figures in Commander Powell's "supplementary report of evacuations from Smyrna and vicinity" show a total of 213,480 persons evacuated from Smyrna by U.S., British, French, Italian, and Greek ships. Powell recorded another 49,107 persons evacuated from "the vicinity of Smyrna . . . Chesme, Vourla, Aivali, Cape Hellas, Kuluk, Makri, Adalia, Port of Alaya, and Rhodes" aboard British and Greek transports and a single U.S. destroyer.[42] The figures for those who were murdered and "deported"—whether Muslim or Christian—have never been agreed upon.

At Smyrna, the massacre of innocents had continued unabated as flames deliberately started by Greek, Armenian, and Turkish arsonists devoured the ancient port. The U.S. vessels would assist in evacuating many thousands, with the remaining Allied nations eventually making valiant efforts as well. Yet thousands more evacuees would be lost to Turkish depredations, their "silent, ghastly processions" winding from the cinders of Smyrna into the somber interior of Anatolia, where their bones have lain unredeemed for the worst part of a century.

In October 1922, a cease-fire was arranged through the Mudania Armistice. This was followed by the Treaty of Lausanne in July 1923, finalizing boundaries for the new nation on Kemalist terms. It was then time for the misnamed "*Odsall*" to move on—from one remote, obscure locale to another just as distant, just as foreign.

With *Edsall*'s presence at the Ionian nightmare no longer required, she was first sent to various ports throughout the Aegean. The U.S. Navy continued to make every effort to avoid creating friction. Although the naval supply base at Constantinople was discontinued, *Edsall*, along with *Bulmer, McLeish, McCormick, Parrott, Simpson, Scorpion*, and a subchaser, was retained until spring. The destroyers were then transferred to the commander of European Naval Forces on May 6, 1924.[43]

Edsall soon went back to the States. Following overhaul at Boston's Navy Yard in the summer of 1924, she departed for the Far East on January 3, 1925. After steaming via Guantanamo Bay, Cuba, for more fleet exercises, the destroyer moved west through the Panama Canal to

San Diego. Then she sailed for Pearl Harbor before being sent on to Shanghai, where she arrived on June 22, 1925.

In Shanghai she would once more find herself part of the U.S. Navy's ongoing mission of protecting the Open Door policy. But in China, as in the Near East, this misguided ethos of Dollar Diplomacy, which the United States paid lip service to, was a clear-cut impossibility. In the end, it garnered nothing but contempt from the Japanese for America. The flushdeckers would still augment various destroyer squadrons in the years to come, giving stellar service as escorts and submarine killers, or converted to high-speed transports and minelayers, but they would never again represent a primary striking arm of U.S. naval forces, except in one region: the small, venerable Asiatic Fleet at the outset of World War II in the Far East.

On the Asiatic Station

We went to G.Q. in the Celebes,
We deployed the fleet on a group of trees—
And ran in circles in various degrees
In the Asiatic Squadron.
    —Sung to the tune of "In the Armoured Cruiser Squadron"

Reconstituted in January 1910, the Asiatic Fleet was based at Shanghai for many years. It was "thoroughly habituated to the routine of summers in Chefoo and winters in Manila."[44] That is to say, four winter months occupied with operations and gunnery training in the Philippines, four summer months undergoing similar training in North China, and the remaining four months of the year "showing the flag" in most of the principal ports between Surabaja, Java, and Yokohama, Japan. Fleet and type exercises were typically held between port visits, with joint exercises conducted in Philippine waters.

Once more, *Edsall* was almost immediately deposited into a hornet's nest. Again troops were put ashore to safeguard U.S. interests, although in this instance, the Nanking Road Incident (a consequence of feuding Chinese labor relations) was by no means a tragedy on the scale of Smyrna. The United States wanted to enforce the Open Door policy in China, too, but there they would face overt opposition from another predator nation with a different view of what "Open Door" meant.

CHINA
Kulangsu
Swatow
FORMOSA
Hong Kong

HAINAN

PACIFIC
OCEAN

INDO-CHINA

Lingayen
Gulf
LUZON

Bangkok

Manila

PHILIPPINE
ISLANDS

MINDORO

SAMAR

Saigon

PANAY
Iloilo
LEYTE

Gulf of
Siam

South
China Sea

PALAWAN

Sulu
Sea

MINDANAO
Davao

MALAYA

NORTH
BORNEO
Sandakan
Jolo

TAWI TAWI

BRUNEI

Celebes
Sea

SARAWAK

TARAKAN

Moluccan Passage

SUMATRA

Singapore

Kuching

BORNEO

Manado

HALMAHERA

EQUATOR

Pontianak

Djambi

BANGKA

Samarinda
Balikpapan

Greyhound
Strait

CELEBES

CERAM

Palembang

BELITUNG

Puting

Gulf of
Tolo

Pomalaa
Kendari

BURU

Ambon

NEW
GUINEA

Krakatoa

Sunda
Strait

Batavia

Java Sea

Makassar

Banda
Sea

Pelabuhan
Ratu

Tjilatjap

JAVA

Surabaja
Jogjakarta

LOMBOK
Tambora

Flores
Sea
ALOR
WETAR

Ombai
Strait

Arafura
Sea

BALI

SUMBAWA

FLORES

TIMOR

CHRISTMAS
ISLAND

DUTCH EAST INDIES

SUMBA
Koepang

Timor
Sea

INDIAN
OCEAN

Joseph
Bonaparte
Gulf

Darwin

0
500 nm

AUSTRALIA

Karimata Strait
Makassar Strait

Topaz Maps Inc.

Along with other Asiatic Fleet destroyers, DD-219 received high praise from the British chargé d'affaires in Peking, Michael Palairet, for her service there:

> The Americans, whatever may be their sentiments regarding the rights of the case, have from the first taken a full share in the defence of the settlement, as they have in the protection of life and property elsewhere. The United States Navy, which happened to have a number of destroyers at Shanghai . . . were among the first to land men, and they have since maintained the largest armed force of any of the Powers.[45]

Edsall would remain a fixture on the colorful, if often seedy, Asiatic Station for the next seventeen years as a "faithful guardian of American interests" in a period of great instability, and nowhere more so than in the lawless, revolution-torn coastal regions of Southeast Asia and China. In 1926 and 1927, amid much civil unrest, there were a number of incidents in China in which rebels and bandits kidnapped and, in some cases, murdered American citizens, often missionaries. Nevertheless, it was good duty for the sailors, yet never really easy for the Anglo-Saxons stationed in a superstitious land, where "the missionary is considered a spy, the business man a rogue, and the naval officer a pirate."[46]

On the morning of May 28, 1927, *Edsall* departed Hankow for Chenglinki, where she was needed to escort the USS *Pinguin*, after that vessel had been fired upon by Chinese bandits. In late October 1927, command of *Edsall*—then a unit in Destroyer Division 39, Destroyer Squadron 15 of the Asiatic Fleet*—was given to Cmdr. Jules James (U.S. Naval Academy, 1908), who "sailed immediately for Hong Kong." In a letter home, James baldly described Hong Kong as "a small barren island . . . ceded to England many years ago," but now a "beautiful English city." A day later, the destroyer left and steamed down the tip of French Indochina, making a leisurely transit across the Gulf of Siam. One writer, flying from Penang, Sumatra, to Bangkok, recorded the following impressions of this part of the Far East:

> The scenery of this part of the journey is very fine. The sapphire sea below is studded with little islands, each a wild uninhabited

---

* Ironically Adm. Mark L. Bristol was the commander of the Asiatic Fleet at this time.

cluster of green palm trees with rocky shores. The islands are not flat like so many coral islands along the Great Barrier Reef or in the calm sea of the East Indies, but hilly, irregularly shaped fragments of land with tiny bays and jagged promontories. Towards the eastern horizon the sea toned to an opal shade and a little below to the west was a low coast-line of brilliant yellow sand with jungle to its edge and blue hills in the distance. As we proceeded north the islands were left behind, the coast became more rugged and the hills of the west grew into jungle-covered mountains.[47]

The little four-piper proceeded on to Bangkok, "about 30 miles up the [Mae Nam Chao Dhraya] river," where DD-219 had "three of the royal princesses on board for tea." The port, upriver from the head of the Gulf of Siam, was, and still is, reached along a winding and contorted channel that offers many navigational difficulties. The Siamese royal family showed their appreciation by inviting Commander James and seven officers to the palace, where *Edsall*'s skipper was presented with an engraved silver cigarette box. Next, the destroyer visited Saigon in Indochina, "a French colony" in which James, a former assistant U.S. Navy attaché in Paris, felt right at home and served as "the interpreter" much of the time.

By November 18, the ship and crew were anchored once more in Manila Bay, where James returned to thoughts "of target practices, torpedo and depth bomb practices . . . full-power runs, etc. till the spring fighting begins in China."[48] In mid-December, after submitting letters offering new methods for improved depth-charge attacks and anti-aircraft fire control, James wrote to Cmdr. Fairfax Leary on the light cruiser USS *Omaha*: "This destroyer game is also new to me. . . . We are here for docking, material inspection, various target practices, etc. until the spring fighting begins. April 1st we go to river patrol."

Two seasons later, *Edsall* was dispatched just before Christmas 1929, along with division mates USS *Bulmer* (DD-222) and USS *McCormick* (DD-223), from Manila to Shanghai once more. Chinese rebels, "brigands," and Communists were battling among themselves and against the imperialist economic forces of America, Great Britain, and Japan, and kidnapping or murdering any number of luckless Westerners who fell into their hands.

When the violence spread into the city of Shanghai, Western citizenry and business interests took priority. Marines and bluejackets were landed, and civilians, rescued from the hinterlands on riverboats and small steamers and protected by the Sand Pebble Navy of the Yangtze Patrol, were then withdrawn. It was obviously not a wholesome period to be a Catholic evangelist laboring to spread the Gospel in missions situated in remote Asian provinces. A priest successfully ransomed and allowed to live might fetch some three thousand dollars, however. That was no small sum in Depression-era funds. As often as not, though, these unfortunates were brutally murdered.

These troubles, or "spring fighting," aggravated by Chinese insularity and suspicions, continued to worsen, especially as the Japanese-inspired "China Incident" grew throughout the 1930s. Disarmament conferences and treaties produced new arms races and allowed those signatories already hell-bent on violence an excuse to portray themselves as victims in order to justify further aggression. Western chauvinism consistently underestimated Japanese technology, pride, and determination, and these failings were highlighted at numerous interwar naval limitations conferences.

"This happy augury for peace," as the 1930 London Naval Treaty was referred to by the U.S. secretary of state, was in fact nothing of the sort. The Japanese were profoundly insulted by its concessions—the so-called Reed-Matsudaira Compromise—and considerable political turmoil resulted in Japan itself. Militarists had gained the upper hand, and in Hirohito, they encountered no meaningful or effective opposition to their aims. Intimidation by the military ruled; elsewhere, supine complacency resulted.

The Western powers, depleted by the hardships of the Great Depression and revolted by the prospect of another world conflict, were again compelled to stand by and await developments. Admiral Montgomery Meigs Taylor, commanding the Asiatic Fleet from September 1, 1931, remarked to a superior that his "sole job out here" was "sitting tight."[49] Her national pride ostensibly at stake, Japan eventually withdrew from the treaty system, refusing to budge from her minimal demands for warship tonnage parity with the West.

By the end of that terrible yet hopeful decade, Japanese arrogance often became outright violence, and no one was spared its effects. There were more brutal clashes with aggressive Imperial Army and Imperial

Navy personnel up and down the war-ravaged coast of China from Hong Kong to Tsingtao. Western diplomatic traffic of the 1930s records an endless chain of disputes between the aggrieved Japanese, the hapless Chinese, and the Anglo-American forces caught in the middle.

Most British and U.S. efforts were reactions to emergencies, hoping to maintain some semblance of status quo. More often than not, however, Japanese patience and inflexibility won; after all, they were operating from a vantage point of military power that Britain, France, America, Germany, and Italy all lacked. Any infraction or perceived transgression, no matter how trivial, was enough to provoke unpleasant overreactions by the Japanese.

In the United States, of all places, these skirmishes should have been recognized for what they were: examples of frontier justice. The Asiatic Station was remote, primitive, and no place for the soft or faint of heart. The Shanghai Crisis of early 1932 was an instructive, albeit negative, example of what would follow throughout the rest of the decade. It was only a matter of time before *Edsall* would find herself caught up in just such an incident.

In 1933, *Edsall* was part of the Yangtze Patrol of the Asiatic Fleet during the Japanese occupation of Woosung. In the last months of that Depression-shrouded year, Cmdr. Jules James, then commanding officer of Destroyer Division 6 at San Pedro, California, received a letter from his friend Cmdr. Warren L. Moore on USS *Black Hawk*, tender for the Asiatic Fleet's Destroyer Squadron 5, of which *Edsall* remained a member. In the letter, Moore requested details of the fleet's advanced torpedo practices held earlier in the spring because "you know we get very little of that Fleet experience out here."

In his response about a month later, James observed, "These destroyers are getting old and we find that a great deal of time must be spent on their upkeep. Even with the present practices we are very much crowded." These sentiments were written a full eight years before Pearl Harbor, at which time the Asiatic Fleet's destroyer squadron was unaltered, comprising the same class of old four-pipers that had served in the Far East since the early 1920s. Indeed, the material condition of the ships was such that a written order had been published forbidding the use of air hammers when the ships went into the Cavite Naval Yard for drydocking. It was feared that chipping hammers might punch holes through their rust-ravaged hulls. And aboard their tender, the ancient

USS *Black Hawk* (AD-9), one crew-member later recalled, "When it showered, it rained to the keel."[50] The ships generally proceeded northward along the coast of China, stopping at Hong Kong, then up to Chinwangtao—the major port through which men and supplies were routed to Peking or Tientsen—before moving on to Taku, Chefoo, and Tsingtao. Some men who had spouses and children were allowed to send them ahead aboard commercial vessels.

In summer 1935, *Edsall* was found at Chefoo, China, escaping the boiling equatorial heat of Manila along with her squadron mates and tender. The harbor and town were situated on the northern side of the Shantung promontory, an enormous curving peninsula where the climate was described as "the most salubrious of all those open to the residence of Europeans on the coast of China, presenting the notable advantages of a dry atmosphere, a thoroughly bracing winter, and sea-air and bathing." One of the only ports in northern China open in the winter months, its harbor was "merely an open roadstead,"[51] some two and a half by three miles with an anchorage capable of taking ships up to a twenty-five-foot draft within a mile and a quarter from the shore.

Sailors who wanted the extra money could use the Chefoo rifle and pistol ranges to improve their marksman rating. For riflemen and pistol shots, "sharpshooters" rated an extra dollar and "expert" marksmen would add three dollars per month to their pay. In this way, enlisted men of the Asiatic Fleet could send a few dollars home to families struggling in the Depression's threadbare economy, as well as subsidize the nipa shacks, joy houses, and breweries of Manila, Shanghai, and Tsingtao through the interwar years.

A major escalation of the Sino-Japanese conflict occurred in the summer of 1937 in and around Shanghai. In August, the U.S. government believed that the situation was serious enough to warrant sending the Asiatic Fleet flagship USS *Augusta* (CA-31) from Tsingtao to Shanghai to protect U.S. lives and property.

While at anchor *Augusta* received near misses from Chinese bombers. She promptly painted large U.S. flags atop her two forward turrets. However, these precautions did not prevent her from being hit numerous times by shrapnel and small-arms fire while moored along the volatile waterfront. Western vessels were often in more danger from errant Chinese shells than from those of the Japanese.

Another Asiatic Fleet veteran dispatched to the region during this crisis was the ubiquitous *Edsall*, also arriving in August 1937. Less than two years later she would find herself embroiled in yet another confrontation with the bellicose Japanese that bore a depressing resemblance to numerous other "troubles" along the Chinese coast.

We were there . . . or were we?

Histories of the Sino-Japanese conflict have reported that on May 13, 1939, *Edsall* and the British destroyer HMS *Scout* were anchored off the small island of Kulangsu, just off the larger island of Amoy, China. Kulangsu housed an International Settlement sheltering some ten thousand Chinese refugees from the Japanese. A Chinese resident of the Amoy Peace Settlement, whose name is given variously as Ang Hip Hoon or Hung Li-Son, had been killed on May 11, and the Japanese Navy landed 150 troops in response, ostensibly to apprehend the murderers. It was a pretext, in fact, because the late Hoon/Li-Son was actually no more than a "head lighterman who had been shot by a rival merchant," but his death gave the eager Japanese another opportunity to further terrorize their fellow Asians, an act they justified by claims of unfair commercial practices, as well as foreign arms being smuggled into China.*

The truth, however, is that the *Edsall* was not then in the Amoy-Kulangsu area but instead spent all of the first half of May 1939 at Swatow (Shantou), China, well to the south. Anchored near Double Island, *Edsall* observed Japanese aerial attacks in support of their ground offensive in the region. At the same time, she entertained commanding officers from various Royal Navy warships also at Swatow, including the captain of HMS *Folkestone* and later the captain of HMS *Falmouth*.

---

* Of course there were immense numbers of arms being sold to the Chinese in their war against Japan. For example, a 1938 secret despatch [F 13881/34/10] from Sir Robert Craigie in Tokyo to Lord Halifax at the Foreign Office in London enumerated the biggest suppliers of arms traffic through Hong Kong. Though the Japanese were convinced that the majority of munitions-carrying vessels were British, in fact, less than half were. One of the foremost sources of munitions was Hitlerite Germany, which in the first half of 1938 alone supplied 70 percent of China's large artillery projectiles, plus 113,250,000 rounds of machine-gun and rifle ammunition. Czechoslovakia supplied more than 5,500 machine guns and 26 million rounds of rifle and machine-gun ammunition. The biggest sales, however, appear to have been with Sweden, which provided 40 percent of all antiaircraft guns, 90 percent of all mortar shells, and 117,670,000 rounds of rifle and machine-gun ammunition. The United States and Great Britain contributed aircraft primarily, and related accessories and spare parts; Great Britain also shipped 25 percent of all the dynamite and gelignite used by the Chinese. British Documents on Foreign Affairs (BDFA), Part II, Series E.

The old British destroyer HMS *Thracian* made an appearance there as well. The Japanese air forces were from the Third Combined Air Unit, with two dozen "ground attack planes" flying from Canton and nine more floatplanes—Type 95 Nakajima E8N2 Daves and Type 94 Kawanishi E7K2 Alfs—being used from the seaplane tender *Kamikawa Maru*, operating out of the Hainan area.[52]

Daily observations in *Edsall's* log noted somewhat nervously the frequent groups of Japanese planes bombing and strafing targets around Swatow. As *Edsall* was anchored with Standard Oil buildings as bearings on May 3, for example, her log records a flight of eight Japanese bombers ("6 light, 2 heavy") flying in from the east to drop twenty bombs on the city.

With the dense smoke rising from Swatow visible at her anchorage, the destroyer's crew found themselves called to air defense stations almost every day. Friday, May 5, saw the mayor, the councilor, and the U.S. consul come aboard the ship at noon for a two-hour meeting that no doubt concerned the rapidly deteriorating local situation. The next day her men observed "six single-pontoon and two double-pontoon" Japanese floatplanes appear to hammer the east end of the city with eighteen more bombs.

On Sunday, May 14, a number of Imperial Navy planes "machine-gunned fishing craft dangerously close to the ship," as the sailors again manned their antiaircraft weapons. No one wanted a replay of the *Panay* or *Tutuila* affairs, but it was clear that the Japanese were not going to be intimidated by a few old, small Western destroyers.

On Tuesday, May 16, officers from the four-piper went ashore to visit General Hua, the local commander of Chinese defense forces in the Swatow area. *Edsall* shifted her anchorage closer to Waglan Island on Friday, May 19, when her sister ship USS *Bulmer* (DD-222) arrived at 8:55 a.m. after a trip to the troubled ports of Amoy-Kulangsu.

Duly relieved, *Edsall* the next day stood out at 11:30, conned by a local pilot, Mr. Woods. She steamed down the coast past Sugarloaf Island, Good Cape Lighthouse, Bill and Green islands, and Breaker Point Lighthouse to anchor off South Nine Pin Island (Nam Kwo Chau), near the main shipping lanes, east of the British Crown Colony at Hong Kong.[53] There she remained briefly, replenishing stores, with the ship's log revealing just how well the destroyer's crew ate. To keep her men, if not fighting fit, at least sated were fresh lobster; a half ton of beef, veal, and liver; 54 pounds of "luncheon meat"; 800 pounds of sweet and dill pickles; 100 pounds of cheese; 400 pounds of apples; 58 pounds of carrots; 60 quarts of milk; "300 cakes assorted"; and spinach, onions, string beans, turnips, and hundreds of pounds of potatoes, all kept cold with 600 pounds of ice.

Back at Kulangsu, a contingent of Imperial Navy warships would have made *Edsall* irrelevant had she been there, but a number of larger Western warships eventually arrived, including flagship HMS *Birmingham*, and HMS *Cornwall*, HMS *Duncan*, HMS *Defender*, the French cruisers *Emile Bertin* and *Lamotte-Picquet*, the U.S. light cruiser USS *Marblehead* (CL-12), the gunboat USS *Asheville* (PG-21), and, again, the flushdecker USS *Bulmer* (DD-222).

Kulangsu had already been a flashpoint. In fact, the year before, in May 1938, the Japanese bombarded and seized Amoy, driving many thousands of Chinese and European refugees into the International Settlement on Kulangsu. This unabashed aggression was followed by more British appeasement, which in turn was met with more bellicosity and arrogance by the Japanese.

Over the intervening twelve months, Western diplomats traded verbose telegrams and documents among themselves and with the Japanese, to no useful purpose, while awaiting the next "incident." This was engineered by Hoon/Li-Son's "murder" when the chamber of commerce president conveniently stopped a bullet during Japanese amphibious landing "exercises."

At the Kulangsu Council, the Japanese consul-general made five predictably unreasonable demands that would have effectively turned the settlement into a colony of Japan. There was an all-day conference aboard flagship *Birmingham*, but the desired compromise was not achieved. The Japanese conceded only to reduce their force ashore to forty-two men.

On May 13, *Bulmer* arrived, with the potential to land naval forces, which disturbed the Japanese, but not enough to deter their coercive tactics. Three days later the light cruiser *Marblehead* was called in. When the Japanese continued with their extravagant demands, the cruiser put ashore a party of forty-two men. A French gunboat had reached Kulangsu the day before and discharged forty-two marines. The British Navy in turn matched this total with an identical number of Royal Marines.

Negotiations then dragged on for some weeks. HMS *Cornwall* arrived, with the British ambassador aboard, and on May 26 *Birmingham* left, taking Admiral Noble with her. The old coastal gunboat USS *Tulsa* (PG-22) arrived to replace *Marblehead*; *Marblehead* embarked her landing party, which was replaced by a contingent from *Tulsa*, and left.

In the estimate of U.S. consul Karl de Giers MacVitty and others, the "general opinion here is that [the] Amoy incident is a dress rehearsal for Shanghai," and it was not the time or place to back down from Japanese threats.[54] MacVitty knew what he was speaking of, for the Japanese seized Swatow in June after bombing the city for weeks, and issued stern ultimatums to Western naval units to depart promptly. This provoked Adm. Harry Yarnell of the Asiatic Fleet and his British counterparts to send more warships to Swatow, including the destroyers *Pope* and *Scout*, which compelled the Japanese to rescind their demands. It was a small victory, of more propaganda than substantive value, but it kept the Imperial forces at bay for the moment.

The Kulangsu stalemate continued into the summer; the Japanese Navy strangling shipping between Amoy and the little island, denying fuel, firewood, and food, and at times cutting off the water supply. The crisis even drew the attention of *Time* magazine in the States.[55]

On July 21, discussions resumed between the commander of the South China Patrol, Asiatic Fleet, Cmdr. John T. G. Stapler, and the Japanese naval officer in charge at Amoy, Rear Adm. Miyata Giichi. Although their relations were friendly enough, Rear Admiral Miyata refused to take any responsibility for the blockade, saying that he was under the orders of Vice Adm. Kondō Nobutake, the overall commander of the Imperial Navy's South China Fleet.*

Throughout the six-month standoff, there is repeated evidence that the prime mover behind these events was the Japanese Imperial Navy, Nihon Kaigun. The Imperial Navy enforced the blockade; fomented trouble at Amoy and Kulangsu by actively promoting rival gangs of Formosans; thwarted efforts of aid organizations such as the International Relief Association; stopped shipping at random without reasonable cause at the least provocation and removed persons at will; conducted door-to-door searches; and was in all likelihood behind the arrests of

---

* The ships of the Asiatic Fleet would encounter Vice Admiral Kondō again some thirty months later and would find nothing resembling the forbearance of the "Kulangsu Standoff" in his actions.

numerous Chinese at Kulangsu, who were reported to have been taken away and shot. Contemporary Japanese newspapers published in China called it a "semi-permanent blockade" that was hardly necessary for the implementation of the New Order in East Asia.

But the Chinese, British, French, Americans, and Dutch continued to parley with the Japanese, and in early August brought in Harry Merrell Benninghoff, second secretary of the embassy in China, who spoke fluent Japanese and had been temporarily detailed to Amoy as consul. His presence seemed to help as the six nations struggled for another ten weeks to reach an "amicable settlement." One historian later wrote that the furious Japanese finally left in the middle of the night, as a face-saving expedient, leaving behind a few troops to guard the consulate.*

In truth, the British and French landing parties left first, but not until September 2, with the advent of the war in Europe. The Japanese immediately adopted an even more truculent position, but British, Dutch, and U.S. negotiators hammered out a settlement, although the letter of agreement was not signed until October 17.

The next day, U.S. and Japanese landing parties withdrew at two in the afternoon. The Japanese demands for greater suppression of anti-Japanese activities in the settlement, plus the addition of a single Japanese inspector and a police sergeant, were met. As soon as these concessions were granted, the Japanese issued new demands to give their navy even greater control of the junk traffic between Kulangsu and Amoy.[56] It was a familiar pattern, repeated at almost every Japanese-controlled entrepôt along the China coast.

By then, however, *Edsall* had returned to southern Philippine waters and was in the Sulu islands resuming her standard Asiatic Fleet routine. Her log at this time reveals little of much note, although small incidents stand out to illustrate the flushdecker's willful qualities.

---

* The version of the Kulangsu Standoff that includes *Edsall*'s presence is in Martin Brice's *The Royal Navy and the Sino-Japanese Incident 1937–41*, pages 117–120. Brice records the following IJN units in the Amoy area at the time: battleships *Kirishima, Ise, Hyuga, Nagato, Mutsu, Fuso*, and *Kongo*; cruisers *Chokai, Natori, Tatsuta, Tenryu, Nachi, Suzuya, Myoko*, and *Katori*; minelayers *Tsubame* and *Kanome*; and destroyers *Shimakaze, Shiokaze*, and *Nadakaze*. Some of these battleships seem questionable participants, and the training cruiser *Katori* had not yet been built. This list may refer to units that had been in the Amoy region over the course of the standoff—that is, between May and October 1939—but a detailed account of IJN operations along the China coast at the time is beyond the scope of this text.

On the morning of September 20, 1939, *Edsall* was anchored off Zamboanga Island. A storm had blown through overnight and the ship's anchor dragged. But her crew and commander should not have had to worry because of "the tremendous strength of the chains issued on destroyers," which was proverbial. "A destroyer captain need have no fear of one parting. Even if he should deliberately try to break one, he will find it quite a job."[57]

The destroyer got under way at 0800 hours and steamed for six hours past the Bolods to another anchorage close to Marongas Island, off Jolo. In the course of this journey, the headstrong flushdecker suffered a casualty: "Chain broken at bending on shackle, resulting in loss of anchor." Although it is unknown whether or not he appreciated the irony, no doubt commanding officer Lt. Cmdr. A. C. J. Sabalot, who was well drilled in the peacetime navy's strict economy, would not have been pleased about this mishap.

Continuing her cruises between Zamboanga and Jolo, where she received stores from the U.S. Army's Quartermaster Corps, the destroyer varied her routine with occasional boarding calls upon steamers, some of which were carrying arms to China.

Her crew was still eating well for the most part: "30 lbs. of string beans, 50 lbs. of cucumbers, 100 lbs. of cabbage, 100 lbs. of bananas, 100 lbs. of limes, 93 lbs. of potatoes, 75 lbs. of pumpkins, 40 lbs. of radishes, 20 lbs. of bean sprouts, 200 dozen eggs" are recorded in this time frame. Yes, the men were well fed; the war was on the other side of the globe; most considered the Asiatic Station as safe a posting as any; and a full stomach after a long day of manual labor would not have inclined many young sailors to scrutinize the future too closely. Of course, their officers knew differently.

It has been argued that events such as those at Swatow or Amoy-Kulangsu, in which the querulous Japanese at times appeared to back down in the face of strong, unified military opposition, may have persuaded some Westerners that displays of force on a strategic scale, reinforced by resolute national political backing, would deter Japanese aggression throughout the Far East. If so, this misguided idea would prove a grievous error.

By January, the scab had been knocked off the wound at Kulangsu, and blood began to flow anew. Yet one more member of the Amoy government, a puppet named Ng Lian Hong, died after suffering wounds in an assassination attempt. Immediately, the Japanese issued new demands for more representation at the Kulangsu Council and for more policemen, and they reintroduced the blockade. The United States saw in this "the same tactics of coercion" all over again.[58] By March 22, 1940, the gunboat USS *Asheville* (PG-21) had been sent back to the little island.

What the Americans called their "sword of Damocles" plan of economic warfare in the Far East was in effect a papier-mâché dagger suspended above a powerful and hungry predator. Or, to borrow a figure of speech used by Claude A. Swanson, secretary of the navy, in an anecdote related by Adm. James O. Richardson, commander in chief of the U.S. Navy, "no sane man would slap a tiger in the face when his other hand is in the tiger's mouth."[59]

That the U.S. Asiatic Fleet had been written off well before the surprise attacks at Pearl Harbor is indisputable. In October 1940, Admiral Richardson met with President Franklin D. Roosevelt (FDR) and Adm. William Leahy, then governor of Puerto Rico (and former Chief of Naval Operations) in Washington to discuss the disposition of U.S. Fleet units in the Pacific.

Richardson doubted the "restraining influence on the actions of Japan" of placing the fleet in Hawaii, and said so. He argued that the Japanese understood that the U.S. fleet "was undermanned, unprepared for war, and had no train of auxiliary ships without which it could not undertake active operations."[60] But President Roosevelt got his way, of course, and fourteen months later Vice Adm. Nagumo Chuichi's lethal 1st Air Fleet's Mobile Force—known as Kidō Butai (KdB)—arrived unannounced off Oahu to validate Richardson's skepticism.

In the interim, however, the U.S. Asiatic Fleet received little, if any, reinforcements. If the commander in chief of the U.S. Fleet had no faith in his Hawaiian battle line as a deterrent to the Japanese, he could certainly see no profit in sending additional units to the smaller and weaker Asiatic Fleet in Manila. This he told to FDR, and Admiral Leahy concurred. As noted by Richardson in his memoirs, on that October day in 1940:

> The President asked Admiral Leahy his opinion about strengthening the Asiatic Fleet and my recollection is that Admiral Leahy said that whatever you sent out will be lost, therefore [he] would send the least valuable combatant ships we have, the 7,500

ton cruisers, but I recommended, I personally recommended that none be sent. A decision to send none was reached.[61]

Less than a year and a half after this conversation, an "old, small, and weak" U.S. warship serving in the luckless Asiatic Fleet would be mistaken for precisely one of these "least valuable" cruisers, and eventually destroyed under the guns and bombs of Vice Admiral Nagumo's KdB. Although *Edsall's* fate may be read as a kind of micro-metaphor for the flaws in U.S. and Japanese war plans and their tragic results, her destruction was in fact an act of gallantry and devotion to duty almost entirely unknown, and without question unrecognized, by the U.S. Navy and the American public.

Not in accord . . .

Our present mission and restrictions as to means are not in accord.
> —Maj. Gen. George Grunert, U.S. Army, Philippine Department

By autumn 1940, the temper of the times and the persistent Japanese aggression made Shanghai untenable, so the blue-water ships were finally withdrawn once and for all to Manila. For three decades this large bay and its harbor, with naval installations at Cavite, were not considered defensible in strategic war plans. Only at the last moment, in the summer of 1941, did the U.S. government allow itself to be persuaded otherwise. Although the causes behind this turnabout were complex and primarily economic, some of the principal players were less than scrupulous in their actions and subsequent accounts.

More than thirty years of healthy U.S. skepticism were reversed by Gen. Douglas MacArthur's messianic fervor and bombast once he had been given command of the U.S. Army forces in the Philippines in July 1941. Much of this enthusiasm centered on his exaggerated, and naïve, faith—which may have been as artificial as his wartime press releases— in the new and unproven Boeing B-17 Flying Fortress heavy bomber. The well-known "pessimism" regarding the defense of the Philippines among U.S. military leaders gave way to MacArthur's charisma and overconfidence as the inevitability of war with Orange (Japan) became clear to all but the most resolute ostriches.* Even Adm. Thomas Hart, the no-nonsense commander of the Asiatic Fleet, was swayed by MacArthur's optimism.

The U.S. war plans—at this period known as WPL-44, or Rainbow-3—were taken to Manila (prior to MacArthur assuming command) on orders from Adm. Harold R. "Betty" Stark in Washington, D.C. They were entrusted to Admiral Stark's personal aide, Cmdr. John L. McCrea, who left Washington on December 13, 1940.[†] His task was to deliver these plans, gauge the combat readiness of the Asiatic Fleet, and assess the condition of its commanding officer. From the West Coast, McCrea departed San Pedro and sailed for Hawaii, then left from there on New Year's Day 1941 for Manila, arriving on January 6. Over the next ten days, McCrea had daily talks with Adm. Thomas Hart, Commander in Chief of the renamed United States Asiatic Fleet (CINCAF), sharing a cabin on the flagship *Houston*. This was as they awaited the return of Capt. William R. Purnell (chief of staff to Hart) from negotiations with the Dutch in Batavia.[62] McCrea also paid visits to High Commissioner Francis Sayres and General MacArthur, finding the former hopeful that war might yet be avoided, whereas MacArthur believed it to be "inevitable" if not imminent. McCrea evaluated Admiral Hart as one of the best thinkers in the navy, and a man of outstanding character. More than thirty years later, McCrea wrote to Hart's biographer, "In my judgement Thos. C. Hart was one of the Navy's best."[63]

The intelligence, backbone, and sense of purpose evinced by Hart during Commander McCrea's visit did not prevent him from receiving a sharp disappointment in the latter part of January when Washington decided finally that the Asiatic Fleet would not be reinforced. Plan "Dog," a memorandum devised by Stark, and the basis for the subsequent war plan Rainbow-5, had given priority to the Atlantic Fleet. Hart would receive no extra ships after all. In his own words, "The Asiatic Fleet had to await attack. It could not attack."[64] The hard, pragmatic conclusions reached by FDR and admirals Leahy and Richardson four months earlier had held up. Nevertheless, British, U.S., and Dutch

---

* Before and after the war this so-called pessimistic cast of thinking was attributed to navy commanders such as Adm. Thomas Hart of the United States Asiatic Fleet. But, then, Hart operated in the real world.

† John L. McCrea later became a naval aide to FDR and directed the White House Map Room in World War II.

authorities continued to grapple with contingency plans for the deteriorating situation in the Far East, which was not helped by the plight of Allied fortunes in Europe and the Mediterranean.

During the ABC talks (American-British Conversations) in Washington, D.C., in February 1941, the British delegation suggested that the United States send at the very least a division of four cruisers to Singapore as support for the anemic Royal Navy presence there. Understandably, U.S. planners again saw no purpose in this move, because it would ultimately mean the sacrifice of these ships to the Japanese with no effective final result and a further weakening of the U.S. Pacific Fleet, which was already believed to be of minimal value as a deterrent.

Some two months later at the ADB talks (American-Dutch-British talks) in Singapore, held April 21 to 27, in which Dutch concerns for the East Indies were directly addressed, the U.S. representative once more came away from the conferences feeling that the British were attempting to subsume Asiatic Fleet units under their command. And again British requests were turned down. On June 7, 1941, U.S. Army and Navy chiefs replied to the British with "a strongly worded rejection of the views expressed at Singapore."

Nonetheless, as set forth in the ADB document itself, the Allies' (or Associated Powers') foremost object "is to defeat Germany and her allies, and hence in the Far East to maintain the position of the Associated Powers against Japanese attack, in order to sustain a long-term economic pressure against Japan until we are in a position to take the offensive."[65] Thus, Chief of Staff George Marshall's oft-quoted remark in a May memo still held true: "Collapse in the Atlantic would be fatal; collapse in the Far East would be serious but not fatal."[66]

Neither the Philippines nor Malaya nor the Netherlands East Indies were believed to be defensible against a determined and thorough Japanese invasion campaign. This is not to say that U.S. propagandists accepted such a defeatist tone; they were compelled by definition to put the best appearance on matters. Yet, even among the best-informed, a large amount of equivocation, not to say delusion, was inevitable.

The U.S. Chief of Naval Operations, Adm. Harold "Betty" Stark, even wrote optimistically to Adm. Husband E. Kimmel in Pearl Harbor that he believed that the British would send several old R-class battleships and a battle cruiser (either HMS *Repulse* or HMS *Renown*), plus four 8-inch cruisers and up to thirteen 6-inch cruisers (about half of them new ships), to reinforce the Royal Navy at Singapore. Again, because Kimmel was very much alone and out on a limb, this was either wishful thinking, or Stark was leading him on with such fantasies.[*]

Throughout much of the spring and summer of 1941, U.S., British, and Dutch planners sought to hammer out new strategic and political agreements to prepare for any anticipated Japanese aggression. In this, however, they plainly failed. The successor, Rainbow-5, was even more contradictory. In the broadest terms, the Rainbow-5 plan reiterated the Europe-first strategy. Most resources were to be directed to the Atlantic, and an offensive against Germany was to be undertaken as swiftly as practicable, with a defensive posture in the Pacific (a subsidiary plan, never enacted, WPPac-46, gave greater emphasis to the defense of the Malay Barrier). For the ships, planes, and men of the Asiatic fleet—the tip of a spear made of tin, as it were—the war plans were straightforward but well beyond their limited means:

3313. The Commander in Chief, U. S. ASIATIC FLEET is assigned the following tasks:
a. TASK
   RAID JAPANESE SEA COMMUNICATIONS AND DESTROY AXIS FORCES;
b. TASK
   SUPPORT THE LAND AND AIR FORCES IN THE DEFENSE OF THE TERRITORIES OF THE ASSOCIATED POWERS. (THE RESPONSIBILITY OF THE COMMANDER IN CHIEF, UNITED STATES ASIATIC FLEET, FOR SUPPORTING THE DEFENSE OF THE PHILIPPINES REMAINS SO LONG AS THAT DEFENSE CONTINUES.);
c. TASK
   DESTROY AXIS SEA COMMUNICATIONS BY CAPTURING OR DESTROYING VESSELS TRADING DIRECTLY OR INDIRECTLY WITH THE ENEMY;

* Appendix I, p. 29 of the ADB Conversations, in April 1941 shows the Asiatic Fleet's primary surface units—*Houston*, *Marblehead*, and thirteen destroyers—based at Singapore and "under orders of Commander-in-Chief, China"—that is, under British control.

d. TASK
   PROTECT SEA COMMUNICATIONS OF THE
   ASSOCIATED POWERS BY ESCORTING,
   COVERING, AND PATROLLING, AS REQUIRED
   BYCIRCUMSTANCES, AND BY DESTROYING ENEMY
   RAIDING FORCES;
e. TASK
   IN COOPERATION WITH THE ARMY DEFEND THE
   PHILIPPINE COASTAL FRONTIER-CATEGORY OF
   DEFENSE "E"
f. TASK
   ROUTE UNITED STATES FLAG SHIPPING IN
   ACCORDANCE WITH AGREEMENTS REACHED
   WITH THE OTHER ASSOCIATED POWERS IN THE
   FAR EAST AREA.[67]

At the same time, in late July 1941, Douglas MacArthur was given command of U.S. Army Forces Far East (USAFFE), with the temporary rank of lieutenant general. He received the Rainbow-5 plans later that summer from his air commander, Gen. Lewis Brereton, and at once began revamping the tasks that U.S. strategic planners had accepted for the Philippines over the previous thirty years. In general, American war plans had envisioned U.S. forces fighting a delaying action on the island of Luzon primarily, then retiring to the Bataan peninsula where they would attempt to hold out until relieved by the navy after the U.S. Pacific Fleet fought its way across from the West Coast and Hawaii; a task that might take up to two years. There were, however, no planned reinforcements of either army or navy forces in the region, and the garrrison on Bataan was not expected to be able to resist for more than six months. In effect, this course meant accepting the loss of the Philippines.

Adopted in midyear, yet never signed and neither approved nor disapproved by President Franklin D. Roosevelt, Rainbow-5 was as hazy in many critical aspects as its metaphoric title. This ambiguity flustered Admiral Hart, who felt that the Asiatic Fleet's requirements must be prioritized because it was "the front line trench," but General MacArthur suffered no such anxieties. He delighted in the attention that his rhetoric and dispatches garnered in Washington.

That Rainbow-5 had not been specific or rigorous in its handling of just how the Philippines were to be held appears to have never crossed his mind. Specificity would have hindered MacArthur's newly minted fantasies for defending the indefensible islands.

Indeed, it is questionable whether MacArthur ever read the plans at all because his own utterances bore so little resemblance to the original aims of Rainbow-5. It was as if he and Hart existed in parallel but different universes. But this was perhaps to be expected from men of similar age and temperament, but dissimilar partisan service values. As Kemp Tolley, one of the most perceptive of Asiatic Fleet officers and historians, later wrote, "The conquest of the Philippines, Malaya, and the Indies by the Japanese was a triumph rendered simpler and quicker for them by Allied violation of the very fundamentals of unified action."[68]

In Adm. Thomas Hart and Lt. Gen. Douglas MacArthur, there is little evidence of unity on any level. Subsequent dispatches by MacArthur complaining about an absence of offensive naval action are valuable for revealing more of his disingenuous nature and his lifelong refusal to accept responsibility; it was MacArthur himself who had denied Hart's command adequate integration with the Army Air Forces then available.

Within three months of assuming command, by the beginning of October 1941, MacArthur requested sweeping alterations to Rainbow-5. These involved significantly increasing the area of the Philippines to be defended by USAFFE, as well as establishing a larger air arm to act in concert with naval forces (but only as long as MacArthur's command retained control of the air units). How to implement these plans, especially the supply logistics, remained the crucial issue that MacArthur, in his apparent wishful thinking, seemed to have happily overlooked.

Rainbow-5 never implied that the lines of communication and resupply to the Philippines could be maintained. That MacArthur's chimerical schemes were accepted, and even supported, by Gen. George Marshall and the Joint Board has been interpreted by at least one later historian as indicative of the Roosevelt administration's desire to paper over its own threadbare plans. It was said to be a case of "plugging another hole that had been overlooked."[69]

Douglas MacArthur's ego led him to believe that the Japanese would accommodate him and not attack before the spring of 1942.

He made bold declarations of the impregnable conditions that would exist in the Philippines by April 1942.* By that time, he envisioned hundreds of B-17 bombers and attack planes under his command capable of striking well out into the South China Seas and destroying any Japanese invasion forces before they reached shore. But the truth about the B-17's bombing capabilities and the Japanese timetable was less agreeable. (In all fairness, MacArthur certainly wasn't to blame for all of these developments.) The decisions that led to the deployment of long-range bombers in another misguided effort to "deter" the Japanese came from Washington, and primarily at the behest of Secretary of War Henry Stimson, although Gen. George Marshall and Maj. Gen. Henry H. "Hap" Arnold were willing accomplices.[†]

Never one to accept a passive role, and emboldened by the new offensive schemes that he believed his air forces could implement, MacArthur abruptly declared that he would forgo the longstanding citadel defense of Manila, and instead meet the enemy invaders on the beaches. Admiral Hart realized that the majority of his ships, many of which were old and vulnerable, could not hope to use Manila as a forward base without effective control of the air.[70] Any chance for reinforcements from the Royal Navy, as had been considered in WPL-44 (or Rainbow-3, an earlier plan, with hopes of at least a cruiser squadron, if not several battleships), had evaporated with the disastrous campaigns for Greece and Crete.[‡]

In an ironic twist, the conclusions drawn from Axis air success against British warships in Churchill's two Aegean mistakes appear to have been faulty as well. Stimson and General Marshall made a gigantic leap of faith when they assumed that the new Boeing B-17 Flying Fortress could effectively deter the Japanese from moving south.

* Contrast this with MacArthur's earlier preparations as military advisor to the Philippines Commonwealth, beginning in 1935, which forecast military self-sufficiency (versus Japan) in 1946. By 1940, these hopeful plans had been largely abandoned, and MacArthur's inadequacies, and high salary, had become a source of great displeasure to then-President Manuel Quezon.

† I am indebted to communications with the historian William Bartsch, author of *December 8, 1941: MacArthur's Pearl Harbor* for additional insights into these somewhat opaque areas in American war plans.

‡ A thorough examination of morphing U.S.–British strategic thinking can be found in Ian Cowman's *Dominion or Decline: Anglo-American Naval Relations in the Pacific, 1937–1941.*

General Marshall's vision of the bombers flying unimpeded over Japan's "paper cities" and setting them afire was equally unrealistic, regardless of the ultimate fate of Japanese urban areas. And MacArthur had neither the time nor the numbers working in his favor, as these augmented plans proceeded according to *his* timetable, and those said that the Japanese would not attack before April 1942. But MacArthur—a born optimist, and never one to suffer unpleasant truths objectively— could hardly be bothered with disagreeable facts in the muddle that passed for his strategic thinking.

These ugly realities were hammered home after Pearl Harbor in the war's opening hours, when MacArthur's waffling allowed the modest air forces then at his disposal to be crushed by unopposed Imperial Japanese Navy bombers and fighters attacking U.S. airfields in Luzon. Just one week into the war, Japan would control the skies over the Philippines and Malaya and southward to the real prize, the Dutch East Indies. By then, Cavite Naval Yard had also been incinerated by Japanese bombs, which destroyed critical quantities of "ammunition, special and general supplies," including the bulk of the Asiatic Fleet's torpedoes.[*]

The pragmatic recognition of Manila's vulnerability by the U.S. Navy and Hart, and Hart's acceptance of the intelligence assessments that culminated in the famous November 26 "war warning," led to a commonsense decision to send his meager forces to the south even before that message was sent.

By the first week of December 1941, Admiral Hart had ordered a "defensive deployment" of his forces, fully cognizant of their vulnerability to sudden air attack by the Japanese. This saved a number of military and merchant vessels and permitted a delaying action to be fought for the next ninety days or so.

Although infuriated by MacArthur's sudden abandonment of Manila and thus of the forward base for submarine operations, "in which lay the main power of the Asiatic Fleet," Admiral Hart seems to have had no illusions about the fate that overtook his forces in late 1941 and early 1942, and he takes responsibility for decisions that he later regretted. On the other hand, MacArthur was justifiably maddened by the inept performance of Asiatic Fleet submarines during the Lingayen

---

[*] Later, in 1951, Hart recalled that the bulk of the torpedoes destroyed at Cavite were not submarine but destroyer weapons. See Louis Morton's *The Fall of the Philippines* in the U.S. Army Green Book series.

landings and let Hart know about it in no uncertain terms. Characteristically, though, no second-thoughts or admissions of culpability deface the otherwise spotless façades of Gen. Douglas MacArthur's post-war reminiscences and reports.*

* Part Five of MacArthur's 1964 memoir *Reminiscences*, which deals with the opening days of the war, goes to pointed lengths to blame others for the fiasco at Clark Field and denies that MacArthur was ever contacted by Brereton's command asking for approval of a strike against the Japanese in the Formosa area. MacArthur also accuses the U.S. Navy of failing to keep open the supply lines to the Philippines, and even makes the ridiculous claim that the navy fought the next two years of the war "without any new ships," implying that they could have saved his command with the vessels they had in 1942, and so on.

Chapter Two

Brothers in Harm's Way

*Don't worry about me and Loys. We are Asiatic sailors and can
take care of ourselves.*
— Charles "Smokie" Parsons, to his family, 1940

Eight weeks after the talks between FDR, Leahy, and Richardson, and
twelve months before the surprise attacks on Pearl Harbor by Vice
Admiral Nagumo's powerful KdB, a young U.S. sailor raised on a farm
in southern Missouri wrote home to his family from the Asiatic Fleet
flagship USS *Houston* (CA-30):

> Well here goes. Calling all pen pals. How are you all by now fine
> I hope. I am just fine. I havent saw Loys in about 2 weeks. He
> was transferred to the U.S.S. Black Hawk. I sure do miss him.
> I tried my best to get transferred with him but no soap. You
> know that's just my luck. Loys has a lot better chance for a rate
> on the Black Hawk though for there isn't so much competition
> he is striking for torpedoman and if he will take care of his con-
> duct he will get to go up for torpedoman third class 1 Feburrary.
> That will mean pretty good money 60 bucks a month.

These homey remarks came from Charles ("Chas" or "Smokie")
Parsons, writing from Manila Bay on December 14, 1940. The "Loys"
to whom he refers is his brother Edgar Aloysius, who had recently
transferred from *Houston* to the destroyer tender *Black Hawk*. The

brothers were an inseparable pair of rough-hewn country boys who by all lights enjoyed what most sailors generally enjoy: drinking, woman-izing, and brawling.

Earlier that fall, as *Houston* received her King Board upgrades at Mare Island, California (additional AA batteries and extra splinter pro-tection, as well as new dual-purpose secondary directors), Charles had written, "Wee know we aint no angels but wee havent got into eny thing worse than going to town & have our fun like a little combat in self defense. We always have ben able to take care ourselves so far."

According to surviving family members, Loys, or "Blackie," was a bigger fellow than Charles, and the surviving full-length photograph of him in his dress blues shows a formidable-looking individual with a ready grin. Surviving letters also reveal that the 180-pound Blackie par-ticipated in wrestling and boxing "smokers" while serving on *Houston*. In one letter home, he reluctantly admits that his back and shoulders were covered in mat burns from his onboard wrestling matches, as if anticipating his mother's alarm and disapproval.

Loys had joined the navy half a year before Charles, in December 1939, but neither he nor his brother seem to have been overly pleased with their decision. And they were clearly discouraged by the fero-cious heat of the Philippines. After *Houston* had arrived in Manila in late November 1940 to relieve her sister ship USS *Augusta* (CA-31) as Asiatic fleet flagship, Loys wrote, "I have been in the Philippines about a week. It is not so good out here so awful hot." His brother next wrote home on December 14 (after Loys had left the cruiser for *Black Hawk*): "Well I guess there may be snow there [at their home in Missouri] and a Christmas spirit. Well we havent either one here. Its hotern hell and these asiatic sailors and tree climbing Filipinos never heard of Christ." These candid assessments are followed by an even more frank—and lurid—admission from Charles:

> Well Dad I had screwed every thing from Frisco to Manila and it was all pretty slop[p]y. So one of my ship mates another Asiatic sailor told me how to get some new meat. Said he, Smokie, the next time you go a shore just go out in the jungle out of sight and grab a tree and shake hell out of it and the first thing that hits the ground run it down and screw it. Well I did and imagine my surprise when I found out it was a coconut.

Five days later, Loys responded with a quick note from *Black Hawk*, also in Manila Bay, just as the mail was to be picked up for the four-day flight to San Francisco. (At that time it took about five weeks for a letter to reach home.) It appears that Loys had left at least one foe aboard *Houston* when he transferred, and Charles had not hesitated to defend his brother's name when the sailor aboard *Houston* "made a remark . . . one of my buddys was telling me about it said when he said what ever it was said old Smokie just got up and hit him 2. They had to pour water on him."

The brothers evidently enjoyed a raucous Christmas and New Year's together: "Sure had some fun . . . Well wee all got to kidding the wops about the greeks chasing the wops all over hell. Wee rubed it in to much I guess. Well they got pissed off & started to slinging bottles. Well wee tossed our selves you know. Eny how it took the shore patrol & police from 5 different nations to break it up." Evidently, the local Italian barflies resented being teased about Il Duce's abortive campaign in Greece.

In spring, the brothers were off to the southern Philippines for longer cruises and more training. Smokie recalled place names—if not their exact locations—torturously, as in this note he scribbled in April:

We got to to to bay [Batu batu at the southwestern end of Tawitawi] stay there for 2 days then we go to Elo Elo [Ilioilo in Panay] & stay there for a few days. To to Bay is just off the coast of Barneo & Elo Elo is on the east coast of barneo. Here a while back we went to Bagio [Baguio City on Luzon] & Zubeck [Sibuco] & up the river. hell, Carl i could write a book all i have saw out there if it wasnt for this asiatic duty getting me.

There is written and photographic evidence from other *Houston* crewmembers at the same time that they were indeed steaming the length of the Philippines, from Santa Barbara, near Agoo on the Lingayen Gulf, where they put a landing force ashore, down to Tawitawi, at the southern extremity of the archipelago, barely fifty miles from Borneo.

Charles had even jokingly asked a friend back home (in April), "has buisness picked up eny since this war scare came along. Well well there aint going to be eny fight now cause me & Loys have got her controll now ha. ha." No doubt such was the frame of mind of quite a few young men cut from the same irrepressible cloth, then serving in that fleet. But for too many, their lives would end in less than a year. The navy brass and Washington had long since written off the Asiatic Fleet, and once things "started to pop," it would be far beyond the means of their raw crews and weathered materiel to "controll" the experienced, razor-sharp Imperial forces of Japan.

In mid-October, Charles wrote from the Manila Army and Navy YMCA after a night on the town: "Am writing this letter at the YMCA have been on a good time all nite after being out at sea for about 2 months i rate a good time."

Yet if they felt that the "good times" were drawing to a close, their youthful optimism and determination to put the best face on things usually concealed such fears. Charles had even written earlier in the year, "I guess ill never die happy until I get to try out a Brownie on a Jap." (Once a researcher becomes familiar, even to a small degree, with the scope and depth of Japanese provocations during the 1930s, super-imposed upon typical U.S. cultural and racial bigotry, the more inevi-table and ingrained such casual prejudice appears.) This eagerness was probably the product of a training cruise he had just returned from in which "wee . . . fired our 5-inch guns & had machine gun practise and wee go out next week and fire the eight inch turet guns."

Before the year ended, though, these "rugged," self-sufficient young-sters would find themselves facing an enemy capable of delivering a great deal more lethal bloodshed, with far more efficiency, than found in a drunken barroom dustup. And these foes would more than match them in righteousness, racism, and violence.

For thirty-five years, U.S. war plans had accepted the Japanese Empire as the unavoidable opponent in the Pacific. These strategic evo-lutions had also long since ruled out any realistic chance of holding the Philippines against a determined southern thrust by Japan. By the early 1940s, the Asiatic Fleet's role was that of supporting the defense of the Philippines "so long as that defense continues," but a retirement to the Malay Barrier was believed to be inevitable.

In the meantime, war planners envisioned the U.S. Pacific Fleet fighting its way "westward from Hawaii, capturing positions among the Japanese-held islands athwart the route," in anticipation of the decisive naval battle to be fought at sea somewhere east of the Philippines.[1] At no time was the undersize and inadequate Asiatic Fleet expected to act as the chief striking force of U.S. naval power against the full might of the Imperial Japanese Navy. Yet that was the fate that befell the three cruisers, thirteen aged destroyers, forty-odd submarines, and associated auxiliaries that made up the U.S. Asiatic Fleet in early December 1941 after the surprise raids on the Pearl Harbor anchorage.

The brash assertion of Smokie Parsons would come back to haunt him and his fellow Asiatic sailors as the war's first twelve weeks unfolded with nightmarish speed.

Charles stayed on *Houston* throughout that "hopeful" year of 1941 and was still serving in F Division on the cruiser when the war broke out. The rambunctious Blackie remained aboard *Black Hawk*, but with personnel shortages acute on many warships, including the smaller ones, he, too, was eventually transferred. On December 18, 1941, he was assigned to the veteran destroyer USS *Edsall* (DD-219), then at Surabaja, Java.

Ten days after Vice Admiral Nagumo's KdB had reduced much of Pearl Harbor to submerged steel, smoking rubble, and ashes, Ensign John Gustin had written home from *Edsall* to his family in Wisconsin, reassuring them of his safety (as well as complaining of the tremendous equatorial heat just like the Parsons brothers):

> We were not in the Manila Area when things started to pop (thank goodness) and we have had all sorts of rumors about what happened. No doubt we shall have to wait until this affair is over before the straight dope will come out. . . . We are all (we includes Jim [John's brother] also) safe and still well and happy as far as circumstances permit.

It is a thoughtful, well-composed letter, as were all penned by this intelligent and conscientious young officer. John also had an older brother, James (U.S. Naval Academy 1937), a lieutenant who was serving aboard the destroyer USS *Paul Jones* (DD-230). Much like the Parsons brothers, John and James Gustin seem to have given each other critical moral support. John frequently mentions his brother's sensible advice as he struggled with the multiple duties and heavy workload of a "fresh-caught" new ensign. However, one paragraph in John's congenial, uncomplaining letter says much for what he and many other young men must have been feeling in that faraway place:

"Several times in the past few weeks I have wished that I might be living on about ten acres of land out in the middle of the South Dakota Badlands. I wouldn't care if the soil grew anything or not."

Two days after Christmas, from "Somewhere at Sea," Gustin typed the final letter that his family would receive. After musing over the relative dullness of his own Christmas and reflecting on the decision he had made to join the navy and his separation from his family—which he accepted with no apparent regrets—Gustin provides a glimpse into the mind-set of the ship's crew at this ominous hour:

> I wish I might tell you of our chasing around and where we go but that might be giving away valuable information if it fell into the wrong hands. We are all keeping logs though and you can be sure that when this is all over we will have some tall sea stories to tell. (!) We haven't been just sitting around twiddling our thumbs since the war broke out but I guess the reason for all of the training that the officers and men get is that it can be put to practice in times like these. You can rest assured we will come out on top. The spirit of the men on this ship is remarkable and certainly gives one a satisfied feeling.

At least one other set of brothers are a part of the story, but unlike the Parsons and Gustin brothers, they served together, both on *Edsall*: the Himmelmanns from St. Louis. Leroy, a twenty-six-year-old torpedo man second class, had joined the navy in 1936. His younger brother, Otto, a nineteen-year-old seaman first class, had followed in his footsteps and joined up in 1940.

On Sunday, March 1, 1942, the Himmelmanns, Lt. Joshua James Nix, and Ensign John W. Gustin, along with both of the Parsons— Loys on *Edsall* and Charles aboard *Houston*—would be killed in two of the Pacific war's most mysterious naval engagements. For years, their families would know next to nothing about these men's deaths.* And although the heroic story of *Houston*'s destruction off Bantam Bay was

---

* Ensign John W. Gustin's letters from *Edsall* were sent to Rear Adm. Edwin Layton by Gustin's older brother, Jim (who served on USS *Paul Jones* [DD-230]), in the late 1970s when he was investigating revelations of *Edsall* survivors picked up at sea by the heavy cruiser *Chikuma*.

more or less understood once the war ended and her nearly three hundred survivors were liberated, for more than sixty-four years a terrible series of errors, omissions, and falsehoods has obstinately hidden what really happened in the final hours of the USS *Edsall*.

It was generally accepted—and many accounts of her disappearance state—that *Edsall* had been sunk with no survivors. Yet this too was a falsehood almost never addressed in official and unofficial reports. And postwar interviews with surviving Imperial Navy officers who claimed to have been involved in *Edsall's* sinking were initially viewed with some suspicion by U.S. investigators.

It was not easy for me to understand this, but once I had entered the historical labyrinth of USS *Edsall*, I began to see the wisdom in maintaining a healthy skepticism concerning everything I encountered.

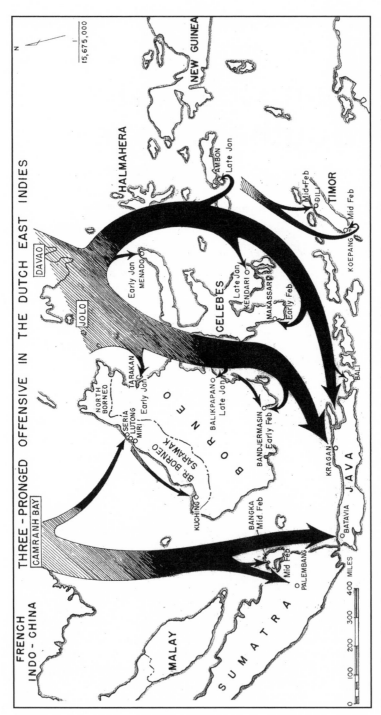

This map derived from Japanese sources shows the enveloping assault on the Netherlands East Indies. *Japanese Monograph No.101 (USAFFE)*

Chapter Three

Rampage in the Southern Seas

The carriers were most terrible of all . . . and their crews did not
need to be told that they could beat anything in the world.
—Stephen Howarth, *The Fighting Ships of the Rising Sun*

Despite avowals by U.S. Navy "experts" to the contrary, the U.S. Pacific Fleet at Pearl Harbor was surprised and devastated by the naval air forces of Japan on December 7, 1941 (December 8 in the Far East). Operations against targets in British Malaya and the Philippines began concurrently with surprising speed and efficiency.* In a matter of weeks, the Japanese had overrun Allied forces from Shanghai and Hong Kong in the Far East to Wake Island in the central Pacific, and beseiged Bataan while swiftly gaining control of the air over much of Southeast Asia. From that point, it was virtually impossible for the Allies to offer meaningful resistance to the Japanese onslaught. Sacrifices would be required in order to buy time, but the final military conclusion was foregone. With the Philippines isolated and Malaya beset by land and air, the central thrust of the Japanese southern advance proceeded on schedule with the East Borneo, Celebes, and Ambon operations.[1]

---

* "The greatest danger from Japan, a surprise attack on the unguarded Pacific Fleet, lying at anchor at San Pedro, under peacetime conditions, has already been averted. The Pacific Fleet is at one of the strongest bases in the world—Pearl Harbor—practically on a war footing and under a war regime. There will be no American Port Arthur." So wrote Capt. W. D. Puleston, U.S. Navy, one-time head of Naval Intelligence, in his book *The Armed Forces of the Pacific*, pp. 116–17.

Following the fall of Manado, in the northeastern Celebes, in early January 1942—coincidental with the invasion of Tarakan on Borneo, 450 nautical miles to the west—the Japanese plans for assaulting and seizing the heart of the Dutch East Indies at Java moved for the most part with smooth celerity. There was one brief delay due to an identification error, but this was sorted out in seventy-two hours or less.* With the Japanese in command of the sea and air around their target areas, these operations faced little substantive resistance. Special airborne assault troops (*Rakkasan butai*) had quickly captured Manado, controlling the area by January 12, and by about January 24 a significant percentage of necessary air forces were operating from the region, projecting air superiority some 360 nautical miles into the Java and Banda seas south of Celebes.[2]

At Kendari, the Japanese invasion followed one of the cardinal precepts of amphibious warfare by approaching under the cover of inclement weather and surprising the Dutch garrison. Six enemy transports had departed their Bangka anchorage near Menado on January 21. The convoy escort was under the command of Rear Adm. Kubo Kyuji in light cruiser *Nagara* (Capt. Naoi Toshio), supported by Destroyer Division (DesDiv) 15 (*Natsushio, Kuroshio, Oyashio, Hayashio*) and Destroyer Division 16 (*Yukikaze, Tokitsukaze, Hatsukaze, Amatsukaze*), along with four minesweepers, two minelayers, two patrol boats, a sub chaser, and one survey ship. They arrived off misty Kendari Bay at 2:00 a.m. on January 24 and began landing troops of the Special Naval Landing Force (SNLF) at 4:28 a.m.

The coveted Kendari airfield was taken in little more than twelve hours. The field's conditions were judged to be "very good" by the commander of the No. 1 Sasebo (Combined) Special Naval Landing Force, Capt. Mori Kunizo; he had some thirty fighters and reconnaissance planes operating out of it by the next day. These were undoubtedly helped by the 30,000 gallons of aviation fuel off-loaded two days earlier from the U.S. seaplane tender USS *Childs* (AVD-1). The ship had been sent to Kendari from Surabaja with the fuel for U.S. Army Air Forces

---

* The occupation of Kendari was delayed by three days owing to reconnaissance sightings of twelve or thirteen "Allied submarines," which proved to be nothing but a pod of whales, but this did not greatly impact the Japanese timetable overall. See USSBS No. 33, Interrogation of Vice Admiral Shiraichi. The official Japanese history noted, "There was not much resistance on the ground" during this operation, and no substantial casualties. See *Senshi Sōsho*, Vol. 26, 210–15.

(USAAF) bombers utilizing the local airfield, situated near the village of Amoito, as "an alternate staging base" in strikes north against Japanese invasion forces.

Kendari's airfield had been considered by the USAAF to be superior to the one at Samarinda, north of Balikpapan on the east coast of Borneo: "It had a dispersal area which could accommodate 35 heavy bombers and near-by fields which could be used by pursuits; construction of extensive living quarters was well under way, and sufficient 100-octane gasoline was available."[3]

Dutch records show that at the beginning of 1942, the field had stockpiles of about 3,000 aerial bombs and more than 250,000 gallons of aviation fuel. These were apparently intended for use by Netherlands Air Force Glenn Martin bombers; but in remote, primitive Kendari, the Dutch colonial forces were even more unprepared than the Americans in the Philippines and the British in Malaya.

"What can we do with four hundred men?" complained Capt. Van Straalen and Capt. A. G. T. Anthonio of the Koninklijk Nederlands-Indisch Leger (KNIL), the Royal Netherlands Indies Army. Fellow officers alleged after the war that this sense of defeatism affected their troops, and an NEI (Netherlands East Indies) historian observed: "The occupation of Kendari was a sad example of a unit that was morally defeated before the first shot was fired."[4]

Childs was also one of the luckiest ships of the Asiatic Fleet during the Java campaign; she escaped from Kendari's bay just as the Imperial Navy arrived, and later survived an air attack by planes from the 11th Seaplane Tender Division during her southward scramble past Buton and the other smaller islands on the southeastern tip of Celebes.[5] Her presence was not unknown to the Dutch colonial soldiers defending Kendari or to locals sympathetic to the Japanese. If a modern satellite camera could have shown these events, it might have zoomed in and caught a veteran Ambonese KNIL infantryman also observing the Allied warship in the small harbor. Having served in Kendari since October 1941, the infantryman recognized the ship as American by the flag on her stern jack staff. He did not think much of this until sometime later, when he heard heavy gunfire coming from the sea after the ship had departed. It had left early on the morning of January 24 just as the dark gray IJN destroyers, minesweepers, and transports emerged through the mist and rain off the bay's northern entrance. The U.S. vessel would have been lucky to have escaped, he thought that morning. And he should have known, being not so fortunate himself; he and his entire unit would be taken prisoner by the Japanese that afternoon.

At each stage of these complex operations, the Imperial Navy's ships and planes played an integral role by supporting the amphibious landings, providing distant cover for convoys, and engaging Allied ships whenever the opportunity arose.* The Japanese, of course, understood that their opponents were forced to guard lengthy coastlines and could never be strong at every potential landing point. And they were aided, unwittingly, by conflicts within Gen. Sir Archibald Wavell's ABDA (American-British-Dutch-Australian) command, which early on showed signs of disunity and worse. Poor organization, faulty liaison, and clumsy dissemination of intelligence undercut ABDA during its short, unhappy life. "During [ABDA's] existence, orders were so vague, the area so vast, and complications so many that responsible American officers rarely really knew what their responsibilities were."[6]

Admiral Thomas Hart of the U.S. Asiatic Fleet, functioning as commander of the ABDA naval forces, or ABDAFLOAT (American-British-Dutch-Australian naval forces), attempted on at least seven separate occasions to counter the enemy's moves with his Striking Force. But the truth is that his aging ships were being "run to death" by the amount of escorting and convoy screening they had undertaken, largely through pressures exerted by the British.[7] These responsibilities wore out men and materiel much more rapidly than Hart believed necessary, kept his ships far from the combat zone, and robbed him of the chance to exploit whatever scraps of good intelligence or reconnaissance he received that alerted him to possible Japanese moves.

Air reconnaissance for the U.S. forces was conducted by the PBY flying boats of Patrol Wing 10, commanded by Capt. Frank B. Wagner, who reported directly to Hart. Dutch Naval Air Force planes carrying out similar missions reported to Vice Adm. Conrad E. L. Helfrich, commander of the Netherlands Navy. According to the memoirs of Gen. Lewis Brereton, "Both of these sailors insisted on keeping their

---

* Almost simultaneously with the Kendari operation, planes from the carriers of CarDiv 2, *Sōryu* and *Hiryū*, struck the Dutch airfield at Ambon in preparation for the seizure of that island.

reconnaissance agencies under their exclusive control. It took twenty-four hours or more for reconnaissance reports to filter through the respective navy headquarters and come to my intelligence section. Opposition to any change was so great that it required an order from General Wavell to make them immediately share their information with us."[8] Obviously, this does not speak well for ABDA's cooperative priorities.

Meanwhile, Hart's ABDA co-leaders neither appreciated nor heeded his objections. And by his own admission, Hart had spoken too bluntly to suit his fellow commanders, who seemed to prefer the blithe verbal insouciance served up by the British, the Netherlanders' stolid resolve, and the overconfident platitudes of General MacArthur. The sands of the hourglass were running out for the Allies—absurd press releases and media posturing aside—and many noncombatant lives would be lost as a result of the false assurances that continued to be broadcast and believed, especially on Java, until the eleventh hour and beyond. For many military personnel, and especially the men of the old Asiatic Fleet, U.S. political vanity would be allowed to trump pragmatism. In the interests of national prestige, they were going to be sacrificed, and nothing could alter that. The tragedy was that their lives would bring so little in return—which was precisely what Admiral Hart had hoped and believed he could avoid.

Elsewhere, Adm. Chester Nimitz, Commander in Chief, Pacific Fleet (CINCPAC), and Adm. Ernest King, Commander in Chief, U.S. Navy (COMINCH), were not optimistic about developments in the Southwest Pacific in early February 1942. However, the aggressive King would brook no talk of Pacific Fleet vessels being "markedly inferior in all types to enemy," and he told Nimitz in no uncertain terms that the Japanese must be kept under pressure by "active operations."[9] CINCPAC got the message, and although the ABDA area was given some token attention, the two men understood that only carrier raids against the mandated islands "will of itself cover and protect Midway-Hawaii line while affording badly needed relief of pressure in southwest Pacific." Their true concern was for holding Australia, New Caledonia, and New Hebrides, but not reinforcing or preserving the expendable units of the Asiatic Fleet in ABDA. They had no desire to throw away more U.S. lives or valuable ships than absolutely necessary to fulfill their political commitment to the Dutch in the East Indies.

*The way in which these operations had been conducted left no room
for doubt regarding the skill, power and efficiency of the Japanese
Navy.*
                              —Steven Roskill, *The War at Sea, 1939–1945*

On Thursday, January 29, 1942, Rear Adm. Ugaki Matome, the
Combined Fleet's chief of staff, wrote in his diary, "Staff Officer Miwa
[Capt. Miwa Yoshitake, operational staff officer, Combined Fleet]
brought in a plan to send the task force off the south coast of Java, where
a second Dunkirk is likely to take place at the time of the Java invasion."[10] After noting a few suggestions that he had made for these plans,
Ugaki does not bring up the matter again until February 7, when he
writes, "The policy which the Second Fleet [under Vice Adm. Kondō
Nobutake] adopted with the reinforcement of the task force is quite
agreeable. It will be interesting to see if a second and third Dunkirk will
take place in the south of Java, as the staff says, so that big British fishes
may be bagged."[11]

Such remarks give the impression of an ad hoc quality to Japanese
planning at this phase of their First Stage operations, and of their desire
for unequivocal propaganda coups as well. Ugaki's diaries also mention
the need for shipping bottoms*—even this early in the Pacific war a critical requirement for the Japanese, who were well aware of their shortages
in that area—and the possibility of augmenting their meager merchant
fleet with captured vessels. One should not imagine, though, that the
men of Nihon Kaigun lacked the desire for a confrontation with their
Western adversaries.

Therefore, the possibility that the Japanese had not yet bombed
Tjilatjap because they hoped the British Eastern Fleet would attempt
another Dunkirk-style evacuation shouldn't be dismissed either. Even
elements of the Dutch and British command on Java suspected as much,
although this was not openly suggested or made explicit at the time.[12]

When KdB was sent south of Java to interdict Allied reinforcements
and refugees, the operational orders would include instructions to not
only "attack and quickly destroy the enemy" but "depending upon the
situation [to capture] transports and convoys."[13] That almost no writ-

---

* The transports and merchant vessels required to move men, materiel, and fuel throughout a nation's or empire's territories.

ten records have survived that dealt with the matter of captured enemy personnel should come as no surprise.

At roughly the same time in Berlin—January 3, 1942—the Japanese ambassador, Baron Oshima Hiroshi, held discussions with Hitler and Joachim von Ribbentrop, Germany's foreign minister, on the very subject of prisoners of war. According to Baron Oshima's later testimony, Hitler himself argued for the ruthless killing of merchant seamen. His thinking appears to have been based on the belief that the British and the Americans were still able to recruit more than enough merchant sailors to man their ever-increasing merchant fleets, and only the knowledge that Axis submarines and raiders were not saving personnel from sunken ships might reduce these enlistments.

On March 1, 1943, a year later, the Imperial Navy's General Staff promulgated Directive 107 (overturning Directive 60, which had allegedly protected the lives of Allied captives), ordering commanders to "completely dispose of survivors."[14] This was also known as First Submarine Force Order and was issued again in written form on March 20, 1943. Stamped *gunki* (top secret), it read: "Do not stop with the sinking of enemy ships and cargoes; at the same time that you carry out the complete destruction of the crews of the enemy ships, if possible, seize part of the crew and endeavour to secure information." Although Directive 107 applied specifically to submariners in practice, it was carried out by countless IJN units throughout the course of the war, from the Bay of Bengal to Wake Island, and from the war's outset until its final moments.

Moreover, this directive was the only evidence of its type to survive the massive, coordinated, and secret destruction of documents under direct orders from Japan at war's end. These top-secret cables were sent to Japanese field commanders across the empire between August 21 and August 27, 1945, stating, among other things, that "personnel who mistreated prisoners of war and [civilian] internees . . . are permitted to take care of it by immediately transferring or fleeing without a trace." The same orders also added that "documents which would be unfavorable to us in the hands of the enemy are to be treated in the same way as secret documents and destroyed."

Of course, many thousands of Japanese had every reason to fear the Allied war-crimes tribunals that they surely knew would be coming. The atrocities committed by the Japanese hundreds of times in China beginning in the early 1930s are difficult to comprehend, and such practices, condoned at the highest levels of all Japanese administrations, did not cease when the Greater East Asia War exploded that fair Sunday morning in Hawaii.

In early 1942, though, such dark eventualities were dimly perceived, if at all, by the men commanding and crewing the ships of Nihon Kaigun. As their operations unfolded with swift efficiency against the weak, disorganized Allied opposition throughout the southward push to secure the Philippines, Malaya, Borneo, Celebes, Sumatra, and Java, the Japanese were intoxicated by what later came to be known as "victory fever." This species of overconfidence blinded senior and junior commanders alike at tactical and strategic levels, resulting in the acceptance of sloppy planning, biased war-gaming, and haphazard execution. Younger officers serving in the Imperial Navy at its apex (such as Fuchida Mitsuo, Tanaka Raizo, and Chihaya Masataka) later acknowledged this malady. Many others, including former "experts" who became inspirational leaders in the Combined Fleet (such as Yamamoto Isoroku and Yamaguchi Tamon, both of whom served in this capacity as part of the Delegation to the London Naval Conference of 1930) as well as men who had led the navy's warships to stunning successes early in the war (as had Nagumo Chūichi and Takagi Takeo), willingly paid with their lives for this failure to fully absorb and profit from the lessons of those initial victories.

It would fall to the diminutive Vice Adm. Nagumo Chūichi to serve as perhaps the most salient example of this hard, paradoxical fate, for it was during his tenure as commander of the 1st Air Fleet's superb Mobile Force, or KdB, that the Imperial Navy's reputation as one of maritime history's greatest fighting fleets was first cast; and it endures, despite its inglorious end, to this day.

> *A very powerful organization in air . . .*
> —Capt. Edwin Layton, U.S. Pacific Fleet Intelligence officer,
> describing Nagumo's KdB during the 1944 Pearl Harbor
> attack hearings

Between December 1941 and April 1942, KdB steamed a third of the world's circumference, leaving in its wake destruction, terror, awe, and an unbroken succession of lopsided victories from one end of the

Pacific to the other: Pearl Harbor, Rabaul, Ambon, Port Darwin, the East Indies, the Indian Ocean, the Bay of Bengal. One by one, the U.S., British, Dutch, and Australian allies were shattered by the relentless hammer blows of Japan's finest ships and seamen and her most aggressive fliers.

At the heart of this force were four of the six fleet carriers that had attacked Pearl Harbor: *Akagi, Kaga, Sōryu*, and *Hiryū*. These were veteran warships ("the cream of the Japanese Navy," according to Layton), crewed by well-trained and proud officers and sailors who knew that they were the best in the world. Although posterity's esteem for KdB is based on a combat career of less than seven months, and its end was spectacular, brief, and violent, a short, general description of these renowned warships is called for.

Akagi was designed and begun as a battle cruiser, then converted in the aftermath of the Washington Conference limiting capital ship tonnage, and completed as one of the world's first large, and potentially most powerful, aircraft carriers. Her half-sister ship *Kaga* had undergone a similar metamorphosis, although from a battleship to a carrier, and she retained the broad beam, heavy conventional gunpower, and somewhat slower speed associated with such vessels. Both carriers underwent extensive refits in the 1930s that increased their size and effectiveness. *Akagi* emerged from her 1938 rebuilding at 42,750 tons full-load displacement, able to make 31.2 knots; three years earlier in 1935, *Kaga* had been reconstructed to a full-load displacement of 43,650 tons and a top speed of 28.34 knots.

Sōryu and *Hiryū*, both launched in the late 1930s, were closely related but with distinct differences. The former was constructed first, and on a somewhat smaller scale, at 15,900 tons standard displacement and full-load displacement of 19,800 tons. *Hiryū*, completed later, was an enlarged version, at some 21,900 tons full-load displacement. She, like the much bigger *Akagi*, had been built with her bridge island on the port side of her flight deck. They were the only fleet carriers operating at that time with this unusual design characteristic. *Sōryu* and *Hiryū* were also the fastest carriers at that time, sprinters each capable of more than thirty-four knots.*

* On trials, *Sōryu*, at 18,871 tons, developed 152,483 shaft horsepower (shp) good for 34.898 knots. Her sister ship *Hiryū*, slightly larger at 20,165 tons, generated 153,000 shp on trials and reached 34.59 knots.

The older and larger pair of carriers formed the 1st Carrier Division; the junior vessels made up the 2nd Carrier Division. All were grouped under the title of 1st Air Fleet, with the carriers known as Mobile Force, or Striking Force—the KdB. (The two other carriers of the Pearl Harbor force, Carrier Division 5, *Shokaku* and *Zuikaku*, were in Japanese waters during this period.) Among the quartet, a total of roughly 250 aircraft—level bombers, dive-bombers, torpedo bombers, and fighters—could be carried. These were flown and serviced by experienced men equal to any in the world, superior to most, and with the self-confidence to match.

However, the ease with which they had accomplished their military objectives also bore the fatal virus of overconfidence, which would contribute to the disasters of Midway in early June. At the time of the operations south of Java in late February and early March, Vice Admiral Nagumo's KdB should have been at the top of its form, and no force that the Allies might realistically have been able to assemble then could have engaged them without suffering serious losses.

Again, though, we may learn from the Pacific Fleet's foremost intelligence officer, Capt. Edwin Layton, who, as early as the fall of 1944, put his finger squarely on the brittleness of KdB in his testimony to Pearl Harbor investigators. Layton emphasized that Nagumo's fleet was in effect a raiding force, and a vulnerable one at that. Although powerful in its air organization, it was susceptible to surface forces at night or under conditions of poor visibility, or to air attack itself.[15] The seemingly unimportant actions of KdB in the operations south of Java also reveal more about its vincibility than earlier histories have recognized, and they, too, are worthy of closer scrutiny.

Although in later years, IJN participants such as Fuchida Mitsuo would argue that these operations were serious misapplications of KdB, many in the Imperial Navy's upper echelons wanted to facilitate a German victory over England and Russia and believed that crushing the Royal Navy's remaining forces south of the Malay Barrier and in the Bay of Bengal would help achieve these strategic aims. Whether political thinking ever matched military capabilities is another issue altogether.

Japanese press releases at the time of Singapore's fall made it clear that there would be "no second Dunkirk" there, and the ships of the Imperial Navy were faithful to those statements. Though not KdB's ships, but those of Vice Adm. Ozawa Jisaburo, they ruthlessly shelled

Organization of Kidō Butai, March 1942

Force	Commander	Composition	Duties
Air Attack Force	CinC 1st Air Fleet V. Adm. Nagumo Chūichi	CarDiv 1: *Akagi, Kaga,* less DesDiv 7 CarDiv 2: *Sōryū, Hiryū,* less DesDiv 27	Attack and destroy enemy fleet(s), transport(s), and convoy(s)
Support Force	Cmdr. BatDiv 3 V. Adm. Mikawa Gun'ichi	BatDiv 3, less 2nd section: *Hiei, Kirishima* CruDiv 8: *Tone, Chikuma*	Escort Air Attack Force; attack enemy fleet
Screening Force	Cmdr. DesRon 1 Rear Adm. Omori Sentaro	CL *Abukuma,* DesDiv 17, 1st section, DesDiv 18; 2nd section DesDiv 4; 2nd section DesDiv 27: *Tanikaze, Ariake, Hagikaze, Isokaze, Hamakaze, Urakaze, Shiranuhi, Maikaze, Kasumi, Yugure*	Screen—attack enemy fleet, transport(s), and convoy(s)
Replenishment Force	CO *Kyokuto Maru*	1st Replenishment Force: *Kyokuto Maru, Kenyo Maru, Nippon Maru, Toei Maru, Teiyo Maru*	Replenishment

Table adapted from Senshi Sōsho, *Vol. 26, Chap. 7, p. 494. Translation by Rear Adm. Edwin T. Layton, 1977.*

scores of small and large vessels, killing thousands of civilian refugees as well as military personnel, and left the Bangka Straits a blood-red waterway. Not to be outdone, KdB and its flank protection, the Main Body of the Southern Force under Vice Adm. Kondō Nobutake, would debouch into the Indian Ocean below Java a mere two weeks later and repeat this slaughter.*

> *Whenever you find hundreds and thousands of sane people trying to get out of a place and a little bunch of madmen trying to get in, you know the latter are reporters.*
> —H. R. "Red" Knickerbocker

That last disorderly weekend of February 1942, dozens of Allied ships fled the beautiful, doomed island of Java, where Dutch obstinacy, or *koppigheid*, had coexisted with the native Indonesian fondness for myth for ten generations. Ships of every shape and description were filled with escaping troops; the seriously wounded; violent, drunken deserters; well-heeled oil-industry executives and their staffs; high-ranking Dutch, Australian, British, and U.S. military personnel; and unnerved civilians, many with young families in tow. All realized that they had probably waited too long before trying to get away, but most had no idea what awaited them over the next few days on the massive swells of the Indian Ocean in their 1,700-mile dash for freedom.

A handful of vessels departed Batavia's Tandjong Priok on Friday, February 27, but most ships that attempted to leave after that were trapped.† There were well-founded rumors everywhere of Japanese submarines lurking just beyond the southern entrance to Sunda Strait and in harbors that still remained in Allied control on the lower coast of Java. At Wijnkoops Bay and at Tjilatjap, under cover of darkness, the plodding merchantmen and remaining warships weighed anchor; negotiated

---

* Kondō (35th Term of Etajima) was senior to Nagumo (36th term) and had overall command. His force consisted of *Kongō* and *Haruna* of BatDiv 3/2; *Atago* (flagship), *Takao*, and *Maya* of CruDiv 4; and the destroyers *Arashi, Nowaki,* and *Hayashio. Kuroshio* and *Oyashio* escorted the oilers.

† This of course includes most famously the Australian vessel HMAS *Perth*, as well as the USS *Houston* (CA-30) and the Dutch destroyer *Evertsen*, all of which were lost on the night of Saturday, February 28, to Sunday, March 1. The final commercial convoy to depart Tandjong Priok was that of *Ashridge*, which left on February 26, escorted by HMS *Stronghold*. (See Gill, Vol. I, p. 579.)

shallow, reef-cramped channels; and stood out, their wakes cutting a serrated path through rising seas. Some went in clusters, screened by small, undergunned escorts. A few tried to get as far away from the Malay Barrier as quickly as they could, and sailed a direct southern route alone.[*] Others were directed to remain approximately four hundred miles south of Java until they received further orders. In a bitter irony, almost all vessels were low on fuel. Even those capable of high speeds had to slow to an agonizing pace so they would have enough fuel for their long, dangerous journey. Others were condemned by the sluggish pace of their respective convoys. Their names recall the diverse and exotic Far Eastern colonial world now imploding by the hour: *Abbekerk, Anking, Bandjermasin, Bintoehan, Duymaer van Twist, Francol, Jagersfontein, Kota Baroe, Le Maire, Poelau Bras, Sea Witch, Tawali, Tung Song, Van Spilbergen, Zaandam.* A few eluded the Japanese maritime dragnet; a number were sunk with heavy casualties; and still others were captured, their crews and passengers to become "guests" of the emperor. Perhaps most fantastic of all, some survivors were able to escape their sinking ships and steer lifeboats to landfall in Java and Sumatra after epic struggles against the Indian Ocean. However, far more remained to be captured on Java, for as veteran United Press (UP) correspondent Harold Guard had put it on Saturday night in Jogjakarta, "I'm afraid the boys who stay are dead ducks."[16]

Until the eleventh hour, they had allowed themselves to be deceived by hopeful Allied propaganda declaring that the island could never fall, and that ABDA forces could hold out indefinitely on the "impregnable" Preanger plateau near Bandoeng. But the Dutch had for decades ignored the warnings in *Max Havelaar*; eighty years later they sounded even more ominous and prescient:

> I have already said that the desire to never send other than good
> news to the Government would be comic if the results of it all

[*] COMSOUWESPAC secret message 281226 [February 28] to other Allied commanders regarding the naval situation shows American and British vessels spread out from the Arabian Sea to Bombay, and Java to Exmouth Gulf, with plans for resistance and reinforcements still ongoing. A day later came the orders, "ALL U.S. AND BRITISH SHIPS LEAVE TJILATJAP AT ONCE X SCATTER BUT PROCEED EAST ALONG THE COAST UNTIL DARK X PROCEED SEA SEPARATELY THEN TO RENDEZVOUS. LAT FIFTEEN SOUTH LONG ONE ONE THREE EAST TO REMAIN THAT VICINITY UNTIL SHIPS JOINED UP THEN PROCEED TO EXMOUTH GULF." Palliser knew that the game was up; Glassford diplomatically waited until told by Helfrich before sending U.S. ships away on the morning of March 1, 1942. By then, however, it was far too late for many of them. (Glassford Files, NARA II.)

were not so tragic. For what correction of so much wrong can be hoped for in the face of a predetermined purpose to twist and distort everything . . . ? Must not the bent spring eventually recoil? Must not the long-suppressed discontent . . . finally turn to rage, desperation, madness?[17]

Even the resolute, "damphool" Western journalists who were washed south by the flood tide of Japanese victories in Malaya, the Philippines, Borneo, Sumatra, and Celebes allowed themselves to be caught up in this tragicomic vortex. Kenneth Selby-Walker of Reuters; Bill McDougall and Witt Hancock of the Associated Press; George Weller of the Chicago *Daily News*; Jack Findon of the London *Daily Express*; and H. R. "Red" Knickerbocker, Frank Cuhel, and Bill Dunn of CBS, just to name a handful, all wanted to believe that the island's defenses would stem the Imperial advance. Regardless, as men committed to reporting facts, they fought daily with censors who wanted only good news to be broadcast. Some were chided by sarcastic Allied censors for their timidity. With fear of ridicule overcoming concerns about the Japanese invasion, these Westerners waited until the last moment to leave. But for a number of them, Fate had by then decreed no escape.* The sinking of the *Langley* and the catastrophic Battle of the Java Sea— both of which took place on Friday, February 27—ended any delusions of "good news" as swiftly and brutally as a Japanese slap in the face, which most Allied survivors would experience firsthand, so to speak, in the ensuing three and a half years.

Smug complacency and stiff-necked pride collapsed almost overnight, if accounts from those who survived the campaign are believed. Even midsize units of Japanese parachutists created no small degree of panic. The success of their operations in Borneo, Celebes, and Sumatra seems to have unnerved the Dutch native forces. Eyewitnesses reported terror-stricken Royal Netherlands Indies Army (KNIL) troops fleeing at the sight of "enemy paratroopers," which turned out to be distant

---

* See *Six Bells Off Java*, p. 94. Of the others, Dunn and Cuhel escaped aboard *Janssens* with Dr. Wassell; Cuhel evaded the Java catastrophe only to die a year later in a plane crash near Lisbon, Portugal. McDougall was shipwrecked after the sinking of *Poelau Bras* and ended up a POW in Sumatra; Witt Hancock went down with the same vessel. Weller and Knickerbocker got away successfully. Selby-Walker refused to flee or surrender and disappeared into the wilds of Java vowing to join guerrillas, never to be seen again.

antiaircraft bursts floating down from the cerulean skies over Bandoeng, Java. It was as if the island's defenses had been buttressed by nothing more than words and images. Perhaps it was fitting that the object of so much Japanese propaganda was defended only by words and taken with such relative ease.

Without question, widespread chaos ruled Tjilatjap on that penultimate weekend (described by Royal Netherlands Navy [RNN] sailor Frans Zantvoort in a 2000 interview as "a madhouse"). Civilian evacuees, journalists, wounded servicemen, oil industry specialists and executives, as well as high-ranking military personnel were attempting to decamp at the last possible moment; many even then failing to recognize what was soon to descend upon them. Narrative after narrative written after the war reveals Dutch citizens and soldiers refusing to believe that they would be captured and imprisoned by the Japanese; instead they clung to the belief that they would be permitted to live in their own homes just as their countrymen in Holland were allowed to do under the Germans. And they failed to believe that their former colonial charges would turn against them and actively support the invaders. One Dutch naval officer refused to assign berths to his fellow countrymen, exclaiming, "I am not going to put you on a ship, I don't want to be a murderer. Let that be enough for you!"[18]

That final weekend, a large number of the oblivious gathered together in the tony nightclubs and hotels of Bandoeng, Batavia, and Surabaja to enjoy a final taste of illusory freedom. Many accounts recall a seductive full moon glowing magically over the East Indies the night of March 1. These memoirs, with the sad clarity of wisdom acquired too late, stress those final nights, for the Japanese controlled the air throughout the East Indies and to travel during the day was to take your life in your hands.

A few hours later, in the huge, featureless seas below Java, during the impenetrable night or in stunning daylight, the fleeing Allies would meet a new paradigm.

Gone but Not Forgotten

On the southeastern coast of Java, a few kilometers inland from "a large bay enclosed by the rocky outcrops of rugged cliffs," a contemporary traveler may find "a strangely misplaced classical Greek temple, inscribed with the words *Gegaan maar niet vergeten*, "Gone but not forgotten."[19]

This memorial at Pacitan recalls the lost colonial empire, culture, and society of the Dutch East Indies—destroyed after three centuries of rule by the Japanese invasion and subsequent occupation.

Few aspects of the history of this dissolution are more shrouded in mystery than the final days of the Java campaign in late February and early March 1942, and the flight from the East Indies by dozens of ships that left from the last operational port on the island.

A comprehensive accounting of all the ships that fled Tjilatjap between February 26 and March 3, 1942, has not been attempted in any English-language history. The reasons for this are apparent enough: It was a period of intense, frenetic activity under chaotic conditions, with poor communications and thousands upon thousands of individuals involved, many of whom were separated from their organizational units or had been hospitalized or otherwise cut off from their fellow servicemen. And of course thousands of civilian refugees were in grim circumstances that could only be described as "every man for himself."

From Surabaja were sent, among others, teenage Dutch marine recruits: "In packed trains, without any food or drink, we travelled to Tjilatjap. Chaos was rife among those who had to withdraw. There was no command anymore. Everybody tried to save himself. Leaving the train was forbidden, however. It would be regarded as desertion."[20]

One Dutch merchant engineer serving on the MS *Abbekerk* and waiting to leave that madhouse later wrote:

> In the course of the day [February 27] men came aboard. A more diverse group of men I never saw before. Aircraft crew with thick jackets, some high officers, a few lower officers, soldiers, sailors, armed and unarmed and some more civilians. A lot of very worried and tired faces...most left family and all they had behind with a very uncertain future...for sure not a place you could escape from easily when things went wrong.[21]

Though nearly everyone expected things to go very wrong, most chose not to speak of their fears. Like many seaman, they were driven by superstitions.

Almost forty merchant ships departed Tjilatjap in this period, along with numerous military vessels. These were ships under Dutch, British, and U.S. control headed for Exmouth Gulf, on the northwest shoulder of Australia, then south along the coast to Fremantle, or west from Java over the Indian Ocean and across the Bay of Bengal to Colombo at Ceylon. (The following examples of such merchant ships are representative, but should not be taken as a thorough or precise inventory.)

Waiting for orders since Tuesday, February 24, at Tjilatjap was the Norwegian merchant vessel *Prominent*. She had arrived in Batavia from Colombo on February 14 to 15 after being diverted from a Singapore-bound convoy (JS 1) when that hollow fortress capitulated. In the chaotic conditions, a number of uninvited Australian refugees suffering from "gang-plank fever" came aboard the merchantman at Tjilatjap. The ship's crew was predominantly Chinese, with Norwegians as officers; the addition of her new passengers gave her a complement of about fifty men in all. It did not take great insight to realize that the defense of Java had broken down, and that chances for evading the Japanese submarines and surface craft in the Indian Ocean were "exceedingly slim."[22]

Late on the evening of February 27, *Prominent* was given an abrupt order to leave immediately. She did so, along with many others, and struck out alone, due south from the port into the Indian Ocean. On March 1, *Prominent* was attacked and sunk in a position approximately 230 nautical miles below Tjilatjap. Records for this sinking, too, are contradictory, with an Imperial Navy submarine, the *I-54*, generally credited with the kill. However, some accounts imply that surface vessels found and shelled the Norwegian ship under. In either case, about fourteen or fifteen crew and passengers were killed outright by the shelling; another five appear to have been picked up by lifeboats from the Dutch freighter *Tomohon*, sunk earlier that day by the destroyers *Arashi* and *Nowaki*. These survivors were eventually rescued by the Dutch passenger ship *Zaandam* and delivered, along with nearly a thousand other passenger-refugees, to Fremantle four days later.

Perhaps thirty other survivors of *Prominent*, including her skipper, Capt. Kristen Gjertsen, escaped into a pair of lifeboats and steered a course for Java. On March 5, half-dead, they made landfall, although only one boat seems to have survived the trip. These "lucky" individuals found willing natives who helped them carry five injured sailors inland to Garoet (on about March 7), where they were admitted to a hospital. In the end, a number were sent by the Japanese to Batavia—because Norway was not officially at war with Japan—but they were not arrested and imprisoned until November or December 1943.

From Tjilatjap's overcrowded harbor, the 10,000-ton Dutch liner *Poelau Bras* (Capt. P. G. Crietee) departed in time to escape the Japanese and had made fair progress on her journey to Australia when she received new orders: "Proceed Wijnkoops Bay. Evacuate military personnel."[23] With a cargo of $2 million worth of war materials still in her holds, *Poelau Bras* returned to the small bay on the southwestern end of Java. There, on March 6, along with an older tramp freighter, the *Siberg*, the liner's crew of ninety-one began embarking some 150 high-ranking Dutch officers and petroleum industry executives and their families: W. H. Oosten, director of Shell subsidiary B.P.M. (Bataafsche Petroleum Maatschappij, or Batavia Petroleum Company); Dr. Anton H. Colijn, manager of the oil fields at Tarakan, Borneo, along with his three daughters *; Rear Adm. J. J. A. van Staveren, former chief of staff to Vice Adm. C. E. F. Helfrich; and Maj. Gen. O. J. D. De Fremery of the Netherlands Army. Captain Gerald Bozuwa, commander of the Netherlands Indies naval air bombers, was also present, along with the former Dutch naval attaché to Japan, Cmdr. J. A. L. Mueller.

The small, rusting *Siberg* refused to risk the trip across the Indian Ocean, but the big liner weighed anchor on the evening of March 6 and stood out into the Indian Ocean under a soothing but deceptive "cover of darkness."† Hoping to put at least 250 miles between herself and the coast by eleven o'clock the following morning, *Poelau Bras* took a south-westerly course, but luck was not on her side. At a quarter past nine on that beautiful, bright blue morning, the ship's whistle blew the alarm three times. From the north, "a Japanese twin-engined plane droned . . . and wheeled in a great circle around the *Poelau Bras*. Our stern gun boomed. The plane disdainfully tightened its circle and banked around us thrice before it headed northeast and disappeared. Every person on board knew what would follow."[24] Little more than ninety minutes later, two nine-plane *chūtai* of dive-bombers from the carriers *Sōryu* and *Hiryū* attacked the liner "in groups of three" and sank her. About

---

* The Colijns were oil royalty, one might say. Anton was the son of Hendrik Colijn, the former prime minister of the Netherlands and chief executive officer of B.P.M. and Royal Dutch Shell. Hendrik Colijn had been deeply involved in numerous unsavory Near and Middle East oil imbroglios with the British after World War I.

† *Siberg* (1,871 tons) would be seized by the Japanese, pressed into service as *Sumerusan Maru*, and later sunk in an explosion at Surabaja in April 1943.

144 persons died during this thirty-minute assault and in subsequent ordeals at sea.

William McDougall nearly perished in those waters; he swam for several hours before being picked up by a drifting lifeboat full of survivors wrestling with an uncooperative sail. The experience altered his life permanently, or "in the Eternal Tense," as he liked to say. Along with twenty-five others, the exhausted but grateful reporter struggled, bailing water and rowing, for six agonizing days to reach land. Two other lifeboats, one with fifty-eight persons crowded into its waterlogged hold, and another with thirty-two, likewise sailed northeast.

On Friday, March 13, McDougall's boat made it to shore on the eastern tip of Sumatra, off Vlakke Hoek, near Semangka Bay. Both of the other boats also fetched up on the southeastern coast of Sumatra, as McDougall and his companions ultimately discovered, but there would be no real escape for any, for in the first days of April all were captured by units of the Imperial Japanese Army. On the evening of Easter Sunday, April 5, after being transported across the waist of Sumatra, the reporter was incarcerated in the Palembang jail. The next dawn broke with a hard, sober clarity: "Night had washed the sky nearly clean of clouds, giving the sun full scope to kindle the day with brilliance. . . . What had been concealed by darkness last night when I entered stood out this morning in harsh reality."[25]

The harsh reality that McDougall had suddenly recognized was about to become much harsher. Although he couldn't have known it, ten days later, a Japanese magazine called *Asahigraph* published photos of the latest achievements of the Emperor's military forces. Many were devoted to the recent East Indies campaign, in which Allied ships and men were "decisively" defeated by the Imperial Navy. There are images of the British tanker *Marantula*, straddled by bombs in Bangka Strait; several more of HMS *Exeter*'s end in the Sea Battle Off Cape Puting; and another showing towering pillars of water exploding around an unidentified naval vessel with four funnels.

Disabusing newly conquered native populations of their awe for the white man was a conscious and deliberate part of the Japanese program as well. The so-called thought war was understood to be of primary importance in successfully exploiting the natural resources that the Japanese had to gone to war to obtain and which were crucial to the strength and well-being of her empire.

As for the psychological aspects of Japanese strategic thinking, these too gave enormous emphasis to public perception and the value of propaganda. This appears to be borne out by the otherwise trivial remarks of Rear Admiral Ugaki in his diary. Whether or not such realizations filtered down through the ranks is a perplexing question. But there is no doubt that the Japanese placed great value on the effectiveness of images and went to extraordinary lengths to obtain and exploit them. At the vanguard of their most successful military campaigns were the dauntless warships of KdB, where one would find many of the most dedicated war photojournalists and correspondents. They were tasked with bringing home rousing accounts and spectacular images of Imperial victories to garner support from a populace that would be asked to make ever-greater sacrifices for the Greater East Asia War. And because mass media was well understood by the Japanese as an invaluable tool for shaping public opinion, vectoring KdB into the waters south of Java would have offered additional possibilities for even greater propaganda coups.

Indoctrinating the semiliterate and uneducated masses of the Nam'po was another task for propaganda, and here, too, the Japanese showed that they were clever in their exploitation of *Sensō* captives and captive senses. They recognized that the great triumphs of Pearl Harbor and Malaya had afforded them invaluable opportunities for potent, iconic photos of Imperial Japan's martial prowess. The cameramen of the propaganda corps were always searching for new images to be seized and exploited, no matter their true military significance or the actual facts behind them.

In the outer Nam'po, the teeming islands of the East Indies known as the Emerald Belt were considered to have the most critical raw materials for the Imperial Way's Greater East Asia Co-Prosperity Sphere, and it was on Java that Japan centered her propaganda machinery for the new southern territories. The Japanese had been wise enough to understand that written propaganda might have negligible impact on a huge region consisting of thousands of islands with tens of millions of poorly educated, primarily rural inhabitants, few of whom shared a common language or culture. They understood, therefore, the value of more basic forms of communication, in particular the sight and sound media of film.

However, beyond such simplistic schemes, the Japanese had given little thought to governing the East Indies, with its culturally delicate, complex, and volatile indigenous populations. Most of their administrative models and propaganda concepts had been formed in the Sino-Japanese war, but the Japanese had had enough contact with Southeast Asian nationalists to realize that they were not going to be dealing with the problems of China in the Nam'po. A significant amount of attention had been devoted to these very issues before the Pacific war, yet in the end, there was more theory than practice, more lip service than actual implementation. "In the absence of a sensible military policy, the Japanese ought to have developed successful modes of civil administration and of counterinsurgency activity. But the central authorities never devised a systematic and standardized approach; local commanders' 'solutions' inevitably stressed force, fear, and intimidation."[26]

At the same time, the Imperial Navy, burdened by its overriding need for fuel oil, demanded that its prerogatives be recognized in the interservice turf wars over resources, and showed not the least inclination to grant any real autonomy to parochial administrations. This had a chilling effect on the creation of viable local governments, and would lead to intractable difficulties and worse in the conquered regions for the duration of the war.

Chapter Four

DD-219 at War

Richardson, we have never been ready, but we have always won.
—Secretary of the Navy Frank Knox to
Adm. James O. Richardson, 1940

In the final weeks before the war broke out, USS *Edsall* (DD-219) and Destroyer Division 57, along with their tender USS *Black Hawk* (AD-9), were sent by Adm. Thomas C. Hart, Commander in Chief, Asiatic Fleet (CINCAF), to Balikpapan, a major oil port on the eastern coast of Borneo. Ordered south with other Asiatic Fleet units from Manila, they departed on November 25 and arrived on the morning of November 30, with vague orders to "linger" in the area while they "ostensibly" sought to refuel. Hart wanted his ships in this "defensive deployment" well south of Manila—which was within range of Japanese bombers flying from Formosa—when "things began to pop." By this time the ship needed to be repainted; the men were ordered to conceal the large white "219" on the ship's bow. They slung stages over her side and broke out the man helpers and buckets of dark-gray paint.

As her deck log reveals, however, *Edsall* was not in port at the time she was notified of the commencement of hostilities—December 8 in the Far East—but at sea with USS *Black Hawk* (AD-9) and the other destroyers of Destroyer Division 57 (DesDiv 57): USS *Whipple* (DD-217), *Alden* (DD-211), and *John D. Edwards* (DD-216). They were supposedly heading for Batavia, but, with the receipt of the war notification, DesDiv 57 was rerouted to Singapore and *Black Hawk* was left behind. The destroyers were to act as an antisubmarine screen for the British ships of Force Z—the new battleship HMS *Prince of Wales* and the World War I–era battle cruiser HMS *Repulse*—sent by

Churchill as a "deterrent" against Japanese belligerence. Sadly, the ships of the Royal Navy's Force Z may be said to have produced the same poor "deterrent" effect on the Imperial Navy that the U.S. Pacific Fleet had exerted at Pearl Harbor.

The positioning of DesDiv 57 at Balikpapan by Admiral Hart was one thing, but the division's commitment to joint operations with the Royal Navy was something else entirely. That it had taken until December 6, when the chilling clarity of Japanese motives was obvious to all, for such an agreement to be reached speaks volumes about the failures of Allied planning. Shared Western cultural backgrounds and values could not overcome immediate economic interests. Britain's interests were not those of the Netherlands; those of the Americans did not match Britain's; and the Dutch were especially concerned with not antagonizing the Japanese after Holland had been overrun by the armies of Nazi Germany in 1940. In terms of experience, many higher-echelon U.S. officers had cut their professional teeth on their own service peers in peacetime internecine turf wars, and lower-level personnel were widely recognized by leaders such as Admiral Hart and General Brereton as used to the lax prewar life in the Far East, leaving them unprepared for the realities of total war against the combat-tested, highly trained, and well-equipped modern Japanese army and navy. The British suffered from arrogance and complacency, and the Dutch were given to both the typical racial prejudices of the day as well as a mistaken, popular belief that the Japanese would never come so far south to seize their thousands upon thousands of isolated and remote islands. They were not the only Western nation to underestimate Japanese determination, energy, and resourcefulness.

As for the four old U.S. destroyers of DesDiv 57, they hadn't much offensive power to add, but the British desperately needed ASW escorts, and at the last possible moment, Hart agreed to release the destroyers. Hart's biographer attributes these decisions to the admiral's probity and to his good relations with and high opinion of Vice Adm. Sir Tom Phillips, the Royal Navy's Far Eastern commander. There was more to it than this, but the arcane and peculiar arrangements between U.S. and British war planners is a subject worthy of an entire volume in itself.*

---

*According to Leutze (see Chapter One, note 2), Hart finally committed DesDiv 57, including *Edsall*, of course, to Vice Admiral Phillips "virtually on the dock" as concluding

According to Hart himself, Tom Phillips was a man he would have gladly served under. Hart made no such comments about Douglas MacArthur. But Hart was the consummate professional officer, and not one to be distracted by petty disagreements, personal vanity, or egoistic trivialities.

Therefore, DesDiv 57 steamed along the southwestern coastline of Borneo, several miles offshore, before turning into the Karimata Strait at high speed. The plodding *Black Hawk* was left behind. Splitting the tapering, needle-nosed lighthouses at low-lying Lengkuas and high Serutu, they could see the dark mass of Borneo to starboard, and off to the northwest the islands of the Karimata archipelago.

Before DesDiv 57 could arrive at Singapore, though, Force Z departed and within thirty-six hours came under heavy air attack by sixty navy Type 96 G3M2 bombers of the Genzan and Mihoro Kōkūtai, and twenty-six G4M1 or 1-*Rikko* land-attack aircraft of the Kanoya Kōkūtai. Flying out of southern Indochina, these planes of the 22nd Kōkūsentai, commanded by Vice Adm. Matsunaga Sadaichi, vindicated the policy of the Imperial Navy to develop long-range bombers.[1] On Wednesday, December 10, 1941, *Prince of Wales* and *Repulse* were quickly and efficiently sunk, with the loss of more than eight hundred lives, including that of Vice Adm. Sir Tom Phillips. It was a mortal wound to not only the naval forces but to Anglo-Saxon prestige across the Orient, and it would leave the Asiatic Fleet flagship USS *Houston* (CA-30), a 10,000-ton "tin-clad" treaty cruiser, as the largest remaining Allied warship between Manila and Australia to oppose the mighty Imperial Navy.

The aging *Houston*; an even older light cruiser, USS *Marblehead* (CL-12); the recently shanghaied new cruiser USS *Boise* (CL-47); the flushdeckers of Destroyer Squadron 29; and what should have been an effective number of submarines made up the bulk of U.S. naval striking power with which Admiral Hart intended to counter the Japanese jug-

their first and only meeting in Manila on December 5 and 6, 1941. The ships were told to operate "under the orders of the British C in C." This is strangely elided by Hart and Capt. John M. Creighton later during the Pearl Harbor attack hearings. Hart told the board that he "sent the ships down to these oil ports ostensibly to get fuel" but didn't elaborate, and Captain Creighton denied any knowledge whatsoever before the Japanese began hostilities. One suspects that the emphasis on extreme secrecy, of which the greatest need was politically driven, concerning American war plans in 1940–41 had not been forgotten by these two officers.

gernaut. Hart's fleet was "old, small, and weak," but it was manned by tough, capable officers of great loyalty, and rugged sailors who prided themselves on their resourcefulness and individuality. And Hart had exercised common sense, heeding the warnings of his excellent Asiatic (as well as Pacific Fleet) intelligence services by dispersing his units to the south just before the attacks on Oahu, Malaya, and the Philippines. This bought some time, although not nearly enough.

The four ships of DesDiv 57 arrived in Singapore early on Wednesday, December 10, standing through the Straits of Johore before falling into column astern of HMS *Stronghold*, which led them to the anchorage. They then moored, and in short order began refueling from the small British oil tanker (RFA) *Francol*. Refueling was completed at about two-thirty that afternoon. In the meantime, a Royal Navy liaison officer, Lt. R. H. H. Webber, and a party of four men came aboard from the cruiser HMS *Mauritius*, which was under repair at the Singapore Naval Base. Just after three o'clock that afternoon, the ships were again under way, "steaming at various courses at various speeds," through the channel and out into the milky blue South China Sea. Until well into the evening, DesDiv 57 attempted in vain to contact the *Prince of Wales* and *Repulse*, but it was too late.

And so *Edsall* and her companion flushdeckers steamed up the coast of Malaya on Thursday, December 11, in the wake of a historic misadventure. Their mission had now been altered from that of antisubmarine screen to one of search and rescue through the area where the two British capital ships had been lost. They moved at a standard fifteen knots before changing to flank speed of twenty-eight knots during the northerly sweep. According to Cmdr. H. E. Eccles of *John D. Edwards*, they soon encountered large patches of surface oil and floating wreckage, much of it scorched and burned, which provided a sobering introduction to the realities of war.[2]

The British had also embarked a liaison team aboard *John D. Edwards* in Singapore, with a young officer, Lieutenant Commander Godwin, and several signalmen and radiomen with books and flags for communications, but their presence was now superfluous. Commander Eccles thought them a competent lot, yet liaison gremlins would bedevil the joint operations of the ABDA forces throughout the next three months. As an example of this, Commander Eccles noted that it took some five to six hours for the U.S. ships to be notified that their mission was "useless" because all of the survivors had already been picked up by British destroyers on the scene, and that this information came not from the Royal Navy, as might be expected, but from Capt. John M. Creighton, the U.S. naval observer in Singapore.*

After an hour and a quarter of fruitless searching in the dead of night, and having passed through another large oil slick at 1:45 a.m., no doubt uneasily, the ships reversed course and turned back. *Edsall,* the last ship in line, was ordered at 9:35 a.m. hours to stop the *Shofu Fu Maru,* a Japanese trawler towing four sampans full of men, women, and children (all under a large Japanese flag, to the befuddlement of Eccles). These they then directed to Singapore's South Channel, where they were turned over to the Australian corvette HMAS *Goulburn.*† After steaming back down the coast along "a green belt of palm-trees, fringing a yellow strand, stretching back to the blue hills beyond,"[3] the quartet of U.S. flushdeckers anchored at the huge naval base just after midday.

No later than 3:35 p.m., moored between *Whipple* and the tanker (RFA) *Francol,*‡ *Edsall* had received 38,000 gallons of fuel oil. She next

---

*Creighton himself is a curious figure. His testimony at the Pearl Harbor attack hearings portray a man overwhelmed with his duties in Singapore and later at Java but who attempted conscientiously to provide Hart with useful intelligence because the admiral felt "he was constantly suffering from a lack of information from home." Yet by the same token, Creighton could remember nothing of a message he had sent regarding arrangements with the British in the event of Japanese aggression. And he blamed his faulty recollection on the large number of classified documents he was forced to burn in Singapore and Java.

† In the deck log of USS *Edsall,* the Japanese trawler's name is as given above; in Royal Australian Navy (RAN) accounts it is written as "*Kohfuku Maru,*" and her capture is credited to HMAS *Goulburn,* one of the 650-ton units of the 21st Minesweeping Flotilla, along with HMAS *Maryborough, Bendigo,* and *Burnie.* The RAN ship is identified as a "destroyer" and her name misspelled as "HMS *Egoulburn*" in *Edsall*'s log for December 11, 1941. Commander H. E. Eccles of *John D. Edwards* later remarked that he believed this to be the first instance of enemy personnel captured at sea by the U.S. Navy during the Pacific war. Later in the war, the *Koh Fuku Maru* would be renamed the *Krait* and would become involved in a remarkable Australian commando enterprise known as Operation Jaywick at Singapore in September 1943.

‡ *Francol,* of 2,623 tons, was sunk in the same convoy as the depot ship *Anking,* MMS-51, and the Australian sloop HMAS *Yarra* on March 4, south of Java, by Vice Admiral Kondō's cruisers and destroyers, not far from the location of *Edsall*'s last action. It was an heroic engagement in which the small RAN vessel, commanded by Lt. Cmdr. Robert William "Oscar" Rankin (KIA) sold herself dearly against overwhelming odds, and it was witnessed, ironically, by four dozen survivors of the old British destroyer HMS *Stronghold,* rescued after their ship had been sunk two days earlier by the same Japanese cruisers and destroyers in another example of poor gunnery. Brought up from captivity to the deck to witness the prowess of the Imperial Navy, these men saw the two heavy cruisers

revictualled from VSIS (Victualling Stores Issuing Ship) *Demodocus*,* taking on 200 pounds of beef, 216 pounds of butter, 40 pounds of cucumbers, 150 pounds of of cabbage, and 75 pounds of carrots. Fresh food would become an ever-rarer commodity as the war unfolded and the Allied situation deteriorated, so over the next couple of days the ship received more provisions, including another 300 pounds of fresh beef. Across the Far Eastern area, Allied forces would see their capacities for reprovisioning increasingly degraded as the Japanese prosecuted the operation known as "A": the southern advance.[4]

Having disregarded the "defeatist" plans of Rainbow-3 and Rainbow-5, General MacArthur had continued throughout the second half of 1941 to make unreasonable, almost irrational, demands on Washington for a "Pacific-first" strategic about-face and for reinforcements (particularly airplanes) that he could neither service nor safely disperse. For purposes of morale and delay, the Franklin Delano Roosevelt administration refused to deny his requests outright; indeed, it was through Secretary of War Stimson and Army Chief of Staff general George Marshall that the fanciful strategic "deterrent" of a long-range bombing offensive against Japan was first concocted and fed to MacArthur.[†] MacArthur's acceptance of Stimson and Marshall's view on the employment of air forces, irrespective of its potential efficacy or MacArthur's enthusiasm, had come at least half a year too late. There was simply not enough time; the Imperial planners had no intention of following MacArthur's timetable. They were prepared to strike before the end of the year, and between the first week of November and that of December, they put into motion their complex plans for simultaneous surprise attacks against Malaya, Hawaii, and the Philippines.

For political reasons, Roosevelt wanted to avoid admitting that the Philippines had long since been written off, or that he had not made adequate preparations for a Pacific conflict, which should have

and two destroyers of Kondō blasting the overmatched *Yarra* at close range, the burning Australian ship returning fire until her decks were awash. Nearly 140 RAN men died as a result of the action.

* *Demodocus*, an Alfred Holt Blue Funnel MV of 6,522 tons, was built in 1912 by Workman Clark in Belfast, Ireland.

† The finest historical account of this period and the destruction of MacArthur's air forces is William Bartsch's *December 8, 1941: MacArthur's Pearl Harbor*.

been seen coming years prior to Pearl Harbor. Naturally, the reality of the Philippine defenselessness was not one that General MacArthur's deeply invested ego could accept, but his "excursions into fantasy" were allowed to continue unchecked. FDR had his own political reasons for not relieving the Far Eastern general, regardless of MacArthur's intractable, even insubordinate, machinations.[5]

The apparent contradictions of Rainbow-5 persisted (Navy: Philippines abandoned; Army: Philippines held and ultimately relieved), and they played themselves out as one might have expected when war came: U.S. Army Forces Far East (USAFFE) under MacArthur retreated to the Bataan peninsula, then to Fortress Corregidor, and fought a stubborn, heroic holding action. The Asiatic Fleet, operating in accordance with its tasks as laid out in Rainbow-5, with its primary base at Manila forfeited by MacArthur, withdrew to the Malay Barrier. As a veteran naval officer wrote many years later of the war against Japan, "An unstated corollary [to Rainbow-5's 'Europe-first' strategy] was the initial loss of the Philippines. This was in the manner of earlier plans for war with Japan alone, for they had also reflected that expectation. . . . The U.S. Asiatic Fleet was to support the defense [in the words of Rainbow-5] 'so long as that defense continues,' but its lack of the strength needed to make such a task meaningful was not indicated."[6] For both service branches, the end result would demand tremendous sacrifices.

The ships of DesDiv 57 remained in Singapore until Sunday, December 14, when they were ordered to Surabaja, Java, at the eastern end of that island, "piled peak upon peak into the blue," several hundred miles away from the omnipresent enemy aircraft. *Edsall* anchored in Surabaja Bay in the early hours of December 16.* A handful of U.S. and Dutch warships trickled into the harbor. But relentless Japanese pressure was driving all Allied shipping even farther south.

On December 21, *Edsall* departed Java, along with *Whipple* and *Alden*, as an antisubmarine screen for USS *Houston* (CA-30), after which the ships of Task Group 5.3 would rendezvous with the Asiatic Fleet support train. Following some milling around in the Bali Sea on December 21 and 22 due to poor communications, TG 5.3 at last met the supply ships, consisting of USS *Pecos* (AO-6), USS *Otus* (AS-20),

---

* Two days later, a young sailor named Loys Parsons, seaman second class, "reported on board for duty with bag and hammock in accordance with ComDesRon Twenty-Nine Transfer Order No. 116."

and, later, USS *Gold Star* (AG-12). These invaluable units were then shepherded south of the Lesser Sunda islands to the relative safety of northern Australia's Port Darwin anchorage.

On USS *Boise* (CL-47)—a more modern cruiser roped into duty with Hart's other ships after she escorted a convoy to the Philippines in early December—an officer overheard a conversation at Surabaja between crewmen of *Ford, Pope,* and *Bulmer* during fueling. At that time, officers were still permitted to keep diaries, and this officer recorded many incidents, large and small, in the opening weeks of the war. "The crews in these old tin cans are pretty darned good. Listened to some of the men batting the breeze on the destroyer forecastles. One of their men, to one of ours: 'How you feeding?' Our man, who is eating very well indeed: 'Not so good. Everything's running out. How're you feeding?' The destroyer man: 'We're O.K. Plenty of dogs and crackers.' "[7] A seaman named Fred Harrison, who transferred from *Edsall* to another ship, recalled sixty years later that the destroyer was indeed short of food during her final weeks. He remembered that one day, stopping a Scandinavian merchantman, *Edsall*'s boarding party was able to acquire a considerable, not to say overwhelming, quantity of sardines. These along with hardtack kept the crew fed for some time before the end.[*]

Fortunately, the Esso tanker *George G. Henry*[†] had also led a charmed life and managed to avoid being hit by Japanese bombs on Manila and Cavite. Over the next few days after the war's outbreak, she was able to discharge some 69,500 barrels of oil for use by Allied forces before departing south. She was led through the dangerous minefields of Manila Bay by USS *Bulmer* (DD-222), then down to the East Indies, where she became an invaluable asset as a fueling vessel to the beleaguered Asiatic Fleet. She arrived in Balikpapan, Borneo, on December 20, and filled her bunkers with 75,000 barrels of precious fuel oil before leaving for Java on Christmas Eve. On the day after Christmas,

---

[*] Harrison thought that the ship was Danish, but this appears to have actually been the Dutch ship *Van Lansberge*, which was stopped by *Edsall*. The destroyer put a boarding party aboard, led by Lt. j.g. Ray Snodgrass, to inspect the merchantman. There are no other recorded events in *Edsall*'s extant logs comparable to this anecdote. *Van Lansberge* herself was sunk before the end of February south of Makassar by the IJN submarine *I-155*.

[†] SS *George G. Henry*, built by the Union Iron Works Company of San Francisco in 1917, displaced 10,840 tons, was 453 feet long and 56 feet wide, and had a cargo-carrying capacity of 78,166 barrels; it had a triple expansion engine and three boilers driving a single propeller and a maximum speed of 10.2 knots.

George G. Henry was in Surabaja's congested harbor. Five days later, she steamed east from Java for Australia. Her convoy was escorted at that time by light cruiser USS *Boise* (CL-47), flushdeckers USS *Pope* (DD-225) and USS *John D. Ford* (DD-228), along with two submarines and the tender *Black Hawk*. The tanker reached Darwin on January 6, 1942, and quickly began pumping 13,900 barrels of fuel into the Asiatic Fleet oiler *Pecos*.

Task Group 5.3 with DesDiv 57 arrived earlier in Darwin—which the U.S. and Australian command believed might be tenable as a staging point—on December 28, along with *Houston, Gold Star, Otus*, and *Pecos*.* On New Year's Day 1942, *Edsall's* assistant engineering officer, Lt. (j.g.) Morris D. "Chick" Gilmore (U.S. Naval Academy 1939), recorded the traditional "poetic" entry in the deck log as she steamed in company with *Houston*, heading for the Torres Straits, along with her DesDiv 57 cohorts:

> Steaming on base course 108 degrees True,
> Condition III watches are being stood by the crew.
> The ship being in condition Afirm Material.
> About the ship all light we are forced to quell.
> With Whipple and Alden, Edsall and Houston,
> Cruising along in their designated position
> With S.O.P.A. in Houston as guide,
> Anti-Submarine screen the destroyers provide.
> The ships maintain patrol in relative position
> Standard speed fifteen knots made to keep station.
> At 166 revolutions the propellors are turning,
> In boilers 1 and 2 the fuel oil is burning
> Around the ship the degaussing coils are cut in,
> In a war with Germany, Italy, Japan we shall win.

---

* British, Dutch, and Australian ships did all of the escorting of convoys into Singapore in the final weeks before that "battleship with no bottom" fell. Only one significant convoy, MS2, which was broken up and transferred to smaller vessels at Ratai Bay, Sumatra, apparently used *any* American warships (the destroyers *Barker* and *Stewart*) and only as cover forces for the transfer at Ratai Bay before the reconstituted convoy (as MS2A) then proceeded on to Singapore (arriving January 24). And after February 19, 1942, Darwin itself could no longer be considered viable as a forward base.

Up to the Blue

In January 1942, *Edsall* would screen two convoys, including elements of the Pensacola convoy, from the Torres Straits area westward into Darwin. And she would take part in a "secret mission" to Kebola Bay, off Pantar Strait, at the island of Alor among the Lesser Sundas. There, she, *Houston*, and *Alden* would encounter a number of Asiatic Fleet units.

On the morning of Saturday, January 3, *Edsall* was anchored at Normanby Bay, in the Torres Straits, awaiting the arrival of what has since become known as the Pensacola convoy. After getting under way, the destroyer spotted these vessels at 9:38 a.m., and took up her station astern. USS *Pensacola* (CA-24), heavy cruiser *Houston* (SOPA), and the destroyers *Stewart, Bulmer, Whipple,* and *Alden*, in addition to two British corvettes, completed the screen. The convoy included the navy transport USS *Chaumont,* the U.S. Army transport *Holbrook,* and the Dutch transport *Bloemfontein,* which were carrying reinforcements originally slated for the Philippines but rerouted to the East Indies as the debacle of General MacArthur's isolated forces began on Bataan.

On board *Bloemfontein* were men of the 2nd Battalion, 131st Field Artillery Regiment, Texas National Guard, who later became known as the Lost Battalion. They were not exactly sure where they were to be sent since their original Philippines destination had been ruled out. After their ship, the Navy transport USS *Republic* (AP-33), was diverted to Suva in the Fiji Islands, and Brisbane, Australia, they were now headed for Darwin and more uncertainty on another ship.

One of their officers, Maj. Winthrop Rogers, of Wichita Falls, Texas, and a 1928 graduate of Texas A&M University, recorded the trip in a small black diary. "Lord what a mess, can't find our stuff, trucks or equipment. Been trying all day to get some ammunition," he wrote. The uneasy artillerymen had brought out their 75mm and 37mm guns on the deck of their transport, the USS *Republic,* during the trip from Hawaii after the war had been announced. Now Rogers saw that they "put four 75s on deck, started 24 hour gun & lookout watch, [and] 28 BAR's for A.A." He also observed the "real swanky" conditions on *Bloemfontein,* writing, "The cabins are really beautiful. Blonde maple, green walls, red beetlemare [Biedermeier] features. Even baths." But he was a soldier and in the next breath again complaining: "Still looking for more ammo. Found 236 shrap[nel], 6000 cal .30, plenty of .45 and .50 wish it was together!"

On Saturday, January 3, 1942, Rogers wrote, "Went around Thursday Is. about noon, met USS HOUSTON, heavy cruiser, 5 destroyers, 2 corvettes. PENSICOLA [*sic*] went back. We are now ordered to Darwin to establish the base. Maybe we stay & maybe not."

At 9:32 p.m. on Monday, January 5, *Edsall* anchored at Darwin, having successfully escorted the valuable convoy into port. Major Rogers on *Bloemfontein* wrote in his diary, "Hot as the devil all day. Zigged & zagged all day . . . Anchored at Darwin about 8 P. Cant see the town but the roads is full of ships." The next evening on January 6, he recorded, "The fleet the Japs claimed they sunk at Cavite steamed in tonite. Not a scratch on 'em." But Rogers' ship would not remain long at Darwin.

These transports also embarked additional naval personnel for the hard-working units of the Asiatic Fleet, many of which had been caught with their complements still below strength at the war's outbreak. *Chaumont* transferred twelve new sailors to *Edsall* on that Friday, January 9. The night before, a quartet of officers on the destroyer "accepted commissions and took oaths of office for promotion in grade. . . . Lieutenant (j.g.) R. W. Meyers, U.S.N., and Lieutenant (j.g.) P. G. Wild, U.S.N. to grade of Lieutenant. Ensign M. D. Gilmore Jr. U.S.N., and Ensign R. C. Dell, U.S.N. to grade of Lieutenant (j.g.)." At this time, some of the men made out their last wills, including *Edsall*'s X.O., Lt. John Fairbanks Jr. After more than a month of retreating, they must have recognized the mortal danger they all now faced.

On Thurday, January 8, escorted by *Boise*, *Marblehead*, and five destroyers, *Bloemfontein* weighed anchor for Java. "We must be valuable or we have a dangerous trip!" Rogers scratched in his neat, tiny writing.

Darwin itself was a red-dirt hellhole. "It had a small naval station, post office, a few little shacks, a small outdoor theatre, and two bars. A large slaughterhouse for sheep and some beef were the cause of great amounts of black flies."[8] With drinking water and decent food scarce, beer became the second-most precious liquid commodity in the region. *Edsall*'s men were allowed to go ashore from time to time, and her log reveals the usual consequences: men returning late to the ship, or drunk and under arrest after brawls, and in a couple of instances, several crewmen missing the ship altogether when she left the port with emergency sailing orders. One or two captain's masts were still held, but the truth is that the ship and her crew were far too busy to get into much mischief.

Everything was geared to pushing men and supplies north, where the fighting was "up to the blue" in Aussie slang.[9]

"Still have the 'Royal Escort' with us and steaming wide open to Java," Major Rogers scribbled on Friday, January 9, followed the next day by, "A very peaceful Sat[urday]! Jap aircraft carrier loose, subs chasing ships a few miles away, changing course & speed. Every one sleeping 'all standing.' That's with clothes on . . ." The ship made it to Surabaya at two o'clock on Sunday, January 11. His final entry for the sea-trip commenting, "Missed Japs only a few miles coming in! Got the 'LIBERTY' instead of us."[10] These submarine worries were legitimate ones, and *Edsall* would have her share of excitement with them as well.

Edsall then accompanied the flagship *Houston*, along with *Alden*, acting as ASW screen, during the second week in January on a rather halfhearted sweep from Darwin north into the Banda Sea. They stopped and searched one Filipino and one Russian freighter on January 13 and 14, with a veteran crewman from *Houston* noting, "We also had a look at some of the women they had on there [the Russian freighter] and they looked like coal heavers. What a size." (Evidently, the libido of the Asiatic sailors had remained intact.)

On Wednesday, January 14, at eleven in the morning, *Houston* sighted a strange vessel fourteen miles distant to the north-northwest and promptly launched an SOC Seagull observation plane under Lt. Tom Payne to survey her. Half an hour later, Payne reported the vessel to be a sinking ship. *Alden* was detached at 11:45 a.m. to investigate while *Edsall* remained with *Houston*. Two hours later, *Alden* rejoined the formation and reported that the wreck found "in latitude 6–51S, longitude 127–50E, to be small Dutch motor ship Poigar." Only the bridge of the fifty-seven-ton coaster, owned by Celebes Kustvaart Maatschappij of Menado, remained above the water. Those on the U.S. ships believed that the coaster had been shelled or torpedoed "not more than a few hours previously." There were no signs of casualties or any survivors. However, unknown to the American vessels, the little *Poigar* had been en route to Surabaja from Ambon and had collided with the Dutch tanker *Juno* in the Java Sea when about eighty miles southwest of Ambon, and all of the crew had been saved. The position recorded in *Houston*'s log would have put *Poigar* between Wetar and the Penyu islands. *Houston*'s diarist recorded, "No survivors in vicinity so we pulled out of there in a hurry as there was a possibility that the sub was still in the vicinity and might try to slip us a fish."[11] He was right; the Japanese submarine *I-124* had spotted the three U.S. ships that day, although it had not been able to close to within torpedo range. Nonetheless, *I-124* would have her own rendezvous with *Edsall* and *Alden* soon enough.

On January 16, Coxswain Madson aboard *Houston* noted in his diary with some frustration, "Cruising slowly along the coast of Timor. We don't know what we are looking for." After these somewhat aimless meanderings, the three ships reversed course and wound their way down through the eastern approaches to the Lesser Sunda islands. A modest striking force of four U.S. destroyers and two cruisers under Rear Adm. William Glassford had been vectored north on about January 15 by the commander of the ABDA (American-British-Dutch-Australian) naval forces (ABDAFLOAT), Admiral Hart, to attack Japanese forces at Kema, in the northeastern Celebes. However, the operation was called off when reconnaissance found that the enemy had departed. It was a case of "another false alarm—rush up at high speed, then retire," as an officer aboard the task group flagship *Boise* wrote in his diary.[12] Hart himself later admitted the ships that then retired to refuel at Koepang, Timor, were sent "too far in the rear."[13]

The trio maneuvered into a remote bay on the island of Alor, where they were to replenish from USS *Trinity* (AO-13), which had moved up from Koepang. *Edsall* and *Alden*, "in compliance with orders," acted for the next nine hours as antisubmarine screen for *Houston*, which then led them into the channel at 9:15 a.m. on Saturday, January 17. Within Kebola Bay, they found *Boise, Whipple, Pillsbury, Paul Jones*, and *John D. Edwards*. It is not known whether the two Gustin brothers were able to visit during this brief rendezvous, but it seems unlikely. Ensign John W. Gustin aboard *Edsall* stood both the 4 to 8 a.m. and the 4 to 6 p.m. watches that day, but his vessel did not enter the bay to fuel until the others had departed. *Houston* fueled from the port side of *Trinity* while *Boise* replenished simultaneously from the starboard side as *Edsall* and *Alden* patrolled. Over all of these evolutions, the pressures of speed, timely intelligence, and missed opportunities loomed like a darkening sky.

At 3:30 p.m., the two big U.S. cruisers with the four destroyers stood out of the bay, anticipating a planned counterstrike against a reported Japanese advance in the direction of Makassar. *Alden* and *Edsall* then immediately entered the bay. By 4:32 p.m., *Edsall* was moored alongside *Trinity* and commenced fueling; she received 47,520 gallons of bunker oil over the next fifty-five minutes. At 5:06 p.m., losing no time, the destroyer was again under way, in company with *Alden* and the invaluable oiler, en route eastward to Port Darwin, zigzagging "on various courses and speeds." They seem to have been in a hurry; *Alden* did not fuel at Alor, but later at sea, on the afternoon of Sunday, January 18, during the return voyage.

The almost chaotic deployment of these various units reveals the communications and intelligence gremlins that hampered the brief ABDA command. There was more than a little resemblance to a Keystone Kops scenario in the seemingly disordered movements of Hart's forces in the week of January 15 to January 21. But even so, the results were not altogether negative. *Edsall* and *Alden*'s routine escort duties with *Trinity* would yield at least one noteworthy action.

The Hunter Hunted: Locating and Destroying I-124

Edsall participated in the first detection, attack, and destruction of a full-size Imperial Navy submarine sunk (at least in part) by U.S. surface forces in World War II. It is one of the relatively few well-documented actions that the destroyer took part in. This does not mean, however, that the episode of *I-124* is without its own mysteries and questions.

Early on Tuesday, January 20, 1942, while escorting the oiler *Trinity* back from Kebola Bay into Darwin, and approximately forty-five miles from the port, *Edsall* and her sister ship *Alden* detected an enemy submarine in the vicinity of latitude 12° 5.5′ S, longitude 130° 5.6′ E. At 5:26 a.m., *Trinity*'s lookouts spotted a spread of torpedoes in her wake. She raised the alarm, and the two flushdeckers promptly began an aggressive, if unsuccessful, initial search. *Alden* laid depth charges at 5:43 a.m. *Edsall*, which also made sound contacts, was ordered to screen *Trinity*. Further contact was broken off, and the trio of ships continued on to Darwin, arriving at 10:07 a.m.

Later that afternoon, once they had shepherded *Trinity* into Darwin, and they lay moored alongside tender *Black Hawk*, *Edsall*, and *Alden* were ordered back out to sea to "attack enemy submarines off Port Darwin."[14] They were under way from the tender again at 4:33 p.m. At about seven o'clock that evening, the two U.S. destroyers sighted three Australian corvettes (HMAS *Katoomba, Lithgow,* and *Deloraine*), which had also been alerted to the submarine presence and were in the process of tracking and vigorously attacking it. HMAS *Deloraine* had been nearly missed by a torpedo from an enemy submarine earlier that afternoon, but "the ship responded quickly and the torpedo passed ten feet astern."[15] Soon a PBY Catalina and two floatplanes from USS *Langley* were overhead helping direct the surface ships to the sub's location. (One of the more confusing aspects of this "kill" is the belief—apparently mistaken—by virtually all of the Allied vessels that they were in fact hunting at least two different submarines.)

As early as 7:15 p.m., on January 20, "a large amount of oil rising to the surface" was noticed, which was recorded in one of the reports made by *Edsall*. After exchanging sighting and keying data with the RAN vessels, the destroyer saw *Deloraine* firing depth charges at 7:33. At 7:40, *Edsall* "crossed middle of barrage at 15 knots," and dropped five more charges "set at 150 feet" herself. (Some historians have credited the depth-charge barrage by *Deloraine* and *Edsall* on *I-124* as the fatal attacks; however, it was not the view of RAN analysts later who gave sole credit for the kill, probably correctly, to *Deloraine*.) *Alden* followed at 7:55 with another barrage of her own. Thereafter, plans for a night search were received from *Deloraine*: The U.S. ships were "to patrol in a direction 000°–180° to the Westward of 130°00' E between the latitudes of 11°58' S and 12°18' S during the night." They were then to rejoin the Australians at eight o'clock the following morning "at Submarine No. 1."*

The Imperial Navy submarine operating off Port Darwin then under attack, *I-124* (Lt. Cmdr. Kishigami Koichi[†], had departed Davao in the Philippines on January 10, with the commanding officer of Submarine Division 9, Cmdr. Endo Keiyu, also aboard. Her mission was to lay mines, intercept enemy shipping, and conduct reconnaissance operations between Timor and northern Australia, which was recognized as a staging area for Allied reinforcements to ABDA warships contesting the Japanese southern blitz.

---

* HMAS *Katoomba* narrative, January 26, 1942, again reveals the belief that two enemy submarines were present and under attack. The Most Secret Message sent by RAN officers at Naval HQ, Darwin, on January 29, 1942, states, "It would appear that three and possibly more Submarines were operating off Port Darwin during these operations. . . . Subsequent investigation suggests that, although one Submarine only can now be claimed to be sunk, at least two others appear to have been severely damaged."

[†] Lt. Cmdr. Kishigami Koichi (52nd term at Etajima) was born on August 23, 1904.

The *I-124*, a *kirai sen* (KRS, minelaying) type, was not a new vessel, having been completed in 1928. She was oversize as well as crowded, and slow and unwieldy when submerged—in brief, a poorly designed boat according to almost all sources.* Her length was in excess of 279 feet, with a 24-foot beam, and she displaced about 1,380 tons on the surface. When submerged, her displacement rose to roughly 1,770 tons. Her optimal speed on the surface was 14.5 knots, and when submerged, about 7 to 8 knots. The boat had four tubes and carried a dozen Type 95 torpedoes, plus more than forty mines that could be laid from two minelaying tubes aft. Her standard complement was seventy-five officers and men. In January 1942, she carried a few more with the inclusion of Commander Endo and staff.[16]

At the war's outbreak, *I-124* had been positioned in the Philippines, and within a day had laid nearly forty mines off the entrance to Manila Bay. According to some records, these mines claimed at least two victims within the month: the passenger ship *Corregidor*, sunk with heavy loss of life (believed to be more than five hundred people), and the Panamanian freighter *Daylight*. *Corregidor* was in all probability lost through the rash decision of her captain to attempt to transit U.S. minefields around the island for which she was named, and not on *I-124*'s mines. Two days after the attack on Pearl Harbor, *I-124* was west of Luzon, where she sank the 1,523-ton British freighter *Hareldawins*. After a brief return to Camranh Bay in French Indochina, she again patrolled the entrance to Manila Bay. In the first week of January, she had moved south to Davao, on Mindanao. With the other units of Submarine Squadron 6 (*I-121, I-122, I-123*), she was ordered to operate in the Timor Sea and northern Australian waters. *I-124* laid another batch of thirty-nine mines in the Joseph Bonaparte Gulf, with an additional twenty-seven mines dispatched off Port Darwin ten days later. On January 14, 1942, the big submarine spotted USS *Houston* (CA-30) and a pair of escorting destroyers, but she was not able to position herself for an attack.† Five days later, *I-124* sent a final message reporting the arrival in Darwin of three transports screened by a destroyer. This is alluded to in the diary

---

* The design of the *I-124* was based on that of a World War I–era German war prize, the ex-*U-125*, a *UE-11* type boat.

† January 14, 1942, was the day that *Houston*, *Alden*, and *Edsall* found the drifting wreck of the Dutch coaster *Poigar*.

of Vice Adm. Ugaki Matome, when he expressed anxiety over not having heard from *I-124* for several days. By then, the boat and her crew of eighty dead men rested in twenty-four fathoms of dark water.

The depth chargings by *Deloraine, Alden, Edsall, Lithgow,* and *Katoomba* on January 20 and 21 had indeed proved fatal. *Edsall* participated in renewed attacks on the morning of Wednesday, January 21, but she experienced problems with her depth-charge racks and "contact was lost with the target. A search was made in an attempt to regain contact in which we were joined by two Corvettes and one plane. At nine o'clock the plane reported no submarine had been sighted and we gave up the search in order to return to the point of original contact the day before."[17] For the next three hours, *Edsall* and *Alden* searched in vain for the contact, but they were forced to abandon their efforts after a heavy rain squall drove off the assisting airplane. It didn't matter, however, for the sole Imperial *sensuikan* then operating off Port Darwin had been eliminated (She was last seen when blown to the surface by *Deloraine's* depth charges. A black bow and a periscope just broke the bubbling, oil-choked surface.), and it remained only for an examination by U.S. Navy divers to supply the postmortem on the cause of her loss.

AIDAC 0202/27: DIVERS HAVE EXPLORED AFTER PART EXTERNALLY CAUSE OF DESTRUCTION APPEARS TO BE DUE TO DAMAGE TO ESCAPE HATCHES BY DEPTH CHARGES. SUBMARINE APPEARS LARGER THAN U.S. SUBMARINES OF SEA-WOLF CLASS. ENTRY CANNOT BE EFFECTED UNTIL FOUR IN NUMBER MOORINGS ARE LAID FOR DIVING VESSEL TO COUNTERACT TIDE. . . . DURING WITHDRAWAL FROM DARWIN OF U.S. SHIPS WITH DIVERS AND DEEP WATER EQUIPMENT NO FURTHER PRELIMINARY DIVING CAN BE EFFECTED WITH LOCAL RESOURCES.[18]

On Sunday, January 25, the deck log of USS *Holland* (AS-3) recorded that at 2245 hours:

Diving party consisting of Lieutenant Hawes, USN left
the ship; Lieutenant J.C. Hatch, (MC) USN; Ch. Gunner
C.M. Cunneen, USN; Way, C.B. CBM. (PA) USN; Empey,
J.F., CSF. (AA) USN; Holley, F., SF1c, USN; Cooney, F.

CM2c, USN; Snyder, R.W., Cox., USN; Stone, L.A., BM1c, USN; Cornic, S.F., SF1c, USN; White, S.N., PhM1c, USN; Mathews, C.D., SF3c, USN; Chandler, R. SF2c, USN.

These men were embarked on board HMAS *Kookaburra* in Darwin harbor and arrived over the dan-buoyed location of the sunken sub ("latitude 12–03 south, longitude 130–09 east") around 0700 hours on Monday, January 26. After dragging operations "apparently made several strikes but nothing certain," the divers groped their way down. Limited to sixteen minutes each on the murky bottom, the first and second divers turned up "no results." The third diver found "a large gully about 15 feet across and 4 to 6 feet deep which [was] believed to be where submarine first hit bottom."[19] The fourth diver was shifted about 150 feet aft of the previous dives and "landed on deck of submarine before reaching bottom." There beneath his feet lay "a large submarine. One hatch apparently blown open. Unable to make any identification. Also located 2 other hatches but did not reach conning tower." A fifth diver descended to the deck of *I-124* and reported:

Gaskets blown out of two other hatches abaft conning tower; a built-in hatch at conning tower with hatch at top. . . . Hatch blown open had dogs bent but no wheel inside for locking as we have. At each hatch there were two pad eye[s] also an air connection. The blown out gasket was cut from the after hatch. The hatch blown open was nearest conning tower. Gasket on second hatch was bulging out. Color of submarine was black. . . . Ship was on even keel. No bubbles visible. No damage of any king [*sic*] noted to hull or decking other than condition of hatches.[20]

The report by the divers of *Holland* also contained a sketch showing a cross-section of a recovered gasket taken from the submarine, which noted, "The gasket is of new rubber and recently installed, showing faint knife-edge markings and the whiteness of its sides unstained. It appears that its surface in contact with knife edge when dogged down is only about ¼"wide, a fatal weakness of design."[21]

Although rumors would persist that confidential documents or codebooks were recovered from *I-124*, the fact is that no such discovery took place. As the secret message from the Australian Navy Department explained, the withdrawal of U.S. ships from Darwin in the first week of February put an end to any thought of salvage operations. A more plausible fact behind these fantasies may be found in the sinking of the Imperial Navy's *I-1* in early 1943 by the New Zealand vessel HMNZS *Kiwi* in shallow Solomons coastal waters, which did result in salvage operations and the recovery of confidential documents that proved to be of considerable value to Allied code breakers.[22]

Back aboard *Edsall*, her skipper, Lt. J. J. Nix, wrote up his confidential report on January 31, 1942. In it he noted, "The personnel reacted most favorably, with sound operator Hegerfeldt, P. W., Radioman first class, deserving of special commendation for his excellent work and efficient operation of the sound gear."

> *He had regretted her neglected condition, a condition—enforced by governmental economy—that her extreme age made increasingly dangerous. Years ago the Department had put her down on its public books as an antiquated, slow creature fit only for coast defence: after which it promptly had flung her into a savage, semi-charted region, where she was called upon to engage in active service, at high speeds, far from bases.*
> —Marcus Goodrich, *Delilah*, 1941

Shortly after the encounter with *I-124*, and with no time to reflect on her success, *Edsall* was eastbound, shepherding another slow convoy to Torres Strait. The destroyer got under way from her Fox One berth at the Port Darwin anchorage on January 23 at five in the morning. She and *Alden* would escort "flagship" USS *Chaumont* (AP-5), *Holbrook*, USS *Gold Star* (AG-12), the liner *Marechal Joffre*, and a dawdling Australian coastal freighter named *Mildura*, given to "sending up a continuous plume of black smoke that could be seen by a submarine twenty miles away."* *Alden* and *Edsall*, as ASW screen, were jittery after their recent engagement off Darwin, and they soon began detecting what they thought were enemy submarines through their hydrophone echo

---

* *Mildura* was a 3,359-ton cargo ship built in 1920 in New South Wales Government Dockyard at Newcastle, Australia. It was launched as *Enoggera* but renamed *Mildura* in 1924. It survived the war and in 1951 was sold to an Asian firm in Hong Kong (as representatives of Tominaga & Co., Tokyo); it was broken up in 1954.

gear. By eleven that morning, *Edsall* was again dropping depth charges. She commenced depth charging at 11:14 and finished fifteen minutes later, with eleven out of twelve charges detonating properly. After this alert, the remainder of the day passed uneventfully, but at 7:38 that evening *Edsall* once more "ceased patrolling station to investigate echo on underwater sound gear." She dropped a barrage of four charges at 7:55, followed by ten more between 8:15 and 8:19 hours after sighting a torpedo wake that "passed ahead of ship, distance 200 yards."

This event was recorded by *Gold Star*'s commanding officer, Lt. Cmdr. Joseph Lademan (U.S. Naval Academy 1920), many years later when he wrote, "At sunset, while entering the Arafura Sea, a destroyer off to port trained a large searchlight on us, flashed 'Torpedo' and started dropping depth charges." The violence of these depth chargings in a channel no more than fifty feet deep left *Gold Star* "dead in the water from the shock of . . . explosions." She was fortunate that her damage was not more severe. "Steam from ruptured boiler fittings filled the combined engine-fireroom. A shattered six-inch auxiliary condenser valve, gushing like a geyser, flooded the crank pit and gave the bilge pumps all they could handle. The main injection valve withstood the shock. Had it let go, it would have been the end of the line for the Goldie Maru."[23] The effects recorded by the old auxiliary also offer a plausible explanation for the type of injuries suffered by *Edsall* (a leaking stern and damaged shaft) but never made clear in previous histories.

The motley convoy "straggled on"[24] to its destination at the islands of Torres Strait. Late on January 26; *Edsall* followed *Alden* into the anchorage off Wednesday Island. The two ships remained overnight before promptly departing the following morning for the return journey to Darwin. In the meantime, *Holbrook* and *Chaumont* evacuated personnel from Thursday Island. Taking a different direction, *Gold Star* and *Marechal Joffre* embarked a pilot for the trip "south inside the Great Barrier Reef into waters where submarines were not able to operate."[25] This took them to Sydney, where they lay to off the Port War Signal Station a week later, on February 2. By then *Edsall* was back at Darwin, preparing for the navy's shift to the last operable deep-water port in Java that was still safe from enemy air attack: Tjilatjap.

By late January 1942, the U.S. Navy had admitted that using Darwin as a forward base was "becoming intolerable." Wanting quicker turnaround times for submarines as well as proximity to NEI oil, a shift to the southern Javanese port of Tjilatjap was made. On February 3, 1942, several Asiatic Fleet units moved from Darwin to Tjilatjap, including USS *Holland* (AS-3), USS *Otus* (AS-20), *Black Hawk*, and *Trinity*. Their escorts were *Alden* and *Edsall*, both of which refueled from *Trinity* while creeping along the southern coastline of the Lesser Sundas, westward past Bali, and on to Java. Deck logs of *Houston* and the old gunboat *Tulsa* between February 6 and 11 confirm *Edsall's* presence in Tjilatjap at this time.* On February 10, the little utility vessel USS *Heron* (AVP-2) followed.

It was at this time that the last known letters from *Edsall's* crew were mailed home. Most were not received in the States until a month or more after the ship had been lost, although many families still held out hope at that point. None wanted to believe that these were the final communications they would ever have from their loved ones.

On February 9, 1942, Blackie Parsons scrawled a brief, hurried note: "Dearest Folks Just a line to all You know that Chas. And me are o.k. I am sorry I cant write where I am are what I am doing but we are knot alowed to write any thing mutch of what we are doing. . . . Just keep the home fires burning and don't worry about me and Chas because we are still coming back to old Mo. One these days Ha. Write to me soon all of you." Eight days later he mailed a form postcard with the preprinted line, "I have received no letter from you (for a long time)" included. Across this yellowing card, as melancholy an object as ever I have held in my hand, are two signatures: "JJ Nix" (Joshua James Nix) below the "Sailors Mail" stamp on the front, and "JWG" (John Webster Gustin) in the lower right-hand corner on the verso. These are, of course, the marks of the ship's censors: the commanding officer and the communications officer. The sailors were allowed no extra messages by the strict censorship imposed at this time. We know that a similar postcard was sent on the same date by another sailor, but these additional restrictions greatly reduce the amount and quality of information we have for *Edsall's* last days.

---

* In the first week of February, another change occurred. The venerable U.S. Asiatic Fleet ceased to exist organizationally; the U.S. ships were now known as Naval Forces, Southwest Pacific Area. On February 14, Admiral Hart was replaced as commander of the ABDA naval forces (ABDAFLOAT) by Vice Adm. Conrad Helfrich of the Royal Netherlands Navy. Rear Admiral William Glassford then took over as Commander Southwest Pacific (COMSOWESPAC), for the remaining U.S. ships.

In less than two weeks, the ship would be more than "half a world away" and, to use a phrase that most of her fractious Asiatic crew would have smiled at, the men would have been "promoted to glory."

On February 11, *Langley* and the Esso tanker *George G. Henry* departed Darwin south for Fremantle, where the old carrier, now a converted seaplane tender, would pick up thirty-two P-40E fighters, which were sorely needed in Java as last-minute reinforcements. *Langley* was refueled by *George G. Henry* before leaving Darwin. *Henry* limped along at her best seven-knot speed, her hull encrusted with marine growth.[26] (Another twenty-seven P-40Es were crated and shipped aboard the U.S. Army transport *Sea Witch*, to follow later.) The ships arrived at Fremantle on February 18; the Warhawks were loaded aboard on the night of February 21. At noon the following day, bearing her planes and their pilots and crews, *Langley* departed and steamed past Rottnest Island, for what would become her final mission, one that provided a graphic illustration of the desperation and confusion of ABDA's last days. The next day *Langley* and her escort, the light cruiser USS *Phoenix* (CL-46), were spotted crossing the Indian Ocean at position 27°57′ S, 112° E by the merchant ship *SS Islander* (Capt. G.H.A. Denne), en route to Australia from Christmas Island with forty-eight evacuees aboard.

There Is No Armor Against Fate
First Act: Tjilatjap

One source states that on February 10, *Edsall* and her sister ship *Alden* steamed east along the southern coast of Java and the Lesser Sunda islands screening the old British steamship HMS *Ban Hong Liong* (1,671 tons) to Koepang, Timor, with a cargo of light antiaircraft guns for the Australian forces there. Other sources show that *Alden* was accompanied by *Paul Jones*. The latter destroyer as second vessel is verified by the logs of *Alden*, *Tulsa*, and *Houston*.*

In any event, we do know that *Edsall* was back at Tjilatjap's uncomfortable anchorage by Tuesday, February 17, because she is logged as escorting *Trinity* from the port on that date, when the oiler was ordered to Abadan, Iran. *Edsall* and the bulk of her crew then had but twelve days left to live.

---

* And somewhere during this period, I came across another small, telling anecdote that reveals more about the spirit of the destroyer's crew. After the bombing in the Flores Sea, *Houston* lost not only her number three turret, cold storage locker, and crew's head as well

Meanwhile, the four-piper had indeed received some damage from her own depth charges during the sub scare on January 23 in the shallow Howard Channel as she entered the Arafura Sea above the Gulf of Carpenteria. *Edsall* was still experiencing leaks in her stern and was therefore kept out of the ABDA Striking Force when it was formed for what became known as the Battle of the Java Sea. Paradoxically, the material deficiencies that prevented *Edsall* from joining the other ships of the striking force for that disastrous battle seem to have eventually led to her being regarded as "expendable" in the last days of Java's defense.

Fellow DesDiv 57 four-piper *Whipple*, which had been laid up for ten days in Tjilatjap having damage to her bow repaired after a February 12 collision with the Dutch flagship *DeRuyter*, was also retained, and was later assigned patrol duty in and around the port.* Already other vessels were being transferred to safer locations. *Black Hawk*, escorted by USS *Bulmer* (DD-222) and USS *Barker* (DD-213) —with both destroyers suffering from minor battle damage and lacking any torpedoes—departed on February 19 for overhaul in Australia. *Edsall* remained in Tjilatjap harbor through Friday and Saturday, February 20–21, nested with *Alden* and *Paul Jones* alongside *Pecos*.

On Sunday, February 22, Rear Adm. Glassford ordered *Edsall* "TO PROCEED TO SEA OFF THE ENTRANCE [TO] TJILATJAP AND RUN ANTI-SUBMARINE PATROL UNTIL ARRIVAL OF ASHEVILLE." She was then to act as a convoy escort until dark, at which point the gunboat would take the ships into Tjilatjap. After that, *Edsall* could return independently, or "REMAIN AT SEA AT YOUR DISCRETION."[27] The final phrase seems to acknowledge the "rat-trap" properties of the

---

as three searchlights and two motor launches; her laundry was also destroyed. At that point the men of *Edsall* volunteered to provide laundry service for the cruiser. Bob Fulton told me that the last time he saw *Edsall* was when his clothes were being lowered over the port side of *Houston*'s quarterdeck to the destroyer. As he put it, "I don't know where that brave ship is today, but wherever she is, my clothes are still aboard."

* In the middle of a squally, pitch-black night on Thursday, February 12, *Whipple*, under way off Java's Segoro Wedi Bay (also called Prigi Bay), southwest of Popoh, was struck by *DeRuyter* "abaft starboard billboard, displacing bow 45 degrees trueo port, damaging bow forward of collision bulkhead, and causing complete flooding of both peak tanks and partial flooding of lower paint locker and chain locker. No leaks aft of collision bulkhead." On Friday, February 13, *Whipple* made her way slowly at six knots, escorted by *Pillsbury*, to Tjilatjap and was towed into a floating drydock, there to remain the next ten days for inspection and repairs. It was another operational accident that the undermanned ABDA forces could ill afford.

port as well. Wisely, Glassford also notified *Edsall* of the proximity of a U.S. submarine, USS *Shark* (SS-174), due in the area at 4:30 on Tuesday, February 24. *Whipple's* log confirms that *Asheville* and *Edsall* both "got underway and stood out" of Tjilatjap's torturous harbor at 6:10 on Monday, February 23. As they left, they may have seen an all-too-familiar sight: An Allied warship—in this instance the British light cruiser HMS *Danae*—had gone aground on one of the numerous shoals at the entrance to Kali Donan, the river that fed into the sea at the port. Just the day before, the flagship *Houston* had struck the same navigational obstacle and wound up on an "extensive, partly drying bank of hard sand" in the twisting channel and spent an anxious hour extricating herself before docking. A week later, this mishap would be repeated by the minesweeper HMAS *Bendigo*, which ran aground as she proceeded into the port, and got under way only by shifting weight forward and steaming full speed astern.*

At the same time, February 23, more than 1,500 miles to the west, a Norwegian oil tanker under British control and another Norwegian steamship departed Trincomalee, Ceylon, escorted by a single corvette bound for Makassar, Celebes. Three to four days after departure, the oiler was redirected to the Cocos Islands, and the merchantman was ordered to proceed to Tjilatjap.[28] Whether or not both of these ships ever received their new orders is not clear, but in the case of *Woolgar*—a 3,060 gross register tonnage (grt) steamship—the confusion and communications failures rampant in the last days of the Java campaign resulted in tragedy. *Woolgar's* consort, the oil tanker *Belita*, was rerouted to the Cocos Islands, yet *Belita* never received, or acknowledged receiving, these orders from Java and instead altered course for Australia, where she arrived safely at Fremantle. The one-sided odds caught up with *Woolgar*, which was not so fortunate.†

---

* Coincidentally, the little Australian minesweeper's war diary shows that she and other members of the 21st Mine-Sweeping Flotilla had been operating out of Merak in Sunda Strait the last days of February. By this time, the Australian sailors recorded, "It is a noticeable fact that Nippon has no need to send fighters with his bombers now." An indication of the inept communications and poor intelligence then dogging the Allied forces was the proximity of these vessels to the Japanese Western Force invasion convoys, and their utter inability to dispute the enemy landings, or to even be aware of them.

† *Woolgar* blundered on in ignorance until March 7, when she was sighted by Japanese aircraft within 150 miles of Tjilatjap, and despite having altered course to the south, was attacked by dive-bombers about two hours later. The ship was struck by at least three

Less than seventy-two hours later, by Thursday, February 26, *Edsall* had also received last-minute orders for the *Langley* operation. This mission should be regarded as among the most ill-conceived and inept actually executed by the Allies during the Pacific war. To make a long and unedifying story short, this operation sent a vulnerable, slow, old ship into harm's way in broad daylight with no air cover and inadequate screening across one of the world's most treacherous oceans on an eleventh-hour mission that had no hope of altering the outcome of Japan's southward push. It was a political decision, largely as a sop to the Dutch, and it cost the United States about as many men as she would later lose at Tarawa, although with far less publicity and anger.* *Langley*'s desperate mission was to ferry thirty-two P-40E Warhawks into Java, along with thirty-three USAAF pilots and twelve mechanics. "The delivery of these airplanes and personnel constituted the special mission of *Langley* on this voyage."[29] As a multitude of shipping fled Java, including *Poelau Bras*, *Abbekerk*, and *Prominent*, the aged, weakly armed, slow seaplane tender was sent back into the combat zone. Her orders were as muddled and contradictory as her mission was foolhardy, and these factors ensured that tragedy would result.

Although the plan was originated by Wavell, Glassford and Helfrich seem to bear the ultimate responsibility for altering this scheme, which risked more than eight hundred lives to transport no more than five dozen fighter planes to an already doomed island. It was the result of a political decision, and one made at higher echelons than COMSOWESPAC or ABDAFLOAT. And it is hard not to recall that

bombs and began to settle; as the survivors scrambled overboard and into lifeboats they were strafed by enemy planes. A few minutes later, after the men had gotten into the boats, *Woolgar* appeared to be hit by another bomb in her ammunition storage. This direct hit caused a "tremendous explosion whereupon she sank by the bow in about 12 minutes." Eighty-eight days later, a single lifeboat with six half-dead men reached Port Blair in the Andaman Islands; the survivors became captives of the Japanese. The details of *Woolgar*'s sinking and the successful escape of *Belita* are drawn from the Norwegian Merchant Fleet 1939–1945 website.

* In the second week of February 1942, Adm. Ernest King reported to President Franklin D. Roosevelt that, in consideration of urgent Dutch appeals for air reinforcements, he did not feel he could release either USS *Ranger* (CV-4) or USS *Wasp* (CV-7) from the Atlantic for duty as ferry ships because they were required for defense against German raiders. Furthermore, with USS *Saratoga* (CV-3) in a shipyard undergoing repairs after a submarine torpedo had damaged her in January, the navy had only three fleet carriers with which to counter Japanese naval airpower in the Pacific. With the British unable to utilize

casual chat between FDR, Admiral Leahy, and Adm. J. O. Richardson in the fall of 1940, when the hard fate of the naval units on the Asiatic Station was decided.

Clamor as the Dutch might about their air forces being augmented with U.S. planes, there was never much likelihood that the United States would have risked one of its precious fleet carriers at that critical juncture. The United States also didn't have any carrier-ready fighters or bombers to fly off as the Royal Navy had in January near Christmas Island. Those British aircraft and pilots were promptly chewed up at Singapore and harried back through Sumatra into Java. For the United States to have thrown more sizable resources into such a meatgrinder with no real chance for stopping the Japanese would have been folly. But a token political gesture, regardless of its futility, made sense to the image-conscious Americans, who were as sensitive to propaganda as their enemy. Like it or not, the remaining U.S. Navy forces were committed to the defense of Java because COMSOWESPAC Glassford understood that his orders placed him essentially under the command of Vice Admiral Helfrich. In the stress of such combined-operations chaos, a desperate plan was hatched in which the almost certain loss of two green USAAF fighter squadrons was considered preferable to the appearance of having done nothing at all.

Vice Admiral C. E. L. Helfrich was never known as a man who would resort to subtlety where brute force could be more easily applied. And his powers as ABDAFLOAT allowed him to send direct orders to *Langley* instructing her to break away from her convoy, ruining her timetable for arriving under cover of darkness and placing her virtually defenseless in the Indian Ocean on her route's final leg into Tjilatjap. Helfrich did not hesitate to do this, and a first-rate catastrophe ensued.

In order to reconstruct the penultimate activities of *Edsall* beyond this point, we must rely entirely on the deck logs; action reports; survivors' statements from *Whipple, Langley*, and *Pecos*; and messages sent by Glassford (although COMSOWESPAC was suffering from radio

one of their carriers, it therefore fell to the aged *Langley*, now reduced to a seaplane tender, to undertake the perilous mission into Java. The evidence shows that U.S. and British planners understood the dangers involved and the unlikely chances of success, but they were determined to make a gesture for their Dutch allies, regardless of the cost in men and materiel. By February 28, however, Lt. Gen. George Brett admitted to General Marshall that sending more pursuit planes to Java constituted "unwarranted wastage."

problems at this time also*). As for her final action, we have only the records kept by her killers.

The two old destroyers, worn but still game, were under way from Tjilatjap at 4:40 p.m. on February 26, *Whipple* with the Dutch pilot Mr. Bruyn at the conn; he left the ship at 5:04 and Lieutenant Commander Karpe then took over. The ships moved on a southerly heading before reversing course to meet the small "sloop" HMS *Kedah*, which was a well-known interisland steamship, limping into Tjilatjap from Batavia, overloaded with superfluous British Royal Air Force (RAF) and Royal Australian Air Force (RAAF) personnel to evacuate important members of Wavell's staff and several score refugees. *Whipple* and *Edsall* escorted *Kedah* in the direction of the port for an hour and fifteen minutes. At 7:47 p.m., they split off from "the little queen of Malacca Straits," [†] altered course to 163 degrees true, and increased speed from ten to fifteen knots, with *Edsall* on *Whipple*'s port beam at 1,500 yards. For the next eleven hours, they headed south into the long swells of the Indian Ocean, built up over thousands of miles of open sea, for their fateful meeting with *Langley*.

Off to the south of the destroyers, solitary, slow, and dreading the exposure that daybreak would bring, steamed the old "Covered Wagon"—as the *Langley* was known—at her best speed of thirteen knots. As her executive officer, Cmdr. Lawrence Divoll, later wrote, "She had no business being there."[30] Nor for that matter did the pair of damaged and elderly four-pipers. But the situation on Java had reached a crisis point, and sacrifices would have to be made, as the Dutch themselves declared. For nearly 650 young American sailors and their families, this would be the ultimate sacrifice.

Edsall and *Whipple*, as ASW escorts, were to meet *Langley* and help bring her precious cargo of P-40E fighter planes into port safely.

---

* See Walter G. Winslow, *The Fleet the Gods Forgot*, for COMSOWESPAC's radio problems at this time.

† HMS *Kedah*, 2,499 grt, was built by Vickers-Barrow for the Straits Steamship Company of the Blue Funnel Line. It was launched on July 16, 1927, and operated from 1927 until 1939 on the Singapore–Penang express route. From December 1939 onward, it was the Royal Navy "armed auxiliary patrol vessel No. FY035." It was armed with two 4-inch guns, one 3-inch AA gun, and depth charge (DC) launchers. In 1940–41 she patrolled the north coast of Borneo and transported troops. One of the last and luckiest vessels to leave Singapore, carrying a heavy passenger load with a large number of RAF personnel aboard, she eluded Japanese bombers and surface units in the Bangka Straits through the skilled seamanship of her captain, Cmdr. J. L. Sinclair, Distinguished Service

Even this seemingly simple assignment suffered from poor planning and poorer communications. *Langley's* carefully considered schedule, which would have brought her into the waters off southern Java and into Tjilatjap under the relative cover of night, was thrown aside by Vice Adm. C. E. L. Helfrich. This led to the ancient tender being forced to approach the island in broad daylight, yet even then she might have arrived safely had the escort details not been muddled as well by Helfrich and Glassford. More time was lost as Dutch and American signals were crossed, and a hobbled Royal Netherlands Navy (RNN) vessel, the *Willem van der Zaan* (Lt. Cmdr. G. P. Küller), a minelayer with leaking boiler tubes—and at that time slower than *Langley* herself—plus two Dutch PBY Catalinas were sent out to escort the U.S. ship into Tjilatjap. This foolishness upset the tender's dicey timetable even more and infuriated her captain, Cmdr. Robert P. McConnell, who recognized the perils of daylight steaming in such proximity to Java. It was yet one more example of the poor choices being thrust upon overextended and fatigued Allied commanders by Japan's swift Southern Advance.

Ultimately, *Langley* was compelled to retrace her steps several times before *Willem van der Zaan* was detached, and so again lost precious hours before Glassford managed to get orders through that definitively assigned the escort task to *Edsall* and *Whipple*. By that time, the estimated time of arrival (ETA) of the seaplane tender with her P-40E fighters and crews had been delayed until five o'clock in the afternoon on February 27, so she would be crossing the dangerous waters south of Tjilatjap during the day. These were well patrolled by Japanese reconnaissance flights out of the newly won air bases on Bali and Sumatra, and the officers aboard *Langley* knew that their odds were not good.

As with much else occurring in the crumbling last days of Java's defense, the operation was doomed to failure.

Regardless of heading, the Allied ships around Java found themselves caught inexorably between Japan's invasion forces closing in from the north and Vice Admiral Nagumo's KdB to the south. Within another two days, a sizable number of these U.S., Dutch, British, and

Order, Royal Navy Reserve. Bombing near misses damaged her machinery, and by the time she reached Java, her speed had been reduced to seven knots. She was ordered to Ceylon, but her engines failed along the way, and she was finally towed into Colombo by the cruiser HMS *Dragon*.

Australian warships, in addition to many merchant vessels and smaller craft, would be leagues beneath the East Indian waves. Their names and stories would later be known at best in jumbled, broken form, like the fractional radio messages transmitted, only partially copied, or lost forever throughout those bleak days and nights.

Second Act

> *It is among war's tragedies that human courage, tenacity of purpose and military skill are sometimes squandered for a useless end.*
> — J. Hetherington, *Blamey, Controversial Soldier*[31]

On the morning of Friday, February 27, *Whipple* and *Edsall*, under orders from COMSOWESPAC to rendezvous with the seaplane tender at "Lat. 9–50 S. Long. 109–25 E," spotted *Langley* at 6:30 a.m. The old ship was plowing along at her best speed of roughly thirteen knots, eight miles distant. It was a fair day with good visibility, a few high clouds, and the heavy swell typical to the Indian Ocean.

When the destroyers closed to within a mile, *Whipple* and *Edsall* assumed positions off *Langley*'s bow. Soon thereafter a submarine contact report was made by *Edsall*, which then left the formation to execute a search. Finding nothing, she returned to the formation at 7:44 as *Langley* and *Whipple* made a twelve-mile-wide detour around the contact. Twenty-six minutes later, much as anticipated, a strange aircraft was seen "bearing 190 T [true]. The aircraft came from the east and departed in the same direction." All but the most naïve men aboard the three ships knew what would soon follow.

Three and a half hours later, Japanese twin-engine planes arrived, flying at more than fifteen thousand feet. These were Mitsubishi G4M "Betty" bombers of the *Takao kōkutai* flying from Den Pasar airfield on Bali: sixteen Japanese Naval Air Force (JNAF) land bombers escorted by some fifteen Zero fighters. At midday they attacked the trio of U.S. ships, concentrating on the lumbering *Langley* for obvious reasons, and flying well beyond the anemic antiaircraft fire of the old tender and her two destroyers.* These high-level bombings were among "the most

---

* Few noticed another drama being played out high overhead between two Dutch patrol planes and the covering Zeros. Around the same time, an unarmed commercial airliner

accurate or the luckiest" conducted against maneuvering ships at sea during the entire Pacific war.[32] When the Japanese bombers and fighters departed at about half past noon, their 250kg and 60kg bombs had left *Langley* a listing, blazing wreck. She had been struck by five direct hits and a handful of near misses and was slowly flooding, with a port list of nearly 15 degrees, her engines gradually incapacitated. In an instant the P-40Es on the main deck and flight deck were set on fire.

Another fierce fire was started on the *Langley* in the starboard side aft, where a bomb penetrated the flight deck and staff officers' quarters and detonated on the deck winch machinery. The "Fleet reserve pyrotechnics had been struck below to torpedo storage" earlier in the voyage, according to Cmdr. Robert P. McConnell, and these no doubt helped fuel the flames. Firefighting mains were destroyed in the bombing, and this undermined almost all damage-control efforts. At the same time, the engine spaces were taking on water, and no amount of counterflooding could correct the list to port. Commander McConnell wrote, "It was decided at this time to abandon ship to save the crew while the escorts were still intact."[33] At 1:32 p.m., or three hours after *Langley* was first attacked, McConnell ordered the ship abandoned. Over the next half hour her screening destroyers, *Whipple* and *Edsall*, rescued all but nineteen of her crew, who had been blown overboard by induced explosions or who jumped to escape the flames; *Whipple* picked up 308 men, and *Edsall* picked up another 177. McConnell later commended these ships and singled out the destroyer captains, writing that:

> They deserve great credit for their skill and daring in maneuvering their vessels, prior to, during and after the action, in screening and in effecting the rescue of the *Langley* survivors. The remarkable high percentage of effectiveness in rescuing the wounded is due to the preparedness and to the effective ship handling on the part of the destroyer captains.[34]

At 1:58 p.m., *Whipple* backed clear of the tender and stood out to destroy her. *Whipple* then delivered two torpedoes into *Langley* at 2:32

strayed into the combat area and was mercilessly shot down by the Japanese fighters. Glimpses of one of these actions were recorded in the report by *Langley*'s commanding officer, Cmdr. Robert McConnell.

and 2:45 after first firing nine rounds of 4-inch/.50-caliber high explosive (HE) into the listing but stubborn hulk. Although the ship was settling, she was not seen to sink, so the two destroyers, with legitimate worries about more bombing attacks as well as enemy submarine activity, decided to steam westward and clear the area.

Overnight, the two destroyers received their new orders (via COMSOWESPAC dispatch 270903) to "proceed to lee of Christmas Island and transfer survivors to *Pecos* and all army personnel to *Edsall*." By eight the next morning, Saturday, February 28, *Whipple* was exchanging calls with the shore station at Christmas Island, and the services of a local pilot were requested. "At 0840 Pilot (Mr. Craig) came aboard." Just before nine USS *Pecos* (AO-6) was sighted.* Ten minutes later the transfer of USAAF personnel from *Whipple* to *Edsall* began, and was completed by 9:20 a.m. Before the other survivors could be transshipped to *Pecos*, though, a trio of twin-engine Japanese bombers appeared. All of the ships "commenced radical changes of courses at high speeds to avoid bombing attack." Within twenty minutes the bombers attempted to drop their payloads on the island's piers near the beach at Flying Fish Cove, but the bombs landed harmlessly in the water offshore.

As the planes departed in a northeasterly direction, they made what appeared to be an attack on *Whipple*. She fired her antiaircraft battery, expending a total of twenty-three rounds of 3-inch AA, 1,050 rounds of .50-caliber, and 287 rounds of .30-caliber as she again maneuvered at high speeds before dipping into a convenient rain squall east of the island. When the three ships emerged from the storm, the menacing Japanese bombers had disappeared.

With the enemy planes gone, *Whipple*, *Edsall*, and *Pecos* were ordered by the senior officer present afloat (SOPA), Cmdr. Edwin Crouch, ComDesDiv 57, "to head south at maximum speed to clear

* After an anxious period of waiting for orders to leave Tjilatjap's claustrophobic harbor, *Pecos* had been directed to Colombo, only to be then rerouted and sent to meet the destroyers and embark *Langley*'s survivors. *Pecos*, escorted by USS *Parrott* (DD-218), had departed Tjilatjap for Colombo, Ceylon, at ten in the morning on Friday, February 27. About three hours later, the oiler began receiving messages concerning the attack and sinking of *Langley*. *Pecos* altered course due west to put more distance between herself and the enemy forces, but later in the afternoon, as recorded by Lt. Cmdr. E. Paul Abernethy, she got a message through *Parrott* to "proceed to the lee of Christmas Island and receive the survivors of the *Langley* then embarked on the USS *Whipple* and USS *Edsall*." Course was changed once more for the northwest tip of the island. *Parrott* left at about 10:30 p.m. "on another mission." At daybreak the island was sighted.

the area." In this instance, top speed was limited to about ten to twelve knots, which was the *Pecos*'s best speed. The three ships, having formed up once more, assumed a base course of 180 degrees true, which was maintained throughout a night of increasingly heavy wind and seas (with the exception of a one-hour course change between eleven and midnight to 150 degrees true).

In the National Archives at College Park, Maryland (NARA II), are files of Vice Adm. William Glassford, and among these are hardbound volumes of the original communications for January and February 1942. On the afternoon of Saturday, February 28, Glassford sent a secret message to Commandant Zeemacht Nederland (CZM), Vice Admiral Helfrich, through the BIMEK channel* concerning the disposition of U.S. surface vessels. It includes the following information:

> X EDSALL [and] WHIPPLE SOUTH OF CHRISTMAS ISLAND WITH LANGLEY SURVIVORS ON BOARD X WHEN TRANSFERRED WHIPPLE PROCEEDS TO COCOS ISLAND TO PROTECT BELITA EDSALL RETURNS TJILATJAP WITH FIGHTER CREWS X PARROTT AND PILLSBURY PERFORMING ESCORT DUTY OUT OF TJILATJAP SPEED OF BOTH MATERIALLY REDUCED DUE TO NEEDED ENGINEERING REPAIRS X.

The next morning, Sunday, March 1:

> In accordance with Commander Southwest Pacific despatch 281737 and Commander Destroyer Division Fifty-Seven orders the transfer of personnel from *Whipple* to *Pecos* began at 0520 and was completed at 0634. The *Edsall* then began transferring personnel and about 0800 transfer was completed. While one destroyer was transferring personnel the other destroyer circled the ships forming an anti-submarine protection.

The bare, terse prose of *Whipple*'s action report failed to note the remarkable job of seamanship by Boatswain Robert Baumker of *Pecos*; he transferred 276 men from *Whipple* and all but 32 USAAF personnel from *Edsall*, or 177 men, in a forty-foot launch through heavy seas in

---

* "BIMEK" was the codeword designating the particular channel. Another such channel was designated by the codeword "COPEK."

the predawn darkness. The indefatigable Baumker made eight trips in all, five to *Whipple* and three to *Edsall*. From the latter he transported two P-40 pilots, 2nd Lt. William Akerman and 2nd Lt. Gerald Dix, each injured in the attacks on *Langley*. These wounds and a good deal of fantastic luck would save both of their lives.

For the men aboard *Edsall*, though, the long seventeen-hour "run to the south" would prove fatal. Had the destroyer been allowed to return to Tjilatjap on February 27 after rescuing *Langley's* survivors, or even from Christmas Island on February 28, she might have had a chance to complete her mission. As it would turn out, the miles put between her and those perceived or anticipated air threats from Sumatra or Bali delivered the old flushdecker and her men into the teeth of KdB.

At roughly quarter past eight on the morning of March 1, the three ships went their separate ways, fanning out in different directions, each according to its orders from Rear Admiral Glassford: *Whipple* was directed to proceed to the Cocos Islands, setting her course for 279 degrees true at seventeen knots. There she would rendezvous as protection for the British oil tanker *Belita*, which Glassford still imagined might be utilized to replenish warships continuing the defense of the East Indies. Unbeknownst to COMSOWESPAC, the tanker never made that rendezvous; recognizing the dangers of vague communications, she altered course to Australia, which she reached safely. *Pecos*, now crammed with almost seven hundred crew and passengers— including men from *Langley, Stewart, Marblehead,* and *Houston*— changed course to 160 degrees true with the intention of passing about 130 miles west of the westernmost tip of Australia before heading south for Fremantle.

Edsall was left with the most difficult, dangerous, and foolhardy mission: that of returning the AAF personnel to Java, where they were to help with the remaining P-40E Warhawks. The much luckier *Sea Witch* completed her journey into Tjilatjap and unloaded her crated warplanes before wisely turning about. She was escorted en route by *Isabel*, as they departed for Australia "under cover of a raging tropical storm." * The presence of a large number of airplane crates at the port of

---

* Controversy still rages over the exact disposition of these P-40Es. Most were unloaded and shipped to different locations, and a few may have been briefly operational. Some appear to have been later captured intact by the Japanese. That they made not the slightest difference in the defense of Java has never been in dispute, however.

Tjiltajap is confirmed by an entry in the war diary of HMAS *Bendigo*, and this information appears to refute later U.S. accounts declaring that the crates had been destroyed or dumped into the harbor.[*]

A final message exchanged between *Edsall* and her sister ship *Whipple* has been reprinted many times, but its lack of rhetorical embellishment cannot disguise the apprehensions felt by all at the eleventh hour. *Edsall* to ComDesDiv 57: "Do you have any further orders for me? Any information on conditions in Tjilatjap?"

ComDesDiv 57 to *Edsall*: "Your 2318 negative. Proceed Tjilatjap. Suggest you keep well off coast today run in about speed twenty tonight to arrive dawn tomorrow."[35]

With these orders, which Ensign John W. Gustin of *Edsall* must have handled, the old four-piper swung about, headed off to the northeast, and was never seen or heard from again by U.S. forces. On her bridge, Lt. J. J. Nix and his navigator, Executive Officer Lt. John "Jack" Fairbanks Jr., surely weighed their options and pondered making the best of a potentially mortal assignment. Any misdirection in her course could lead to detection and catastrophe.

On gun number four, atop the after deckhouse, Seaman 2nd Class Loren Stanford Myers probably hoped to get some rest at his battle station. But he, too, knew that the crews of gun boss Lt. Phil "Oscar" Wild Jr. had to operate efficiently if the ship was to make it through the Tjilatjap gambit. The black gang in *Edsall*'s engine spaces commanded by Lt. Dick Meyers and Lt. j.g. Morris "Chick" Gilmore struggled to keep the worn pumps, boilers, and turbines functional and efficient. At one set of her triple twenty-one-inch torpedo tubes, a tough young Missourian named Blackie Parsons would have ached to deliver a blow against the enemy along with the other torpedomen under Lt. j.g. Russell Dell.

Exhilaration competed with fatigue as the dutiful crew of *Edsall* steamed northeast to complete their task. For the thirty-one Army Air Force remaining pilots, feelings must have been mixed, to say the least, caught up as they all were in a mission that many had openly described as "suicidal." Although rumors after the war circulated that these men

---

[*] This information is per the official U.S. Navy Combat Narrative: *The Java Sea campaign*, which stated, "there was no time to assemble the crated planes. It was reported that they were destroyed in their crates to prevent their falling into enemy hands when Tjilatjap was abandoned." Recent investigations by Jos Heyman and Gordon Birkett repudiate these reports.

were sent back as ground troops, there is no evidence beyond hearsay to support the contention that they were returned to Java for any reason other than as pilots for the P-40Es.

The day was largely clear, with a light haze and a few scattered clouds, the long swells running beneath the wind blowing from the southeast. The men of *Edsall* would have preferred storms and rain squalls in which to conceal themselves and their ship on that journey, for they well knew that enemy forces, surface and submerged, were operating in those waters. Yet her greatest battle was hovering just over the horizon, less than eight hours away.

Gone but not forgotten . . .

As *Whipple* proceeded to the northwest and *Edsall* to the northeast, *Pecos* continued south on course 160 degrees true at her best speed of twelve knots. Within an hour, Glassford (COMSOWESPAC) sent another message to his bedraggled forces. The game was up, and following an early-morning conference with the Dutch commander, Vice Admiral Helfrich, and Rear Admiral Palliser of the Royal Navy, Glassford ordered the U.S. ships to "clear the region." It appears that this communication went out sometime before 0930 hours.

Simultaneously, a slow Dutch merchant ship attempting to flee the doomed East Indies found herself being shadowed by a Japanese airplane. Her position at that hour was given as 12° 40′ S, 106° 40′ E, which would have placed her close to *Pecos* as well as *Edsall*. Too close, in fact. Forty-five minutes later she was spotted by the dark-gray ships of KdB's Support Force. From one of the flanking Japanese destroyers a flag message signaled: "Enemy transport sighted." The time was 0955 hours. The heavy cruiser *Chikuma* opened fire on the helpless merchant ship eighteen minutes later. From the decks of the carriers a number of pilots and aircrew watched this "firing exercise." They saw the shells close in on the vessel, which then appeared to vanish altogether. "The water columns looked like a chunk of spray, converging excellently almost to one point. . . . In the blink of an eye, the transport disappeared completely beneath the horizon, as if by some magic."[36] However, it was not as clean-cut as that. *Chikuma* expended more than four dozen 8-inch/20cm armor-piercing shells, but the heavy shells went straight through the merchant ship's thin sides, failing to sink her. Boiling with fury, the frustrated Japanese commanding officer moved his ship in closer and fired a single torpedo, which "instantly" sank the vessel. For this *Chikuma* received a "harsh reprimand" from Vice Adm. Abe Hiroaki, commander of Dai Hachi Sentai, in *Tone*: "We may encounter an enemy fleet at any moment. Under no circumstances [is] launching a torpedo at a merchant ship tolerated. Never waste even one torpedo any more."[37]

Although the Dutch merchantman sank, she left at least two dozen or more crewmen alive in the choppy Indian Ocean. They were picked up by another of the Japanese ships of Vice Admiral Nagumo, but precisely which one is uncertain. It was then about 1030 hours; at this time yet another report was received from a Japanese patrol plane of a "special service vessel" off to the west southwest moving south.* This was the heart of the former Asiatic Fleet train. The dive-bomber squadrons from all four carriers of KdB, without fighter escort, would attack this solitary unfortunate. And, based on the times from the carriers' records, an argument can be made that the ships were much closer than has been previously recognized.

Approximately an hour later, the first strikes were flown off, with the *chūtai* from *Kaga* under Lt. Watanabe Toshio, leading the way. The VBs (dive bombers) from *Kaga* would reach the "special service vessel" in little more than thirty minutes ("soon after take-off," according to dive-bomber pilot Yamakawa Shinsaku), which says much for just how close this ship was to Nagumo's carriers that morning.

On the Allied ship, the men knew that they were "in for serious trouble." They had seen plenty of it lately; the ship was of course USS *Pecos* (AO-6), and everyone aboard her understood the lethality of Japanese air attacks. For there was not only the crew of *Pecos*, but survivors from *Langley*, sunk two days before, along with men from the abandoned flushdecker USS *Stewart* (DD-224), left behind in Surabaja, where it would eventually be salvaged by the enemy. A signalman third class named Lowell Barty, who had spent two and a half years aboard *Langley*, was now wedged in among those already on *Pecos*. Remembering that he and the other "newcomers" occupied virtually every square foot of open deck space, he recalled, "I thought I was pretty safe. . . .

* The action report of the USS *Pecos*, written by her commanding officer, Cmdr. E. Paul Abernethy, on March 7, 1942, states "a single engined Japanese observation plane, wheels retracted, was sighted approaching from the northeast" at about 1000 hours. *Pecos* altered course at 10:40 to 225 degrees true for thirty minutes and then due south again. The time given above corresponds to Allied vessels; for the IJN it would have been noon.

I wasn't too sure, but I thought I was pretty safe."[38] If this sounds like wishful thinking, it was.

There were also many stragglers, along with walking wounded from the cruisers *Houston* and *Marblehead*, victims of devastating bombing attacks in the Flores Sea on February 4. Commander Abernethy had refused to allow any but ambulatory patients to embark on *Pecos*. He understood that the poky oiler's chances were slim. In the end, his reservations proved well founded. More than two decades later Abernethy would write, "Although we had definite knowledge that a Japanese Task Group was operating south of Java, our lack of air reconnaissance left us with no indication as to their location or size."[39] Tragically, the Japanese force was much closer and far larger than anyone ever imagined.

Among the injured men allowed by Abernethy to board and crowded in like cattle "all over the deck"[40] with the others, was a storekeeper second class from *Houston* by the name of Vincent G. Koenig. Although only scant details of his fate are known, what is known is worth reproducing, if only to commemorate one life lost among many. Vince Koenig's story is representative in a number of significant aspects.

What Became of "A Quiet Fellow"

Vincent Gerhard Koenig (pronounced CANE-ig) joined the navy in late 1936 after a childhood and youth in desolate Baker, Nebraska. Born on February 14, 1916, he was a twin; his twin brother was named Albin. There were twelve children in the Koenig household, seven boys and five girls. Farm life in a remote community in Boyd County during the Depression was difficult at best. Lifelines were rigged from farmhouse to the privy and barn during blizzard season to keep family members from getting lost and freezing to death in the heavy winter snows. Jobs after high school were few and far between. The U.S. Navy actively sought out these rugged farm boys from the Midwest as sailors, and the paper-soled economy of the Great Depression did the rest.

Vincent was the first of the Koenig boys to join the military, though all seven would eventually serve during World War II. He enlisted on December 28, 1936, and went in at Great Lakes Naval Training Station, north of Chicago, Illinois. By 1939, he was serving aboard the submarine tender USS *Holland* (AS-3), and had been able to send enough money home to contribute to a down payment on a new car for his family. He also helped pay for the education of his twin brother, Albin, in dental school. In the summer of 1940, he reported aboard the cruiser *Houston* for duty; his name, rating, and service number (316 48 32) were given in the ship's newspaper, *The Bluebonnet*, on July 17. Over the following year and a half, Koenig's name would appear regularly as a member of *Houston*'s shore patrol party, which if nothing else indicated that he could take care of himself. Another young sailor from the Midwest was likewise a storekeeper on the cruiser, and many years later recalled Koenig: "Vince was a stand-up guy. If you needed him to go to bat for you, he would. . . . He was a quiet fellow who did his job well."[41] These understated remarks, coming half a century after the fact, are fine tributes to a former shipmate, and high praise by the standards of the Asiatic Fleet sailor, known for hardy but taciturn self-reliance.

The war caught up with Vincent Koenig around midday on February 4, 1942. He, along with a number of his fellow sailors on *Houston*, "saw the elephant" when that ship was attacked in the Flores Sea by Japanese bombers flying out of Kendari, Celebes.[42] Forty-eight others were not as lucky; they were killed outright or died of wounds soon thereafter. Although the cruiser had avoided many attacks that day, she was finally struck by a single errant 250-kilogram (551-pound) bomb that detonated next to her aft eight-inch turret after deflecting off her mainmast. The bomb's pathway left dead and injured before and after its explosion, with one seaman, Bruce Adkins, cut almost in half as he lay prone on the floor of searchlight control. Nearly the entire turret crew died in the resultant fires, with turret officer Lt. George E. Davis Jr. being blown to pieces by the blast. Only quick thinking and good training prevented the destruction of the ship; two sailors, Gunner's Mate 2nd Class Czeslaus Kunks and Seaman 1st Class Jack Smith managed to isolate and flood the aft magazines.* Aviation Machinist Mate 1st Class John W. Ranger sprinted aft and, entering the gunhouse without any breathing apparatus, played carbon dioxide canisters against the flames while another crewmember drenched him with a firefighting hose. The mount was a charnel house of dismembered and burned bodies. On the deck below, virtually all of the after damage control party were slaughtered in the explosion.

---

* Jack Smith survived the engagement and the war; Czeslaus Kunks died on August 23, 1943, in 100 Kilo Camp in Burma during construction on the so-called Railway of Death.

One exception was Electrician's Mate 3rd Class Howard E. Brooks, who had been called from his action station to help repair a malfunctioning 5-inch shell hoist just moments before the bomb struck. Brooks, along with Electrician's Mate 2nd Class Lawrence Wargowsky, had been ordered forward by Chief Warrant Officer ("Bosun") Joseph Bienert during the bombing attacks to work on the port-side hoist aft of the 5-inch handling room in D-401-M. The overtaxed hoist's malfunction saved the lives of Brooks and Wargowsky. Hearing and feeling the tremendous "thud" as the bomb struck, they moved quickly back through the crew's messing space and living quarters to the site of the explosion. There they found those already dead from the concussion, and those dying from shrapnel, burns, and internal injuries—including the veteran Bienert, a "plank-owner" from USS *Lexington*, and the senior warrant officer aboard *Houston*—as well as the critically wounded. The perforated barbette itself looked "like it had been made out of butter splashed with steel."[43] One of the twenty wounded young men (probably a victim of burns) was Storekeeper 2nd Class Vincent G. Koenig.

United States war correspondent George Weller, posted to Java covering what many hoped would be the first serious reversal for Imperial Japanese forces, wrote, "In Tjilatjap's small cemetary lay, under walnut-colored wooden crosses, the bodies of American sailors who died defending Java. Others were there alive, the wounded with reddish scarifying marks from bomb blasts."[44]

Two days later, as the dead were buried, the deck log of the gunboat USS *Tulsa* recorded Koenig's name, rank, and service number when he was transferred to shore with the other wounded from *Houston*. Within another few days, he was recovering at the Christian Petronella Hospital in Jogjakarta.* The few available details concerning this period come from Dutch nurses, interned by the Japanese, and from a single RAF ground crewman named P. W. Wears, who was in the same hospital suffering from a tropical skin ailment. A half-century later, Wears wrote:

In Feb. 1942 I was in [a] Dutch Hospital in Jogjakarta with a minor skin complaint on my face when I heard a lot of noise coming from another ward. On investigation I found it filled

---

* Today, Rumah Sakit Bethesda in Yogyakarta (now the predominant spelling) is still a well-respected, Protestant-run hospital.

with wounded and badly burnt survivors from an attack on the *Houston* and *Marblehead*.[45]

Due to a shortage of nursing staff, Wears lent a hand:

Medical staff were very sparse—it was left to Javanese boy orderlys [sic] to fetch & carry, they could not understand English (or Texan) so I, self-appointed interpreter who had only taken up learning Bahasa Indonesia a few months earlier, requested the piss bottles & bedpans where they were needed. I also cleaned their teeth, & shaved a few over the next few days.

After noting his admiration for the stoicism with which these young Americans bore their wounds, Wears concluded, "I was discharged from Hospital after a week but before I left I was given a photo I think of the *Marblehead* (4 stacks?) pasted in a small folder & on the cover autographs of 15 from *Marblehead* & 7 from USS *Houston*." With the fall of Java imminent, Wears' RAF group wandered about aimlessly "for days" before they "finally got to Tjilatjap which was being dive bombed when we got there."

Wears and his companions did not escape; they were captured in West Java and ended up back in Jogjakarta ("to repair the aerodrome we'd previously sabotaged"). Then they were shifted from place to place, and finally sent to the huge "Jaarmarkt" POW camp at Surabaja. Wears endured many horrors throughout his imprisonment, worst and most memorably as part of the British and Dutch contingent sent to the Moluccas in April 1943 aboard the *Amagi Maru*.* Forced to work as slave laborers building an airstrip on Haruku, three hundred prisoners died "in the first few weeks, dysentery mostly." Wears' return journey from Ambon to Surabaya in late 1944 was an even more hellish experience. The voyage, which beggars description, should have taken no more than two weeks; it instead lasted some sixty-seven days. According to Wears, of the 650 POWs who left the Moluccas, 307 were buried at sea.

---

* The SS *Amagi Maru*, 3,165 tons, was completed on May 31, 1924, by the Yokohama Dock Company in Yokohama. The ship was a prewar regular on the Nippon Yusen Kaisha line between Japan and the "South Seas Islands Passenger and Cargo Service" (Kobe to Davao, Menado, and the Mandates). It was torpedoed and sunk in May 1944 by HMS *Tantalus* off the Andaman Islands.

Among the names of the seven sailors from *Houston* who signed the card sometime between February 6 and February 27, is "Vince Koenig SK 2/c." This means, among other things, that Koenig was in Petronella Hospital on Valentine's Day 1942, his twenty-sixth, and final, birthday. Fifteen days later, he would lose his life in the Indian Ocean along with far too many other young men.

The wounded under Dr. Wassell's care at Jogjakarta were split up once they returned to Tjiltajap. Some went aboard the submarine USS *Sturgeon*, a few went on the Dutch vessels *Janssens* and *Abbekerk*, and others were allowed to board *Pecos*. Of the *Houston* men who were with Vince Koenig at Jogjakarta, a marine corporal, Kelton B. George, would also die in the sinking of *Pecos*.*

For Vince Koenig's twin brother, Albin, it would be a heartbreaking loss from which neither he nor his family would ever fully recover. Like numerous other American families with loved ones serving in the Asiatic Fleet, the Koenigs first received a missing in action (MIA) notice, and much later, a killed in action (KIA) notice, but that was about the extent of the information received.† Albin died in 1997, and even until his death the dentist from Nebraska could not address the subject of his twin brother's fate without profound anguish.

The Bitter End of the Line: Exit *Pecos*

> *And so the grief and sorrows piled up, a portent of the fearful end that awaited the Heike.*
>
> —The Tales of the Heike

On the morning of March 1, *Pecos* lumbered due south at her best speed of roughly eleven to twelve knots. Aware that she had been sighted, her crew fully expected to be attacked. After being shadowed sometime around noon (IJN time), a breathing spell of not much more than an

---

* Oscar M. Rudie, machinst mate second class, from *Marblehead*, escaped on *Abbekerk*; Bob Clark was evacuated on *Sturgeon*; and Cmdr. William B. Goggins, *Marblehead*'s executive officer, along with several others, succeeded in reaching Australia aboard *Janssens* with Dr. Wassell.

† Vincent Koenig was the war's first casualty from Boyd County, Nebraska. A Requiem High Mass was held for him at St. Mary's Catholic Church in Spencer, Nebraska, on Monday morning, May 4, 1942.

hour ensued for the exhausted sailors aboard *Pecos*, most of whom had slept in the open beneath the stars the night before.

The carriers of KdB, duly alerted, had decided to fly off four *chūtai* Type 99 Vals—one group each from *Kaga, Sōryu, Hiryū,* and *Akagi.* The mission was not expected to be difficult, and the *kanbaku* flew without fighter escort. This has been interpreted to signify the relative ease with which the attacks were supposed to be carried out, but another factor may have been the sheer proximity of the oiler to KdB. *Pecos* was probably not more than forty miles distant, if that. Unknowingly, the Americans and Japanese had almost steamed atop each other.

The first nine-plane group lifted off from *Kaga* at 12:55, led by Lt. Watanabe Toshio. All of the Type 99s in *chūtaichō* Watanabe's unit carried a single 250-kilogram (551-pound) "No. 25 ordinary" semi-armor piercing bomb. A mere twenty-six minutes later, at 1:21, they sighted *Pecos*. Commander E. Paul Abernethy, commanding officer of the ship, recalled, "Just before noon (corresponding to 1:30 IJN/ Tokyo time) three Japanese glide bombers with nonretractable wheels appeared out of the sun. Each dropped one bomb and all missed the ship." The times are confirmed by the Japanese report, which states with characteristic overconfidence, "bombed it [*Pecos*] from 1327 to 1330 (nine 250-kg. bombs), scored one direct hit, and 8 near-misses. Tanker observed sinking after attack. Four planes were hit, but all returned."

Although rarely examined closely, the combat records of the U.S. Navy and its Japanese counterparts match up remarkably well throughout this action. However, *Pecos* had not been fatally damaged by Lieutenant Watanabe's *chūtai*, and though her gunners had hit four *kanbaku* with AA fire, her durability along with this unexpectedly severe AA fire would necessitate three more waves of air strikes from KdB before the oiler would finally succumb. The next group of attackers would not be long in arriving.

A second *chūtai*, from carrier *Sōryu*, led by Lt. Ikeda Masatake,* took off at 1:06 and sighted *Pecos* as it was under attack by the first group of D3A1 Vals from *Kaga*, which reinforces the data indicating just how close these ships were to one another. Circling overhead as the *Kaga*

---

* The first name of Lieutenant Ikeda (IJNA, 61st Term) is given variously as Masatake (Wenger and Sugahara), Masahiro (Parshall and Tully), Masayori (Sugahara), Shoi (Ashworth), and Masi (Messimer). The name agreed upon by Wenger and Sugahara is used here.

Vals completed their attacks, Lieutenant Ikeda then led his stocky dive-bombers down upon the oiler in three orderly waves at three-minute intervals between 2:24 and 2:33. They dropped nine 250-kilogram bombs, delivering the most accurate and damaging attacks of the day. Lieutenant Commander Abernethy's report described the Japanese planes as "painted dark brown and the wheels were not retracted." He mistakenly credited them with making two dives each against his ship, dropping one bomb in each attack. Although this was not the case, he did note that the second wave of attacks led to several hits. Abernethy wrote that *Pecos* suffered "four (4) hits and one (1) near miss that were damaging" at this time, and these reduced the ship's already modest speed to "about 10.5 knots."[46] One Japanese report says they made three hits, including one "in the side which caused the tanker to list 15 degrees true to port and sink." *Pecos* did not sink, but she did indeed take on about a 15-degree list, according to her captain, which was countered by letting go of the port anchor and chain and pumping oil overboard from tank No. 18 on the port side. A large number of men on the oiler were wounded or killed in this, the most precise and deadly attack by KdB that afternoon.

There was also an outbreak of panic among several groups of men described by Abernethy as "passengers in the crew's quarters aft," who somehow heard an order to abandon ship. No such order was passed by any officers or through an authorized source, but before this rumor could be countermanded, two whaleboats and four life rafts were lowered and thrown over the ship's side, promptly followed by a considerable number of men who jumped overboard. This reaction occurred as the ship was under heavy air attack, suffering numerous explosions and near misses, and with all of her AA guns and small arms returning fire against her antagonists. All of the individuals who left the ship prematurely—perhaps as many as a hundred men if an eyewitness survivor from *Marblehead* is to be believed—were never seen again.

Thanks to a sloppy day for the plane-handling crews and aviators of the carrier *Hiryū*, a lull of more than an hour would then follow, allowing Abernethy and crew aboard *Pecos* some time for damage control. This "heroic work" was organized and implemented by the oiler's executive officer, Lt. Cmdr. Lawrence McPeak. In the engine room more heroics "enabled the ship to continue at a speed of about 10 knots. The damaged boiler was secured without fire or flareback, and maximum steam was carried in the fireroom for the remainder of the action."[47]

Sōryu's planes meanwhile had "sustained hits from two dual-purpose guns and many machine guns, but all returned [to the carrier] at 1501." Due to some unexplained "mix-up," *Hiryū*'s *chūtai* did not take off until 3:15.[48] The nine planes were commanded by Lt. j.g. Shimoda Ichiro. Within forty minutes, they sighted *Pecos*, still heading south at a sluggish but resolute twelve knots, showing surprising staying power.

In the interval between the second and third waves of bombings, damage control parties had worked with herculean fortitude to return *Pecos* to a more even keel and also increase her speed slightly. The doctor aboard *Pecos*, J. L. Yon, his assistant, Chief Pharmacist's Mate D. Ashcroft, and *Langley*'s doctor, Robert B. Blackwell, all labored under impossible conditions in the sick bay and the improvised dressing station to stabilize as many wounded as possible. These medical officers later estimated that as many as "fifty (50) men were killed and one hundred fifty (150) injured as a direct result of this action."[49]

After the first wave of attacks, which were made "from the direction of the sun," as doctrine would have suggested, the Japanese planes came at the oiler "from almost any relative bearing," which was clearly the case with the *chūtai* from *Hiryū*. Sighting *Pecos* at 3:55, the nine Vals of Lieutenant Shimoda dropped down at less extreme angles, almost glide bombing, from all points and unleashed their bombs in quick succession. They scored no direct hits but two serious near misses. One damaged the bridge area, wounding several men; a second miss on the starboard side aft killed and wounded a number of men there. At 4:20 the nine *kanbaku* of *Hiryū* began their return flight, arriving back aboard the carrier at five o'clock and claiming six hits. Yet seven of the nine Type 99 Vals were holed by the infuriated gunners from the mortally damaged oiler. It had not been a stellar performance for the *Hiryū kanbaku*, but they were not yet finished for the day.

The final wave of attacks on *Pecos* came from the carrier *Akagi*, her *chūtai* led by Lt. Chihaya Takehiko (brother of the former IJN officer and future historian Cmdr. Chihaya Masataka). Nine Type 99 Vals launched at 3:20 from the flagship of the Pearl Harbor attack force, and twenty-five minutes later, at 3:45, they spotted *Pecos* through the clouds.

Circling above as the *Hiryū* bombers completed their attacks, the *chūtai* from *Akagi* patiently awaited their turn like the veterans they were.

In the meantime, between 3:44 and 3:58, the radiomen aboard *Pecos* began transmitting calls for help. These were off-frequency, but they appear to have been copied, at least in part, by the destroyer *Whipple*, then steaming on a parallel course some seventy miles away. At 3:54 *Whipple* had changed course from 225 degrees true to 180 degrees true after receiving "numerous messages . . . from Commander Southwest Pacific relative to retirement from Java and in expectation of change of orders from same sources." The flushdecker knew that her fleet mates on the oiler were under attack and well understood the perils involved in a return to the scene. Nevertheless, due to more confusion regarding orders from COMSOWESPAC and the rapidly deteriorating situation on Java, it would be another full hour before *Whipple* turned and changed course "left to 112 T [true] and speed increased [from 12] to 20 knots towards the PECOS' position."[50] It was fortuitous that she did. At about that time, the fourth assault from KdB *kanbaku* was about to hurtle down upon *Pecos*, and the battered oiler would not recover from this last attack.

Lieutenant Chihaya's nine-plane *chūtai* waited for a break in the clouds, and for *Hiryū*'s bombers to complete their mission, before attacking at 4:25. *Akagi*'s bombers swooped down "diving from almost every direction," recalled Abernethy. He also thought that individual Japanese planes made more than one dive, dropping a single bomb on each dive, but in fact what the captain of *Pecos* probably saw was an earnest attempt by one or more of these youthful and still rather naïve pilots from *Akagi* to release their bombs satisfactorily. This would have exposed them to antiaircraft fire repeatedly and may account for the high number of Vals hit in the engagement.

Such daring did in fact take place, according to memoirs written many years later by a D3A1 pilot from *Kaga* (Yamagawa Shinsaku) and another from *Akagi* (Iizuka Tokuji). Yamagawa swept down to strafe *Pecos* and was struck by AA fire, suffering considerable damage to his machine. The determined Iizuka made not two but three dives against the oiler, which netted a bomb hit along with bullets in his engine and a face full of oil and windshield glass. Both men struggled back to their respective carriers, and both acknowledged that the proximity of these ships had much to do with their survival.[51]

Seven of the bombs missed. Perhaps the *Akagi* planes had been unnerved by the intense AA fire still being directed on them—four of the Type 99 Vals were hit—but the last two bombs slammed into the sea next to the oiler's bow and stern, causing severe and irreparable damage. *Pecos* began to settle by the bow, and between 4:30 and 5:00, Commander Abernethy at last admitted that

> the ship was doomed. I authorized the communications officer [Lt. Joseph L. LaCombe] to open up on the radio distress frequency and any other frequency possible, and request help. Our superb navigator [Lt. Francis B. McCall] kept the ship's position plotted to the end. Our position was broadcast, knowing the Japanese, having tracked us since 1000 [1130 IJN time] already were well aware of our exact position.[52]

There is irony in this statement, too. One may question just how well the Japanese understood the position of *Pecos*. Lieutenant Chihaya's plane, piloted by Petty Officer 1st Class Furuta Kiyoto, circled over the stricken ship until 4:55, then, convinced that "the tanker apparently sank," began its return flight. They landed with their *chūtai* successfully on *Akagi* at 5:10p.m.* For Petty Officer 3rd Class Iizuka, it was touch and go as he flew back. With the Val's engine hemorrhaging oil and his eyes gradually swelling shut from the impact of obliterated windshield glass, he crouched behind the instrument panel, scarcely able to breathe in the air stream. "I was saved because my carrier was in the vicinity," he wrote years afterward. This, too, confirms how close the ships were that day. Iizuka's superiors barked at him after he landed, telling him "it was not necessary to try [to drop his bomb] three times." He was told, "Drop your bomb. Even if it misses, it's okay."[53]

Pecos did not sink swiftly, but with the waves washing over her main deck forward as the sea poured into her fractured bow, all aboard knew that it was time to get off. At five o'clock, Commander Abernethy ordered "Abandon Ship." This began a more or less "orderly evacuation" in which "all the men acted well and most of them were over the side by the time the ship sank." The final radio call for help, sent by Charles Snay of *Langley*, who had been helping in the radio room of *Pecos*, went

---

* All of the times in the flight data compiled by D. Ashworth for Abernethy's article in *Proceedings* match up precisely with the *kōdōchōsho* of KdB's attacks for March 1.

out at 5:08; it was copied by *Whipple* at that time and is worth reproducing for its gallows humor, so representative of the gritty Asiatic sailors who manned these ships:

LONG 10630 PICK UP SURVIVORS CQ CQ DE NIFQ SENDING
BLIND SENDING BLIND CASNAY RAD U.S. NAVY SENDING CQ
CQ DE NIFQ COM LAT 1430 LONG 10630 PICK SURVIVORS OF
LANGLEY AND PECOS CQ CQ DE NIFQ . . . SINKING RAPIDLY
AND THE JAPS ARE COMING BACK TO GIVE U.S. ANOTHER
DOSE OF WHAT THE U.S. IS GOING TO GIVE BACK IN LARGE
QUANTITIES.[54]

Not more than ten minutes later, with her shattered bow plunging into the sea almost vertically, "leaving her stern poised high in the air," a single massive propeller still rotating slowly, *Pecos* hesitated "for an instant before finally sinking." The time was then 5:18 p.m. Miraculously, the ravaged ship never suffered any serious fires throughout the engagement or afterward, but "many men and much debris and oil were to be seen," wrote Abernethy in his article nearly three decades later.[55] In another letter written to Kemp Tolley in 1972, Abernethy remembered, "When the survivors of *Langley* were transferred to *Pecos*, they were in generally excellent condition, having been transferred almost wholly by boat. But not so when they were again rescued. . . . Then they were in bad shape indeed."[56]

Sometime later, as he and his men fought against the oily sea and a mounting sense of despair, Abernethy noted sounds booming out over the Indian Ocean from the northeast. Were his combat-dazed senses playing tricks? Evidently not, because other survivors in the water heard and felt the same "rumbling and shock waves."[57] Ensign Michel Emmanuel from *Langley* and fighter pilot Lt. Gerald Dix* both agreed with Abernethy's recollection when he later wrote, "Toward twilight

---

* Dix, a pilot of the 33rd Pursuit Squadron, was the only man who lived through World War II who had been aboard *Edsall* that day. Akerman, his fellow pilot also picked up by *Edsall* after surviving the sinking of the *Langley*, was later killed during a training mission in the States. Groggy from morphine, Dix remembers little of his time aboard *Edsall*, but he did recall hearing three or four salvos from heavy naval guns while in the oily water after *Pecos* sank. Rescued twice in three days, he wound up flying fighters out of New Guinea before moving on to Europe. There, two days after D-day, flying with the 355th Fighter

I heard what seemed to be bomb explosions in the distance. It may have been bombs bursting on the *Edsall*—nothing was heard from that proud ship or anyone on board her after that fateful day."[58]

Unknown to Abernethy, or the other American survivors in this string of catastrophes, they had come as close to the carriers of Vice Admiral Nagumo's formidable KdB as had any surface force in the Pacific war that lived to tell of it. But no more than thirty to forty miles away, another solitary U.S. warship was steaming toward their position, perhaps expecting to arrive in time to rescue the survivors, and unaware, it would seem, of the Japanese task group's proximity. Her crew would be afforded the unique honor of engaging the redoubtable "Nagumo Fleet" in its one and only surface action of the war, but this fact would not be properly recognized in postwar histories for more than six decades.

Group, and after strafing ground targets in France, his P-51B Mustang (43-7164) clipped a power line and crash-landed in an orchard. Still the uncanny luck of Lieutenant Dix prevailed: he survived, and sat out the remainder of the war as a POW in Germany.

Chapter Five

Fiasco

Then Fortune changed and failed them.

—Virgil, *Aeneid*

And so it came to pass on March 1, a day of few clouds above the slight surface haze veiling the sea, that several thousand young men from the farmlands of America's Midwest and the hinterlands of Japan, from Eta Jima and Annapolis, found themselves occupying the same Prussian-blue waters south of Java. That afternoon, eighteen Type 99 Val dive-bombers floated down like embers from a conflagration to the carriers *Hiryū* and *Akagi*, returning from their final strikes against the fleet oiler USS *Pecos*, in two nine-plane *chūtai*. They were back aboard their respective carriers at 5:00 and 5:10 p.m. Damaged earlier that day in previous attacks by Vals from the other carriers of KdB, *Kaga* and *Sōryu*, and blasted to a foundering standstill around 4:30 by the *Hiryū* and *Akagi* squadrons, *Pecos* fought and died stubbornly before finally sinking at 5:18.*

As the *kanbaku* of carrier *Hiryū*, banded in blue identification markings, under Lt. j.g. Shimoda Ichiro, were in the process of landing, nine more Vals, with red fuselage bands and under Lt. Chihaya Takehiko, touched down on flagship *Akagi*. Almost simultaneously a lone mast top was spotted by the Japanese at a distance of about thirty kilometers (16.2 nautical miles) to the northwest. This small, solitary vessel, hull down, bearing 335 degrees, had maneuvered in behind the IJN forces that were moving away from it in a southerly direction, preoccupied with their attacks on *Pecos*. It must have been at the extreme limits of visibility, but soon enough, above the dark-blue swells and in the shimmering light, four funnels could be seen.

---

*Times are IJN/Tokyo unless otherwise noted; deduct ninety minutes for U.S. Navy time.

At 5:22, Vice Adm. Nagumo Chūichi, in *Akagi* (Capt. Aoki Teijiro), who could not have been pleased with the proximity of this interloper, gave the following orders to his Support Force commander, Vice Adm. Mikawa Gun'ichi, in battleship *Hiei*: "Support Force attack and sink the enemy light cruiser steaming behind the fleet." (A second copy of the Japanese text in my possession provides the alternate translation "tracking to the rear.")

What was the identity of this ship, and how had it managed to close undetected to within less than twenty miles of the mighty Kidō Butai? With its four stacks, the identification as a "light cruiser" was logical enough for a Japanese lookout. The presence of "*Marblehead*-type" ships operating with the Asiatic Fleet was widely known. The Japanese later acknowledged that even Lt. Cmdr. Ono Jirō, a flight commander on *Chikuma* and an authority on ship identification, had mistaken the vessel for a light cruiser.*

However, the ability of this ship to slip in behind the Japanese fleet also speaks ill of KdB's air-patrol arrangements on March 1. And to have approached to within such a range would have galled Nagumo, already on edge, one would assume, from the lackluster performance of his *kanbaku* against the slow, lightly defended *Pecos*.

Shien Butai comprised upgraded and re-engined 36,000-ton battleships of Sentai 3, Section 1, *Hiei* (F), and *Kirishima* (Capt. Iwabuchi Sanji), both capable of more than thirty knots, and armed with eight 14-inch/356mm guns, and numerous secondary (6-inch/50-caliber) and AA (5-inch/127mm) batteries. Also included were the great white sharks of Dai Hachi Sentai (8th Cruiser Division), the newest oversize cruisers of Nihon Kaigun: the sister ships *Tone*, flagship of Rear Adm. Abe Hiroaki (Capt. Okada Tametsugu), and *Chikuma* (Capt. Komura Keizo). Each heavy cruiser was more than 640 feet long, displacing 15,200 tons, carrying a main battery of eight 8-inch/203mm guns in four turrets—all situated forward of the bridge superstructure,

---

* This misidentification prefigures other IJN identification problems with deadly consequences. For example, at Coral Sea, Rear Admiral Takagi's attacks on the oiler *Neosho* and destroyer *Sims* echo the events of March 1, as would the fatal miscalculations at Midway. Even sixty-three years after, there remains confusion regarding the precise tracks of the KdB carriers that day. Earlier that morning, two of the screening destroyers, presumably with carriers *Kasumi* and *Shiranuhi*, had allegedly attacked the merchantman *Modjokerto* after the vessel blundered into view. But *Modjokerto* escaped, damaged, only to be allegedly found later in the day by the submarine *I-154* and sunk at 12° 40′ S, 106° 40′ E. These coordinates place the Dutch ship right in the path of KdB.

which gave these ships a sinuous and sinister profile—plus a secondary complement of eight 5-inch/127mm dual-purpose guns, and a full set of twelve torpedo tubes for their prodigious 24-inch/610mm Type 93 Long Lance torpedoes. With speeds in excess of thirty-five knots, these vessels, along with their fast battleship units, were the swiftest, most powerful heavy ships then operational in the Imperial Navy, and more than a match for any Allied warship still afloat in the East Indies.

At first contact, the Mobile Force was some 240 miles south of tiny Christmas Island, on a bearing of about 150 degrees, prowling the Indian Ocean below Java in search of fleeing transports, convoys, warships, or reinforcements foolish enough to venture into the region. Their mission was to annihilate the enemy's warships and to capture, where possible, his transports and auxiliaries.

This fleet, the Kidō Butai, with its Kushi Butai of carriers, Shien Butai of fast battleships and cruisers, Keikai Tai of one four-funneled light cruiser and ten destroyers, and all-important Replenishment Force of oilers, had staged at Staring Bay in the southeastern Celebes, near the small port town of Kendari. With them as flank protection went the Southern Force of Vice Adm. Kondō Nobutake, made up of the other two fast battleships of Sentai 3, *Kongō* and *Haruna*; the heavy cruisers *Atago* (F), *Takao*, and *Maya*; and three destroyers.*

Kidō Butai departed on Wednesday morning, February 25, 1942, at 8:30, steaming unhindered in majestic single file across the flat, tranquil Banda Sea, with its schools of flying fish and knotted masses of sea snakes. After negotiating the wide and deep Ombai Strait (8° 30′S, 125° 00′E) between Timor and the island of Alor—near the rendezvous of *Edsall, Boise, Houston, Trinity*, and others barely five weeks earlier—the forces entered the long, inky swells of the Indian Ocean at 9:30 on Thursday, February 26. From that point the ships headed west, along a heading of roughly 260 degrees, to a position well below Java, where on Saturday, February 28, they began sweeping south. On the morning of Sunday, March 1, Kondō's Southern Force and Nagumo's Kidō Butai had separated and were respectively about 70 and 320 nautical miles south southwest of Tjilatjap. First the unlucky *Modjokerto*, then the

---

* Vice Admiral Kondō was in fact superior to Vice Admiral Nagumo and had overall command of these IJN forces. The battleships *Kongō* and *Haruna* had departed Kendari with Kidō Butai, but split off below Java to join Kondō. Needless to say, Vice Admiral Nagumo exercised tactical control over his forces.

plodding *Pecos*, would provide KdB's surface and air forces with a few hours of sport that day. Their third victim could run and fight back; disposing of her would be neither simple nor swift.

The enemy light cruiser that was detected at a range of almost thirty-three thousand yards and misidentified at first because she had four funnels like the older *Omaha*-class light cruisers (such as *Marblehead*) was, in fact, the USS *Edsall* (DD-219). She was "old enough to vote," as Asiatic Fleet commander Tommy Hart liked to quip, but the good fortune that had served her well throughout her twenty-one years, from Smyrna's holocaust to the Sino-Japanese conflict, was soon to expire, although not without a memorable struggle. During her last ninety minutes, *Edsall* saw more action than many ships saw during the entire war. This remarkable last engagement has never been well understood, and more precise information was lacking until very recently. *Edsall* was without question in the wrong place at the wrong time, largely due to one of the Pacific war's most foolish operations, but I believe her reasons for being there were above reproach.

> *Many wondered why the destroyer* Edsall *did not come to the rescue [of* Pecos].
> —Walter G. Winslow, *The Fleet the Gods Forgot*

> *But, in war as elsewhere, the noblest and bravest actions are not always the most famous.*
> —Michel de Montaigne, *Essais*

How *Edsall* happened to be at the point given on the IJN chart (approx. 14° 9' S, 106° 38' E) raises other questions. Given the locations recorded for the sinking of the *Pecos*, it is probable that DD-219 was spotted less than twenty-five to thirty-five nautical miles from the oiler's last position, and she was coming from that direction when first seen by IJN surface vessels. No one has ever suggested that the old flushdecker was attempting to do the same thing that her sister ship, USS *Whipple* (DD-217), was undertaking at the same hour—that is, steaming to the rescue of several hundred men who had been able to get off the *Pecos*.

The time for making such a case is long overdue.

Knowing what we do now about the period of time between when the three ships parted earlier that morning (at 8:30, U.S. Navy time), the transmission of COMSOWESPAC Glassford's "withdraw from Java" message (sent between nine and ten o'clock), and the distances and likely speeds, it is conceivable that *Edsall* read the distress signals of *Pecos*. These may have begun as early as 12:47, and seem to have been received by *Whipple* at 1:24, when she altered her northwest course to 180 degrees true. Even the troopship USS *Mount Vernon* (AP-22), en route from Colombo to Fremantle, and many hundreds of miles to the south southwest, read the distress calls from *Pecos*: "A few days out of port the ship's radio intercepted a distress call from a supply ship pursued by enemy subs, [*sic*] headed for our destination, and on our course to Fremantle."[1] *Mount Vernon* picked up a number of these broken transmissions, which are recorded in Commander Abernethy's report, written aboard the troopship as it journeyed from Australia to the States a week later. These partial messages show that *Pecos* had been under attack for several hours and was struggling to remain afloat, and her radio was being jammed. It is not unlikely that *Edsall* may have received the messages as well.

If so, *Edsall*, like *Whipple*, began charting a new southward course—that is, assuming *Edsall* had already turned back from the original mission into Tjilatjap (with the Army Air Force personnel from *Langley*) upon copying at least one of the first Glassford messages. *Whipple* allegedly copied a signal ordering *Edsall* to clear the region.* Traveling in a south southwest direction at an average speed of roughly fifteen knots for six to seven hours would have placed *Edsall* in the area in which she was ultimately detected. The indisputable proximity to *Pecos'* final position seems too close to be mere coincidence.

The weathered ship and her spirited but exhausted crew, spared at the last moment from a death-sentence appointment in Tjilatjap, had

---

* The records of *Whipple*, though, state that *in anticipation* of receiving orders that morning from HQ (Glassford) "relative to retirement from Java," ComDesDiv 57, Commander Crouch, made the course change to 180 degrees true. *Whipple's* action report itself contains several contradictions regarding the transmissions from *Pecos*, stating that they received a number of them between 1:15 and 2:28. *Whipple's* report states that she had responded at 1:25 hours to *Pecos* with "Roger," but she did not believe that the oiler received it. *Whipple* also noted that *Pecos* was transmitting "off frequency" and thought it unlikely that any other ships heard the message. This is difficult to accept because of the number of messages copied by *Mount Vernon*. *Edsall* was probably no more distant from *Pecos* than was *Whipple*, and indeed must have been closer because she was intercepted by Nagumo's Support Force nearly three hours before *Whipple* arrived on the scene. This suggests that *Edsall* had probably copied some of these messages herself, either before or after she received the "scatter" order from Rear Admiral Glassford in Bandoeng. (*Whipple* Action Report, p. 4, and *Pecos* Action Report, March 7, 1942.)

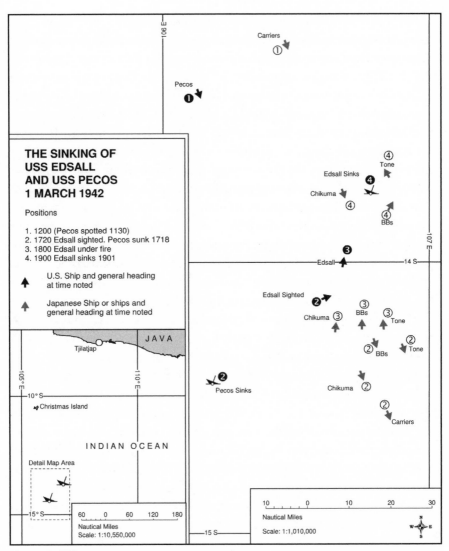

Vincent P. O'Hara

turned about and headed at the best economical speed for Australia. Already on edge from recent nerve-wracking events, the crew may have been subjected again to the sounds of distant explosions as they steamed south. That morning—if able to distinguish the ominous noises from the roar of the sea and the vessel's overworked engines—they could have heard wind-driven heavy gunfire booming across the Indian Ocean as the *Modjokerto* was attacked by floatplanes and shellfire. They would have continued making for the relative safety of Australia until the early

afternoon, when suddenly copying the faint, fragmentary calls from
Pecos, with whom *Edsall* had parted company just a few hours earlier:
"NERK NERK V NIFQ ANS PLS MAYBE SINKING S 15 106 K K K." *

Seventy-five nautical miles to the northwest, moving in the opposite direction, ComDesDiv 57, Cmdr. Edwin M. Crouch[†] (a former
commanding officer of *Edsall*), held a brief conference aboard *Whipple*
with its captain, Lt. Cmdr. Eugene Karpe,[‡] before altering course for
their long, arcing return to the dying oiler's last known position. What
exchanges or debates, if any, took place among the officers aboard *Edsall*
that day remain forever hidden from our knowledge, yet there is ample
cause to believe that her men would not have left the scene, as close to
their fellow servicemen as they must have known they were. After all,
this damaged ship's crew had refused to be taken out of the combat zone
and had rescued 177 men from the port side of *Langley* as she settled on
the afternoon of Friday, February 27, before transferring them to *Pecos* at
daybreak on Sunday, March 1. *Whipple*'s report later noted the eagerness
and heroism of her own crew in preparing for and engaging in the rescue
of the men from *Pecos*; there is no reason to imagine that *Edsall*'s crew
were any different. One may envision them rigging lifelines and preparing knotted ropes and cargo nets (as specified in divisional rescue bills) as
they approached the area where they believed the oiler had been sunk.

Recall, too, those *Pecos* survivors in the water who later reported
hearing gunfire and the hailstorm of explosions "toward twilight" in
the direction taken by *Edsall* earlier that day (northeast). This also
makes sense; the destroyer might have been as close as twenty-five to
thirty-five miles at 5:22, and the extrapolated positions appear to place
DD-219 bearing about 45 degrees true from *Pecos*' point of sinking. If

* *Pecos*' navy call sign was NIFQ, as shown in the messages received on *Mount Vernon*.

† Edwin Mason Crouch, U.S. Naval Academy 1921, had the misfortune to accept a ride to
the Philippines from the Marianas with a former academy classmate commanding a heavy
cruiser in the closing weeks of the war. The classmate was Capt. Charles Butler McVay,
the ship was USS *Indianapolis* (CA-35). She was torpedoed by the Japanese submarine
I-58 on July 30, 1945. Only 317 of the 1,196 men aboard her survived the sinking and the
subsequent four days in the water waiting to be rescued. Captain E. M. Crouch was not
among the survivors.

‡ In the early 1950s, while working as naval attaché to the Balkans, Capt. Eugene S. Karpe
fell to his death from a train—the fabled *Orient Express*—under suspicious circumstances
near Salzburg, Austria.

this is approximately accurate, *Edsall* needed but another hour's worth of steaming to begin reaching the men in the water.

To use her fuel as efficiently as possible, she would have been steaming on two boilers, which could still provide power for more than twenty knots, and in some ships for almost twenty-seven knots. A regular watch on the "smoke telegraphs" (or indicators) was considered essential—however, only with well-trained men. "Appreciable steady light black smoke, without heat waves, should be coming from the stacks at all times. It is all very well to say you want a light brown haze, but such orders will result in a clear stack most of the time. Get some smoke you can actually see—then there is no question about [it]." For full-power runs, the other two boilers could be cut in during acceleration, which should have given full speed in less than twelve minutes.[2]

Edsall would not have abandoned her fellow servicemen on *Pecos*. Sometime just before four o'clock in the afternoon, a lookout in her crow's nest seventy-five feet above the water would have called down through his phones: "Bridge, Spot One. Masts on the horizon bearing Red—" It is quite possible to imagine his words cut short at that very moment, as Japanese shells could have already been screaming through the air toward *Edsall*.

She did manage to get off at least one transmission, however, for her "signals"[3] are mentioned in a long-forgotten report by A. S. Voorduyn, master of the Dutch merchant ship *Siantar*, sister-ship to *Modjokerto*, after he reached Sydney—his own ship having been sunk by a Japanese submarine off the western coast of Australia just two days after *Modjokerto*, *Pecos*, and *Edsall*.

Good men with poor ships are better than poor men in good ships.
—Alfred Thayer Mahan

A bungling attack is more effective than the most skillful defense.
—Yamamoto Isoroku

"At full speed like an arrow, trailing black smoke behind her," *Edsall* was sighted by the westernmost Japanese ship *Chikuma*, which reversed course and swiftly brought her main battery to bear. Minutes later, at 5:33, the heavy cruiser opened fire from a distance of twenty-one thousand meters (about twenty-three thousand yards). This was most likely a ranging salvo to measure the distance to the small target, as Imperial Navy doctrine for battleships and cruisers favored opening gunfire at maximum range.

The U.S. destroyer, realizing her closeness to the enemy, had also reversed course, "skillfully [laying] smokescreens from time to time," as she "frantically attempted to escape at high speeds of over 30 knots." At 5:37 the flagship of Sentai 8, *Tone*, signaled "All forces charge," and the two cruisers took off like bird-dogs after a spooked quail.

It is unlikely, to say the least, that *Edsall* was ever able to attain a speed of thirty knots within such a brief period of time, even if she had been capable. But pushing her engineering plant to its limits had never been more necessary, and in the next hour and a half, the old ship's panting boilers and turbines showed that she still had enough speed and agility to foil the gunnery of the Japanese ships tasked with destroying her.

According to Japanese records, the wind was brisk ("10 meters per second," or twenty knots) from the southeast (at 130 degrees), so the pursuing IJN ships would have had their own gun smoke blowing between them and the U.S. destroyer. There were also typical Indian Ocean mists and rain squalls that day of limited size and duration, but a lame World War I–era destroyer shouldn't have been a real challenge—even when mistaken for a light cruiser. "However, this enemy ship," wrote one of *Chikuma*'s young midshipmen acting as an assistant navigator, "was extremely maneuverable, and repeated changing speeds and courses, and ran away like a Japanese dancing mouse."

Turning to join the hunt, the battleships launched three Type 95 Nakajima E8N "Dave" floatplanes at 5:45 to aid spotting fall of shot. Three planes from carrier *Sōryu* were already aloft as "upper air patrol," suggesting that that carrier had drawn the role of "duty ship," but these evidently took no part in the action. It is possible, though, that *Edsall* was first spotted by these planes overhead.* The attack signal was given by Vice Admiral Nagumo—who must have been well beyond visual range of the destroyer—at 5:22 (or four minutes after Commander Abernethy watched *Pecos* take her final plunge), with the Support Force vessels sighting the four-piper a few minutes later.

---

* The Pythagorean calculation shows that a plane at no more than seven hundred meters in altitude could have easily spotted the ship from thirty kilometers. *Senshi Sōsho* gives surface visibility on March 1, 1942, as thirty-five kilometers.

At 5:47 the battleships commenced firing with their main batteries (14-inch/356mm), the range given by *Hiei* (Capt. Nishida Masao), a colossal 27,000 meters (about 29,500 yards), or almost fifteen nautical miles, which would have been near the limits of their main battery rangefinder's optical horizon. Firing at this tremendous range when aided by spotting planes also adhered to standard IJN gunnery doctrine for day action, which favored outranging, and specified, "When visibility is very good, for a while Battleship Squadrons will fire at long range with the angle of elevation of the main batteries at about maximum."[4] The splashes from Kirishima's *chakushokudan* (pillar-coloring shell) sent towering columns of blue-dyed water into the air, whereas those of flagship *Hiei* were unmarked.

At 5:48 Battleship Division (BatDiv) 3/1 completed a series of turns, from course 250 degrees to 290 degrees—gingerly, so as to launch the Daves, and also not throw off the fire-control teams—before settling on a north northeast heading of 35 degrees. Vice Admiral Mikawa then gave the orders "Full speed," and at 5:50 followed this with "All forces charge." What transpired over the next seventy minutes was one of the Pacific war's most conspicuous examples of "target fixation."

These maneuvers positioned the two fast battleships of Vice Admiral Mikawa east of *Edsall* but still within main-battery range, which cut off an escape by the destroyer to the northeast. The "Full Speed" order probably indicates that the two battleships began accelerating at that time from fourteen knots or so up to full speed, which should have been around eighteen to twenty knots, *not* their maximum speed, and that such an increase might have consumed at least another fifteen to twenty minutes.

In the meantime, *Tone*, also working up to speed, bent on a course east of and beyond the battleships, acted as the right claw of the Support Force pincers. *Edsall*, as recorded in *Chikuma*'s Detailed Action Report at this time (5:52 p.m.), was making smoke as she fled. An eyewitness from the cruiser wrote, "Soon, the destroyer deployed [a] smoke-screen, which made it more difficult for us to aim, and we missed many more shots."[5] A few minutes later—Japanese sources say between 5:56 and 5:57—an unexpected turnabout occurred, when *Edsall*'s skipper, Lt. J. J. Nix, yanked his shuddering old four-piper around in a 180-degree turn and headed directly for the nearest antagonist, *Chikuma*. DD-219's gun crews would have bellowed their well-practiced drill, "Load . . . Bore clear ... Ready One ... Commence firing, Commence firing ..." as the prow swung toward the enemy. With a terrific crack the main battery's 4-inchers fired, and with the pointers and trainers frantically trying to "match bugs" while the ship turned, hot shellmen caught the ejected brass casings and threw them overboard; first shellmen slammed another projectile into the breech and gun captains snapped their handles down to seat the round properly before repeating the firing evolution again. *Edsall's* gunnery officer, Lt. Phil Wild Jr. directed the return fire from his position on the open signal platform above the bridge, where a five-foot rangefinder was situated forward of a rudimentary gunnery computer known as a "Baby Ford."

These weapons had a maximum range of just under sixteen thousand yards, which the Japanese easily outranged, so all of the U.S. shells dropped short. Or did they? IJN accounts state: "1756 DD headed toward *Chikuma* & opened fire—Near misses." The aging "Sea-hornet" fought back actively. "Moreover, if the enemy destroyer found opportunities, she repeated counterattacks by launching torpedoes and gunfire. Fortunately, we were beyond the range of the enemy gunfire, and all shells fell short of our fleet."[6] It's not certain whether Lieutenant Nix wanted to strike back at the enemy, who as phantoms had tormented his ship for so many weeks, or whether he simply wished to allow his gun crews an opportunity to vent their anger no matter how futile the gesture.* What is certain, though, was the courage displayed in that brief counterattack.

As it turned out, their opposite numbers on *Chikuma* were by no means such hardened combat veterans that they felt nothing at all: "Even though we were out of range of the enemy gunfire and we knew we would not incur any hits, there were some who [hunched] their shoulders instinctively when they saw the flashes of the enemy gunfire."[7]

It seemed likely that J. J. Nix may have been trying to put himself in an advantageous position for a torpedo attack, or to at least bluff such a tactic by firing booster charges, as several four-pipers escaping through Bali Strait had done when they ran into Japanese pickets. J. J.'s grandson,

* Two notes by the commanding officer of *Whipple* in his action report of March 4, 1942, bear this out: No. 21, "it is believed that the morale of the crew would be greatly impaired if not allowed to open fire"; and No. 22, "It is not believed that the A.A. defense would be very effective against dive bombers but from information received, it is believed that dive bombers can and will be hit by determined gunners." (Lt. Cmdr. Edwin S. Karpe, "USS *Whipple*—Activities Between 26 February and 4 March 1942," Serial CF-015.) Imagining this maneuver is aided by viewing prewar 8mm film footage of Lt. J. J. Nix and others

James Tallent Nix, thought they would have been "derelict" had they not fired their torpedoes at the Japanese pursuers.

That there had never been any mention of torpedoes being fired was one more mystery in this enigmatic story. Extant DesRon 29 documents from the Java campaign show that the U.S. ships' torpedoes were prone to malfunctions if fired at speeds "much above 20 knots," but the same report also notes that "At high speeds we should fire at targets as far aft as possible."[8] One would have thought that *Edsall*'s antagonists were well placed for at least one torpedo salvo—assuming that *Edsall* then carried any.* Sixty-five years later, the Japanese finally answered this question, too.

Having experienced his first and only surface engagement from *Chikuma*'s bridge, the young assistant navigator, Haraguchi Shizuhiko, later wrote: "The wakes of the torpedoes the enemy destroyer had launched passed the side of our ship, while we [watched] them holding our breath: we were intact." The gritty destroyer still had a few tricks up her sleeve, and a fistful of fight there as well. She had retained her torpedoes and knew how to use them. As it turns out, the torpedo attack and counterbattery fire distracted the inexperienced Japanese; this may well account for some of the poor marksmanship and failure to close the range decisively in this action. "The AA lookouts, whose duty was to watch the sky above, were [reprimanded] and called down badly, because they completely forgot to watch the sky, and were watching the torpedo wakes under the water surface instead after they heard the report, 'Enemy launched torpedoes, wakes are coming toward our ship!' "[9]

After *Edsall*'s torpedoes missed and her shots fell short, she quickly doubled back, wrapping herself in an effective smokescreen as she gyred. Almost simultaneously *Chikuma* ran into a dense squall line and checked fire at 6:00.

Below, at the forward store-deck level in the gunnery computer room (*shageki-ban shitsu*), a young Ensign Candidate (*shoi kohosei*)

from USS *Black Hawk* taking target practice at Chefoo. Nix actually fires the last clip of his .45-caliber pistol from the hip, like the Western gunfighters that any red-blooded American youth would have been raised to emulate, particularly one born in Fort Worth, Texas, with a fondness for pulp fiction.

* Although it isn't known precisely which type of torpedo was carried on that day by *Edsall*, the ship had been originally fitted with 21-inch Mk.8–3B weapons, and these had a range of sixteen thousand yards at thirty-six knots. This appears to agree with Japanese records that say *Chikuma* had managed to close to within such a distance.

named Sasaki Masao, along with the other IJN sailors and officers stationed there, had been doing his best to keep *Chikuma*'s main battery of eight 8-inch (20cm) guns on target against the skittering little four-funneled vessel in the distance, but the destroyer's wild maneuvers had so far frustrated their efforts. *Tone*'s track chart and that of BatDiv 3/1 show that they also had ceased fire between 6:00 and 6:09. Wreathed in her own smokescreen, *Edsall* darted out of view. The flushdecker, it would appear, had once more escaped.

> *Vigorous pursuit is recommended. . . . The routed enemy will be pursued. He will be engaged and destroyed.*
> —Imperial Japanese Navy Battleship and Cruiser Doctrine, "Day Action and Outline of Combat"

Through their adrenaline, *Edsall*'s crew may have felt a sense of relief, which they nevertheless understood was at best only momentary. One hundred and fifty-three officers and crew, plus some three dozen USAAF pilots and enlisted men, were aboard the veteran tin can when the fighting tops of Nagumo's Support Force ships began appearing along with the freight-train roars of the Japanese shells.

In actions that took place on the same day several hundred miles to the north in the Java Sea, in the Battle Off Cape Puting, another U.S. flushdecker, the USS *Pope* (DD-225), and a British destroyer, HMS *Encounter*, experienced a similar fate. They were cornered, pursued, and dispatched with the aid of air strikes in lengthy stern chases by a larger force of Japanese warships. By coincidence, officers survived from both of these ships' gunnery divisions; the men were ideally placed to observe their respective engagements and later published fine accounts of their experiences.

Aboard *Pope*, Lt. j.g. John "Jack" Michel was aloft in spot one (the cramped crow's nest) and was amazed to find the ship suddenly alone after a long period of combat, and seemingly safe within the dark womb of a blinding squall.

> The rain was so heavy it was impossible to see more than fifty yards. Now I had nothing to do but think of our situation, and I realized that I was scared. . . . Our only salvation was in flight. . . . I had been so engrossed in spotting and making various

reports that the precariousness of the situation did not bother me. But now that we were trying to run away, I had an insecure feeling.[10]

Meanwhile, Michel's opposite number, Sam Falle, in the main battery director atop the bridge of HMS *Encounter*, found himself in much the same situation:

Suddenly a storm came up and hid us from the enemy and them from us. The firing stopped. It was uncanny. We were suddenly silent and alone, with the teeming tropical rain and dense cloud. We could not even see *Exeter*, while *Pope* was further away from us, to port of *Exeter*. It seemed like a miracle and we hoped we could disappear under cover of the storm. The ocean, even an enclosed sea like the one we found ourselves in, seems wide and one does not feel so hemmed in as a surrounded army must. . . . But the storm was all too brief. It cleared as suddenly as it had come. There they all were, those stark menacing ships.[11]

Encounter went down with her sister *Exeter* early that afternoon. *Pope* lasted longer, separated and at a greater distance from her pursuers, but then she too sank. Surely the *Edsall* action was much the same, as she pounded north by northeast, fleeing four of the Imperial Fleet's fastest battleships and cruisers. Time was now running out as irretrievably as the ship's fuel oil during that long run to the north. She and most of her crew, including the hapless Army Air Force passengers, had no more than an hour left on the surface of the slate-colored sea as they were relentlessly pursued by the dark gray shapes astern.

Was *Edsall* really able to send out a radio message in that brief space? No such messages were logged by U.S. ships, but the operator serving aboard *Abbekerk* that last weekend as she steamed through the same waters noted "the staggering number of SOS calls broadcast from ships all around us."[12] It is possible that Ensign Gustin's "radio gang" made an attempt to get off a signal of some type, but concussion, atmospherics, or Japanese jamming may have negated these efforts.*

* Ensign John Gustin noted in a letter home to his family in November 1941 that his radio crew numbered seven men, including himself. They included Sam Cassady, Wallace

Then, too suddenly, *Edsall* scampered into daylight again, a graying old fox flushed from cover once too often. More than five thousand finely trained Japanese sailors and airmen were now in pursuit of the hamstrung destroyer. Clearing the squall at 6:09, *Chikuma* reopened fire, but by then Vice Admiral Nagumo had seen enough. Generally placid, but also known to possess a hot temper, he finally ordered air strikes ("seething with rage," read the IJN notes) from three of his four great carriers. The *kanbaku* crews were equal to the job.

Between 6:00 and 6:05, as the men aboard *Edsall* would have feared and expected, seventeen dive-bombers in two *chūtai* lifted off from the pitching flight decks of *Kaga* and *Sōryu*. From the former, eight Vals under *chūtaichō* Lt. Ogawa Shōichi, and from the latter, nine more *kanbaku* led by Lt. Koite Moriyuki. The *kōdōchōsho* (combat reports) of Kidō Butai also record that nine more D3A1s commanded by Lt. Kobayashi Michio, a veteran airman considered one of the IJN's most capable and *buntaichō* (leader) of *Hiryū*'s carrier bomber unit, had launched at 5:20. But this means that these planes were climbing into the air when the ship was first sighted, and therefore airborne for almost an hour and a half before attacking *Edsall*, while the other *chūtai* struck the fleeing four-piper within forty to forty-five minutes of taking off.

This discrepancy may be nothing but a typo. It's one of the last serious questions remaining to be ciphered out in *Edsall*'s final action. If not another "clerical error," it almost suggests that either Nagumo had lost faith in his Support Force's "big guns" before the actual stern-chase began or that Captain Kaku—or perhaps Vice Adm. Yamaguchi Tamon, a man not known for his patience—had jumped the gun and flown off his VBs prior to receiving orders or before the destroyer was sighted. This might imply that the Japanese may have felt that the obstinate *Pecos* needed another visit. And then there was that reference to a "foul-up" aboard *Hiryū* earlier when Lt. Shimoda Ichiro's *chūtai* had been late taking off and arriving for the strikes against *Pecos*.

However, based on the evidence regarding carrier doctrine early in the Pacific war, it hardly appears possible that *Hiryū* could have landed nine *kanbaku* at 5:00 from the *Pecos* strikes, and then promptly launch another nine Vals at 5:20. Therefore, a simple typo may be the culprit. Be that as it may, one might charitably say that Japanese coordination

Gilman, Paul Hegerfeldt (although he was later a soundman on the ASW detection gear), Kenneth Jones, Harold Rice, and Dale Westwood.

in such operations, like their target identifications, still left something to be desired. Conventional wisdom holds that Kidō Butai possessed superior airstrike doctrine at this time. One could argue that the events of March 1, 1942, refute such a description. Yet, as the overall picture *is* one of several closely related, almost overlapping actions that would put any carrier battle-group to the test, perhaps *Hiryū*'s *kanbaku* were searching for other potential vessels to attack in the area.

The *Senshi Sōsho* text, originally translated by Edwin Layton and adhered to for the past quarter of a century, stated that the Vals were armed with 250-kilogram (551-pound) or 500-kilogram (1,102-pound) bombs. This data appears to be in error: Research of primary IJN carrier records indicates that all of the dive-bombers were carrying one 250-kilogram (Type 99 No. 25 Mk.1) semi-armor-piercing bomb. And, in contrast to Layton's faithful recording of what now appears another clerical mistake repeated in the *Senshi Sōsho* volume, no evidence has come to light that Vals from *Akagi* were used against *Edsall*. An examination of the timelines involved in the air strikes earlier that same day against the oiler *Pecos* confirms that the D3A1s from *Akagi*—their *chūtai* led by Lt. Chihaya Takehiko—were indeed the last to arrive back on board the four carriers under Nagumo and were thus too late to be rearmed, refueled, and flown off again for the attack on *Edsall*. It does appear that time was the critical factor, although it is also possible that the D3A1s were held in reserve for any other threats or targets of opportunity.* Finally, the *kōdōchōsho* do not show that the attack from *Sōryu* was led by the celebrated "god of dive-bombing," Egusa Takeshige, as has been alleged in other works.

The three *chūtai* of Kobayashi, Ogawa, and Koite climbed into the late afternoon sky, wheeling to the north in search of the solitary little vessel. It should have taken them only about thirty minutes or less to reach the ship, but the light was failing and the enemy, even if fleeing, was assumed to be armed with torpedoes, which the Japanese ships rightly feared. She could not be permitted to escape.

At 6:14, belatedly, heavy cruiser *Tone* at last found the range against the U.S. "light cruiser" and commenced firing, the distance still an

---

* The clarification of the air strikes launched against *Edsall* (and *Pecos* also) is relatively recent (spring 2005) and has been among the most difficult to obtain and evaluate. This information, taken from primary IJN sources by J. Michael Wenger, enabled the vital pieces of the puzzle to fit together accurately. (Mike Wenger's other notes appear in Appendix II at the end of the text.)

excessive 23,500 meters (25,700 yards); not surprisingly, her salvoes missed. Official notes in Layton's translations of the track charts and sketches read "unable to make any hits . . . the surface forces bombardment not achieving its objective." Even so, nothing appears to have dampened the IJN gunners' determination. Conserving shells (or precious fuel oil for that matter) was not the top priority. That these crack ships in vaunted Nihon Kaigun, with its most advanced fire-control system(s) and three planes spotting shell splashes, had made only a single hit—and even that not before 6:24—must have disturbed and baffled the senior officers. One junior officer present that afternoon claimed to believe "that our superiors wanted to get close in and let the secondary guns practice firing using her as a target." If true, they were willing to squander a huge amount of fuel oil and ordnance for this "practice firing."

At 6:18, *Chikuma* ceased fire; she reopened fire at 6:23. For her part *Hiei* (and possibly *Kirishima* as well) had unleashed four-turret salvos at the destroyer beginning just before 6:25, when they altered course northwest from 20 degrees to 340 degrees. At 6:33, BatDiv 3/1 fired with only one turret each, undoubtedly attempting with this "partial salvo firing" to spot their own salvos amid the torrent of shells raining down from the two cruisers. But after that time their small, "jinking" target was probably obscured by other splashes: emerging from the failing light of dusk, the *Aichi* D3A1 Vals had at last reached *Edsall*.

The Damned Die Hard

> *All bullets do not hit their mark and there is a great deal of space
> above and around a man.*
>
> —Prosper Mérimée

"*Totsure, totsure, totsugeki taisei tore!*" signaled the *chūtaichō* once the Type 99s arrived over the small target. "Take up attack position!" The first plane would perform its primary role as leader by indicating "the target, its course, and speed; the wind direction and speed; the point of aim; bomb release altitude; direction of retirement; and rendezvous point." At that moment, each of the planes separated from the tight V formations and "dove according to the judgment or instinct of its pilot." The rest of the *chutai* followed the lead plane, watching its bomb drop and correcting on their observations.[13]

From about 6:40 until 6:57, the twenty-six *kanbaku* flown by the crack dive-bombing pilots of Kidō Butai swarmed on the swerving little ship in waves. Assuming they reached altitude, the planes approached in multiple Vs at between 10,000 to 15,000 feet, then glided and circled down several thousand more feet before being pushed straight over into harrowing dives at 50 to 60 degrees from less than 5,000 feet. The sturdy *Aichi*s screamed down to their release point at 1,000 to 1,500 feet, dropping their ordinary 250-kilogram bombs at a 45-degree angle.[14]

Although hitting the narrow vessel squarely as it battled through the swells (and in poor light) would have been challenging, the flush-decker—whose limited AA capabilities consisted of a single 3-inch/23-caliber "pea-shooter" on the afterdeck, and whatever number of .30-caliber and .50-caliber machine guns her crew had been able to jury-rig topside since the war's outbreak—appears to have suffered mortal damage rapidly. In addition to any direct hits, near misses would have wrought severe damage just as surely.

The inferiority of the aft 3-inch/23-caliber AA gun was well known: It lacked range, tracking ability, and rate of fire to be effective against modern warplanes. Although a maximum ceiling of eighteen thousand feet at 75 degrees elevation is given in technical books today, these old weapons were probably useless at half that altitude, especially against a sizable number of attackers. (The action report of USS *Pope* [DD-225], though, proudly claimed that its 3-inch AA fire kept ten Mitsubishi F1M2 Pete floatplanes attempting to glide-bomb the ship at bay for some time.)* Navy veterans have described the weapon as a relic of the Spanish-American War that had been designed to be broken down into pieces for transportation overland on mules. It also kicked like a mule: "The combination of a 3-inch bore and a short 70-inch barrel resulted in an unbelievable impact when it was fired. Every time it was fired it felt like you had been hit in the face by a boxing glove."[15]

On occasion the old destroyers fired their main-battery 4-inch guns, loaded with "shrapnel," at low-flying attackers, presumably as the planes retired, which was often done at low altitude. Some water-cooled Browning M2 .50-caliber machine guns had been mounted aboard four-pipers

---

* These planes attacking *Pope* were from the seaplane tender *Chitose* of the 11th Seaplane Tender Division, commanded at this time by Capt. Furukawa Tamotsu. An interesting coincidence, in view of later events.

prior to the war, but they too had neither the range nor the punch to be of much use, although it does appear that these weapons must have damaged the planes of Yamakawa Shinsaku from *Kaga* and Iizuka Tokuji of *Akagi* earlier in the day in the attacks on *Pecos*.* As for the venerable .30-caliber Lewis guns, which were also "borrowed" from various sources and probably in use as well in sundry lashed-up mountings, were stopgap measures. An aircraft moving at 250 miles per hour would traverse the effective range (five hundred yards) of a Lewis gun in about four seconds; the gun's rate of fire (550 rounds per minute) meant that in such a period, not much more than three dozen rounds—hardly a killing burst—from its forty-seven-round drum could be squeezed off.[16]

Attacking out of the sun that late in the day would have been impracticable, so the Vals probably hit the destroyer head-on in order to avoid as much of her AA fire as possible. From a height of roughly twelve thousand feet, the pilot would wait until the ship could be seen off to his left, ahead of the engine that blocked much of his forward view. That was the direction in which the *kanbaku* fliers preferred to turn, "because the propeller was revolving to the right," so they generally banked to the left before beginning their descent.[17]

To achieve the desired 60-degree angle, they would use what one pilot called a "visual yardstick" to guide them to the critical moment when the dive began. This moment was achieved when the target reached the front edge of the Type 99's distinctive elliptical wing. At that instant, the dive would begin, preferably at about a 45-degree angle. This angle would be increased as the dive proceeded, with the target kept in view through the cross hairs of the bombsight mounted in the front windshield. Headwinds, tailwinds, and crosswinds also factored into the calculus of dive-bombing as the *kanbaku* hurtled down at an optimal speed of 450 kilometers per hour before reaching the release point. With the rear-seat observer calling out altimeter readings and wind conditions to the pilot—"*Happyaku* (eight hundred meters), *Roppyaku* (six hundred meters), *Yohi* (ready)"—a point slightly in front of the ship, which in this case was moving at high speed, had to be calculated.

---

* *Whipple's* action report for the *Langley* sinking, and those of other attacks, shows that she fired 1,400 .50-caliber and .30-caliber rounds in defending the old seaplane tender on February 27, and another 1,300-plus rounds against three Japanese planes that surprised her along with *Edsall* and *Pecos* off Christmas Island on the morning of February 28.

All of this needed to be done in a matter of seconds and in the face of antiaircraft bursts "filling the bombsight with their red fireworks." At about four hundred meters, the observer would give the signal "*Teh!*" ("Release bomb"; an abbreviation of "*Uteh!*" an imperative meaning "Hit it!"), and as the bomb's 551 pounds broke free, the pilot would begin to pull the heavy plane up from its dive. Gravitational forces would take over at that instant, the flier seeing hundreds of stars as his eyesight darkened, but the sensation would pass rapidly as the plane gradually nosed up to 30 degrees. At low altitude and full throttle, the *kanbaku* would dart away over the ocean, evading AA fire in short dips and climbs.

The planes from *Kaga* struck first, at 6:40, followed by those of Lieutenant Kobayashi's *chutai* from *Hiryū* at 6:45, and finally the *Sōryu* group at 6:50. It was a one-sided business, of course, and could end with only one result. "[Our] dive-bombers attacked the enemy ship . . . suffering many direct hits and near-misses . . . causing fires to break out and the speed of the enemy ship to be immediately reduced," reads the account in *Senshi Sōsho*. In *Edsall*'s early war logs, her firefighting drills show that the first water streams flowed within a couple of minutes. She may have again seen such alacrity from her damage control teams in this instance, but nothing would have saved the ship once her steering and propulsion were compromised.

Although there is a certain amount of ambiguity in IJN records, they show that when the Vals made their attacks, the distances between pursued and pursuers were still formidable. According to the official source, Sentai 3/1 was at 25,500 meters (almost 28,000 yards) and *Tone* no closer than 20,500 meters (more than 22,000 yards). Only *Chikuma*, which had been the closest initially, seems to have narrowed the gap, being at 14,900 meters (about 16,200 yards), apparently aided by *Edsall*'s own counterattack nearly an hour earlier.

However, another officer aboard the flagship *Hiei* later claimed, "Prior to the firing [of the battleship's secondary guns] I saw the *Edsall* attempting to run away from place to place desperately at a distance of about 15,000 meters." And, during the bombing attacks, "the distance to the *Edsall* was about 10,000 meters or so." His visual recollections were still acute after sixty-four years: "In the meantime the Vals dove on her, and all the bombs scored hits. I was watching this scene, and saw the smoke and the fire shoot up as the bombs exploded. Later on, I learned that the eighteen Vals* were from the carrier *Sōryu*."[18]

It would be easy to assume that the initial misidentification, at least on the part of the first ships to sight *Edsall*, was the reason why the Japanese did not attempt to close the distance as aggressively as might be expected, if in fact they imagined themselves chasing an *Omaha*-class light cruiser armed with 6-inch/53-caliber guns, which had a maximum range of approximately twenty-three thousand yards.† But their gunnery doctrine called for just such tactics, and, in any event, whatever the Imperial Navy gunners may have lacked in their ability to "measure" the U.S. ship, they more than made up for in tenacity. (A handwritten note in English in the margin of one of my copies of the *Senshi Sōsho* text reads, "What a patient, courageous, and painful engagement." Whether this refers to the Japanese or the Americans or both, it is searingly apt.)

Mathematicians, navigators, and those obsessed with such details may divert themselves with calculations showing how these distances between principals work out, given time, speed, and range variables. It appears that, as in the action against *Pope*, little real closing occurred (with the exception of *Chikuma*) before the bombers entered the picture. A simple measurement of the distances covered in the track-chart in *Senshi Sōsho* suggests that *Edsall's* speed may have averaged little more than 15 knots, however, but that could be explained by her radical manuevers to elude the Japanese shells.‡

Although the old four-stacker was obviously dying by then, (*Chikuma's* detailed action report (DAR) notes: "1845 [hours] DD on fire."),

* There were not eighteen planes, nor were they all from *Sōryu*.

† Also see *Mr. Michel's War*, p. 76, for Lieutenant Michel's comments on the Japanese cruisers and destroyers in action against *Exeter, Encounter*, and *Pope*, and their reluctance or refusal to close the range. Michel assumed that the Japanese were content to engage at long range, knowing full well that the Allied ships could not possibly escape, and thus they protected their own vessels from needless risk. This is more or less verified in *Battleship and Cruiser Gunnery Doctrine* documents. There are many parallels between *Pope's* final action and that of *Edsall*, and these similarities both clarify and cloud matters.

‡ These speeds rely on reminiscences of a former crewmember of *Edsall*, Fred Harrison (d. 2005), whose life was spared when he was transferred in February 1942 to the *Sea Witch*. He recalled that by then the destroyer had "a serious vibration in shaft no. 2," in addition to sagging firewall bricks in one or more of the boilers, and "could not exceed 26 knots. Original documents also show that DD-219 had received damage to her stern due to the depth of the water (eight fathoms) in which her depth charges were dropped in a submarine alert on January 23, 1942, in the Howard Channel. Certainly damage to her shaft

the Japanese feeding frenzy continued with shelling, even closing to within range of their secondary and AA batteries. The Japanese notes in the Supplement to *Senshi Sōsho* say, "Our surface ships, whose gunfire had moderated during the dive-bombing attacks, immediately closed the enemy which now had practically lost its fighting power, and again opened gunfire on it." This adopts a martial tone, but doesn't really convey the ugly math of an execution carried out against a virtually defenseless foe. These actions, however, are entirely consistent with the promulgated "Doctrine for Conduct of Day Action": "In the strike or mop-up phase the entire force will close the enemy attacking fiercely."

In the brief interval between the bombing attacks and the coup de grâce, those still alive aboard *Edsall* would have had their only chance to abandon ship, which was clearly settling by the stern, and get as far away as possible from it and the deadly impact of detonating projectiles in and around the target area. How many men were able to escape the ship is not known, of course. It seems fantastic that any Americans survived the engagement at all. *Hiei* was firing with all four turrets at 6:44 p.m., but that was reduced to one at 6:46. The secondary guns (all of the *Kongō*-class battleships had carried a dozen or more 6-inch/50-caliber guns in casemates, betraying their World War I origins) opened fire at 6:52, when her main battery ceased fire. This ship fired the fewest number of main battery shells during the engagement, but a clear explanation for this has yet to be reached.

First Lieutenant Motegi Meiji, was securely ensconced behind 254 millimeters of steel in the cramped forward conning tower of flagship *Hiei* along with members of Vice Admiral Mikawa's staff. An assistant to the battleship's executive officer, Motegi was observing the action through a periscope ("special binocular") that protruded through an aperture that had been unscrewed in the conning tower's armored roof. According to his account, the secondary battery fired on the immobile destroyer when she was "already . . . capsized and dead in the water, showing her red bottom" at a distance of "about 4,000 to 5,000 meters." *

struts would have been consistent with such explosions, and the severe shock experienced by *Gold Star* as documented by her commander. That *Edsall*'s war readiness was affected at all was explicitly denied by Lieutenant Nix in surviving records—again, perhaps, an indication of her crew's spirit.

* Mr. Motegi's account of this action, the first eyewitness report ever given apart from that in *Senshi Sōsho*, was arranged through historian and translator Kan Sugahara—coauthor,

As Sentai 3/1 would have been pursuing the U.S. destroyer from the southeast, with the ship then wallowing and unable to maneuver after the fatal dive-bombing on a southerly heading, and with a gradual starboard list (as revealed in the film footage shot from aboard one of the Japanese ships), First Lieutenant Motegi's memory strikes me as faithful. The flushdecker would have shown "her red bottom" had she been rolling over to that side as the battleships approached. *Hiei*'s 6-inch guns used *Edsall* for "practice firing" for some seven minutes, expending several dozen more shells. *Chikuma*'s chart shows that she checked fire at 6:56, but Cruiser Division (CruDiv) 8's flagship *Tone* continued firing on the stationary vessel until 6:59.

This three-minute gap between *Chikuma*'s cease-fire and that of her sister ship, along with the higher expenditure of 8-inch projectiles (and a lesser number of 5-inch shells) fired by *Tone*—in conjunction with the positions of the ships as represented in the *Senshi Sōsho* track chart and the angle of the targeted flushdecker in the film footage—seem to indicate that *Tone*, not *Chikuma*, was the ship that filmed what appear to be the last salvos landing on *Edsall*. But by any reckoning the only IJN warship whose orientation precisely matched the movie's perspective was *Tone*.

As shown on the IJN chart and in the film, USS *Edsall* (DD-219), having fought the good fight, died hard, her end far more violent and spectacular than that of *Pope*. Elusive to the last, even when immobilized and riven by shellfire, *Edsall* finally, slowly, almost steadfastly, capsized and slid under the waves, exhaling clouds of steam and dark smoke from 7:00 to 7:01.[*]

The location of her sinking is given as 13° 45′S, 106° 47′E.

Aftermath

At 7:35 p.m., *Sōryu*'s dive-bombers returned to their ship; those under Lt. Ogawa Shōichi landed on *Kaga* at 7:46. By eight o'clock, twenty

---

with Ichiro Matsunaga and Gordon J. Van Wylen, of *Encounter at Sea and a Heroic Lifeboat Journey*—who painstakingly translated questions into Japanese for Mr. Motegi, then retranslated his Japanese answers back into English.

[*] Kan Sugahara's translation of *Senshi Sōsho* reads, "At 1901, the enemy destroyer went down to the bottom of the sea." David Thomas' account in *Japan's War at Sea*, p. 84, reports, "She sank at 1906."

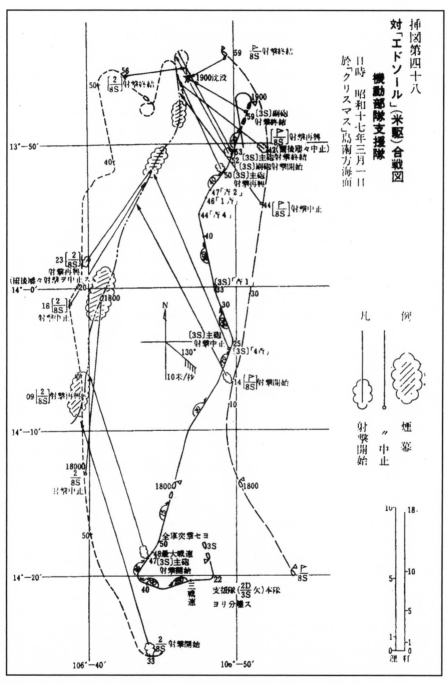

The track chart of the final engagement of USS *Edsall* (DD-219) against the Support Force of Kido Butai on the afternoon of March 1, 1942. *Senshi Sosho Vol. 26, p. 497*

minutes before sunset, Lieutenant Kobayashi's *chūtai* had landed back aboard *Hiryū*. March 1, 1942, had been a long, hectic day for the air groups and carriers of KdB, although not an especially dangerous one—for them. But *Modjokerto, Pecos,* and *Edsall*, to name but three of their victims, were all now entombed miles beneath the waves. One might have expected even more victims in that target-rich environment, but the ocean was large and most ships took their own courses, often aided by rain squalls and fissured cloudcover.

Perhaps less than fifty miles away, floating in rising seas only slightly calmed by tons of heavy bunker oil, were several hundred survivors of *Pecos*. More than a few of these men heard and felt the gunfire and explosions from *Edsall*'s desperate last action as she led Kidō Butai's Support Force battlewagons and cruisers northward, away from the helpless survivors of the oiler's sinking and a fuming Vice Admiral Nagumo and his carriers.[*] At least two of the men treading water were U.S. Naval Reserve officers who had traveled to Manila before the war in the SS *Harrison* with, among others, Ensign John W. Gustin, *Edsall*'s communications officer. Afterward they, too, reported hearing "heavy gunfire from the direction the *Edsall* had taken . . . later in the day."[†] At 8:52, they and other *Pecos* survivors, who by then had grown "very depressed," were the recipients of one of the Pacific war's great unsung acts of courage as the distinctive outline of a four-piper appeared in silhouette above the dark seas. It was the *Whipple*.

Having risked everything to re-enter the area, *Whipple* first sighted flares in the distance and then clusters of men in the water. One *Langley* survivor, Signalman 3rd Class Lowell Barty, recalled, "[We] were scattered out on the water as far as you could see. There was probably close to 800 men in there. You could see them as the waves would go up and

---

[*] *Edsall*'s pursuit may also have permitted *Whipple* to re-enter the area some hours later and pick up as many men as she did. Commander E. Paul Abernethy himself wrote in "The *Pecos* Died Hard": "Toward twilight, I heard what seemed to be bomb explosions in the distance," as he struggled to stay afloat in the oily and "obnoxious" seawater.

[†] This information is from a letter written in January 1979 by James Gustin, older brother of Ensign John Gustin of *Edsall*, to Rear Adm. Edwin Layton. Thirty-seven years after the fact, Jim Gustin, himself a former Asiatic Fleet officer aboard the four-piper USS *Paul Jones* (DD-230), was still attempting to grasp the convoluted mystery of *Edsall*'s last hours. The story of how he received this small piece of data is representative of the fragile, interconnected fates of the ships transiting the Indian Ocean during the NEI's last days. The two reserve officers, who were not named, were from *Langley* and had been rescued by

down." At 9:05 *Whipple* began hauling the exhausted, oil-covered, and traumatized survivors of *Pecos* from the black, pitching waves. *Whipple* took aboard some 220 men and would have rescued many more, but a submarine contact was made around 10:00. Already jittery from previous alerts, and the known proximity of Japanese carriers—which for some reason they imagined were at least one hundred to two hundred miles distant—Commander Crouch, in agreement with Commander Abernethy, decided to clear the area.

It is estimated that more than 450 men died in the sinking of *Pecos*, either killed in the bombing attacks or lost in the water. A number who perished were hard-luck survivors of *Langley, Houston,* and *Stewart.* Signalman Barty from *Langley* thought the number of casualties was even higher: "We had to get under way and leave about 600 men there in the water. And none of them was ever heard from again." He had disobeyed orders from an infuriated naval officer in the balsa life raft that he and a dozen other men were clinging to by swimming with his friend Reginald Mills to the four-piper on the horizon. The two exhausted sailors just made it. Lowell Barty was dragging himself up a cargo net on the side of *Whipple* when a panic-stricken sailor climbed over him and knocked him back into the water. Too tired to regain the nets, he wrapped a chain around himself and two sailors on the destroyer hauled him up. Barty and Mills—a gunner's mate third class on *Langley* who was later cited for bravery by Commander Abernethy—were among the last men pulled out of the oily water. Years later Barty remembered, "Mills and I made it, but none of those that was on that raft were picked up. We told the other men in the water we would come back for them, but they all perished."[19]

And where, after all was said and done, were the four carriers of Kidō Butai when the contact with *Edsall* was first made? Midway through my research, I came upon the book *Japan's War at Sea,* by David Thomas,

---

Edsall, put aboard *Pecos*, sunk a second time, picked up by *Whipple*, and taken to Australia. Then, during a stopover in New Zealand, they encountered a Goodyear Rubber family from Singapore, the Mayers, being sent to the States after many harrowing adventures, to whom they related their experiences. The Mayers family had met Jim and John Gustin in late February 1942 at Tjilatjap, Java, prior to being evacuated to Melbourne on a Dutch ship. On Easter 1978, Jim Gustin happened to speak with W. M. Mayers, in Milwaukee, Wisconsin, and heard the comments of the reserve officers for the first time. (From the Edwin Layton Papers, Naval War College Library, MS Collection 69, Box 37.)

which has a short reference to *Edsall*'s fate that includes the following: "On her way to Tjilatjap she [*Edsall*] stumbled into the mighty Nagumo Striking Force. At 1747 in a position 14 degrees 34′S 106 degrees 51′E the battleships *Hiei* and *Kirishima* and the cruisers *Tone* and *Chikuma* detached themselves from the main body and chased *Edsall*. She was never heard of again." I noted down the coordinates, and once home quickly unrolled my improvised track chart: the positions fit like a naval officer's white gloves. There at last, on my homemade map, along with the locations of *Pecos*, *Edsall*, *Modjokerto*, and the Japanese Support Force, appeared what one must assume to be Kidō Butai's position, roughly ten nautical miles south of the heavy cruisers of Sentai 8 and the two battleships of Sentai 3/1.*

It was also in Thomas' book that a reference was found stating that the ships of KdB may have been as close as thirty miles from *Pecos* when contact was made earlier in the morning. (This is in sharp contrast to Dwight Messimer's source, which states that the distance was eighty miles. However, it is possible that the ships were on parallel but slightly converging courses.) This, too, appears borne out in my rough track chart, and may be inferred from the takeoff, attack, and landing times of the VB *chūtai* from the carriers that day. Surprisingly, no more detailed records from the attacking Vals survived. Volume 26 of *Senshi Sōsho* contains several explicit schematics taken from the same carriers' air groups after the Indian Ocean raids of April 1942, which show the number and location of their bomb hits on the cruisers HMS *Dorsetshire* and HMS *Cornwall*, the carrier HMS *Hermes*, the old destroyer HMAS *Vampire*, and the corvette HMS *Hollyhock*. One would think that such records should exist for the engagements against *Pecos* and *Edsall* as well.

But the Support Force had different reasons for remembering *Edsall*. The Japanese archivists note with particular thoroughness the appallingly inaccurate and wasteful expenditure of ordnance. The figures are not flattering, and it appears that no one accepted the "alibis" and "excuses" (Edwin Layton's terms) later made by officers of the

---

* The carriers of KdB may have been cruising in a box configuration with perhaps four to five kilometers between units, and the Support Force cruisers and battleships spread out perhaps twice again as far.

Support Force—such as Japanese claims that *Edsall* was making speeds of more than thirty knots. Here are the actual numbers:

Battleship *Hiei*: 210 rounds of 14-inch/35.6cm, and 70 rounds of 6-inch/15cm
Kirishima: 87 rounds of 14-inch /35.6cm, and 62 rounds of 6-inch/15cm
Cruiser *Tone*: 497 rounds of 8-inch/20cm, and 8 rounds of 5-inch/12.7cm
Chikuma: 347 rounds of 8-inch/20cm, and 54 rounds of 5-inch/12.7cm

Many years later, contributing to the gargantuan Japanese Defense Agency history, a former *Chikuma* officer, thought by Edwin Layton to be Sasaki Masao,* wrote of this action: "These highly unsatisfactory results of gunfire . . . For two high-speed battleships and two of our newest heavy cruisers to have been able to make only one hit, and for the enemy to be finally disposed of by the assistance of dive-bombers was indeed a fiasco."[20]

The "alibis" and "excuses" alluded to—but not translated—by Edwin Layton were not known to me until a separate translation of the section in BKS (*Boeicho Bōeikenshūjo senshishitsu*, or *Senshi Sōsho* project) came into my possession some time later. They appear to have been translated in 1983 by an individual from Japan with a slightly imperfect understanding of English. But they are workmanlike and worth reproducing here nonetheless:

The following impressions of the battle was [*sic*] given by 3rd Combat Squadron [Sentai 3/1] and 8th Combat Squadron [Sentai 8]:
Comments by 3rd Combat Squadron
1. The fact that the enemy was a single destroyer and relative to the distance, it did not have to consider demonstrating its fire power. Therefore, it maintained free movement, enforcing

---

* Sasaki Masao, who helped compile Volume 26 of *Senshi Sōsho*, also worked on Volume 54, "Naval Operations in the Southwestern Area" (1972). Mr. Sasaki, who was still alive in mid-2008, says he did *not* in fact write this so-called Supplement.

evasive maneuvering and creating smoke screen (approximately every minute, it continuded [sic] "jinking" or it appeared that it kept switching course based on its judgement of our firing).

2. Firing range was approximately 28,000 or 24,000m. [Projectile] flight time was rather long (approximately over 45 seconds) and the range of firing was long so this made it easier for the enemy to conduct evasive tactics.

3. When firing commenced, *Hiye* and *Chikuma* were able to detect that the enemy was not a light cruiser and that it was a destroyer. They fired accordingly.

Kirishima and *Tone* had held suspicion as to the enemy identification, but, nevertheless, they took action as enemy to be a light cruiser (Marbel head Class [sic]).

Comments by 8th Combat Squadron

1. The movement of the enemy vessel was free and took to evasive tactics. Firing range was long and the strike rate was poor; therefore, unexpectedly, large quantity of projectile was exhausted.

Based on this experience, it has been judged that for this type of artillery engagement, the following conception is required:

(1) Close in on range and execute artillery engagement. It is judged that appropriate firing range is within 10,000m for the princpal [sic] gun used on this type ship.

(2) If the situation is difficult to wait and achieve the appropriate range to fire, firing should be conducted in a moderate way and watch the enemy situation. When firing is determined to be effective, then immediately conduct an all-out (simultaneous) firing.

2. Efforts are required to confirm the classification of enemy ship before artillery engagement is commenced.

Tone was under erroneous assumption that the enemy ship was a "Marbel head Class" ship. Therefore, it experienced considerable disadvantage in artillery engagement and in measuring.[21]

Translation difficulties aside, it is another significant small piece of the larger puzzle, and it disproves the notion that Japanese veterans have deliberately avoided all discussion of the ship's fate. And, as First Lieutenant Motegi wrote:

> When we sighted this destroyer, the people in the bridge must have thought she was a U.S. cruiser and over-estimated her. . . . I believe that our superiors wanted to get close in and let the secondary guns practice firing using her as a target. Since the firing practice was conducted at such a great range, there was not a single shot hit the *Edsall*.[22]

"Firing practice" or not, the conclusion drawn by David Thomas in his seminal *Japan's War at Sea* still rings true: "Kondo and Nagumo, their powerful forces intact, returned to Staring Bay in the Celebes: the only scar of battle borne by the warships was blistered paintwork on overheated gunbarrels."

J. J.

The waters were his winding sheet, the sea was made his tomb.
—Richard Barnfield

Far from last or least, one must admire the evasiveness of the destroyer herself, which was naturally an extension of the ship-handling skills of Lieutenant Nix and crew as they drove across the heavy swells. Dusk was coming on; perhaps they might outlast the Japanese ships, ducking in and out of the mists and squalls, chasing salvos, cloaked in their own smokescreen whenever possible. Her stout crew refused to go down without a fight.

It has been said that Joshua James Nix was a man who could really think on his feet. A standout guard as an underclassman on the Annapolis football team, and possessing the largest chest dimensions of any cadet, J. J. was nonetheless nimble footed—attributes verified by recently discovered 8mm home movies. He was an avid reader of mysteries; the 1930 Lucky Bag, the Naval Academy yearbook, noted that "for J. J. [mysteries] meant 'literature.'" Little could he have foreseen the mystery that he, his crew, and his ship would become.

Instances of any vessel, regardless of type, eluding the enemy under similarly lethal circumstances for such a period of time are quite rare. That two fast battleships, two spanking-new heavy cruisers, and four aircraft carriers should have been so frustrated by *Edsall* ought to have inspired some more thoughtful coverage in U.S. histories of the naval war in the Pacific. But the U.S. Navy's initial response to IJN claims of the little destroyer evading Japanese battleships and cruisers for two hours seems to have been one of skepticism instead of pride in its men.

Viewing the event from another perspective, and indulging in a bit of simplistic number mongering as well: divided by the eighty-nine minutes that the Japanese records state *Edsall* was actually under fire, those 1,335 projectiles work out to a stunning average of fifteen shells per minute landing around the ancient destroyer.* What could the commanders of the Combined Fleet make of such gunnery? By no alchemy can such abysmal numbers be transmuted into propaganda gold. But if the figures themselves wouldn't lie, human beings might, and images could easily be made to—or at least be made convincing enough for the gullible and the half-educated.

In the end, that cruel week was the death knell for the U.S. Asiatic Fleet. The flagship USS *Houston*, the tender *Langley*, the destroyers *Pope*, *Pillsbury*, and *Edsall*, the oiler *Pecos*, and the China Station gunboat *Asheville* were all sunk in that grim period from Friday through Wednesday. And when the antiquated *Asheville* was overtaken, at her best twelve-knot speed, crushed by cruisers and destroyers of Vice Adm. Kondō Nobutake, only a single bewildered second class fireman, Fred Louis Brown, survived, the lone Ishmael-like witness to his old ship's destruction. (He perished, however, in a Japanese POW camp at Makassar late in the war, in March 1945).

Similarly, but even more completely, USS *Pillsbury* (DD-227) was lost, having steamed directly into Kondō's cruiser force on a squall-swept night. In another harsh irony, *Pillsbury* was following the guideline coordinates for Allied ships sent by Rear Admiral Glassford in his "scatter" transmission; when attacked, she appears to have been right where she had been told to be. Glassford's message said for ships to assemble

---

* I recognize, of course, that the firing against *Edsall* was irregular and at times the number of shells falling around her might have been greater, and at other times far less. With so much shelling, spotting would have been maddening, exacerbating an already inherently pernicious gunnery problem.

at "15 deg S, 113 deg E," and the records of the Japanese cruisers give the coordinates 15 degrees 38 minutes S, 113 degrees 13 minutes E for the destroyer's ambush. She was smothered in concentrated 8-inch gunfire at close range, 170 shells at 5,200 meters (5,700 yards), by *Atago* (F) and *Takao*. The four-piper—also misidentified, as was *Edsall*, as a "*Marblehead*-type cruiser"[23]—seems to have suffered catastrophic damage; she sank a mere seven minutes after firing was commenced. *Pillsbury* had been able to return fire from her aft batteries, "but the shells hit nowhere near [us]."[24] Not one soul was known to have been rescued. Even the men who sank her were literally and figuratively "in the dark." During postwar interrogations of Japanese 2nd Fleet staff personnel, this action was referred to in passing as an attack on "a Dutch destroyer" and the sinking of "a Dutch destroyer . . . thought to be the American cruiser *Marblehead* at the time."[25]

The Imperial Navy's Striking Force, at sea so far from even their advanced bases—in this case, Staring Bay, south of Kendari, in the Celebes—wanted little to do with prisoners of war. The Striking Force appears to have occasionally fished a few men from the water to determine a sunken vessel's identity, but beyond that, it had no desire to save any of their victims. (And, without question, there could be no thought of the real facts of the action off "*Ku-ri-sa-ma-su-shima*" reaching the public.) It was also known that units of Kidō Butai's carrier forces were conducting training operations at Staring Bay during this period. Yet First Lieutenant Motegi, in response to a question I asked him concerning the *Edsall* action, remarked:

> As we were busily engaged in getting ready for the subsequent major operations, no crewmembers talked much about the battle that had already been over, and carried out their respective duties. The fleet headquarters did not seem to have had an idea of rescuing the survivors of the sinking ship. We hurried straight on to the subsequent battlefield.[26]

That "subsequent battlefield" would remain the waters south of Java for several days before a return to Staring Bay on March 11. The planes of Kidō Butai were flown off several hours prior to the ships' arrival. The same aircrews that sank *Edsall* were therefore present at the newly won airfield when the survivors of the old destroyer were brought in to Kendari aboard *Chikuma*. In the meantime, salvage operations continued in northern Staring Bay on the submarine *I-5*, stranded on a coral reef, the milky water slapping against her black hull; she would not be ready for combat operations again until after the third week in March.

In early March 1942, Japanese "victory fever" was mounting daily. With ABDA's opposition nothing more than token resistance after the Battle of the Java Sea, a lack of concern for the welfare of Occidentals who had surrendered much too readily in the eyes of the conquerors is hardly surprising. Capitulation and survival after the fact weren't qualities that the "noble Bushido code" extolled anyway, and "compassion" was too often meted out with a *katana* blade.

The Strange Ride of Lieutenant "Fergie" Ferguson

In those last disordered days of the Java campaign, Rear Adm. William R. Purnell, former chief of staff to Admiral Hart, having already reached Australia, had enough presence of mind to insist on another attempt to locate the large number of men who had survived the *Pecos* sinking. As surviving Allied ships began dribbling into the ports of western Australia, Purnell contacted Lt. Cmdr. J. V. Peterson of Patrol Wing 10 in Exmouth Gulf on Wednesday, March 3, and expressed his desire for some means of finding the men. He was likewise heedful of the uncertainty that many of the Allied ships then fleeing the East Indies would have been facing; they were instructed to head for Exmouth Gulf, but already this location was thought to be too close to the Japanese. Purnell and Glassford knew that the ships would have to be sent south. But Purnell could not let the men who had been aboard *Pecos* perish without some final effort at finding them. He told Peterson to do whatever he could. This led to a little known event, for Peterson's battered contingent of PBYs was far too war-weary for such a dangerous assignment, but he had one additional unit that could make the flight into the perilous area south of Java where the old oiler had battled to the last.

As bad luck would have it, an unarmed but otherwise serviceable Consolidated XPB2Y-1 Coronado flying boat had just arrived at 1800 hours that evening from Perth on its way north on a resupply flight. The fall of Java now made the original mission pointless, so Peterson decided to send the huge four-engined Coronado, which had better range than his PBYs anyway, across the Indian Ocean in search of survivors. The plane was soon secured to a buoy, and the bowser crew from USS *Childs* went to work refueling it.

Lieutenant John A. "Fergie" Ferguson and his men were more than a little shocked by their orders to fly the big Coronado into hostile airspace. As a transport plane, the XPB2Y-1's gun stations had been left plated over to save weight. Anything but a combat-tested crew, they were dumbfounded when told of the likelihood of encountering enemy fighters: "But surely the Japanese wouldn't fire on an unarmed plane?"[27] One wonders whether the Australian and Dutch commercial airliners that strayed into Kidō Butai's air patrols over the Indian Ocean were asking themselves the same question when the Zeros' aerial cannon shells began tearing them apart.

At 1:18 a.m. on March 4, Fergie Ferguson and his young crew took off for *Pecos'* last known position. They wanted to arrive just after daybreak, scout the area, and if need be, scoop up any survivors while hopefully eluding the Japanese before returning to Exmouth Gulf. At about 7:00 they reached the last coordinates given by *Pecos*. They saw no men in the water, but they did spot several Japanese cruisers and destroyers escorting a carrier just as her morning combat air patrol (CAP) was taking off. The Coronado must have been a fat and tempting target because the screening vessels of Kidō Butai soon opened up with their AA batteries. Lieutenant Ferguson knew the better part of valor and turned the big flying boat east to Exmouth, the crew no doubt as relieved and disappointed as Commander Peterson himself. But he and his men had done what they could do, and there was simply no realistic alternative. And although it will never be known with absolute certainty, by then—Wednesday afternoon—the men from *Pecos* (and *Edsall*) would have been in the oil-covered water for nearly seventy-two hours: Surely most had died by that time. Commander Abernethy later wrote that he didn't think the men would have survived the Indian Ocean's harsh conditions (enervating days and chilly nights) for much more than twenty-four hours. No one appears to have thought about any potential survivors from *Edsall*, but at that point the navy knew nothing of her whereabouts or fate.

The XPB2Y-1 returned to Exmouth Gulf at 5:00 p.m., and was again promptly refueled. Under orders from COMSOWESPAC Glassford, who had escaped to Perth, Combat Patrol Wing (ComPatWing)

10 and staff were to move south to that city for the time being to resume command of Patrol Wing 10. At 10:00 p.m., the Coronado lifted off and headed south with Commander Peterson and twenty-three other men, along with the plane's crew. The next day, March 5, Peterson met briefly with Cmdr. E. Paul Abernethy of *Pecos* and Cmdr. Robert P. McConnell of *Langley*, who had arrived at Fremantle on *Whipple* about seven o'clock the previous evening, and told them of his flight. According to Abernethy, "The young lieutenant said he arrived just at dawn and clearly saw the Japanese carrier task force headed into the wind, flying off the morning patrol. As his was one of the last three PBYs [*sic*] operable in that area, he turned and beat a hasty retreat back to [Exmouth Gulf]."[28]

On that anticlimactic note, the "*Pecos* tragedy," as Abernethy called it, ended. There remained only the sufferings of family and loved ones. Their pain, unassuaged by official apathy and bureaucratic indifference, would persist for decades.

Chapter Six

What Numbers Cannot Tell Us

Mathematics has the altogether false reputation of furnishing infallible inferences [Schlüsse]. Its whole certainty is nothing more than identity.[1]
—Goethe

Clearly, men *were* picked up from *Edsall*. This was not a case of the entire crew perishing outright, as many later histories have claimed and as some U.S. records continue to claim even to this day. Records from heavy cruiser *Chikuma* (Capt. Komura Keizo) revealed that "some" or "a few" (the Japanese word, as noted by Edwin Layton in his translation, was *jakkan*) survivors of the battle were rescued and interrogated aboard this ship, "on orders"—although no mention is made of whose orders they were acting on. Because this particular information appeared only in the anonymous Supplement/Annex to Volume 26 of *Senshi Sōsho*, an awareness of Japanese sensitivity to possible war-crimes allegations can be inferred.* However, it was an act of courage to record these details.

---

* One of the foremost American experts in Imperial military history, Professor Alvin D. Coox, of San Diego State University, and a former participant in the U.S. Eighth Army's Japanese Research Division during the postwar period, has spent a lifetime cultivating relationships with Japanese veterans. Coox notes in his book *The Unfought War: Japan 1941–1942* the survival of secret, classified, and rare reports that were simply "appropriated" by former officers at war's end. Although he restates the old saw about the skies over Japan being "blackened" by burning documents in 1945, he also paradoxically claims that large numbers of such confiscated papers probably still exist, and might be elicited from their owners with the correct mixture of patience and respect. Ruth Benedict's *The Chrysanthemum and the Sword* offers as good advice as any about the subtleties and intricacies of these interpersonal dealings with the Japanese that Westerners have often failed to apprehend.

The name associated with this rare information, as recorded by Edwin Layton, was Sasaki Masao, who was said to have been an assistant gunnery officer on the cruiser *Chikuma.*

I was naturally inclined to believe that Sasaki Masao himself must have helped in the interrogations of these survivors. After a good deal of time, effort, and research, an interview with the elderly Mr. Sasaki—the first and only ever conducted—was arranged. My gut instinct was thus confirmed. According to remarks in the so-called Supplement and his answers to my questionnaire, these survivors were questioned on *Chikuma,* telling their captors that their ship was the old U.S. destroyer *Edsall*—the name is written in *katakana* on the IJN track chart as "*E-do-soo-ru,*" which suggests that perhaps the Japanese heard the name as "Edison"—and they related the following about their evasive maneuvers to frustrate the Japanese gunners:

1. Course was changed when the Japanese force was seen to fire
2. Large changes of course were made, including some 360-degree circles*
3. Speed changes were also made—from full speed ahead to stop
4. Smoke screens were laid at the same time that an evasive maneuver was begun

Mr. Sasaki remembered asking these men "about the methods of evasive maneuvers they employed." Their responses led him to realize "that their maneuvers involved much greater and more abrupt changes in course and/or speed than the changes the IJN had used in gunfire training." He concluded, "In other words, their evasive maneuvers were far beyond the normal procedure of the IJN."

Japanese reviews of the action involving *Edsall* later freely admitted that fire was opened at much too great a distance; the time of flight for projectiles was initially "45 seconds and upwards," which they perceived gave the enemy adequate time to alter course. After this are "opinions" from the Yokosuka Gunnery School addressing the gunfire problems as related in the previous chapter.

* It is conceivable that *Edsall*'s "counterattack" against *Chikuma* was such an evasive circling turn. The track chart provided by the Imperial Navy indicates that *Edsall* probably traveled not much more than twenty-five nautical miles in her engagement of some ninety minutes, which gives an average speed of roughly fifteen knots—hardly the "over thirty knots" stated in *Senshi Sōsho.*

Edwin Layton did not deal with these remarks. He did observe that no reference to *Edsall* by name, or to rescued survivors or interrogations, could be found in the primary text of Volume 26 of *Senshi Sōsho*. But why was no mention made of these? There were nearly 1,000 men each aboard *Tone* and *Chikuma*, and another 2,600 or more aboard the two battleships, and several hundred involved in the air strikes during the long, clumsy engagement. To believe that most of these men did not discuss the action or compare notes and experiences seems, at best, naïve. And *Edsall* was not the only victim of the Support Force that day.

For some reason, and despite Edwin Layton's efforts, the April 1980 clarification in *Shipmate* did not grasp the connection between *Chikuma* and the bodies discovered after the war near Kendari on the island of Celebes. This is perplexing but not altogether unprecedented. Before now, little exact information has ever been disclosed publicly regarding the precise details of these recovered remains.

However, we do know that the heavy cruiser operated as part of Kidō Butai for several more days after the action against *Edsall*; her floatplanes took part in the March 5 attacks on Tjilatjap. On March 7, elements of Vice Admiral Kondō's Main Body bombarded Christmas Island before turning their bows eastward again for the return journey to Celebes. On March 11, 1942, *Chikuma* and her sister ship *Tone* were back at Staring Bay, on the southeastern coast of the spider-shaped island, with the other Task Force vessels, where they replenished stores and munitions for the upcoming Indian Ocean raid (Operation "C"). At this time men from *Edsall* must have been disembarked and taken to a compound at or near Kendari.

Mr. Sasaki, in reply to my questions, noted, "I remember the survivors were transferred to the Naval garrison there after we made a port of call at Staring Bay." (He had not recalled the name of this bay until I supplied it to him through my contact in Japan.) The remainder of his answer to my question, and his amplifications concerning whose orders were responsible, are worth including here:

> They were husky guys, and it would cause a lot of trouble if they rampage[d] around aboard our ship. There was no adequate place to detain them. A guard had to be placed where they were detained. In addition, we were on our way to engage in the Indian Ocean Operation. As *Tone* was the flagship of Sen-

tai 8, *Chikuma* could not leave them at Kendari on her own [judgment]. The Sentai 8 Headquarters aboard *Tone* and the Garrison Headquarters in Kendari might have contacted [each other] and decided to leave them at Kendari, and notified *Chikuma* of their decision accordingly.*

Reading between the lines of this somewhat oblique final sentence, whose indirectness is by no means unusual (or representative of evasion) in Japanese, it seems probable that the decision ordaining the ultimate fate of *Edsall*'s small number of survivors came from Vice Adm. Abe Hiroaki, commander of Sentai 8. This officer survived the Pacific war but died a few years after it ended, and to my knowledge no evidence has ever surfaced to show that he was suspected of war crimes. It would be fruitless to speculate about this until any concrete, specific evidence to the contrary emerges.

Kendari: Captured by Death

As noted, Kendari had fallen easily to the Sasebo Combined Special Naval Landing Force on January 24, 1942, under the command of Capt. Mori Kunizo.† A token force of approximately four hundred KNIL (Koninklijk Nederlands-Indisch Leger: the Royal Netherlands Indies Army troops) under Capt. F. B. van Straalen was defeated, with the majority surrendering early in the morning. Two Japanese soldiers were wounded in taking the airdrome, but, as indicated in the Official War History, it was operational by the next day. Quoting *Senshi Sōsho*:

There was not much Allied resistance on the ground. Captain Mori, Kunizo, Commander of the landing operation, sent a message at 0305 hrs on the 25th [Jan.] "At 1700 on the 24th we occupied the airfield." The conditions of the base were very

* The questionnaire/interview with Sasaki Masao was conducted at his home in Hayama, Japan, by Kan Sugahara, who also translated the information.

† The Sasebo Combined Special Naval Landing Force (SNLF, or *Rengo Tokubetsu Kaigun Rikusentai*) consisted of Sasebo 1st SNLF, commanded by Lt. Cmdr. Shiga Masanari, and Sasebo 2nd SNLF, under Lt. Cmdr. Hashimoto Uroku. These detachments were then sent on to offensive operations against Ambon and Makassar, respectively, by the end of February 1942.

good. The Captain sent another report, "The base can accommodate 30 fighters immediately. . . . I don't see any problems with using this airstrip for mid-range air raid[s].[2]

When seized by the Sasebo Combined Special Naval Landing Force, Kendari boasted one of the finest airfields in the NEI. Although initially used by the 21st *Kōkūsentai* (Air Flotilla), the airfield was headquarters to the 23rd *Kōkūsentai* for most of 1942 and after.* Southwest of the town of Kendari, twenty kilometers distant, the field was some two kilometers from the village of Amoito on the edge of the Boroboro mountains.† A small airport had first been constructed near Amoito in the late 1930s by the Dutch, which made it a strong attraction for the invading Japanese.[3] By the time the war broke out, the airfield and its three landing strips had been built up significantly and housed stockpiles of high-octane aviation fuel and bombs. Construction was under way on barracks to house up to five hundred men. In many Allied texts and maps, including Dutch sources, this field at Amoito was referred to as "Kendari II."[4] It was said to be an "excellent airfield with poor defenses" ("*Uitstekend vliegveld met zwakke verdegiging*") by the Dutch themselves, which—in view of later events—was an accurate statement.[5]

The remoteness of this outpost, its poor communications, and the small number of troops allocated to its defense combined to make the enemy's task much less difficult than it might have been. There was a clear, and lamentable, failure of leadership by the Dutch commanders, Captains Anthonio and Van Straalen, on the scene. Captain

---

* This was not necessarily on March 11–12, 1942, the date on which *Chikuma* and other Support Force vessels returned to Staring Bay from their operations south of Java. There was still a good deal of flux among IJN air forces, with elements of the 23rd Kōkūsentai utilizing Kendari's airfield when it was not being used by the 21st Kōkūsentai, while other units leapfrogged ahead to Koepang, Timor, or were dispersed to different bases at Ambon, Makassar, and Bali. According to Capt. Shibata Bunzo, senior staff officer of the 21st Kōku, at that time the 23rd Kōku "did not operate east of the Celebes; main bases were at Tarakan, Balikpapan, and Bandjermasin." It would have been during this period of intense and somewhat confused activity that the survivors—whatever the actual count—from *Edsall* would have reached Kendari.

† Amoito is also referred to as "Amoitou" in other documents. Mondonga is spelled "Mandongan" in Nortier.

Van Straalen in particular impressed all who served with him as inde-
cisive, confused, and given to passive complaints rather than exercis-
ing a proactive role. Another KNIL officer serving there, sublieutenant
Schalen, informed the captain, "It is urgently necessary that you need
to assert leadership in order to avoid anyone erecting fortifications or
bunkers willy-nilly. It is logical that there should be one commander,
not four or five. This is true for the present situation and whatever may
happen after an invasion."[6]

These remarks seem to have produced little effect, because Captain
Van Straalen relocated his immediate command, consisting of roughly
twenty fifteen-man brigades, away from the air base to a village called
Konda (Komda) to the east, a position he referred to as "the reserve."
Later, immediately prior to the invasion, he moved once again, this time
to native housing along the main road to Kendari itself. Dutch historian
Nortier wrote, "His tactical reason for this move was a riddle to everyone. The general consensus was that, by being close to the road, it was
an excellent place to flee."[7]

The Japanese paratroop operations at Palembang, Sumatra, and to
the north at Menado, had unnerved the Dutch and the local population as well. Reports about Japanese brutality had already filtered in,
and some native and KNIL infantry soldiers at Kendari had deserted
their posts on January 13 and 14 after an insignificant aerial attack.
Two brigades of KNIL soldiers were further squandered in a search for
the deserters. When the KNIL brigades made contact with the derelict
troops, a firefight ensued in which two men were fatally wounded. At
the time of the invasion these brigades were still up country and in no
position to aid with the defense of Kendari or Kendari II. (They wound
up in the village of Motaha, some twenty-five kilometers to the west of
the airfield.)

It is conceivable that anti-Dutch propaganda had already begun to
gain a foothold. Without question, the local population lacked faith in
their Dutch overseers: "Help from the natives was virtually nonexistent.
Contributing factors may have been fear of the Japanese, but the Dutch
forces also did not leave a favorable impression. From a distance the
military was taunted with remarks such as, 'The military does not know
what to do. . . . The marines have no courage.' "[8]

By the third week in January, the Dutch, led by Captains Van Straalen and Anthonio, had but three units in place to fight the Japanese: 105 men (seven brigades) in the town of Kendari itself, under Captain Anthonio; another 105 men under Van Straalen at the air base (Kendari II); and 90 more men (six brigades) under the command of 2nd Lt. T. E. Aronds between the airfield and the seven-kilometer mark on the road from Kendari to the airfield. The latter were to be held in reserve and also used to act if the enemy happened to come ashore near Sampara, which is precisely what they did. However, the Dutch were caught by surprise, and their poorly conceived defensive plans were immediately overwhelmed by the sudden appearance of the Japanese.

No concerted attempts were made by the Dutch to combat the CSNLF, which outnumbered the Dutch units by some five to one, as it moved southwest from its landing zone. Had the end results not been so heartrending, one might almost smile to describe the vaudevillian maneuvers of the KNIL on January 24. But by late afternoon the town and airfield were in enemy hands, and they would remain there for the next three and a half years.[9] Within a couple of days the Japanese were operating twenty-five fighters and twenty-seven bombers out of Kendari II.

At the field itself the Japanese would have been able to examine the remains of Lt. J. L. "Duke" DuFrane's B-17E (41–2459), which had been forced to land at Kendari II after an attack in mid-January against Japanese shipping in the Philippines. The battered USAAF bomber was further damaged by Japanese strafing and became completely disabled. DuFrane and crew escaped and were later evacuated to Java, but the ruined B-17E was still at the field when the Japanese forces took it a month later.

Murders by the Japanese began immediately, as they had in Menado. On the day of the invasion, two KNIL sergeants who were leading a group of soldiers and citizens out of Kendari were captured and beheaded.[10] Dutch-Indonesian captives also gave eyewitness accounts after the war of POWs murdered by decapitation in the vicinity of the airfield. There were killings as well near a village called Diji, close to Mondonga, where the Imperial Navy's 29th Aerial Torpedo Unit was later based. Whether or not this implies that JNAF personnel were involved in these killings is all but impossible to say. There were documented atrocity cases in the war's final year that definitely record naval air base personnel asking that POWs be sent to them from Kendari for execution.[11]

At the time of the *Edsall* engagement, though, Special Naval Landing Force (SNLF) personnel seem to have been in the Kendari area as well. These SNLF, or *Tokubetsu Rikusentai*, had been at the forefront of the fighting to seize critical East Indies oil fields, port facilities, and airfields in the First Stage operations. They were also among the most hardened and ruthless soldiers in the Imperial military and would be widely implicated in numerous war crimes, including several occurring in the NEI early in the conflict. The Australian National Archives houses documents that list copious allegations against various SNLF units, many of them involving brutality perpetrated by SNLF troops against Allied wounded, unarmed civilians, members of the clergy, and women and children, as well as POWs.*

Some Dutch and KNIL troops fled into the jungles around Kendari, where a halfhearted guerrilla resistance was attempted; within another few weeks almost all of these stragglers had given up or been captured. A few eluded the Japanese and made their way to Palopo (Captain Van Straalen) and Enrekang (Captain Anthonio); one group led by a Sergeant Major Bruijnius is said to have escaped to Timor.[12] By then the Japanese had brought in the First Construction Party, under a civilian named Ohmizo Toyojiro, to build additional facilities and housing at the air base, which was situated in the fork of two small rivers.† The construction party had been delayed in mid-January, which led to a brief postponement of the operation.[13] At the end of March, the Japanese rounded up local Dutch women and children and transported them aboard ships to the *Goa weg* women's internment camp near Makassar, before settling them eventually at Kampili.

---

* The infamous Ambon executions of Australian and Dutch prisoners after that port fell (at about the same time as Kendari) were a notable, if appalling, example. See "Summary of Laha Massacres of Australian POWs in Ambon 6–20 February 1942." [NAA A 705/15 Item 166/43/989]. There were also SNLF atrocities in Borneo, Menado (Celebes), and New Guinea.

† This unit had not been part of the assault echelon. In the early stages of the Pacific war, ten Navy Construction Parties (*Kaigun Setsuei Han*) were formed. The First through Sixth and the Ninth served in the NEI. Beginning with the Eleventh, they were called Navy Construction Units (*Kaigun Setsuei Tai*). Typically these organizations were mostly civilians employed by the IJN. The commander was a navy technician; he had three technical assistants, a secretary, some forty working employees, and as many as three thousand laborers. If needed, a doctor, a paymaster, and up to a dozen IJN sailors were also attached. Thanks to Akira Takizawa ("Taki") from Japan for these details.

The Dutch on Java began surrendering on Sunday afternoon, March 8, and the formal declaration took place the next day.* Japanese military forces in the East Indies inaugurated a new command structure at once. The Imperial Navy had been granted administrative control of much of Borneo, all of Celebes and the Moluccas, as well as parts of the Lesser Sunda islands. The forces stationed in the southeastern Celebes were under the command of the Southwest Area Fleet (formerly 3rd Fleet), headquartered at Surabaja, with Vice Adm. Takahashi Ibō as commander, and Rear Adm. Nakamura Toshihisa as his chief of staff.[†]

On about March 10, Captain Mori became the commanding officer of the 23rd Special Naval Base Force, with headquarters in Makassar. In May, he was promoted to rear admiral. A division of *Otori*-class torpedo boats operated out of the port, ushering various merchant ships across the Java Sea, which was still a fertile hunting ground for Allied submarines. Rear Admiral Mori's old troops of the Sasebo 2nd SNLF, then converted to the 3rd Guard Unit, once more came under his command at Makassar that spring. On May 29, Mori also insituted new rules to prisoners and internees for the proper etiquette in greeting their Japanese captors. Severe corporal punishment was promised for all who failed to heed these rules.

Later Mori and his staff "with 6 cars" were briefly seen inspecting Makassar's POW camp on July 10, 1942, "and were gone in a minute," according to a Dutch prisoner.[14] This attentiveness appears to have been a consistent trait in Admiral Mori,whose tour of duty reads like a southwest Pacific map of Hell. One infernal posting follows another. After commanding the 7th Auxiliary Base Force at Lae on New Guinea in 1943, he would wind up as the ranking Imperial Navy officer on the little island of Chichi Jima in the Bonins. He reached this post in February 1944 to command the Special Naval Base headquarters located there.

During Mori's tenure, several U.S. naval aviators were captured, tortured, and murdered, and their bodies were cannibalized by various

---

* As noted, though, sporadic anti-Japanese guerrilla activity on rugged, remote Celebes lasted for some months, primarily some 130 kilometers northwest of Kendari in the Tawanga-Asenoea-Sanggona triangle of *kampongs*. DeJong states that Captain Anthonio's group went to Ambakari, which is also nearby.

† At this time, Vice Admiral Takahashi held commander in chief positions concurrently for the Southwest Area Fleet and the Southern Expeditionary Fleet in addition to the formal title of "Governor-General."

members of the Imperial Japanese Army and Navy.* Mori, who was fed
their viscera but claimed to have been unaware of just what type of meat
he was eating—even though he had remarked to his peers upon the
medicinal properties of human liver, having learned of such delicacies
while serving in China—subsequently defended himself by hazily stating that his responsibilities were purely defensive, and his naval personnel would never have conducted themselves in such a barbaric manner.

The U.S. court at his trial on Guam in the late summer of 1946 spared
Mori, described as "a somber individual [who] enjoyed the beauty of life
more than the bloodshed of war" and "wrote poetry and looked upon
the world as a vast wonder of creation." This poetic, if peculiar, officer
(artistic sensibilities notwithstanding) was found guilty and sentenced
to life imprisonment at Sugamo Prison.[15] Although mention has been
made of this unseemly fate, some may find Mori's incarceration all the
more ironic, for the name of the little officer with the large head and
pointed face, coincidentally, means "to die" in Latin.

But if Mori breathed a sigh of relief when so sentenced, he had
relaxed too soon. Fate was not done with him yet. On April 22, 1949,
Vice Admiral Mori—the officer Okada Fumihide later described as "an
extremely charitable person" who treated his prisoners of war "with
kindness"—was hanged at Makassar by the Dutch for war crimes committed under his command early in the war.

Across the Gulf of Bone, along Celebes' southeastern tentacle, a
cluster of naval units was situated in and around Kendari in early 1942.
In the complex (some Westerners would argue incomprehensible)
arrangements of the Japanese military, these various units were subordi-
nated to several different higher naval commands. The 23rd Air Flotilla
(*Kōkūsentai*) was subordinate to the regional 11th Air Fleet in Manila.

Similarly, naval installation departments, aeronautical arsenals, and
naval munitions departments had regional headquarters in Surabaja,
Java, with subsidiary branches in Kendari. All of these came under the
control of the Second Southern Expeditionary Fleet, based in Surabaja,
which in turn was part of the Southwest Area Fleet, with headquarters in Manila. The 11th Air Fleet, and later the 1st Air Fleet, based

* One U.S. Navy "flyboy" who had a narrow escape from the madmen at Chichi Jima was
a future president, Lt. j.g. George Bush, U.S. Naval Reserve, whose TBM *Avenger* flying
from USS *San Jacinto* (CVL-30) was shot down in a glide bombing attack on September
2, 1944. Lieutenant Bush was rescued by the submarine USS *Finback* (SS-230) and spared
the fate of other Allied POWs at Chichi Jima.

in Luzon at Manila, also held jurisdiction over the 23rd Air Flotilla in Kendari, as it did for the 29th Torpedo Adjusting Unit, based in the small village of Mondonga.

The 23rd Special Naval Base Force, commanded by Rear Admiral Mori at Makassar, would have also controlled the so-called 23rd Special Base Force Dispatch Unit at Kendari, and the two anti-aircraft units defending the airfield at Amoito. By 1944 these were the 53rd Air Defense Unit, with its medium AA (75mm) guns, and the 103rd Air Defense Unit, armed with heavy machine guns. Operational and administrative duties were not clearly defined, and the chain of command was so convoluted that determining individual responsibility was difficult at best.[16]

Although it never became a major target for the Allies, Kendari was quickly known to be a "principal enemy feeder base in the eastern part of the NEI." After insubstantial early attacks in January and February, Kendari was first bombed by B-17 Flying Fortresses of the Fifth Air Force on June 30, 1942. Within a week rumors had spread to the civilian internment camp at Makassar of this and other attacks, with casualties reported to be "160 dead, 216 wounded."[17] Such attacks would be sporadic throughout 1943, but by the next year B-24 Liberators and B-25 Mitchell bombers would begin to attack the Kendari area more often. There were also frequent missions flown in this region by PBY Black Cats and P-38 Lightning fighters as the Allies swept clean the skies over the NEI and submarines dominated the sea-lanes below. By August 1944 the 23rd Air Flotilla had been reduced to a maintenance and air defense unit with no planes.[18]

Such successes, however, came with a mortal price. Any Allied fliers, or any Allied personnel in general, who were captured and unlucky enough to end up in Kendari would later meet an unequivocal and gruesome fate as the war turned against Japan.*

---

* One notable exception to this was the 380th Bombardment Group's B-24 "Fyrtle Myrtle," shot down in a raid against Pomalaa's nickel mines by Zeros on October 26, 1943. Six to eight of her crew survived; apparently two were taken to Kendari, but in the end all were shipped to Japan, where they survived the war. Diary entries by Dutch internees at Makassar record several of these men being brought there for a brief period in mid-November 1943. A postwar investigator later found a drawing of the B-24 Fyrtle Myrtle with her name written below, and a crewman's name, "T/SGT O. Sleighter," scratched into the wall of a *Tokkei Tai* holding cell in Kendari. Howard Sleighter was the radio operator for Fyrtle Myrtle.

Avenger's Tragedy

As for those *Edsall* men deposited in Kendari in early March 1942, the story again seemed to reach an impasse. When I started my research on *Edsall*, I didn't know precisely when its men were killed and I didn't know why. Official silence and outright deceit—by the United States as well as Japan—have had much to do with this. All I was left with often amounted to speculation derived from extrapolated, circumstantial evidence.

The voyage across the seas below Java saw dozens of Allied vessels of every description and size intercepted and destroyed by Kondō's and Nagumo's forces. And unlike their counterparts to the north in the Java Sea, these Japanese task groups took few prisoners, preferring instead to abandon their victims to the merciless Indian Ocean.

Although the bulk of the crews of USS *Pope*, HMS *Exeter*, HMS *Encounter*, and USS *Perch*, plus a large number from the Dutch flagship *DeRuyter* and a handful from the old cruiser *Java*, were rescued after being sunk in the Java Sea battles, the warships under Vice Admirals Kondō and Nagumo were, of necessity, less magnanimous.* Although some ships with their entire crews were seized, hundreds of victims were left to perish, and those few Westerners who were plucked from the sea had no assurances that they would be allowed to survive.†

As elsewhere in the newly won territories, the Japanese in the East Indies had given little if any serious consideration to the matter of prisoners of war. Rescued Americans, British, Dutch, Australians, Chinese, Malays, and Eurasians alike found themselves held captive by an enemy with a deserved reputation for cruelty. Still, there were rare examples of uncommon decency, such as that experienced by Sam Falle of *Encounter*, but any benevolence shown at sea by the Imperial Navy early in the war was not the general rule once prisoners reached land.

Did the Japanese imagine that, as U.S. naval personnel, the *Edsall* crewmembers were more highly trained and of greater value to the war

---

* The IJN destroyers *Inazuma* (under the command of Lt. Cmdr. Hajime Takeuchi) and *Ikazuchi* (Lt. Cmdr. Kudo Shunsaku) deserve particular credit; the former picked up more than five hundred men from *Exeter* and *Pope*, and the latter picked up several hundred more from *Exeter* and her escort, HMS *Encounter*.

† The Dutch merchant vessels *Bintoehan, Sigli, Duymaer van Twist,* and *Tjisaroea* were captured between March 1 and March 4 by the Imperial Navy, and their personnel were made prisoners of war.

effort, and as such a greater potential threat to be liquidated? Or did the Japanese fear possible embarrassment if they were to release surviving *Edsall* crewmembers into the general POW population? The men from old "*E-do-soo-ru*" had led four of the Imperial armada's newest and most powerful surface vessels on a messy chase before being halted by air strikes from the carriers of Vice Admiral Nagumo. If permitted to live, they might well have shared this unflattering information with fellow POWs. Many captives and civilians elsewhere were murdered for less substantial reasons. Ample evidence exists showing Japanese hypersensitivity to any contact between POWs with information unfavorable to the Imperial war effort—or perceived war effort—and with other prisoners or locals who were being sequestered, or kept in the dark.*

It is also undeniable that the navy's secret police force, the *Kaigun Tokubetsu Keisatsu Tai*, or *Tokkei Tai*, was deeply hated and feared by local populations under Japanese rule. A "confidential" U.S. Navy translation released after the war documented excerpts from a training publication issued by Imperial Japanese Navy HQ Second Southern Expeditionary Fleet describing the establishment and role of the Tokkei Tai. It asserts that the force was "established on 18 July 1942 with the appointment of Naval Judicial Police Officers by the Navy Ministry."[19] This date coincides with the arrival in Makassar of the chief regional civil administrator, *Sokan* (governor) Okada Fumihide, who reached the port via the *Kamakura Maru* on July 7, 1942.

Okada's memoirs state that he had been delayed by the military's concerns over shipping to the Southern Region (Nam'po) in the aftermath of the Doolittle Raid in April, the sinking of the *Taiyo Maru* in May, and the defeat of Nagumo's Kidō Butai at Midway in June. It appears that Japanese worries about their security arrangements were intensified at this time, which is understandable; hence the establishment of the Special Naval Police Force.

One study notes that "Tokkei personnel in Western Borneo had previously served with the Naval Base Force in Shanghai, where they had arrested many communist sympathizers, and readily accepted the

---

* Later in the war these very reasons were determined to be instrumental in the deaths of the nine PBY crewmembers; they could have been sent to Makassar—and were in fact told by their captors that they would be—but in truth the Japanese were not about to allow these POWs, with their late-1944 knowledge of the war, to be placed among hundreds of POWs with early-1942 perspectives on the conflict.

idea that the Chinese in peaceful Pontianak were involved in hostile activities."[20] In Borneo, too, the Tokkei uncovered more Communist plots and dealt with them as they had in China: They massacred hundreds. In other words, they brought their paranoias, bigotry, and reactionary methods with them from China to remote Borneo and, finding themselves again in a culture with a large Chinese component, allowed their old fears to run rampant in a new setting. Having learned nothing in China, the Tokkei were able to import complacency and violence once more, with similarly negative results.

The Tokkei Tai was also involved in establishing brothels in the East Indies areas under naval control and keeping them supplied with females. This was usually effected under coercive tactics, and local families with sisters or daughters thus forced into prostitution could be severely mistreated if any attempts were made to escape the brothels.* This, too, shows the baleful impact of the Chinese Incident on Japanese behavior in the Nam'po.

There is ample evidence to suggest the Tokkei Tai at Kendari during the war were just as harsh. Eyewitnesses in the various war-crime trials later against IJN personnel there remarked on the prevalence of spies, beatings, and murders. And though it is not clear whether the Tokkei Tai had officially been installed in the time frame of the *Edsall* sinking, an Imperial Navy officer took charge of these men and was ultimately responsible for their fates. His name, too, was Nakamura.

This officer's name was given in one postwar atrocity investigation as "Capt. Teitje Nakamura." I briefly felt that Nakamura's first name was a version of the unusual Japanese name Teiji. But in an earlier statement made to war crimes investigators, one may read the name as signifying a rank—"Teitjo"—which I thought might have been a corruption of "Tai-sho," or "general." Allied translators noted that the native Malay language, such as spoken by the witness giving the statement, did not have distinguishing words for different military ranks. This clarifies little enough, though, because *Taisho* is also the Imperial Navy term for admiral. In this sense *Taisho*, meaning either admiral or general, might have been applied to any commanding officer within the context of a

---

* See IMTFE Exhibit 1702, "Report on Enforced Prostitution in Western Borneo, NEI during Japanese Naval Occupation," by Capt. Charles Jongeneel, NEFIS. Batavia, July 9, 1946. There was a clear reason for these arrangements: The Japanese were adamant that their forces not have contact with local Indonesian or Chinese women. However, the investigation also shows how closely the Tokkei Tai and *minseibu* coordinated their efforts.

specific incident recalled by the witness. Later, this eyewitness did make a point of clarifying Nakamura's identity as a Japanese naval officer, with the rank of captain.[21]

As long ago as 1612, the East India Company merchant Jacques Specx wrote, "In their own country the Japanese are lambs, but outside of it they are almost devils." One should not overlook the significance of a seventeenth-century Dutchman in the East Indies making such a statement; Japanese mercenaries aided the Dutch in their subjugation of the East Indies. In May 1621, these mercenaries were involved in one of the worst atrocities against indigenous peoples then on record when they beheaded and quartered forty-four defenseless prisoners (including eight *orang kaya*, or prominent leaders) of the Banda islands while serving under Jan Pieterszoon Coen.[22] Dutch reports of the event may be seen as terrible foreshadowings of the murders that would occur 320 years later. An Indonesian eyewitness would recount these crimes but the victims, in this case, would be Westerners. And like the baffled U.S. sailors serving aboard *Edsall* two decades before at Smyrna, this Indonesian, too, would be compelled to become a passive witness to atrocities that defy explanation.*

There is another layer of harsh irony to confront here: At that time, early March 1942, British and U.S. Navy intelligence services were tracking, with varying degrees of accuracy, the whereabouts of several Imperial Navy units. And British and U.S. code breakers understood that some of Nagumo's carriers, as well as others (for example, CarDiv 5, *Shokaku* and *Zuikaku*) were in the NEI region, probably preparing for a strike into the Indian Ocean. The British could use this information only to keep their ships at a safe distance. Their attempts at a Midway-style ambush nearly led to disaster as two heavy cruisers; an old, undersize aircraft carrier; and several smaller warships were crushed by KdB. Royal Navy losses might have been much worse had they not retired to the west in the face of Nagumo's overwhelming air superiority. The Americans could do little but watch and wait.

* Observations among some scholars of the Japanese military suggest that for the common soldiery in the "China Incident," messianic fervor swiftly turned to murderous rage when thwarted. There is much worth serious consideration in this reading. Many of the officers in the Imperial Army and Navy who were deployed to the Southern Regions were veterans of the fighting in China, as were the men under their command. For many, the well-known "Asia for the Asiatics" slogan was more than mere rhetoric; the men believed that ridding Asia of Western imperialism was a sacred cause, and they had little time or compassion for those who could not or would not share their convictions or who opposed conversion.

At that point the East Indies was passing into the hands of the Japanese military, and virtually all surviving Allied vessels were in desperate flight to Australia or Ceylon. So, if the Japanese felt that the survivors of *Edsall* represented an intelligence risk, they were mistaken. Their security shields had already been compromised.

Where *No One* Wanted to Be

The way of the world is to bloom and to flower and to die but in the affairs of men there is no waning and the noon of his expression signals the onset of night. His spirit is exhausted at the peak of its achievement. His meridian is at once his darkening and the evening of his day.
                                          —Cormac McCarthy, *Blood Meridian*

And thus, as Col. (later Sir) Laurens van der Post, himself a POW for more than three and a half years in Java, wrote in his "Secret Report to the British Secretary of State for Foreign Affairs" at the end of 1946: "Allied intelligence, elsewhere so good, had failed lamentably in this remote and cloistered theatre of operations. In fact British and Dutch prisoners of war have left it on record that . . . they felt like the inhabitants of some backwater of Mars, so darkly did they appear to know and to be known."[23] To the United States naval command, the Southwest Pacific area was considered "a theater tantamount . . . to a leper colony."[24] But after the war there would be no U.S., British, or Dutch POWs located at Kendari, a town described two decades earlier as rows of houses built on stilts over the harbor's waters, with tame deer wandering the main street (they were the pets of skilled Chinese workmen who produced extraordinary gold filigree work). Nothing but the buried remains from a human abattoir are left behind on "this gruesome island."[25]

The first Allied investigations undertaken in Kendari were concerned with killings that took place much later in the war. These included the beheadings of nine U.S. Navy crewmen captured from a downed PBY in November 1944, and the execution in January 1945 of a single U.S. Air Force officer, Maj. John Z. Endress, whose P-38 Lightning had been shot down over Kendari during a sweep of the airfield. The Endress case was dismissed for lack of evidence—an explanation was posited and accepted at the time that made pursuing the matter impracticable—but the murders of the PBY crew resulted in a series of four trials, beginning on October 1, 1946, in Manila with the prosecution of Vice Adm. Ohsugi Morikazu. These trials left a large, if difficult, paper trail, and along that uncertain path of documents I was able to uncover a handful of clues. They weren't much to go on, but they were enough to stimulate my imagination and curiosity, which in turn deepened my investigations and led me to what I believe to be a plausible account.

Finding information on any crimes committed at Kendari in the first months of the war would prove much more taxing. So far as I knew, no in-depth attempts were ever made to ascertain exact details of the killings of the men from *Edsall*. I would find little to counter this first impression, but I did find a good deal suggesting that more might have been and could have been done.

There is also plentiful evidence that the overworked and under-staffed Graves Registration units (of the U.S. Army's Quartermaster Corps) did not or could not cooperate with adequate speed in the work of the War Crimes Commission. For example, in the case of the Kendari murders of the nine PBY crewmen, although a postmortem ID of one of the murdered U.S. Navy men had been completed in October 1946, this data wasn't provided until the final trial of those charged with the killings, in the summer of 1948.

And, as if the post-war situation wasn't turbid enough, local frictions after the Japanese surrender in 1945 had eventually metastasized into civil war between Nationalist rebels and Dutch anti-insurgency forces in the southeastern Celebes by 1948, and travel there had become even more difficult and perilous.

Java itself was torn by numerous kidnappings, murders, and assassinations, not to mention vitriolic exchanges between British South East Asia Command (SEAC) administrators and the Dutch. The latter clung obstinately to dreams of regaining their lost East Indies empire while fighting tooth and nail among themselves, the British, and rebellious Indonesian nationalists who were struggling to throw off three centuries of Dutch domination. Under this tumultuous insurgency and extremism, British, Australian, Indian, Dutch, and U.S. forces moved into the outlying regions of the vast East Indies, and the more deeply they pushed into these tenebrous areas, the more horrors they uncovered.

Liberation of POWs and civilian internees was the primary focus of the military forces then, but this took time and, in some areas, delicate negotiations with skeptical Japanese. At Ambon the liberators were turned away by disbelieving, though polite, Japanese forces. It took several days to straighten out matters, at which point the ships were reinvited by the senior surviving Allied POWs. And at Menado, in the northern Celebes, some 334 internees—110 women, 145 children, and 79 men, all ravaged by malnutrition—were carried to Morotai on September 14, 1945, in HMA ships *Glenelg, Rockhampton, Bowen, Junee,* and *Latrobe.* One week later, the 21st Infantry Brigade of the Australian 7th Division landed at Makassar, transported by HMAS *Barcoo,* and *Inverell, Grass Snake, Alatna,* and HMS *Eduardo.* Two days after that, HMS *Maidstone* arrived to help remove POWs. These included about 460 survivors of HMS *Exeter,* HMS *Encounter,* and HMS *Stronghold. Maidstone* remained anchored seven miles offshore as the men were quickly ferried out, due to "strong anti-Dutch feelings."[26] To the east, at Kendari, the Japanese who had been involved in war crimes against Allied POWs were mulling over the possible consequences, and, in accordance with official directives sent out after the cessation of hostilities, began destroying evidence and fabricating explanations. But of course there would be no living Allied POWs released from captivity at Kendari.

Different Knowing

Initial research into the numerous murders that took place at or near Kendari began with an Australian investigator, Flight Lt. Martin T. O'Shea, of the RAAF Contact Party "Makforce" in October 1945. Possible atrocity cases were being researched by joint groups of British, Dutch, Australian, and U.S. teams. The Australians had established reasonably good relations with the Indonesians (with whom they empathized) in the course of their occupation, and were less reviled than the Dutch. Celebes at that time had declared for the nascent Indonesian Republic, which Soekarno and others proclaimed in mid-August 1945 in Java. It was, nonetheless, quite a dissimilar situation to that on Java, and the Celebes Republican administration lacked the organization and military power to successfully oppose the returning Dutch once the British and Australians departed in January 1946. In the interim, Westerners ventured outside of heavily staffed and policed centers (such as Makassar) only with caution.

Lieutenant O'Shea traveled from Makassar—where the British were already looking into allegations of war crimes—to the Kendari area.

In his brief visit, he uncovered evidence that formed the basis for the PBY crimes, "Australian Case No. 7, Beheading of Nine Americans at Kendari," dated October 19, 1945. There was sufficient cause for the U.S. Army to begin its own investigation through its War Crimes Branch, but there was at that moment no inkling of navy captives killed earlier in the war.

Data collected by O'Shea during this short trip was first laid out in a rough, preliminary three-page document entitled "Information Obtained At Kendare [*sic*] 19th October '45."[27] There were ten separate pieces of information recorded, including eyewitness accounts in addition to evidence he had seen himself "scratched on the walls of prison cells" at the Kendari Tokkei Tai compound. Some of these cells "had been recently demolished" by Allied bombing, claimed the Japanese, although O'Shea noticed that it was "a very neat bomb hit. Not a cracked or broken piece of masonry anywhere in the vicinity." The cell walls were covered with bloody fingerprints and smears. There is also considerable overlapping and redundancy in these entries, but each must be considered as carefully as the pieces in a multidimensional jigsaw puzzle.

Number 7 on O'Shea's list mentioned "information obtained from TOMASOEA—former Ambonese soldier at Kendare [*sic*]." Although the bulk of this individual's claims dealt with the PBY crew captured near Salabangka in 1944, and a number of other Allied aircraft crashes in which all of the crews were killed, there were also curious, fragmentary references to anecdotal accounts of captives seized at sea much earlier in the war and brought to Kendari to be murdered.

Another pair of Eurasians, former employees of the Dutch colonial government, named Mesman and van der Vrighoef (spelled Vrichoff elsewhere) provided more information on the PBY murders, as well as names of a group of Japanese alleged to have been guilty of atrocities. But beneath their list is a single, stark line: "At Amato [*sic*], 12 miles from Mondonga—eleven graves of American sailors." There is no elaboration regarding whom these sailors may have been, or the identity of their ship.

O'Shea ended this section (Number 8) with an observation that he had himself "inspected the grave of Major ENDERS [*sic*] U.S. A.A.C., who died in hospital in Kendare, [*sic*] Pilot of a P38." O'Shea concluded his report:

When confronted with all of this evidence, the Japs went through the usual stalling and lying procedure, and as they always do in such cases, finally passed the responsibility to Jap officials who have since returned to Japan. We were told that no one there at present had anything at all to do with the apprehension or detention of prisoners. We know different.

Search-and-recovery missions must have taken place in the "execution grounds" of Kendari over the course of the next twelve months, following statements and affidavits by the few witnesses who could be found. No doubt it was a dangerous, laborious, disheartening task. Three years later, prosecution and defense lawyers would still be arguing over whether or not all of the almost one hundred bodies allegedly recovered in the Kendari area had yet been identified.

My best original guess—and it was no more than speculation—was that the discovery and identification of the remains of *Edsall* crewmen seized by *Chikuma*, and later killed in Kendari, must have occurred between the surrender in fall 1945 and spring 1947. That was when five bodies of the lost PBY's crew—including Bill Goodwin—were discovered in a common grave a few hundred meters behind the compound administered by the Tokkei Tai, the "feared and hated" naval secret police force.

Time Regained

> *But how is it that this lives in thy mind?*
> *What seest thou else in the dark backward and abysm of time?*
> —William Shakespeare, *The Tempest*, Act I, Scene 2

After the war ended, remains of U.S. servicemen recovered in the Southwest Pacific were taken to Barrackpore, India, where they were kept until positive identification could be made, if possible, through identity tags, dental records, or in some cases clothing.* This often took many months, or even years, and with deleterious consequences to war-crimes proceedings as well as to thousands of information-starved families at home.

---

* "Every article of clothing shall be clearly marked with the owner's name, using black paint in marking white clothes and dungarees, and white paint on blue clothes, or with pen and indelible ink. . . . The name will be legibly inscribed." From "Regulations For Mark-

USS *Edsall* (DD-219) was
christened at her launching by
Mrs. Bessie Edsall- Bracey, the
sister of Norman Edsall, on
July 29, 1920. *Nara II,
College Park, MD*

Edsall in San Diego Harbor, California, in the early 1920s. *Naval Historical Center Collections*

Edsall, probably in San Diego Harbor, undated. *Naval Historical Center Collections*

Sailors on one of *Edsall*'s four triple torpedo mounts. *Collection of E. W. Stuart*

Prewar firing of a 21-inch torpedo from *Edsall*; the original caption says these would "wreck anything smaller than a battleship." *John P. Loveridge*

Taken from *Edsall*, a division of four-pipers on maneuvers off the Philippines in 1937. *Collection of E. W. Stuart*

Edsall with Destroyer Division 39, probably in San Diego Harbor, 1921. From right to left: *Edsall*, *McCormick* (DD-223), *Bulmer* (DD-222), *Simpson* (DD-221), *MacLeish* (DD-220), *Parrott* (DD-218), and, in background, *MacKenzie* (DD-175) and *Hogan* (DD-178). *Naval Historical Center Collections*

Capt. Walter Collier Nix, son of Lt. J. J. Nix.
Jim Nix

Lt. Joshua "J.J." Nix (as USNA senior, 1930),
commanding officer, *Edsall*.
Author's collection

Lt. John Fairbanks Jr., executive officer.
David Wright

Lt. Richard Meyers, engineering officer.
Jim Nix

Lt. Phillip Wild Jr., gunnery officer.
David Wright

Lt. (jg) Ray Snodgrass, first lieutenant.
Carolyn Sparks

Ensign John Gustin, communications officer.
Elizabeth Gustin-Hinkley

Coxswain John Burgoyne. *Jack Burgoyne*

Coxswain Elmore Duff. *Timothy Duff*

S1c David Handy. *Jim Nix*

S2c Loren Stanford Myers.
Rear Adm. Kent Riffey USN (ret.)

F1c Jack Noe. *Father John Noe*

S2c Loys Parsons.
Jo and June Gallagher

Charles Parsons, Loys' brother, USS *Houston*.
Jo and June Gallagher

EM1c Henry Thaw.
Kelley Geary

S1c Ralph Rowland.
Capt. Chris Hampton,
U.S. Army

MM2c Allen Wilson.
Delores (Miller) Wilson
via Jim Nix

SK2c Vincent Koenig, USS *Houston*. *Mike*
Keenan

Lt. (jg) Albin Koenig, Vincent's brother,
USNR, DC-V(G). *Mike Keenan*

Crew photo taken September 28, 1940, in Shanghai. *Edsall*'s skipper at this time was Lt. Cdr. Edwin Crouch, who later commanded DesDiv 57 aboard USS *Whipple* (DD-217) during the *Langley-Pecos* operation. *Jim Nix*

Identified Personnel
1. 1. Lt. (jg) Richard Meyers
2. Lt. Cecil Caufield, executive officer
3. Lt. Cdr. Edwin Crouch, commanding officer
4. Lt. (jg) Phillip Wild Jr., gunnery officer
5. S2c Loren Stanford Meyers
6. MM2c Allen Wilson
7. MM3c Donald Donaldson

USS *Langley* (AV-3) was sunk in a foolhardy attempt to ferry P-40E fighters into Java in late February 1942. The mission also led to the loss of *Pecos* and *Edsall*, and over 650 American lives. *U.S. Navy*

The Asiatic Fleet oiler USS *Pecos* (AO-6) "died hard" on March 1, 1942, requiring four airstrikes by dive-bombers from *Akagi*, *Kaga*, *Sōryū*, and *Hiryū*. *U.S. Navy*

Kidō Butai departing Kendari, Celebes in late March 1942. The carriers of Vice-Admiral Nagumo's command lead the four *Kongo*-class battleships, with screening vessels in the distance on the flanks. *Kojinsha Publishers*

The Dutch merchant ship *Modjokerto* was sunk by *Chikuma* the same day as *Pecos* and *Edsall*. Her survivors were also taken to Kendari, where they, too, were executed. This rare wartime image shows the old ship armed with a 3-inch gun on a bandstand at her stern. *Jakob Baggus/Baggus.org*

IJN carrier *Soryu*. Note aircraft on aft deck (at left). By early 1942 she boasted some of the finest dive-bomber crews in the Imperial Navy. They were instrumental in the attacks on *Pecos* and *Edsall*. *Kojinsha Publishers*

IJN heavy cruiser *Chikuma* at flank speed during a gunnery exercise before the war. On March 1, 1942, *Chikuma* fired 49 main-battery projectiles to sink the Dutch merchantman *Modjokerto* and another 347 in the long pursuit of *Edsall*. *Kojinsha Publishers*

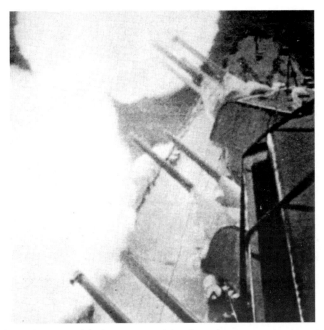

The forward 8-inch turrets of the heavy cruiser *Tone* firing during a gunnery exercise. On March 1, 1942, *Tone* expended 497 main-battery projectiles against *Edsall*. *Kojinsha Publishers*

Sister ships *Tone* and *Chikuma* at high speed in pre-war exercise. The enormous bow and stern waves attest to the speeds these powerful ships could attain. *Kojinsha Publishers*

The *Shoi Kohoisei* (ensign candidates, or midshipmen) of the *Chikuma* in late 1941, in their winter blues. Sasaki Masao is on the far left standing in the second row; Haraguchi Shizuhiko stands third from the right. *Dr. Haraguchi Shizuhiko via Kan Sugahara*

Chikuma's midshipmen on April 13, 1942, returning from the Indian Ocean raid. Sasaki Masao is sitting second from the left in the second row, and Haraguchi Shizuhiko is in the same row sitting second from the right. In the back stand Matsuda, medical officer Lt. (j.g.) Kazuki, and Ensign Kiuchi, immediate superior of Haraguchi. These young men were ordered to pick up *Edsall's* survivors and to interrogate them aboard *Chikuma*. *Dr. Haraguchi Shizuhiko via Kan Sugahara*

Vice Admiral Nagumo Chuichi, commander of *Kidō Butai*. Controversial to this day, Nagumo led the carriers of KdB during the period of their greatest achievements, although the actions of March 1, 1942, showed little evidence of their true prowess. *Naval Historical Center Collections*

Vice Admiral Abe Hiroaki commanded the two heavy cruisers *Tone* and *Chikuma* on March 1, 1942, and probably gave the orders to pick up *Edsall*'s survivors, as well as to disembark the men at Kendari. *Mike Wenger*

Lieutenant Kobayashi Michio of *Hiryū* led the 26 *kanbaku* (divebombers) of *Kidō Butai* in the strikes that eventually brought *Edsall* to a halt. Kobayashi was a courageous veteran pilot who perished three months later leading *Hiryū*'s counter-attack against USS *Yorktown* at the Battle of Midway. *NHC #81560*

Motegi Meiji, IJN, circa 1941. First lieutenant Motegi's action station was the forward conning tower of the battleship *Hiei*, flagship of *Sentai* 3/1, where he was an eyewitness to *Edsall*'s last battle. *Motegi Meiji via Jim Nix*

The last stand of the *Edsall* was captured on film and distributed in a *Nichiei* newsreel. Compare top image with propaganda still on opposite page. Finally, at bottom, she appears to have slipped beneath the waves, only the rising smoke remaining. *Film captures by permission of* Nederlands Instituut voor Beeld en Geluid, *Hilversum, Holland*

The infamous *Nichiei* newsreel image doctored for use as a still in the April 15, 1942, issue of *Asahigraph* magazine, as well as in the propaganda booklet "Victory on the March" in December 1942 as "the British destroyer HMS *Pope.*" *NARA II, College Park, MD, 80-G-178997*

There was speculation that this rare image of Allied POWs could have been *Edsall* personnel. It was in fact taken at Makassar, and probably shows men from either HMS *Exeter*, HMS *Encounter*, HMS *Stronghold*, USS *Pope*, USS *Perch*, or the Dutch cruiser *Java*. *Roger Pineau Papers, NHC, via Mike Wenger*

The grave of Loren Stanford Myers in the Punch Bowl, Honolulu, Hawaii; he is the sole *Edsall* crewman buried there. His remains were interred on March 31, 1950. *David F. Kehn*

The ambiguous marker for five identified *Edsall* sailors and the partial remains of five unknown AAF pilots interred together at Jefferson Barracks National Cemetary near St. Louis on December 20, 1949. *David F. Kehn*

On November 25, 1945, the U.S. Navy declared all crewmembers from USS *Edsall* (DD-219) "presumed dead." This finding of presumptive death by the Navy Department was fixed in order to take care of settlements and dependents. At that point no one yet suspected that survivors from the destroyer were among a number of victims of war crimes that took place at the remote base in the southeastern Celebes. And as it turned out, many more bodies would yet be found at Kendari.

Another entire year passed before the remains of five more Americans recovered in the NEI were identified as those of naval personnel by their clothing and identity tags. In the same month that SEAC was disbanded, these remains were quietly reinterred in the U.S. Military Cemetery in Barrackpore, India, on November 12, 1946, in Plot 3, Row R, Grave 15. Along with them were believed to be "three Unknown bodies." By November 30, a more lengthy "Report on Reinterment" had been submitted, and although it acknowledged that there may have actually been "at least 9 individuals" recovered, it expressed skepticism, saying that the extra fibula and left tibia found were probably mixed in "inadvertently" at the time of recovery in Kendari.

The initial reports from HQ American Graves Registration Services (Calcutta, India) speculated that all of these remains were from either USS *Perch* (SS-176), a submarine lost in the Java campaign, or from USS *Houston* (CA-30). This early report, by Capt. W. O. Hudson, also began with more confusing and gruesome details from the search-and-recovery teams sent to Kendari. These tell of a large group of Americans and Chinese seized at sea off Java by the Japanese, and brought to Kendari, where they were killed together and their remains thrown into a "mass grave." It was due to the large number of bodies found in a single site that the real difficulties of identification began.

Two months passed, and on February 6, 1947, a memorandum was sent from the Office of the Quartermaster General (QMG) by their naval liaison officer to the Bureau of Personnel identifying the five sets of remains (from among the "eight" complete skeletons found) as crewmen from the vanished USS *Edsall* (DD-219): "These names check with the names on the five identification tags recovered with the remains." This correspondence also states "that it is doubtful that the

ing Clothing," *The Bluejackets Manual* (p. 204). To my surprise some Asiatic Fleet vets recalled that they wore dog tags of some type. Other survivors from *Houston* said that they did not wear such identification discs. The *Edsall* remains appear to confirm the former.

remains can be separated into individual groups. Therefore the burial is being changed to a group burial." One week later, on February 12, the Navy Department noted these findings in a document by the director of the Dependents Welfare Division.[28]

It would be another three years before these young men's remains came back home to the States, and when they did, only their immediate families would know. By then, Supreme Allied Commander MacArthur and his G-2, Maj. Gen. Charles Willoughby, were well on their way to limiting war-crime prosecutions, as one dismayed Australian investigator put it, "in order to spare Japan the odium and contempt of the world."[29]

The status of the five men's remains, those found and identified, was later changed to "determined dead." As given in these official documents, their names (with their addresses and family data added) are:

1. Amory, Sidney Griffith F1/c, 256 32 84 (Family address: 1050 W. Washington Street, Charleston, West Virginia)
2. Andrus, Horace Welburn MM1/c, 359 83 94 (Family address: 1140 Prairie Street, Beaumont, Texas)
3. Cameron, J. R. MM2/c, 287 11 75 (of Burnside, Kentucky; parents Mr. and Mrs. Arthur Cameron)
4. Vandiver, Larry MM3/c, 283 39 00 (of 354 Union Place, Akron, Ohio; mother Mrs. Lela P. Kelly)
5. Watters, Donald Franklin F1/c, 328 71 49 (of 395 Marshall Avenue, St. Paul, Minnesota)

In the colorful firsthand account *Another Six Hundred*, by J. Daniel Mullin, a gunner's mate first class aboard USS *John D. Ford* (DD-228), there is a brief, anecdotal reference to the discovery of these bodies: "In 1946, a priest showed an American searching party a common grave containing five bodies on the southern shore of Java. There was enough evidence to establish that they were from *Edsall*, one officer or CPO, and four enlisted. Separate identities could not be established. They had been beheaded."[30] Where Mullin came across this information is unknown. There were two Japanese Catholic clerics in Makassar at the time of the surrender: Bishops Yamaguchi and Ogihara, both sent from Flores as the war came to an end. But, as we now know, there were no officers or CPOs identified among the bodies at Kendari. And they were clearly not on Java's southern coast. But Mullin was absolutely correct about the identification problems.

These five men were probably from the Engineroom Branch, two firemen and three machinist mates, which in turn suggests that there was enough time for some personnel belowdecks to abandon ship and escape the hurricane of Japanese shells. This may not have been as improbable as it might at first appear.

> Egress from either of the firerooms [on the flushdeck-type destroyers] was fairly easy, via an air lock and then up about a 12 rung ladder to a hatch on the main deck. As for the engine rooms, egress from the forward space was quite easy up an inclined ladder. In the after space it was up a vertical ladder at the after bulkhead and a throttleman there would have a longer exit route. Those in a space that was hit had no chance at all but in an adjoining space there was a chance to make it . . . the blast from an explosion was likely to vent to the atmosphere.[31]

Some of the information given to their interrogators regarding *Edsall*'s evasive maneuvers could have come from the "black gang." Other aspects of their replies suggest that members of the bridge or at least some whose action stations were topside may have been among those rescued.

Here, too, there is a poignant irony worth noting. Two of the letters in Rear Adm. Edwin T. Layton's papers from the library of the Naval War College are from a surviving sister of Lt. j.g. Morris D. Gilmore (U.S. Naval Academy 1939), the destroyer's assistant engineering officer. She notes that her father, himself a graduate of the class of 1911, explained carefully to the family that "boiler room personnel were least likely to survive in the circumstances." That the majority of men who were lucky enough to have escaped may have been from the engine rooms is irony enough; that they were picked up and murdered "in cold blood" soon thereafter casts yet another shadow over the crew's fate.

Gravedigger as Witness: Tomasowa's Testament

The struggle of man against power is the struggle of memory against forgetting.

—Milan Kundera

In the book *Shobun*, by Michael J. Goodwin, is a key—or perhaps key additive, as code breakers might say—that would prove instrumental in deciphering many of the mysteries of *Edsall*'s survivors.[32] In *Shobun*, Goodwin investigates the murders of nine American fliers from a downed PBY who were captured later in the war, in October 1944. One of these captives was Goodwin's own father, Lt. j.g. William F. Goodwin Jr.

A sparse and unrelated vignette near the beginning of the book involved another casual and vague account of the execution of U.S. Navy personnel from a sunken and unnamed warship who were brought as POWs to Kendari in early 1942. The precise date given, January 24—the day that this remote town and air base fell to Japanese forces—seemed exact enough to serve as a kind of verification, but instinctive skepticism grabbed me later when I reread the account in search of information on the war in the East Indies.

I had first been drawn to Goodwin's book because it mentioned the Celebes region, and such references were rare. Only later would I realize how important a role *Shobun* would play in my own research, for without Goodwin's dogged research, far less about the events that occurred in Kendari a half-century before would have ever come to light. Glancing through the short text a few years later, I soon realized that important scraps of information were buried within its overall narrative. In one of those moments of inspired, if accidental, insight, I suddenly saw that these bits of information might be relevant to my search for answers to the *Edsall* mystery.

But I could find no records of any U.S. vessel lost around that time in the vicinity of the southeastern Celebes—or anywhere in the Java Sea either—and that struck me as peculiar, arousing my skepticism. These hapless figures, with IJN personnel present alongside intimidated locals who were captured or pressed into service, were all made to kneel at hastily dug graves before being decapitated one by one—who could they be?

Later, based on my reading of *Shobun*, it appeared that a single eyewitness, the captured KNIL soldier Johan Tomasowa—a figure as baffling as the events in which he became enmeshed—had alone revealed these truly mysterious killings. This was of course the same soldier, spelled as "Tomasoea," noted in O'Shea's early report in 1945.

During the PBY trials in the Yokohama Courthouse in June 1948, when first asked about the whereabouts of his fellow KNIL prisoners who were also pressed into gravedigging duty, Tomasowa sparked a courtroom controversy by grimly stating, "all of them were beheaded." The defense attorney who was representing an accused Japanese naval officer, Rear Adm. Furukawa Tamotsu,* was so "upset" by this reply that he instantly moved for a mistrial. Sly professional indignation notwithstanding, his motion was denied.[33]

What I did not know until well into my research was that Tomasowa had given multiple statements to Allied investigators *before* the Furukawa trial, including several in 1947 in conjunction with a pending case against Capt. Taniguchi Gosuke, who had been commander of the Kendari Tokkei Tai detachment in 1944 and was under prosecution for the same crimes against the captured PBY crew. None of these other accounts by Tomasowa are specifically identified in *Shobun*.

Western prosecutors and defenders encountered many serious communication difficulties during the war-crime trials because of the bewildering language differences. With questions and responses translated from the Malay language into Dutch, and from Dutch into English, and into Japanese as well, some important information was likely lost in the process.

The initial statement given to Dutch investigators in early 1947 was an oral one, in Malay, which was recorded by the military prosecutor, J. R. F. Apontoweil, and read back to Tomasowa. "After this statement has been read out to him in the Malayan [*sic*] language, the witness deposes to desire to stick to his statement, not wishing to add anything or change anything."

Subsequently the statement was transcribed in Dutch, after which it was translated into English by Capt. J. N. Heijbroek (a KNIL reserve officer).[34] At later hearings in Manila during the Taniguchi trial, Tomasowa answered questions posed to him in Malay and translated

---

* Rear Adm. Furukawa (Naval Academy Graduate, 43rd class) had previously been the commanding officer, with the rank of captain, of the seaplane tender *Chitose*. This vessel operated throughout the NEI during the First Stage operations, including the Kendari area. Furukawa also appears to have commanded the light carrier *Hiyo* later in the war.

back into English for U.S. prosecutors. It does not take much effort to imagine the potential for inaccuracies and factual errors to creep into such depositions.

Tomasowa's trial testimony in the Furukawa case, all eighty pages of it, reveals defense and prosecution staff often stymied, at odds over a response, and pausing to consult the interpreters. U.S. defense attorneys made energetic and persistent interruptions to quibble over the smallest nuances of language. The Dutch translator Capt. Gerrit J. Jongejans and the Indonesians Raden Suwanto and Sudarmo Martonago were sworn in on different days. Additionally, a Japanese translator, Mr. Sumiyoshi, appears in the record from time to time. The defense haggled, debated, and emphasized superfluous minutiae against the clear and incontestable evidence. Arguments about verb tenses took precedence over the bones of the murdered.

Documents regarding the Kendari war-crime trials contain multiple explicit references to Tomasowa's questionable "reliability" as a witness. But these appear to stem more from language and translation disparities than anything inherently problematic in the man's character. In one of his 1947 interrogations, Tomasowa was said by the Dutch "summoner" (Special Constable Gerrit Gelijn Jochems) to be "a little bit confused by the many hearings about the matter," which seemed a fair assessment because Tomasowa himself had admitted in an earlier statement, "I mixed several facts and so I made an incorrect statement. So I kindly ask you to undo that statement."[35]

It is not hard to imagine how bewildering these question-and-answer sessions must have been to Tomasowa, coming five years and more after the events he had witnessed. And there were probably political reasons for opposing his testimony, although there seems to be scant direct evidence of this. Finally, a historian must make judgments regarding the general spirit of a person's recollections as distinct from their ability to state specific facts, numbers, and statistics in what the researcher feels is an accurate manner. As filmmaker Werner Herzog observed, "Facts do not create truth; facts create norms. . . . They do not create illumination."[36]

The Sole Survivor

In the summer of 1948, Tomasowa was twenty-nine years old, five feet six inches tall, and a private first class in the Dutch East Indies Army, in which he had served for more than thirteen years. At the time of his first statements in early 1947 he had been at the "Training School for Paratroopers" at Hollandia, New Guinea. Born in Meester Cornelis (present-day Jatinegara), a suburb south of Batavia, on August 29, 1918, he was a member of a KNIL unit sent to Kendari in the fall of 1941 and lived there with the other soldiers in military barracks. He had been captured on the first day of the Japanese invasion, January 24, 1942, when his automatic weapons unit—one of only two units to actually fire their weapons, and the last to capitulate to the Sasebo Combined Special Naval Landing Force troops—"ran out of ammunition at about 3 o'clock in the afternoon."[37]

About 105 men were interned at first, but most were soon sent on to Makassar, several hundred miles to the southwest, where the Japanese established POW camps and imprisoned Dutch Army, Royal Netherlands Navy, U.S. Asiatic Fleet, British Royal Navy, and Royal Australian personnel together.* Tomasowa, however, was kept in Kendari, where "[I] had to work for one Captain Nakamura who was the first one to enter Kendari." This shadowy individual, an officer in the Japanese Navy, and whose name may or may not have actually been Nakamura, figures prominently in many early events at Kendari recounted by Tomasowa. "I and my companions had to work for the Japanese clearing up roads, building roads, etc. We were held confined first for a few days and then they started using us for work, and from that time on there were more soldiers captured, more Allied soldiers captured by the Japanese and they joined us."[38]

Tomasowa's statements of January and June 1947 formed the basis for the *Shobun* version of the murders of American sailors in early 1942. These documents are riddled with inaccuracies, red herrings, and errors, yet the KNIL private—who had more on his mind than remembering precisely the nationalities or names of men whose horrific killings he witnessed—obviously saw Allied prisoners murdered and was called upon to bury their remains. And it *is* possible to make sense of the contradictions without destroying the fabric of his testimony.

Tomasowa was confined each night to a cell at the small Kendari prison compound, although working daily for the Japanese and was

---

* The number of men (105) matches the Dutch records of seven fifteen-man brigades defending the air base at Kendari II. The men in the Makassar camps—from the ships *DeRuyter, Java, Exeter, Encounter, Pope,* and *Perch,* among others—were not known with certainty to still be alive until after the war.

released from this internment on April 29, "the birthday of Emperor Tennoheika," he testified. He then rented a house in Kendari, "from a Buginese," only to find himself thrown back into prison a month later when "someone" found a forbidden Dutch flag in his home.

For this (very serious) offense he was seized, incarcerated for one hundred days, then sentenced to twenty years hard labor.* He was still serving out this sentence, living at the Tokkei Tai—as the compound also came to be known—two and a half years later when the nine PBY crewmembers, including Lt. j.g. Bill Goodwin, were captured in October 1944 and brought to Kendari. By that time Johan Tomasowa was one of the few KNIL soldiers still alive who had been interned since the fall of Kendari.

That he was available for so many postwar statements is explained by the fact that he was the only Ambonese kept at Kendari town who had not been murdered in July 1945 as the Japanese saw the end of the war coming, and with it the inevitable war crimes tribunals. Tomasowa stated to Allied investigators later that he had learned of a plan by the Japanese to execute all thirteen Ambonese soldiers being held by the Tokkei Tai in Kendari. Although he said he urged his fellow soldiers to try to escape, not one was willing to take the chance, and many professed a strange and fatalistic resignation: "They answered that if the time comes they would die."[39]

When interrogators quizzed Tomasowa about this inexplicable behavior, he responded, "I can't understand why the other twelve did not run away. I told them to run away but they were afraid to do so." Terrified or not, Tomasowa decided to try to save himself. During a break for the *benjo* (latrine), he bolted out the back of the compound, "through a small river behind the camp up the hill," into the jungle nearby, and there he remained, "hiding in the woods until the Australians came" a few weeks later. It is a fantastic anecdote and could be viewed with much skepticism if not for even more outlandish stories of Allied POWs who fled their Japanese captors in the war's final weeks after they learned of plans for their elimination.† And Tomasowa's story

* E. A. Fricke's *The Unknown History of the Child Soldiers* records the seizure and execution of a nineteen-year-old Ambonese soldier at Makassar for the "crime" of possessing a photo of Queen Wilhelmina.

† The most striking such example of POWs fleeing their captors is that of two USS *Houston* (CA-30) survivors, Lanson Harris and Red Huffman, who escaped near Phet Buri, Thailand, in July 1945.

agrees with a variety of postwar histories that reveal that often a small number of Japanese occupiers were able to control, and often terrorize, entire communities and regions.

Johan Tomasowa was an Ambonese Protestant Christian and had taken a Christian oath to tell the truth in his testimony.* As a scholar traveling to Sulawesi wrote in the 1980s after encountering a helpful, earnest Ambonese while stranded in Surabaya: "It is always slightly shocking to be in a country where Christianity is regarded as a serious religion, and not merely a euphemism for godlessness."[40] Laurens Van Der Post wrote, "These sturdy native soldiers . . . were the finest soldiers in the old Netherlands East Indies Army, devout Christians, and born mercenaries in the best sense of the word. They and the Menadonese, so akin to them, were almost the only Colonial troops who had seen action."[41]

There is terrible poignancy in Tomasowa's testimony affirming that he, and he alone, had survived among the Ambonese KNIL soldiers first caught at Kendari. Other accounts written by Allied participants later recorded the excellence of these troops, the Black Dutch as they were sometimes known, and how they continued to sing their somber Dutch hymns—"Blyft met my Oh Heer!" (Abide with me, Oh Lord!)—deep in the jungle. Their fidelity and enjoyment as "Christians in a Moslem setting" has also been noted.[42]

The diaries and memoirs of Dutch POWs and internees at Makassar and elsewhere in the Celebes record that many Ambonese were murdered by Indonesian extremists as soon as the war ended. This suggests that the Indonesian nationalists, many of whom *were* overt collaborators, had not forgotten those who resisted the Japanese invaders and who aided Western prisoners throughout the war. It might well explain Tomasowa's betrayal to the police in the house rented from a Bugi, who was surely Muslim.

There are other accounts of Muslim administrators (in the south-central region of the island, near Makale) betrayed to the Japanese by vindictive Torajan Christians under almost identical circumstances. In the "atmosphere of mutual suspicion and recrimination that characterized

---

* Many KNIL troops had an Ambonese Protestant Christian background and were considered more reliable by the Dutch because they *were* Christians and therefore less susceptible to non-Christian nationalist rhetoric. A few also had European legal status, if not practical equality, under the law. For the same reason, they were distrusted by the Japanese and were much more likely to be persecuted or imprisoned.

the transition to Japanese rule," such private vendettas were far from uncommon.[43] The anarchy of a political interregnum provides a breeding ground for settling old personal scores. It is not hard to imagine half-educated locals who had swallowed the propaganda line of the day—which may have included declarations that the Japanese themselves were also Muslims—finding an irresistible target in a Christian soldier loyal to the hated Dutch. And *Ambonezen* were not shy about openly flouting their loyalties.

Tomasowa was subjected to concerted efforts by the American defense attorney to discredit and undermine his testimony. But although he admitted making some erroneous statements, he nevertheless remained firm in his convictions about the atrocities he had seen. The lawyers reviewing Furukawa's case later in 1949 noted Tomasowa's problems as a witness, although the trial record did show that both sides spent an inordinate amount of time quibbling over the niceties of translation interpretation and comprehension.

The U.S. defense attorney for the Japanese made a point of confronting Tomasowa repeatedly with accusations of lying—"He is a crafty witness"—and the possible consequences for such. The accusation seems fairly ironic considering the craftiness required by all prisoners to simply survive under their brutal and arbitrary keepers. One can only imagine the bitterness with which such accusations must have struck this faithful individual who had survived so many horrors, and the uneasiness he would have felt—alone and unsupported in, of all places, Yokohama—far from his family and native land.

As part of the "grave-digging detail" made up of Ambonese captives, Tomasowa was a firsthand eyewitness to multiple executions of Allied POWs throughout the war. The issue of divided loyalties aside—when Tomasowa had been released in the spring of 1942 he signed a pledge for his Japanese captors—he had also been at Kendari from the beginning of the war, and his descriptions, at least initially, seemed detailed and precise.*

Could it be possible that the men executed "on the first day of the Japanese occupation" had in fact been the *Edsall* crewmen plucked out

---

* Tomasowa's descriptions seemed a little too precise, in fact, for investigators. In January 1947 he was asked a round of questions to clarify an earlier report of atrocities. When queried about how he remembered "the days, hours, and names so exactly," Tomasowa told the Dutch military prosecutor at Hollandia, "I made some notes in a pocketbook." Apontoweil Statement, 1947.

of the Indian Ocean by *Chikuma*? Tomasowa had made mistakes rec-
ollecting dates in other parts of his testimony.* If postwar graves registration units had recovered the remains of between five and eleven
individuals, and native witnesses saw seventeen actually beheaded, with
the remainder, another nineteen U.S. Navy men captured off the same
unnamed ship reportedly sent to work as slave labor in "nickel mines on
the island," such a scenario seemed plausible.

The account in *Shobun* is not part of the Tomasowa trial testimony
but is taken from an earlier statement to investigators, in which it was
said that the men were executed at three graves. In mathematical terms,
this might suggest that recovery teams later found only two of the three
burial sites—that is, roughly two-thirds of the total number of bodies. (In
Shobun, Goodwin makes a persuasive argument that more Allied remains
are probably still there and could be found if someone were to make the
effort. With modern DNA testing technology, the odds of identifying
them are better now than they were in the years 1946 to 1949.[†])

After more research—none of it encouraging—I still could not
locate one Allied vessel sunk with survivors captured in January 1942
near Kendari. Granted, USS *Childs* (AVD-1)—seen in Kendari's harbor by Tomasowa[‡]—had undergone a nerve-wracking adventure there
between January 22 and 24. The converted tender narrowly eluded the
Japanese invasion force, having unwittingly provided the invaders with
thirty thousand more gallons of aviation fuel that she had deposited at
Kendari's airfield, but she had left no crewmen there. Later, when piec-
ing together the facts behind the atrocities he had seen, Johan Tomasowa
assumed that the men whom he had witnessed being murdered were in
fact sailors captured from this vessel, which he believed had been sunk
by the Japanese Navy. But *Childs* had made good her escape, although
by the slimmest of margins.

* Most notably in an erroneous assertion that Rear Adm. Furukawa Tamotsu had been
present in Kendari in April 1944. Rear Admiral Furukawa was then commander of
Kasumigaura Air Base in Japan.

† Also, an individual born in Menado, Celebes, suggested that the men may have been
worked to death alongside natives (*romusha*), and buried with them, or perhaps, if
involved in highly sensitive work, killed and buried in "secret graveyards" for just such
victims. This explanation appears almost proverbial among the occupied populations of
the NEI/Indonesia.

‡ "About a week before the invasion of the Japanese at Kendari, an American warship
entered the harbor of Kendari and remained there till the day of the invasion" (Jochems
Warrant, June 1947).

The American servicemen's bodies that Johan Tomasowa had buried with his own hands—after witnessing the executions—had to have been from another vessel, lost on another date. And the only U.S. sailors' remains discovered and identified at Kendari were men from *Edsall*.

There is no question that U.S. submarines were operating in the vicinity of Staring Bay throughout the spring and summer of 1942. One, USS *Sculpin* (SS-191), had succeeded in torpedoing the Japanese destroyer *Suzukaze* off Kendari in the first week of February. This vessel was severely damaged, with nine crew killed, and it remained at Staring Bay under repair until the end of March 1942.* U.S. Navy intelligence knew of the increased activity of important IJN units in that area, and many attempts were made to ambush these vessels, but with no success.

As for merchant ships, that track also seemed cold, with a single line on page 30 of the USAFFE Military History Section's "Japanese Monograph No. 101 (Netherlands East Indies Naval Invasion Operations)" containing a brief reference to a "small merchant ship sunk south of Boetoeng [Butung or Buton] Island" at the time of the Kendari operation. Were there no others? Not in that immediate region, although some Western vessels were seized south of Java as the island fell. Most of these are recorded in *Senshi Sōsho* as Dutch ships, but there has always been confusion and disagreement regarding the identities and fates of these ships and their crews.

Would Tomasowa have been able to distinguish between Dutch, British, Australian, and American captives? He admitted he could not speak any English, but as a member for nearly a decade of the KNIL he surely knew some Dutch, and although language differences between the British, various Commonwealth personnel in the region, and Americans could have escaped his understanding, there is not much evidence that any Westerners apart from U.S. and Dutch POWs were brought, even briefly, to Kendari.†

---

* For this information thanks to www.combinedfleet.com's Allyn D. Nevitt, who has recorded the TROM (tabular record of movement) for most IJN destroyers during the war.

† One exception to this is the bizarre story that Tomasowa told of a single white woman discovered in a life raft in late December 1944 off Wowoni Island. She was, he said, kept for a few days doing odd jobs before being decapitated by a Tokkei Tai warrant officer named Abe. Slightly different versions of this story appear throughout Tomasowa's various statements and testimony. One other statement also mentions a single British sailor captured early in the war, brought to Kendari, and summarily dispatched.

. . . melted into air, into thin air.
        —William Shakespeare, *The Tempest* Act I, Scene 2

In a fantastic twist in the already outlandish history of USS *Edsall*, the prosecution's star witness, this very Johan Tomasowa, managed to disappear in the midst of the Furukawa trial in the summer of 1948, never to be seen again. *Edsall's* story now reads like a scenario from some pulp-novel or one of the B-grade noir films popular at the time. Even so, the possibility of malignant, lethal actions cannot be ruled out.

> The Trial Commission had adjourned for a month in order to allow an attempt to gather additional evidence at the site of the crimes. . . . The witness Tomasowa, together with representatives of both the prosecution and defense staff, journeyed by plane [from Yokohama] to the Celebes, for that purpose. While there, the witness Tomasowa became separated from the rest of the party.[44]

Tomasowa convinced prosecutors that he had kept written notes during the war, with details on the Japanese executions of POWs.* Naturally the prosecutors were eager to see these notes, and permitted him to travel to Java to retrieve them. A group involved in the case (defense and prosecution attorneys) also went, intending to revisit Kendari in search of more evidence, but they got no closer than Makassar. From there, Tomasowa was sent on to his home in Batavia (Djakarta), where he said the notes were kept in his footlocker. After reaching Batavia he wired back saying he had been delayed, having missed his return flight. At that point, Johan Tomasowa disappeared as utterly as the *Edsall* had six years earlier.

Had Tomasowa been swallowed up in the convulsive political events then sweeping through Java, perhaps murdered by rebel militants (many of whom belonged to groups with paramilitary training provided by the Japanese during the occupation), or killed by Dutch anti-insurgency

---

* "I used to make notes of all the things at the time I was in Kendari," said Tomasowa. These notes, "small papers which [were] sewed together," may or may not have existed, yet they could account for the precision of some of Tomasowa's recollections. He also claimed that he had referred to them when he was first interrogated in 1945 during "the Australian investigation." The U.S. prosecution attorney, Mr. Fisher, was as stunned by this revelation as the defense lawyer, Mr. Shandler. (Tomasowa Testimony, 185.)

troops? Could Japanese sympathizers have caused his disappearance? A number of Japanese units were still being utilized in Java as security forces. Or was Tomasowa giving false testimony against the Japanese who had held him in Kendari for those three nightmarish years?

Perhaps Tomasowa was exhausted and traumatized by the rigors of his interrogations and simply wanted to go home. And the tinderbox ward of Meester Cornelis in Batavia was itself an unsettled and dangerous place for any Christian at the time.

Tomasowa had been subjected to long, grueling cross-examinations, and several harsh accusations from the defense attorney for Rear Admiral Furukawa, yet he had resisted being dissuaded from the truth as he had seen it. Threatened with a charge of perjury, he refused to alter his story to any substantial degree. And under questioning by defense attorney Shandler in the Furukawa case in 1948, Tomasowa could still recall with precision the date of his first interrogations "by Australian investigators." He said it was October 18, 1945, and so it was.[45] Without his testimony, regardless of its inconsistencies, we would know absurdly little of the atrocities conducted throughout the war in the southeastern hinterlands of Celebes.

The more I reflected upon Tomasowa, the more I believed he was a loyal soldier and good Christian, a witness committed to telling the truth as he experienced and recalled it. On the surface, the raw facts, as they often do when examined at first glance, remain less convincing. His abrupt disappearance remains unexplained, creating another murky vacuum in the *Edsall*'s story. All the same, I like to imagine Tomasowa survived the "era of gangs" that followed and that perhaps he might have been one of the *many* KNIL Tomasowas who left Indonesia in 1951 and were transported aboard Dutch ships to Holland, there to live out his days peacefully among other Moluccans who had faithfully executed their duty to the utmost of their ability.

"... *jakkan*"

As if another bewildering note in the discordant history of *Edsall* were needed, one more crewmember had been taken to Kendari and killed, but his remains were found at a later date, and in a different location, it seems. He was the pointer on gun number four, Seaman 2nd Class

Loren Stanford Myers, the sailor who was holding *Edsall*'s life ring in the 1940 crew photo at Shanghai.

Myers' remains were interred in the picturesque National Memorial Cemetery of the Pacific in Hawaii. His interment in the Punch Bowl seemed to imply the participation of his family or next of kin, but here, too, were riddles: In National Cemetery Administration accounts, Myers' burial is marked by an asterisk, which indicates that actual interment records may not have been verified. Quests through United States Naval Casualty lists revealed that he came from the small town of Virden, Illinois (b. April 10, 1920), not far from Springfield (or St. Louis) but half a world away from Honolulu, where he was buried in Section P, Grave 424, on March 31, 1950.

Loren Stanford Myers made six *Edsall* crewmembers "positively" identified, plus "five unknowns" suspected to be Army Air Force personnel. In any case, this suggested that at least six men, and probably as many as eleven, if not more, were "rescued" on March 1 by *Chikuma*. That Myers' remains were found separately from the others has puzzled his family, but it is not inconsistent with evidence from war-crime trials, which yield many instances of groups of POWs being broken up and sent to different Japanese units for execution.

Eighteen months into my research of the *Edsall* saga, I made contact with an individual who provided powerful new information from official communications of half a century ago that explain the discovery of Stanford (as he was known to his family) Myers' remains, and much greater clarification concerning the other bodies, too. These communications were sent to me by Rear Adm. Kenneth "Kent" Riffey, U.S. Navy (Ret.), the son of Stanford Myers' oldest sister, Revah. Although the communications imply more contradictions, they deliver clues as well as factual answers to the mystery of *Edsall*'s survivors, and they pointed me to a small handful of relevant documents at the National Archives. Their sparse, grim details were consistent with my early suppositions.

Two documents of crucial importance were among the papers that Riffey sent. The first he described as "a poor copy of a Department of the Army document, Form 319 Burial Information, dated November 12, 1946 that states 8 bodies were recovered at Japanese Headquarters at Kendari No. 2, Celebes and identified 5 Navy personnel among them by name . . . the other 3 being unidentifiable."[46]

To be precise, however, this document, which is faded and difficult to read, makes no mention of these remains being men from *Edsall*. They had not yet been identified as such. Still, it provides a good general idea of when the bodies were found after the war's end. And although it does refer to "Jap Military HQ, Kendari, II, Celebes," this standardized Form 319 contains another small, unobtrusive, and tantalizing clue: In the box marked "Date of Death" is typed "Dur. Feb. 1942." Such information, even if inaccurate, could only have come from a witness.

A second letter, lengthier, dated March 10, 1949, notes the "Suspension of Board Proceedings" regarding five former crewmen of *Edsall*, whose remains had been identified, along with "Five (5) unknown persons." These remains were designated as "Unknowns X-254A through X-254J" (that is, ten individuals) who had been interred at Barrackpore, India, before being stored in Schofield Mausoleum No. 2 in Honolulu. Quoting from the document itself:

2. Board Proceedings and Letter of Approval . . . have been temporarily suspended by this Office pending further action for the following reason:

a. Additional information received by this Office definitely associates subject Unknowns with AAF personnel transferred from the stricken ship USS *Langley* on 27 February 1942 and declared as missing from USS *Edsall* on 1 March 1942, South of Tjilitjap, Java.[47]

Because AAF men from *Langley* had been on board *Edsall* when she disappeared, and their remains found later, the military wanted to wait until the unidentified remains could be reprocessed through the Central Identification Lab (CIL) in case some of the remains of the AAF personnel could be identified. This report is valuable for one other piece of information: it lists the missing AAF men known lost in the *Langley* operation, an additional nine were ground crew personnel thought to have died aboard *Pecos*. This list does not suggest that all of these men's remains were ever found, though, and ultimately no individual identifications were made.

However, the Riffey papers also included a letter from the Navy Department dated February 15, 1950, to Rear Admiral Riffey's mother

(Stanford's oldest sibling, Revah) with the following information, which struck me like a thunderbolt when I first read it:

> Navy Department records show that after the USS *Edsall* sank, your brother and about 40 other members of the crew were picked up from the sea by the Japanese just off the coast of Tjilatjap, Java. They were taken by Japanese boat to Kendari, Celebes, and held one night at Japanese Military Headquarters, Kendari No. 1. The following day they were transferred to the headquarters at Kendari, No. 2, and were executed.

This was the first and only documentation that I had been able to find that appears to verify the grim recollections concerning the thirty-six murdered U.S. Navy survivors.

According to Tomasowa's testimony in *Shobon*, these survivors and twelve locals, Tomasowa among them, were kept "in the Dutch Guard House that would soon become the prison compound," assumed to be HQ Kendari No. 1. After interrogations "by the highest-ranking Japanese present, Teitje Nakamura… they were lined up on the parade ground of the newly captured Dutch Army camp. Nakamura called the names of seventeen Americans, who stepped forward one by one." These prisoners were loaded into one truck, while Tomasawa and the eleven Indonesian prisoners went separately in another truck, and "Nakamura and his staff rode in a car. The little convoy traveled a few miles to the village of Amoito," near the air base, or HQ Kendari No. 2. The account continues:

> At Amoito the twelve Indonesian prisoners were ordered to dig three large holes. At each hole, Nakamura stationed a Japanese officer with a drawn sword. At the orders of Nakamura, the Americans were blindfolded, brought forward, and forced to kneel. They were then beheaded, and their bodies thrown into the graves. The Indonesians were ordered to fill in the graves. The remaining American prisoners in Kendari were held for about two weeks and then shipped off to work in nickel mines on the island.

It now seemed more certain than ever that Tomasowa must have witnessed the executions of survivors from USS *Edsall* (DD-219) that day. The Navy Department letter of February 1950 proved as much; in his war-crimes statements, Tomasowa alone testified to such a number of POWs captured and killed. If killings on such a scale took place, it would have been virtually without precedent, and may well have been the largest single mass execution of survivors from a U.S. warship in the Pacific war.

How and why this execution was never investigated remains the deepest mystery of the *Edsall* tragedy. Although Rear Admiral Furukawa himself denied knowing of the executions of thirty-six U.S. sailors at Kendari in one of two preliminary statements taken in February 1948, there was a strange, cryptic remark by Furukawa's defense attorney during the June 2, 1948, controversy over Johan Tomasowa's testimony concerning his murdered companions. The defense attorney declared, "I submit that this should be carefully done [that is, questioning Tomasowa and controlling his testimony so as not to prejudice the evidence] in view of the fact that there is before this court evidence of the fact that there was one incident involving a large number of executions."[48]

Beyond this statement there is no clue as to which incident this refers to. Why so little interest in these atrocities? Were the complexities involved so overwhelming? Even if not, the implications of the push by the Supreme Commander of the Allied Powers (SCAP) to "wind up" war-crime trials by 1948 or 1949, and the machinations of his "brooding intelligence tsar," Maj. Gen. Charles A. Willoughby—that most reactionary of unwavering MacArthurites—should be given close consideration.

High-strung, volatile, and as autocratic a militarist as any in Germany and Japan, Willoughby admired Benito Mussolini and Gen. Francisco Franco, and viewed those who were not as conservative as himself or his fascist idols as virtual Communists. MacArthur's G-2 also helped mastermind the deals that allowed Unit 731's Japanese scientists to escape war-crimes prosecution in return for cash and "invaluable" technical research, including thousands of tissue pathology samples taken from their human victims.

As noted elsewhere (and based on the remarks of war-crimes investigators sickened by the atrocities that they were still uncovering), by 1948 and 1949 Willoughby appears to have been reluctant to expend more SCAP resources on any trials that might have reopened old wounds. It is also known that at this time Willoughby had become embroiled in a pre-McCarthyite witch-hunt for "subversives" within SCAP itself ("the leftist infiltration," as he called it) and would not have been devoting as much attention to obscure and remote war crimes as to the vicious infighting within his own command.[49] By any reckoning, this was not a man who displayed a nuanced sense of justice, but then the absence of these qualities may well have been just what endeared Willoughby to MacArthur, who after all called him "my lovable fascist." Nor was either man known to have had any great affection for the U.S. Navy.[50]

That no Japanese were interrogated postwar about the *Edsall*'s survivors might also be explained by the constant turnover of personnel at the Kendari bases during the war. This would have been especially true at the time of *Edsall*'s loss because the Imperial air forces were then still pushing southward throughout the NEI, in the drive to secure Java and establish a defense perimeter from the Andamans in the Indian Ocean to the central Pacific atolls.*

Furthermore, it was doubtful that the men guilty of participating in the "blood carnival" against Allied POWs in March 1942 would still have been stationed at Kendari in August 1945. Whatever scant evidence later retrieved by Allied officers of War Crimes Investigating Detachments concerning *Edsall*'s men must have come from local native eyewitnesses such as Johan Tomasowa, if not the man himself. For years I felt—incorrectly, as it turned out—that the remains were discovered by accident in the course of searching for other known bodies to which investigators had been led. The complete absence of records in IMTFE documents and the Yokohama trials, and the paucity of Graves Registration Unit material, too, appeared to imply this.

But I was incorrect. It hadn't occurred to me that Japanese suspects might well have been questioned about these killings without U.S.

---

* The fluid situation in the Nam'po was exemplified by the commissioning of Okada Fumihide, as *sokan* (chief civil administrator) of the South Western Fleet *minseifu* (civil administrative office) well after these areas had been taken by Imperial forces. In his memoirs, privately published in 1974, entitled *Dotō No Naka Koshū* (A Lone Boat on the High Seas), Okada relates that "the administration of the Occupied Territories was by no means an easy task." The Borneo *minseibu chokan* (regional chief administrator), Inoue Kojiro, collapsed from a nervous breakdown and had to return to Japan, and Okada's own chief secretary, Mizuike, "lamented that the Japanese were more difficult to control than the natives." Theft, drunkenness, army-navy turf wars, personality clashes, private vendettas, and much worse appear to have been commonplace, judging from Okada's narrative, although he makes it clear that *he* was floating well above these sordid doings. Nonetheless there were well-substantiated war-crimes allegations by the Australians against the *minseibu* after the war.

investigators or the Japanese themselves having any knowledge of the identity of the victims or their ships. Nor for that matter had it dawned on me that *Edsall*'s POWs might have been executed with a mixed group of captives taken from different vessels sunk during KdB's strike south of Java. That possibility made itself clear as I continued my research into the Java campaign.

"Darkness Visible": The Mysterious Death of *Modjokerto*

The end of February 1942 marked the start of a series of naval massacres on the Indian Ocean below the Malay Barrier. It was the destiny of many noncombatant Allied vessels to be intercepted and destroyed by the ships and planes of the twin task groups of Nihon Kaigun's Southern Force, under Vice Admirals Kondō and Nagumo.

The seeming opportunity to flee then enjoyed by many of the Allied ships was little more than the freedom of fowl running loose in a henyard. Or, as one Japanese naval aviator aboard the carrier *Akagi* later wrote, employing Kidō Butai was "using a big sword just to kill a chicken."[51] Naturally, some birds were more elusive prey than others.

One such hapless merchant fowl that could neither run nor fight was the 8,806-ton Dutch freighter *Modjokerto* (Capt. Jacobus Verhagen), built in 1922 by W. Gray and Company Ltd. for the Rotterdamsche Lloyd, a large shipping company in Holland. At her optimal speed of fourteen knots, she wasn't going to outsprint anyone, least of all the swift, powerful predators of Kondō and Nagumo.

Fate would find the old ship at Tjilatjap, on Java's southern coast, on February 4, 1942, unloading her cargo of defense materiel "at a snail's pace," according to one account.[52] Within a couple of days another old ship stood in to the harbor: USS *Edsall*. Three weeks later, with the end in sight to everyone but the most foolish and unyielding—such as the U.S. military press censor in Java, Captain Zimmerman, who "personally guaranteed" that the island could not possibly fall to the Japanese at about the same hour as the transports carrying the Imperial Army's 16th Division were approaching their landings at Merak and Bantam Bay—*Modjokerto* proceeded out of Tjilatjap's crowded, winding harbor with a number of other ships attempting to flee. Within the next few days more than half of these vessels would be crumpled on the floor of the Indian Ocean.

On the morning of March 1, several hundred miles south of Java, in broad daylight *Modjokerto* met a fate that rivals the tragedy of *Edsall*.

Her precise killer is uncertain, the exact location of her sinking a mystery, the details of her crew's subsequent disappearance never made clear. (Indeed, the very fact of their rescue was completely unknown until after the war.) Unlike *Edsall*, however, *Modjokerto* sent several distress signals, which were copied by at least three other ships. The Dutch merchantmen *Van Spilbergen, Siantar*, and *Tawali* picked up her initial message; later signals were garbled and read only intermittently.

It would appear that the merchant ship steamed across the search path of Kidō Butai planes before midday, for she broadcast messages saying that she was being shadowed or pursued by an enemy aircraft about 330 nautical miles south southwest of Tjilatjap at about 9:40 or 10:00 (10:40 or 11:00 IJN time).* More than twenty minutes after this first signal was received, a second was picked up, but only by her sister ship, *Siantar*. This signal reported that a warship was chasing *Modjokerto*. Then, some thirty minutes later—around 10:50 (11:50 IJN time)—*Siantar*'s radioman logged a signal "on a rather unusual wavelength" sent using the ship's emergency transmitter. This final signal received by *Siantar* included the word *sinking*.

According to a document compiled by Kapitein Luitenant ter Zee H. M. van Bemmelen in May 1942, *Siantar*'s captain, Vooduyn, believed the ship's location was "roughly 11°30′ S, 107°30′ E." However, van Bemmelen's *Memorandum* also contained a statement by "A. Kokkee," former captain of the sunken 7,135-ton freighter *Boero* (the ex-French *Dupleix*), which was torpedoed by a Japanese submarine south of Sunda Strait on February 25. Forty-four members of this vessel made it safely to Java Head in the ship's boats and were rescued by the Australian minesweepers *Bendigo* and *Burnie*, and taken to Tjilatajap on Saturday, February 28. One day later the captain was given passage to Australia on the merchant ship *Zaandam*. This, like so much else regarding the evacuation of Tjilatjap, was a confused episode because *Zaandam* had gone to sea at the same time as *Modjokerto*—the night of February 27–28—only to be recalled, returning on March 2 and then immediately going to sea again. (*Zaandam* would arrive safely in

* We now know that the battleship *Kirishima* had launched a Nakajima E8N Type 95 Dave floatplane early on March 1, and this plane had dropped its pair of 60-kilogram (132-pound) bombs on a fleeing Allied merchant ship that morning (per *Kirishima*'s tabular record of movement [TROM] at www.combinedfleet.com). It is possible that this vessel was *Modjokerto*.

Australia on March 6 with nearly nine hundred British, Australian, and civilian evacuees.) Nonetheless, when she was approximately three hundred nautical miles south of Tjilatjap on March 1, *Zaandam* had copied parts of *Modjokerto*'s signal, which announced she was under attack by a surface warship ("*bovenwater-oorlogsschip*") and giving her position, then afterwards transmitting, "I AM SINKING."[53]

It is tempting to view these sketchy details through the frame of the reminiscences of *Kaga*'s dive-bomber pilot Yamakawa Shinsaku because they then seem to make some sense. Yamakawa stated that in the morning a destroyer reported sighting an "enemy transport," at which point the Support Force warships were allowed to destroy it with gunfire.[54] One version of Yamakawa's account—there seem to be at least two— says that the "big warships'" guns disposed of the blundering merchant vessel in short order. This particular account says nothing specific about which ships were involved.

A different version (or translation) notes that the battleships did the firing with their 14-inch main batteries.[55] There is no mention of this in the logs of *Hiei* and *Kirishima*, or any recollection of it in the interview conducted with Lt. Motegi Meiji in 2006. But there is an account of a merchant ship being sunk by 8-inch (20cm) gunfire in the action report of heavy cruiser *Chikuma* at just the times one would expect: Dai Hachi Sentai (8th Division) recorded sighting a merchant ship in position 12° S, 106° 40′E around 11:25; opening fire with 20cm guns at 11:43; and sinking the ship at 11:55 after expending a total of forty-nine rounds. These times match up closely with the distress signals received by the various Dutch ships that morning. (Yamakawa notes that at virtually the same time, the carriers received a report from a reconnaissance plane of a "special service vessel" approximately eighty nautical miles to the west: This was the lumbering, overcrowded *Pecos* still plowing southward at twelve to thirteen knots.)

Yet other accounts credit the destruction of *Modjokerto* to an Imperial Navy submarine, the *I-54* (Lt. Cmdr. Kobayashi Shigeo), although nothing appears to substantiate this other than a vague recollection later by an evacuee aboard *Zaandam* who claimed to have heard of radio signals from the freighter saying it had been torpedoed and gunned by a submarine.* There is no specific corroborating data from the submarine.

* From C. B. Droste, *Tot Betere Dagen*. This account, by the former harbormaster of Tjilatjap, apparently contained a description of the attack by a Japanese submarine and the surrender of the ship's crew based upon "SOS signals." This strikes me as fanciful, to say the least.

Kernels of truth can be found in almost every account. In this instance, as in that of *Edsall*, it would require the memoirs of an officer aboard the cruiser *Chikuma* to sort out the facts. For that warship had indeed attacked *Modjokerto*. This officer wrote of the event many years later:

> On one occasion, [all hands on a Dutch merchant ship refused to] abandon the ship. Some crewmembers remained aboard, and counterattacked us with a gun installed near the bow. Of course, this ship was no match for our vessels. As our commanding officer ordered [us] not to aim at the crewmembers near the bow, the shells of our gunfire concentrated on the ship's stern, and the ship began to go down stern first. However, some crewmembers clung to the listing forward deck, [and] kept firing until she was under water. However, the range of the enemy gun was short, and the shells fell [well] short of our vessels, [shooting] up water pillars between both sides in vain.[56]

Although the Japanese officer records that they were impressed by the courage of these Dutchmen, "who were a credit to that maritime nation," during the war the Imperial Navy dealt severely with merchant crews who resisted. I had not formed any basis for the execution of her survivors, however, until I came across a Dutch painting depicting *Modjokerto*'s sinking, and I received the new material from Japan. The painting shows the old freighter sinking by her stern, with survivors in boats and rafts, under fire from the enemy, and a gun mounted on her forward deck. My skepticism regarding this armament was further lessened when I found a wartime photo of *Modjokerto* that clearly reveals a gun mounted in a tub on the stern of the ship, and what appears to be another small weapon positioned forward. *Senshi Sōsho* claims that Nagumo's forces indeed sank *Modjokerto* that day, and that she was armed with "one 3" A/A gun and two machineguns." On a map in the same volume she is said to have been sunk by *Chikuma* and an unspecified destroyer division.

These revelations suggest that the ship may have indeed resisted when approached by the Japanese task group, and this might well account for the fate of the survivors.

After the war, sometime "in the second half of 1946," graves were opened in Kendari, Celebes, and twenty-five bodies from the vanished

Modjokerto were discovered and identified by company insignia on their clothing. On the basis of information from the Netherlands War Graves Foundation (Oorlogs Gravenstichting, or O.G.S.), it appears that these bodies were found in two mass graves at Kendari. The remains were reinterred in the Makassar War Cemetery in 1947. In the 1960s, Indonesia "requested that the mortal remains be concentrated [in] war cemeteries on Java." This was accomplished in 1968, when the men were moved to two cemeteries for the war dead at Ancol near Jakarta and at Kemang Kuning near Surabaja.[57] The reason for the separation of these men's remains into two different cemeteries is not known. Seventeen other crewmembers of *Modjokerto* were never found.

The absence of more primary records at O.G.S. was another disappointment. But embedded within the meager details in the second list was an invaluable piece of data: the date for the killing of *Modjokerto*'s survivors. It was not January 24, but March 24, 1942.

Does it seem an improbable assumption that the fates of the men from *Edsall* and those from *Modjokerto*—both sunk by Vice Admiral Nagumo's Support Force and with specific associations to the heavy cruiser *Chikuma*, and their bodies all recovered near Kendari following the end of the war—were somehow intertwined? The original U.S. report on reinterring the remains mentioned the presence of Dutch Army doctors at the time of the bodies' discovery. There must have been a connection, even if only a tenuous one.

It is doubtful that the submarine *I-54* picked up *Modjokerto*'s survivors, or that the veterans of *Chikuma* rescued these men, or that the battleships would have condescended to rescue them. Perhaps the survivors were found by the escorting destroyers that have been mentioned in connection with this action: *Kasumi* and *Shiranuhi*. Both have been connected to the sinking of "an unidentified merchant ship" south of Java on March 1, 1942, and both destroyers returned on March 11 to Staring Bay with the other IJN vessels under Nagumo and Kondō. Nonetheless this remains nothing but conjecture. The only certainty is that the men from *Modjokerto* somehow ended up in Kendari, the "Japanese execution ground," and there they died.

From a purely mathematical perspective, there could be a plausible equation: twenty-five bodies from *Modjokerto* plus eleven more from *Edsall* add up to thirty-six, the exact number adhered to by the sole eyewitness, Johan Tomasowa. His report of seeing another seventeen men brought to Kendari at the end of May and executed in the same manner does not fit as neatly into the mathematician's box. Tomasowa recalls speaking with a "Malay crewman" from "an English merchant-man" shipwrecked at sea some weeks before "in the neighborhood of Tjilatjap." Seventeen sailors in all—"ten white men, four Malayans, and three Chinese"—were picked up by a Japanese ship that transported them to Kendari. The man's name, according to Tomasowa, was Mard-jono.[58] Had the troubled Ambonese gravedigger perhaps confused the man's name with that of his ship, the *Modjokerto*? The suspicion that these seventeen men allegedly brought to Kendari in late May were from the Dutch merchantman cannot be dismissed out of hand. Such lengthy voyages in open boats from sunken merchant vessels across the Indian Ocean to Java, Sumatra, and the Lesser Sundas most certainly took place.

Those Who Were Spared

Another question remained unanswered: Why were fifty survivors of HMS *Stronghold*—who were initially taken to Kendari—allowed to live, and those *jakkan* from *Edsall* and *Modjokerto* executed? The Royal Navy (RN) men, their ship sunk in the late afternoon of March 2, were transferred to the Japanese cruiser *Maya* after being rescued at sea the following morning. This warship, a member of Cruiser Division 4 with the other *Atago*-class vessels, was not scheduled to participate in Operation "C," so it remained at Staring Bay only from March 7 until March 11. But those British captives were never disembarked there.

According to two accounts written after the war by a survivor from *Stronghold*, Able Seaman John Francis "Spud" Murphy,* a rating from New Zealand, thirty-seven crewmen from the destroyer and thirteen evacuees in transit on that vessel had been "picked up at about 1000 hours the next day, 3 March, by a small Dutch merchantman [believed to have been *Bintoehan*] which had previously been captured . . . when a cruiser came along and prevented his rescuing any more. We were trans-shipped to the cruiser called Maia [*Maya*], or a very similar name."[59]

Murphy went on to write that "the treatment afforded us was excep-tionally good for Japanese standards as we subsequently found out. We

---

* Murphy's accounts were supplied by historian John Bradford of Perth, Australia, who had found and copied the first account, a letter written in longhand, as well as the second account, published in *Smith's Weekly*. I am most indebted to him for his aid.

were given medical treatment for wounds and allowed on deck to have a smoke several times daily."[60] The following day, in the morning, Murphy and his fellow captives were "herded below under guard"[61] when the Japanese force, which consisted of the heavy cruisers *Atago* (flagship of Vice Adm. Kondō Nobutake), *Takao*, and *Maya*, accompanied by two large destroyers, *Arashi* and *Nowaki*, sighted a small Allied convoy. This was the luckless HMAS *Yarra* group.

Murphy's second report, which was printed for an Australian weekly in late 1946, gave a terse eyewitness account of the bloody conclusion to this action, one of the most famous in the history of the Royal Australian Navy:

> We, the survivors from *Stronghold*, were locked below decks for most of the action, but later were taken on deck with much ceremony to be shown the might of Japanese Navy. When we reached the deck, HMS *Anking* had sunk, *Francol* was burning fiercely, and *Yarra* was burning, but her guns were still firing at the Jap destroyers that were circling her and pouring fire into her.* Silently we stood and watched the little sloop, white ensign flying and guns blazing against the hopeless odds of the Jap force. We were allowed to watch her until she finally went down and all that was left was a pillar of black smoke reaching high in the sky.[62]

The three Japanese cruisers then "formed line ahead and steamed away from the scene."[63] They did not bother to pick up survivors from *Yarra*, but for whatever reasons they rescued two men from *Anking* and about fifteen from *Francol*.

"Spud" Murphy next wrote, "We were aboard the cruiser three more days and were transferred to a merchantman in a base harbour. I don't know where it was for certain. [It was Staring Bay, the outer harbor of Kendari in the southeastern Celebes.] The force remained intact until it arrived at the base I previously mentioned. There were battleships, carriers, submarines, cruisers, etc. and all we could see of the surroundings was tall bush covered hills."[64] These men were some of the only captured

---

* The stubborn counterbattery fire from *Yarra* was by all accounts the work of Acting Leading Seaman Ronald "Buck" Taylor (b. 1918), who refused to abandon ship and remained at his gun, "firing slowly and defiantly" until he was killed by the hail of Japanese projectiles from *Arashi* and *Nowaki* as the sloop sank.

Western service personnel to actually see the shadowy vessels of KdB in the first months of World War II and live to tell about it.

Possibly the fact that the men had been shown the Imperial Navy at its most impressive—at least by its own peculiar standards—offered them some protection from the overweening and volatile pride of their captors. If this was the case, it is clear that the men who survived *Edsall*'s last action would be granted no such reprieve. Able Seaman Murphy later speculated that the Japanese were in too much of a hurry, "on what was obviously a swift strike south, and back,"[65] to burden themselves with prisoners, and this explained why they left so many to die in the ocean.

By March 18, *Maya* had returned to Yokosuka, along with *Takao*, her consort. The carrier *Kaga*, her hull slightly damaged, also steamed back to the home islands, accompanied by the destroyer *Hayashio*, arriving at Sasebo on March 22. *Atago*, Vice Admiral Kondō's flagship, took a more leisurely route, visiting Makassar on March 23 to 24, with destroyers *Arashi* and *Nowaki*, on an inspection cruise before steaming back to home waters. After "four days of hell in the coal hold of the Japanese merchant ship," the men of *Stronghold* at last wound up in Makassar. Did they ever realize how close they had come to the compassionate spirit of Bushido? Perhaps not, but as it turned out they were still to face more than three years of inhuman treatment at Makassar in a POW camp dominated by a Japanese seaman named "Yosh," whose brutality and unstable character were legendary.[66]

But most of these men survived. From an account by Bill McDougall, a U.S. news reporter captured in April 1942 after suffering a shipwreck in the Indian Ocean and incarcerated in various Sumatran jails for the next three and a half years:

> Not only did the fate of a prisoner vary according to the individual Japanese who found him but also according to the particular moment the Japanese found him. The Japanese soldier seemed to possess the personality of a Dr. Jekyll and Mr. Hyde. He could be a gentleman or beast with equal naturalness and facility. However, except for wartime conditions on battlefield or in prison camp, the gentleman prevailed in all the Japanese I have ever personally known. In their own country, where I worked before the war, I never experienced an unkindness or a discourtesy.[67]

* * *

It would be an obvious mistake to assume that only the Japanese committed war crimes in the 1930s and 1940s, but what is more perplexing is the viciousness of the atrocities. Perhaps it is best that we do not know all of the details concerning the fates of the survivors of *Edsall*. In too many instances such facts have revealed only cruelty and malice badly veneered by transparent lies and duplicity. But the human heart clings with obstinacy to its deepest scars, and so hope still persisted in the official silence. The mother of Lt. j.g. Ray A. Snodgrass imagined that he might yet appear following the war's end but, finding the home in which he grew up no longer occupied—the family had moved after the war—might wander disconsolately in search of his loved ones. Most families seem to have been afforded no real explanation; their relatives had been declared MIA, followed by KIA, and that was that.

Even now, in the seventh decade following the ship's disappearance, families continue to recall the laughter of brothers, uncles, fathers who went away and never returned. Tears are still shed for these young men. There were twins who lost siblings in the East Indies archipelago during the war's early months who later deliberately joined naval forces sent to the remoter areas of the Asiatic theater in hopes of locating a long-lost brother "somewhere in the Pacific." (Even the grandson of *Edsall*'s commanding officer said that as a youngster he often imagined that J. J. Nix had sailed in a small boat to an uncharted tropical isle, where he lived out his days with a native wife, trouble free and thoroughly acclimated in the ultimate "gone Asiatic" dream.) When other Allied POWs who did survive the war reappeared, it was seen as a miraculous deliverance and inspired the hope that other miracles could take place. Stranger events had occurred, and not merely in the pages of pulp magazines.

Blue Sea of Blood

> *The sounds and the smells disappear ahead. . . . There is only endless darkness without width or depth and a blue sea of blood at the bottom from where the suffering of countless people can't be heard above.*
>
> —*Dogura Magura*, Yumeno Kyōsaku, 1935

And what of the Japanese warships engaged in the pursuit and sinking of *Edsall*? They would not escape their fates either. The four superb carriers succumbed within thirteen weeks of the old flushdecker, destroyed by U.S. intelligence and carrier planes at Midway.

There are haunting ironies here, too; both Vice Adm. Nagumo Chūichi, and Rear Adm. Takagi Takeo had been in combat situations in which misidentification led to their sending substantial air strikes against targets hardly worth the effort. In both cases those attacked were U.S. oilers (*Pecos* and *Neosho*) and single destroyers (*Edsall* and *Sims*): these events occurred during the so-called mopping-up operations south of Java in March, and the Battle of the Coral Sea in May. In June at Midway, problems with misidentification and lax ship-sighting reports would have mortal consequences. In 1944 both admirals would sacrifice their lives in the defense of Saipan, far from the heady victory fever of the war's opening months.

The battleships *Hiei* and *Kirishima*, sister ships in many operations, died within two days of each other off Savo Island, in mid-November 1942, during the furious engagements for Guadalcanal. *Hiei* was reluctantly scuttled after suffering tremendous battle damage from U.S. destroyers, cruisers, and aircraft; *Kirishima* was disemboweled the next night by as many as twenty 2,700-pound, 16-inch armor-piercing shells from USS *Washington* (BB-56), fired at the point-blank range of 5,800 yards.

Sibling cruisers *Chikuma* and *Tone*—among the most active units in the Imperial Navy—lasted longer, engaging in most of the war's major naval contests. The former perished in late October 1944 at the fateful Battle of Leyte Gulf (the Shō Gō operation) under circumstances imperfectly understood to this day (which might be said to rival the lingering questions about *Edsall*'s loss). *Chikuma* was brought to a halt off Samar as she pursued the U.S. escort carriers in their pall-mall dash from Kurita's Centre Force.

Struck by bombs and torpedoes from American planes, after which she capsized suddenly, *Chikuma*'s crew was picked up by the destroyer *Nowaki*. Nemesis, or its Eastern (albeit Indian) analog, karma, kept pace with the Japanese survivors, however, for that very night the loyal destroyer was overtaken by U.S. surface units and sunk with heavy loss of life, including the cruiser's commanding officer. Only one member of *Chikuma*'s entire crew of more than 1,100 men was eventually rescued by the Americans.[68]

Last, it was the fate of *Edsall*'s executioner to be sunk in the shallow waters off Etajima on July 24, 1945, mere weeks before the war's end. *Tone*, "the most powerful and successful cruiser in the Japanese Navy," according to Fukui Shizuo, was reduced to defenselessness by Japan's oil shortages and Allied air superiority. After being bombed and bottomed, she was towed in and beached near Etauchi with her bow toward the northern shore of Nomijima. She was dismantled from April 1947 through September 1948, the same time that the Japanese war-crime investigations and trials were taking place.

Lest We Forget

Think of a way,
a way which you must take alone, permitted
Neither to join the number of the dead
Nor dwell among the living. Die, yet die not . . .
—Seneca, "Oedipus," Act V

Why were *Edsall*'s survivors—whatever the actual number—murdered? One rational explanation could be that the Japanese had neither the time nor the inclination to keep them alive. An academic study offered the following analysis, troubling enough but by and large still rational:

The fortunes of a prisoner of the Japanese depended very largely on the caprice of the officer in charge. He might be summarily shot, or otherwise executed, or he might be "merely" beaten, starved, or tortured. He would certainly not escape ill-treatment of some kind. . . . The defeated, especially those who simply surrendered, were regarded as being beneath contempt. . . . There are really very few things one can do about prisoners. They can be killed or ransomed—the common practices of the ancient world—or they can be incarcerated and then perhaps repatriated. The Japanese did not quite resort to any one of these as a policy: instead they "kept" their prisoners—if this is the appropriate term—in conditions that were often tantamount to a living death. They worked until they dropped. It was an achievement just to survive in these circumstances. The Japanese do not seem to have had any compunction about the execution of the vanquished or moral qualms about ill-treatment in general.[1]

In the end, rational though they may be, such explanations are no more satisfactory than appealing to the superstitions of southern Java in order to get at the heart of *Why?* But even if reasoning falls short of penetrating these terrible acts, there yet remain representations that can enlarge our understanding, if not heal those bone-deep wounds suffered so many years ago.

In practical terms, the action of March 1 may be seen as the fallacy of the traditional Japanese saying: "When a tiger attacks a hare it uses all of its strength." The Imperial Navy expended far too much—in resources, in energy, in time—on this insignificant military target, as well as others. Indeed the entire mopping-up operations south of Java were ultimately wasteful and counterproductive; one might argue that the Japanese learned nothing from their small successes there.

In the quick victories of December, January, and February, the Imperial Navy sealed its own doom and that of the Japanese nation by failing to perceive what was concealed behind these achievements: there was nothing truly decisive about any of them. On the contrary, even an action that was in every meaningful sense minor, such as that involving *Edsall*, should have alarmed the commanders of Nihon Kaigun. The poor scouting, lax identification, and shoddy execution betrayed fundamental weaknesses that would only be amplified in more serious engagements. And so they were, as the Battle of the Coral Sea and Midway both proved.

The *Edsall* engagement encompasses sundry elements of what has been deemed "constructed consciousness," from the falsified reality of the Victory on the March photo to the alibis and excuses of the ineffectual Kaigun-ners, from deadly enticements to East Indian *romusha* throughout the Nam'po to the terrible fate of those few survivors from *E-do-soo-ru*.

Granted, there was an immediate semirational response to such waste (as shown by the changes in long-range gunnery engagement rules), but this wasn't the deeper, mortal lesson to be drawn. In 1914, Adm. Akiyama Saneyuki of the Naval Affairs Division of the Navy Ministry had told a task force commander going to the Nan'yo, "If you do a job that expends large sums of money, at least get some profits."[2] This might be another way of viewing the photographs and films acquired in the First Stage operations; they at least offset to some extent the heavy expenditures of fuel and ammunition. But the overall pursuit of the

Southern Area fantasy, so seductive and elusive, with its proponents crying "*Minami-e!*" (Southward, ho!) since the turn of the century and before, was as wasteful and misguided as trying to sink the slippery old four-stacker at long range:

> Unfortunately for the inhabitants of the South Seas area, the Japanese who had established themselves as entrepreneurs and successful economic agents of empire, and the allies that fought back the Japanese military offensive, the navy's aggressive strike south in 1941 solved none of Japan's problems that naval planners suggested it would. Rather, it led to hardship, suffering, and economic calamity. It is perhaps the greatest irony surrounding the rise of the Japanese navy in the late nineteenth and early twentieth centuries that the ideology which its leaders helped create from 1870s onward, in no small part to justify its independent existence and budgetary expansion, eventually led the navy on a ruinous course that took with it the very empire and domestic security for which much [*sic*] of its vessels and sailors had been developed and trained to protect.[3]

That the Imperial Navy ever acquired new insights into deficiencies for the tactical doctrine utilized by Kidō Butai is another matter, and a questionable one. Tanaka Raizo, former rear admiral, wrote an incisive article for the *U.S. Naval Institute Proceedings* in the 1950s, which contained the following criticism of Japanese military thinking:

> In belittling the fighting power of the enemy lay a basic cause of Japan's setback and defeat in every operation of the Pacific war. Enemy successes were deprecated and alibied in every instance. It was standard practice to inflate our own capabilities to the consequent underestimation of the enemy's. This was fine for the ego but poor for winning victories.[4]

If "under-estimation of the enemy" was a chronic problem with the Japanese military machine from the beginning, so was the navy's strategic and economic chimera of *nanshin*, the Southern Advance, which transformed Teikoku Kaigun into a serpent devouring its own tail.

*   *   *

Long life and short life are made all one by death.
                                                    —Montaigne, *Essais*

Japanese nationalist ideology of 1942 required an idealized meaning, and it is embodied in the famous propaganda photograph "HMS
Pope." This visual trope may be construed as ceremonial violence first—
that is, celebrating a sacrificial act:

> Sacrifice . . . is performed in the name of the official ideology . . .
> in sight of all and to everyone's knowledge. The victim's iden-
> tity is determined by strict rules. . . . The sacrificial victim also
> counts by his personal qualities, the sacrifice of brave warriors is
> more highly appreciated than that of just anyone. . . . The sacri-
> fice . . . testifies to the power of the social fabric, to its mastery
> over the individual.[5]

When one perceives *Edsall*'s last image in these terms, it is that
much more difficult to view it without feeling the wastefulness of war
at its most piercing.

Previously thought to have first been published in December 1942
for the propaganda booklet "Victory On the March," in honor of the
anniversary of the Pearl Harbor attacks, the image of *Edsall*'s destruction was in fact first released in the April 15, 1942, issue of *Asahigraph*
magazine in Japan. That is, a mere six weeks after the fact. Japanese sailors
carried these magazines with them in the war's opening months, and on
occasion sought to impress their foes by showing their images to them.

Unlike ceremonial violence, the second mode of violence is hidden
and concealed because it "threatens to reveal its essential contradictions
and weaknesses."[6] This is what should be perceived as "massacre violence," and it is never represented if at all possible.

> [It] reveals the weaknesses of the same social fabric . . . hence
> it should be performed in some remote place where the law is
> only vaguely acknowledged. . . . The individual identity of the
> massacre victim is by definition irrelevant (otherwise his death
> would be murder). . . . Unlike the sacrifices, massacres are gen-
> erally not acknowledged or proclaimed, their very existence is
> kept secret and denied.[7]

The *Edsall*'s intentionally mistaken identity and the enduring, well-concealed execution of her survivors are paradigms of this mode of "massacre violence." No more perfect emblem of these contradictions exists in the history of the Pacific war.

There is no known other instance in which as many survivors from a single U.S. warship were rescued, only to be murdered so hastily with or without any clear reason. And this applies whether or not one accepts that there were no more than a dozen men taken prisoner, or as many as forty. Remember that these killings occurred more than a month before the Doolittle Raid, an event that later gave the enemy an excuse to legitimize the murder of POWs. Explaining this ruthlessness through rational analysis is impossible, even though very considerable minds have attempted to do so.*

As noted, perhaps the security-conscious Japanese, chronically secretive to a fault, even paranoid regarding their naval programs, felt that these men from "*E-do-soo-ru*" already knew too much, or had seen more than was acceptable while aboard *Chikuma* as they returned to Staring Bay. The task forces were preparing, training for the major operation (Operation "C," or Indian Ocean Raid), which would also take them deep into the Bay of Bengal, where they hoped to destroy even more Allied shipping and eradicate whatever naval vessels and planes were present in this "British lake," expelling the Royal Navy's bothersome presence once and for all.[8]

It is also plausible that the navy simply washed its hands of the survivors as soon as they could in Kendari, turning these doomed captives over to the hardened naval garrison or Tokkei Tai administrators there. In other areas (Ambon, for example), Allied prisoners who had fought well against the invaders were methodically butchered for nothing more complex than revenge by enraged, second-tier Japanese service personnel.[†] An American publication containing excerpts from

---

* The most thorough and impressive attempt is Professor John W. Dower's *War Without Mercy: Race and Power in the Pacific War*.

† The facts concerning mass killings of Dutch and Australian POWs that took place in February 1942 at Laha airfield were not revealed until very late in the course of Allied war-crime investigations—after 1950—and were exceptionally ugly and savage. Hundreds of helpless men were decapitated under the most horrific circumstances, primarily by crewmembers of a sunken Japanese minesweeper, lost in the Ambon invasion. Eyewitness accounts appalled even the hardened Australian investigators from the War Crimes Section under Lt. Col. D. L. B. Goslett. (See Ambon Massacre, File 85, H. 851.

wartime Japan—in this instance a magazine article—reveals more of this rage:

> The ultimate objective of the Imperial Navy in the Greater East Asia War is the absolute annihilation of the American and British Fleet: not a single American or British warship is to be left floating on the sea. . . . The Imperial Navy is burning with the fiery determination that its guns will not cease firing until the final objective is fully attained." (*The New Order in Greater East Asia* magazine, April 1942).[9]

This is relatively well-mannered, but still reminiscent of a threatening, and disturbed as well as disturbing, note sent by the Imperial Navy to British sailors embroiled in one of many "incidents" along the China coast in 1939:

> Your kindest Sailor of Britain. Perhaps you don't know why you came here. Mr. Chamberlain (do you know, the Prime Minister of Britain) never order such a navy action. If you are only brutal barbarian no need of word to you, Sir. We declare we derive you Anglo-Saxon from Asia. We are very sorry you belong to this category. We have warned your friend here to go back to his native village of Britain. The same warning message still be also to you. We will politely teach you for first greet.
>
> Do you know sacrifice Armada. This is the name given to you Far East Fleet of Britain by your respected Admiral not by Foreign authority. Do you challenge us?
>
> Perhaps you can kill us free as you want. But do you do it glory to kill disarmed people in your unjust reason as your same deed in Arabia? God never be a word. Do you challenge to the furious Invincible Armada of World of Japanese Navy Force? Perhaps you never be such a Dunglike foolish boy. If you challenge we will glad to throw you back your grave. But you shall be know the meaning of the Sacrifice Fleet. You had best know the fish of the China Sea is thirsty for blood.[10]

Behind the Monty Pythonesque insults that the British sailors are said to have found rather funny at the time, one cannot fail to apprehend darker drives, which would soon turn Greater East Asia crimson under a sun of blood.

On December 20, 1949, the remains of the aforementioned five *Edsall* crewmembers, along with five unknowns (now known to be Army Air Force), were interred at Jefferson Barracks National Cemetery, about ten miles outside of St. Louis, Missouri, in Plot 79–0 340A-C.* No mention of *Edsall* is made on the marker. Their final resting place seems only slightly less obscure than the distant grave of their ship's namesake— who had likewise been decapitated on a tropical island, in 1899—or the two-thousand-fathom-deep abyss in which the old destroyer, her courageous commander, and her steadfast crew now sleep eternally.

Every action has its share of ritual and its share of improvisation.
—Tzvetan Todorov

Although I have attempted in this history of a mystery to clear up a number of misconceptions and falsehoods that surround the ship and her loss, her final story may still be as elusive to history's detectives as she was to Nihon Kaigun's frustrated gunners, always deftly skipping just out of range whenever we feel we've arrived at a definitive account. Certainly my research has taken unexpected twists and turns along the way.

I first met Dutch filmmaker Niek Koppen at the 1993 and 1994 reunions of the Lost Battalion, which included men from the 131st Field Artillery Regiment, 2nd Battalion, Texas National Guard, and survivors of USS *Houston* (CA-30). Niek described his work in progress, and we discussed not only the Lost Battalion and *Houston* but also an overaged, doomed destroyer. He seemed to know something of *Edsall*, but the name was only mentioned in passing conversation.

How much more surprised, not to say astonished, was I in 1997—at our annual memorial reunion in *Houston* honoring our city's namesake cruiser and crew—when Niek's documentary was screened (along with Vic Campbell's two-part history of USS *Houston*) in the hotel's darkened ballroom. The work in progress he had mentioned three

---

* Even in this, the *Edsall*'s story had ambiguity: The grave marker first lists the *Edsall* crew—Amory, Andrus, Cameron, Vandiver, and Watters—with their ranks, and then below that are the words "Five unknowns." Whether this was meant to refer to the five men already identified (i.e., "Here lay five men, previously unknown") or to five additional sets of unidentified remains was unclear; ultimately, Rear Admiral Riffey's documents straightened this out.

555

years earlier, which had just been released on video, was his 1995 film *De Slag in de Javazee* (The Battle of the Java Sea), which tells the story of the battle from the points of view of participants interviewed in America, England, Holland, Japan, and Australia. It incorporated a good deal of rare archival footage, and within the somber opening minutes of the movie appeared a flickering, bluish-tinted snippet of film showing a four-funneled ship motionless on the sea, repeatedly straddled by large-caliber naval shells, the huge white splashes vivid in the twilight.

The scrap of film, cropped down to twenty seconds in *De Slag in de Javazee*, is without question the same seen in early 1952 by the preproduction staff and naval experts—including Lt. j.g. Donald R. Morris*— of the groundbreaking television series *Victory at Sea* (1952–1953). It matched in almost every respect the written descriptions given in an August 1952 article in *All Hands* magazine (a monthly periodical for navy personnel), which also reproduced two stills taken from that film that precisely match the footage in *De Slag in de Javazee*.

The *All Hands* piece in turn formed the basis for Hanser's article, "The Mystery of the Missing Destroyer," for *Bluebook* magazine: "These films [*sic*] were the only known motion pictures of a United States warship being sunk by enemy gunfire. But they were more than that."[11] Hanser had been a cowriter with Henry Salomon for *Victory at Sea*.

In November 2004, more than seven years after first seeing *De Slag in de Javazee*, I recontacted Niek in Holland. A couple of excited e-mails produced the source of this little-known strip of film—the Netherlands East Indies. Niek acknowledged that the original information that claimed the film showed "the sinking of one of the Dutch ships" had to be "nonsense."[†] But the Netherlands East Indies source made perfect sense.

---

* I spoke with Morris about *Edsall* in 1993. At that stage in his life, Morris had left the *Houston Post* newspaper, where he had written an op-ed column for more than twenty years, and was semiretired but still producing "The Donald R. Morris Newsletter," by subscription only. We talked over the phone two or three times, and in person as well when I ran into him at a Rice University–area scale model shop. He mentioned sending me original materials from the 1952 investigation, but all I ever actually received was a subscription form to his newsletter.

†Along the same erroneous but understandable lines was a mistaken belief that the cruiser *Ashigara*, flagship of Vice Adm. Takahashi Ibō, CinC of 3rd Fleet, had picked up and delivered *Edsall*'s survivors to Kendari. This probably stemmed from the fact that this cruiser had been in NEI surface actions and had at various times quartered ABDA survivors taken from sunken warships. This in turn had to do with the

When I finally received a DVD copy of the rare Japanese Nichiei newsreel from the Nederlands Instituut voor Beeld en Geluid, I was in for more surprises: There was half a minute of extra footage of *Edsall*'s end that had not been incorporated by Niek Koppen into his documentary; given the poor quality of the images, it wasn't hard to understand why he had not used it. Even so, the Nichiei newsreel proves that the famous photo of "HMS *Pope*" is in fact a combination print, thanks to photographic special effects. There is *no* major salvo splash on the forward section of the ship when it is hit by the four shells around its stern. And there was the original Japanese-language soundtrack.

Immediately before the *Edsall* footage is shown, there are inserted segments of prewar film, with various Imperial Navy units, including "Special Type" destroyers and at least one *Atago*-class cruiser. The narrator recounts early-war successes to the accompaniment of selections from Wagner's more martial passages. One can make out the spoken names of various Allied warships sunk during the NEI campaign: *Houston, Exeter, DeRuyter*. Then appears that "scrap of blurred and wavering film," with its undeniable ninety seconds of combat footage, over which no voice intrudes—just the booming echoes of heavy guns.

After the final major salvo lands around the ship's stern, the film freezes. This cinematographic device is used elsewhere in the newsreel. Then, strangely, the frame comes to life again, like a marble statue shifting into animation in front of one's eyes, and the towering shell splashes collapse around the stricken vessel. There is one more cut, and then the four-funneled ship is no longer visible. One sees white smoke and what appear to be much smaller disturbances on the surface of the sea (perhaps tertiary gunfire?) before a large, dark cloud billows up from the water, as if soot from the stacks and boilers was forced out as she sank. The quality of the footage as shown in the Japanese newsreel is even poorer than that of the excerpts in Niek's film. One must view everything repeatedly in order to make heads or tails of the actual events. Yet the footage reveals the dogged determination of the *Victory at Sea*

flagship's need for swift intelligence, as these were primarily ABDA officers being interrogated, but there is no hard evidence that *Ashigara* made port at Kendari, and not the least suggestion she ever disembarked POWs there. (I am indebted to Tony Tully's research in tracking this ship's movements.)

producers—Lt. j.g. Donald R. Morris and company—in 1952. This rarest of naval warfare footage is so with good reason.*

So, whether misnamed at Smyrna's destruction or mistaken for a British destroyer, a light cruiser, or one of the Dutch ships lost in the Java Sea, the *Edsall* has accumulated fables and misapprehensions over the years, and has only now grudgingly discharged some of her deeply stored secrets.

In those disheartening days when the United States had had more than its fair share of bad news, it was imperative to acknowledge the great sense of righteous anger felt throughout the country. The heavy naval losses suffered in the Java campaign were not scrutinized for the military achievements they were not, but for the inspirational acts of sacrifice and devotion to duty that they were. In this they were closely related to the army's men being sacrificed in the Philippines.

In October 1942, an article in *Time* magazine featured Admiral Hart's views on the campaign after he had returned to the States. For public consumption Hart implicated the Dutch command in U.S. naval losses, but this was not the opinion he offered in his 1946 "Supplementary," in which he declined to blame Vice Admiral Helfrich. The magazine article contains sad half-truths and wishful thinking:

> Hart had deployed his Asiatic Fleet as far south as Borneo before the war began. He contends it would have been "footless" to bring his destroyers and cruisers into Luzon waters after control of the air had been lost. Twice—at Balikpapan and Bali—the Asiatic Fleet stalled the Jap drive southward, but (after Hart was relieved) "disaster soon followed and in the end we lost heavily—the *Houston* [cruiser], *Pillsbury*, *Edsall* and *Pope* [destroyers] were all lost in surface ship action at sea under circumstances about which we know little. . . . Yes, ships were lost, but it was not footless. They took a good toll from the enemy. . . . The submarines caused much loss and unfortunately have taken some themselves. Not much ever gets said about it for their personnel share, with the entire Navy, the description, 'the silent service.' They really overdo it."[12]

* The footage seen by U.S. researchers in 1952 must have been the original sixty feet (about ninety seconds) of 35mm film, and not the farrago of prewar, staged, stock, and actual footage of the 1942 Nichiei newsreel.

Restoring morale, not fault finding or finger pointing (the purpose of the Roberts Commission, in the eyes of many), was the order of the day. This was the dark subtext of that "iron necessity"[13] that has passed into popular usage through the facile expression "they were expendable." Expendable, of course, if duty demanded, but not forgettable—the United States would not replace "lest we forget" with "best we forget," would she?

From Ensign John W. Gustin's last letter home from *Edsall*, December 27, 1941:

> I doubt very much if it is necessary to warn you about what to believe and what not to believe in regards to the reports you may receive concerning the war. Propaganda is naturally running rampant and the other day we had a very good example of what I mean. The Tokyo news broadcast reported that the Asiatic Fleet had been wiped out. We all got quite a kick out of that. . . . Don't believe anything unless it has been officially put out by the powers that be in Washington.

All unusual actions are subject to sinister interpretations.
—Montaigne, *Essais*

Second-guessing is not my intention; Helfrich, Glassford, Wavell, Hart, Brereton, et al., were not policymakers but professional soldiers doing the best they could with what they had. *Edsall*'s loss and the death of those young men was a sacrificial offering to the gods of political expediency. Yet, later, only Adm. Thomas Hart had the courage and honesty to openly admit how painful the Asiatic debacle had been to him personally, and the guilt he felt for having abandoned so many of his officers and men in their hour of need.

Hart, snubbed and insulted by MacArthur on more than one occasion, even went so far as to invite the son of slain Capt. Albert H. Rooks—USS *Houston*'s skipper killed in the melee off Bantam Bay—to his home at Christmas after Hart had been relieved as ABDA's naval leader, in order (or so speculated Hal Rooks in conversation more than sixty years later) to make his peace with a human consequence of those hard decisions.

The first one hundred days of the war in the Pacific were among the most tragic that U.S. military forces have ever suffered. As clichéd as it sounds today, in a time of callous pride and diminished memory, the elements of classical tragedy were writ large in the Netherlands East Indies campaign, particularly among the Dutch forces and the ships and men of the old Asiatic Fleet. And nowhere is that somber cloud of fate more pronounced, more impossible to escape, than in the example of *Edsall*: a ship that perished attempting to support the Dutch, and whose few survivors had an even more absolute connection with these Allies.

> *Duty. In the Navy, the only acceptable standard is performance of duty to the limit of one's ability.*
> —*The Naval Officer's Guide*, 1943

My hope has been that re-telling this story would draw attention to the sacrifices made by the men of the Asiatic Fleet and rescue their stories from neglect—another form of undeserved suffering. Their relatives and descendants deserve nothing less.

Yet there was a "curious fitness to *Edsall*'s death."[14] The ship's namesake, Seaman Norman E. Edsall of Kentucky, had been killed on Easter Sunday, April 1, 1899, by Samoan native rebels while struggling to return his wounded lieutenant to safety. The official records concerning this incident tell us that Seaman Edsall "showed a spirit of bravery and self-sacrifice in keeping with the standards of the United States Navy."

Little known before, Norman Edsall died after landing forces from HMS *Tauranga* and USS *Philadelphia*, totaling some 110 men plus "150 friendlies," were ambushed by 800 heavily armed Samoan warriors near a German-owned plantation east of Apia. Vaguely described by Rear Adm. Albert Kautz of the U.S. Navy in a contemporary press article as "a reconnoitering party," about sixty Royal marines and British sailors commanded by Lt. A. H. Freeman of HMS *Tauranga*, and an American contingent of another fifty-six U.S. Marines and U.S. Navy sailors armed with a Navy Colt Model 1895 machine gun and led by Lt. P. V. Lansdale of *Philadelphia,* marched out to disperse the rebels. However, "on its return this force was suddenly attacked in the rear and immediately afterward on the left and in the front. The Colt gun jammed and became useless, and the friendlies bolted."[15]

Being surrounded and out-gunned, Lieutenant Freeman ordered a retreat, but he was soon killed by a sniper hidden in the trees. As Lt. Phillip V. Lansdale attempted to free the machine gun, he was struck in the thigh by a rebel bullet, which shattered the bone. Dispirited by the loss of their two leaders, and under severe fire, the men "retired to the beach, under cover of fire from HMS *Royalist*."[16]

Ensign J. R. Monaghan was last seen alive defending Lansdale against the Samoans with his revolver. Norman Edsall perished in the firefight as he tried to either aid the wounded Lansdale or recover the bodies of the slain officers. Five other sailors from HMS *Royalist* and two more U.S. seamen from *Philadelphia* were also killed. Their dead bodies were beheaded and mutilated by the triumphant Samoan warriors, "according to the barbarous custom that their best friend among civilized men, Robert Louis Stevenson, deplored and did his best to abolish," wrote the *New York Times*. Later that night French priests brought the decapitated heads back to Apia.

Given *Edsall*'s career, and the fate of the old destroyer forty-three years later, it is ironic that the young U.S. sailor for whom the ship was named gave his life in a cause that has been termed America's first serious breach of the Monroe Doctrine, and criticized by U.S. Secretary of State W. Q. Gresham as the "first departure from our traditional and well-established policy avoiding entangling alliances with foreign powers in relation to objects remote from this hemisphere."[17] But the military serves at the pleasure of the president and Congress, and theirs is not to reason why.

The ship named in Norman Edsall's memory more than lived up to the highest standards and best traditions of the naval service. She and her crew sold themselves as dearly as possible on March 1, 1942, and their actions may have saved the lives of scores of *Pecos* survivors. In the future, that remarkable spirit should always be kept in mind whenever this story is reexamined and retold.

Postscript

The Revelations of Dr. Haraguchi

That's the historian's dream: fresh information that illuminates a dark problem.

—Edward Drea, former chief, Research and Analysis Division, U.S. Army Center of Military History

Perhaps it is fitting that the extraordinary mystery of *Edsall*'s end, and that of her survivors, much of which had been secondhand or speculative, should find a final voice through one of the men who actually lived through those events in March 1942: an ensign candidate (*shoi kohosei,* or midshipman) aboard the heavy cruiser *Chikuma*. His general quarters placed him in an ideal location to witness the pursuit itself, and he was later ordered to participate in the rescue, interrogation, and transfer of the U.S. destroyer's captured crewmembers. In the end, my supposition concerning the large number of IJN personnel involved in the engagement had a reasonable basis that yielded results.

After more than two years of research, I was able to locate and interview—through my friend in Japan, Kan Sugahara—two officers from *Chikuma* who had been eyewitnesses and participants. And to my amazement and delight, they were neither reticent nor evasive, but offered valuable and poignant insights. One of these was Sasaki Masao, former assistant gunnery officer stationed in the *shageki-ban shitsu* (gunnery computer room). The second witness, Haraguchi Shizuhiko, an ensign candidate and assistant navigator, was on *Chikuma*'s compass bridge among the *kokai-ka* (navigation personnel) during the battle. His direct superior was the chief assistant navigator and head of the 7th Division, Ensign Kiuchi Tetsuro.* This assistant navigator had been aboard the cruiser with ten other *shoi kohosei* from the beginning of the war. They had been present for the Hawaii Operation against Pearl Harbor and the invasion of Wake Island, as well as later attacks in swift succession on Rabaul, Kavieng, Ambon, and Port Darwin. These young officers were also tasked with picking up *Edsall*'s survivors, and afterward interrogating them.[†]

Stepping forward after sixty-five years, Dr. Haraguchi Shizuhiko published an eight-page account he called "The Sea Battle Off Tjilat-jap." And while one may question memories from a man now well into his eighties, careful sifting separates important new information from the less relevant.

After outlining the movements of Sentai 8 from the Hawaii Operation through the attacks on Wake Island, Rabaul, Kavieng, and Darwin, and merchant raiding in the Indian Ocean south of Java, Haraguchi sets the stage for the encounter of March 1, 1942: "The mission of our Kidō Butai was to locate and sink the enemy vessels attempting to flee from the Southeast Asian areas into the East Indian Ocean, and to bomb and destroy the enemy vessels taking refuge in the harbors of Java island." He goes on to describe the harbor of Tjilatjap as "heavily congested with the Allied warships and merchant ships" swept before the advancing Japanese, which, he writes, resembled the Allied debacle at Dunkirk.

With their floatplanes and the scouts of KdB searching south of Java, numerous Allied merchant ships were driven into the Imperial Navy's net to be sunk by shellfire and bombs or, in many cases, by the torpedoes and deck guns of submarines. Yet, Haraguchi frankly admits, "For our conceited Kidō Butai (regarded as the very best fleet in the world) it was undeniable that (our) sinkings were mostly unarmed merchant ships, and we had more time on our hands than needed every day. . . ."

* Ensign Kiuchi's superior was *Chikuma*'s *kokaicho* (navigator), Lt. Cmdr. Okihara Hideya (51st Term of Etajima). Lieutenant Kiuchi, who served later on submarines, survived the war.

† Dr. Haraguchi, a retired otolaryngologist, published an anthology of his writings in Japan based on his wartime experiences. This particular one about *Edsall* tells a story never before revealed in the West. All quoted passages are from Dr. Haraguchi's account as translated by Kan Sugahara.

He continues his description:

Only one time, did our Kidō Butai encounter an enemy surface vessel and engage in a gunfire and torpedo battle. It was the
first and last, and the only ship-to-ship battle that I have ever
experienced in my whole life. It was on the evening of March 1,
1942, when our fleet was off Tjilatjap harbor, underway down
to the south after completion of the operations along the southern coast of Java Island.

A warship was in pursuit of our fleet from the north, at full
speed like an arrow, trailing black smoke behind her. As Chikuma was at the rearmost of the fleet, the lookout of our ship
spotted her first. Hurriedly, signal flags were hoisted high up
on our mast, "Enemy light cruiser is in pursuit of our fleet...."
In response to the signal of "sighted the enemy," the flagship
CV Akagi ordered the 3rd BB Div (Hiei and Kirishima) and
the 8th CruDiv (Tone and Chikuma) to immediately reverse
course and intercept her.

Over the next hour and a half, *Edsall* eluded most of the Japanese
salvos as Lt. J. J. Nix and crew put on one of the Pacific war's finest examples of ship handling under fire. And she fought back as she went:

As soon as the enemy destroyer was within our gunfire range,
we opened up. However, this enemy ship was extremely maneuverable, and repeated changing speeds and courses, and ran
away like a Japanese dancing mouse, and we could not score
any hits. Soon, the destroyer deployed [a] smoke screen, which
made it more difficult for us to aim, and we missed more shots.
... Moreover, if the enemy destroyer found opportunities, she
repeated counterattacks by launching torpedoes and gunfire.
Fortunately, we were beyond the range of the enemy gunfire,
and all shells fell short of our fleet.

Haraguchi's memoir even acknowledges the trepidation experienced by some of the young Japanese sailors in their first naval combat
as they watched torpedo wakes pass by their ship. And the fact that they

were out of range didn't keep them from hunching their shoulders as the *Edsall*'s guns flashed in the distance. Haraguchi goes on to describe "blunders" committed by the inexperienced crew of *Chikuma*, such as failing to keep an adequately sharp lookout for airplanes, due to their wariness about *Edsall*'s torpedoes. And he recalled a curious fragment of conversation overheard on the cruiser's bridge concerning the four-piper's evasiveness. His superiors apparently deduced that *Edsall* must have had a special type of boiler that enabled radical course changes and rapid shifts from high to low speed: "In addition, the use of special boiler called Belox (in Kana *be-ro-kku-su*) which could withstand rapid changes in the combustion areas, thus enabled such high mobility." ("Belox," which naturally sounded strange to the young navigator, may well have been "Babcock-Wilcox.")

Frustrated, perplexed, and running out of daylight, fuel, and ordnance, the Support Force yielded to the mighty carriers of Kidō Butai once more: "As the twilight deepened, there were the possibilities of letting the enemy escape, or allowing her to launch [more] torpedoes at us, [so] the Fleet headquarters finally decided to launch the carrier-based planes." The Vals brought the old ship to a halt at last. "[Soon] several bombs dropped by the dive-bombers hit the enemy destroyer, damag[ing] her rudder, and she lost maneuverability. Then each ship concentrated gunfire on her, silenced her, and gave her the coup de grace."

Haraguchi then itemizes the enormous expenditure of shells in the engagement and records the name of the U.S. ship: USS *Edsall*. He concludes, "In my personal opinion, it was a very expensive battle to sink only one destroyer. We paid an extraordinarily high price and took an [unexpected amount of] time."

So far, the information in Haraguchi's memoir is largely within the realm of current knowledge, either acquired or deduced. The next pages, which bring the Haraguchi narrative to an end, take us into *terra incognita*, yet the landscapes there are familiar, if heartbreaking.

All days travel toward death, the last one reaches it.
—Montaigne, *Essais*

As the enemy destroyer [was] listing heavily, and was about to go down, the commanding officer of the ship gathered his men on the deck with the Abandon Ship order, and appeared to give his last instruction as the commanding officer.* Some of the crewmembers lowered the boats and got into them. Most of them jumped into the sea one after another. The person [who] appeared to be the commanding officer, however, walked on the listing deck and returned to the bridge. It is believed that he shared the fate of his ship.

Although one may view this heroic finale with some skepticism, Haraguchi makes a point of stating that the survivors of *Edsall* and two different IJN officers on *Chikuma*—Special Service Ensign Washio and another unnamed man—corroborated this version of Lt. Joshua James Nix's last moments:

> Later, Special Service Ensign Washio told me that he had clearly witnessed the courageous deed of the commanding officer through his large binoculars from beginning to end. . . . Thereafter, we, the junior officers, interrogated the POWs. According to what they told us, the commanding officer of the enemy destroyer returned to the bridge alone, after he ordered all hands to abandon ship.

There was little time for reflection, though. *Senshi Sōsho* records that *Chikuma* was "on orders" (in all probability from Rear Adm. Abe Hiroaki in Sentai 8's flagship *Tone*) to pick up survivors. As shown on the track chart, *Chikuma* made a 360-degree turn and slowly steamed back to the area in which *Edsall* had disappeared. "The battle was over, but what came after the battle was no simple matter at all! In the vicinity where the enemy ship had sunk, we found many crewmembers who had gotten on the cutters, lifeboats, or were clinging to rafts and buoys, and swimming with their clothes on. What a pitiful sight! As we were ordered, the rescue work began."

Haraguchi, with the remaining *shoi kohosei* of *Chikuma* and other sailors, began dropping knotted lines over the sides of the cruiser's aft decks to pull the bedraggled survivors of *Edsall* from the water. Yet no

---

* This reference to the listing ship verifies the memories of 1st Lt. Motegi Meiji aboard the flagship *Hiei*, and distinguishes *Edsall's* end from that of *Pope*, as well as confirming the identity of the capsizing flushdecker as *Edsall* in the Japanese film footage.

sooner had they rescued a small handful than they received a submarine alert and new orders: "Discontinue rescuing the survivors immediately, and join the main body." The remaining men were left to the dubious mercy of the sea. Haraguchi states that he and his companions felt pity for the large number of U.S. "crewmembers left to the sea," but he hoped that the mild weather and relative tranquility of the Indian Ocean at that time of year might permit some to reach land alive. Although Haraguchi says "many crewmembers" were still alive in rafts as well as boats, none were ever seen again.

"We had to discontinue the work after we had picked up 8 survivors. . . . Those POWs who had been injured were treated. All of them changed from their soaking wet clothes to IJN fatigues* and were accommodated in the enlisted men's quarters." Only eight? So it seems. In another correspondence I was told that it was possible that "one or two" might have been rescued by *Tone*. There is no amplifying or supporting evidence to back this up, however.

What is indisputable, though, is the number of American remains associated with *Edsall* found in Kendari after the war. There were eleven skeletal sets—six full and five partial—six sailors from *Edsall* and five bodies believed to have been airmen from *Langley* traveling aboard the destroyer. Were there more? Had there really been forty? I have concluded that there were not. The balance appears to have been the unfortunate twenty-five merchant officers and crewmen taken from *Modjokerto*.†

In any case, Haraguchi's document claims that these few survivors were well treated while aboard the cruiser. "Our enlisted men were very kind to the POWs. They took good care of them. For example, in the morning, instead of miso-soup, they went a long way to prepare soup for them. [They] served them with canned pineapples for dessert, which they had carefully laid aside for future use. As to the meals . . . the *Chikuma*'s enlisted men envied them." The reminiscences of Sam Falle,

---

* This detail agrees with the testimony of Johan Tomasowa, who saw the American sailors brought in wearing white shorts (and with their hands bound).

† Ultimately all of these survivors were disposed of in a decisive manner by their captors. It is important to bear in mind such bland and misleading statements as those found in the so-called Nagumo Report regarding U.S. Navy aviators "rescued" during the battle of Midway. One flier in particular was described as dying following interrogation, after which he was "buried at sea," when in fact he was brutally murdered with an ax and his body thrown overboard.

Jack Michel, and Spud Murphy, among others, revealed that the treatment the survivors received at the hands of the Imperial Navy while at sea was good by later standards. So it seems that Haraguchi's recollections deserve respectful consideration.

Next came the interrogation of *Edsall*'s few survivors.

We Ensign Candidates were instructed to carry out the POW interrogations. The POWs were so submissive, and told us everything. There was 1 petty officer, and 7 sailors and the Navy Department civilians. They knew practically nothing about the war. About the Japanese attack on Pearl Harbor, they said, "Nonsense!" and would not believe what we told them.

That the canny Asiatic Fleet sailors may have answered their questioners at times disingenuously comes as no surprise. On the other hand, remarks in *Senshi Sōsho* reveal that they appear to have given truthful information regarding their evasive tactics during the battle. What is fascinating here is the strange reference to "the Navy Dept. civilians" who were rescued in addition to eight sailors.

These must have been the Army Air Force fliers whose bodies were also found at Kendari in 1946. There have been some accounts that state that "stragglers" boarded *Edsall* before her last mission, but I have yet to see any good evidence of this. Why these men would have described themselves as "civilians" from the navy is another unanswered question.

Then Haraguchi records several all-too-human details that, whether believed or disregarded, contain more than a semblance of truth.

The POWs were quite happy and cheerful. The petty officer's name was Wilson, which reminded me of the President Wilson of the USA. He was quite soft-hearted (good natured). A young sailor told us that he had a good-looking fiancée in his hometown in Texas. There was a sailor whose job was a painter. At first, we thought he was an artist following the Navy. From his gesture, however, we understood that he was a painter (whose job was painting the ship).

The final muster roll of *Edsall* in fact shows three sailors named Wilson aboard the destroyer on March 1, 1942. Which specific individual this may have been is not known. That the name elicited an image—of President Woodrow Wilson—in the mind of the young ensign candidate gives this remembrance authenticity. As for the sailor with the attractive fiancée, one of the bodies recovered was that of Machinist Mate 1st Class Horace W. Andrus, known as "Dutch," who was a native of Beaumont, Texas. Andrus was the only Texan among the men whose remains were recovered at Kendari.

The prisoners were held aboard the cruiser for ten days, including the severe air strikes against Tjilatjap on March 5 that finalized that port's fate. KdB then returned to its anchorage at Staring Bay outside Kendari. At that time the fate of these men appears to have been decided. "As we could not detain the POWs aboard *Chikuma* for an indefinite period of time, they decided to transfer them to the land force." Once again these orders in all likelihood originated, if not from Vice Adm. Nagumo himself, from Rear Adm. Abe Hiroaki, the commanding officer of Sentai 8.

The survivors of *Edsall* were then transferred to the Special Naval Landing Forces (SNLF) at Kendari. Haraguchi's memoir spells this out unequivocally:

> Just then, near the harbor, one of the units of the navy paratroops that had landed on Manado in mid January was here to construct an airfield. A decision was made to transfer the POWs to this construction unit for the time being. Another ensign candidate, five enlisted men, and myself were ordered to take charge of escorting the POWs for this transfer.

What followed was the prisoners' grim but inevitable recognition of their fate:

> Although the POWs had become fairly friendly with Ensign Candidates and the enlisted men who took care of them, when we told them that they were going to be transferred to another unit, they lost their peace of mind and became restless. Before they were transshipped from *Chikuma* to a launch, they were blindfolded, which made their anxiety peak. They had been so happy and cheerful until then, but [then] their faces twitched and turned pale. We had to blindfold them, because we did not

want them to see the scene of our entire Kidō Butai in the harbor while they were being transferred.

All of this confirmed my suspicions about the security concerns of the Japanese during this period. However, just three or four days prior to this, the survivors of HMS *Stronghold* had been spared, despite having viewed the enemy's warships in Staring Bay, when they were sent on to Makassar in the grimy hold of a merchant vessel. This again seems to imply that after the "fiasco" of March 1, the Japanese did not want these men alive among the general POW population.

The concluding paragraphs in Dr. Haraguchi's account are profoundly sad. It is clear in this, if in nothing else, that he "preferred not to" imagine with too much precision what would befall these young sailors after they were turned over to the construction unit of the SNLF.

> However, they must have thought they were going to be killed at last. It was an impressive scene I still recall, which made me feel the sorrow of [the vanquished] who were deprived of their right to live. Our launch reached the mouth of a river, and then we further went upstream along a small river for about ten minutes, and landed. There, we took off their blindfolds, and all of them gave a sigh of relief.

Around this same time, somewhere in the shabby little port town or at the airfield on the jungle's green fringes, a confused and undoubtedly frightened group of twelve Royal Netherlands Indies Army (KNIL) prisoners, including an infantryman named Johan Tomasowa, were instructed to pick up their shovels and prepare to climb into a truck.

> From there on, we roped the POWs together and surrounded them with seven of us; one ahead of the line, another aft, and a few on each flank, and proceeded in the jungle toward our destination, the Headquarters of the Construction Unit. We heard reports now and then from a distance, and an ominous air prevailed in the jungle. As we walked toward our destination, it got darker around us. From nowhere, about ten or more big fireflies appeared, and joined us blinking their luminescent lights. What would their fate be? The line of the POWs looked

like a funeral procession. They were walking silently with their heads drooping. The fireflies flew following about; ahead of, behind, and around us as though they were guiding us to our destination. The scene was very beautiful, but very sorrowful as well, and I shall never forget it.

On the surface, this melancholic rendering of the final moments of *Edsall*'s survivors is notable for eliding the foregone conclusion of the POWs' fate. But this almost fairytale vision also contains nuanced suggestions based on distinctive Japanese folklore and symbolism.

In Japan, the firefly (*hotaru*) is emblematic both of life's impermanence and of the transfigured form of soldiers killed in war. These singular insects, with their brief lifespan of two to three weeks, are associated with water, and often found near streams, rivers, and lakes. One specific type, called the *Heike-hotaru*, is named in honor of the souls of an ancient family, whose members all perished in a famous twelfth-century naval engagement.*

Apart from a few brief remarks in which he acknowledges his own wishful thinking that some of the prisoners from *Edsall* actually survived the war, Haraguchi's remarkable memoir ends there. The assistant navigator from *Chikuma* had been under no obligation to divulge *any* of these matters, still less to share his feelings, and he admitted that he had not anticipated finding much public interest in his written wartime experiences. That he came forward to tell this extraordinary if imperfect tale with as much candor as he has should be reason enough for our gratitude whether we accept all of it as literally factual or not.

Edsall, understood as an engine for Western colonial interests, was present at two great junctures of colonialist deconstruction—at Smyrna for the climax of the Kemalists' "Turkey for the Turks!" reaction to Western territorial ambitions and, two decades later, at the fall of the Dutch East Indies under the Japanese slogan of "Asia for the Asiatics!"—and therefore occupied a uniquely tragic position in the complex historical narrative of the twentieth century. USS *Edsall* (DD-219), that emblem

---

* This engagement served as the historical basis for one of the most durable and potent Japanese narratives, what some have called the most representative work of Japanese national literature, the *Heike monogatari*, with its famous opening line: "The proud do not endure, they are like a dream on a spring night; the mighty fall at last, they are as dust before the wind."

of fidelity and fortitude, certainly earned the sentiment expressed by Cmdr. John Alden, the preeminent historian of flushdeckers, when he wrote that "deep in their hearts, old destroyermen know that somewhere in the wide reaches of the oceans, one of their number still carries on, and when the truth becomes known, she will be seen in full fighting regalia escorting the Flying Dutchman into port when he completes his endless seafaring rounds on Judgment Day."[1]

Without suspending disbelief entirely, I accept Dr. Haraguchi's revelations, with their symbolic suggestions, although offering a single, personal adjustment to his last image of *Edsall*'s survivors: I prefer to imagine these young men holding their heads up as they were marched into the darkness, for in the story of this unforgettable ship and crew one must state with finality that in their service and end there was "neither dishonor, nor cowardice, nor failure to do all that becomes a seaman."[2] And it is with such respectful understanding that their memory should be guarded and regarded by future generations.

Appendix I

Final Muster Roll for USS *Edsall* (DD-219)

The following Final Muster Roll of USS *Edsall* (DD-219) is taken from microfilmed records at the National Archives (NARA II) and reproduced here with service numbers for the entire crew to facilitate further research by family members and descendants. The source is Record Group 24 (2520), Box 121, Reel 1439. The list of pilots was created by Mark E. Horan and is not part of the ship's final muster roll.

Photographs are included as supplied by families and fellow researchers. In particular I would like to express my thanks to Jim Nix, Carolyn Sparks, Elizabeth Gustin Hinkley, Jack and Peggy Burgoyne, Father John Noe, Rear Adm. Kent Riffey, Jo and June Gallagher, Kelley Geary, Edward Rogers, David Wright, and Capt. Chris Hampton.

As written on the original document, "This report shows the final disposition of the 'entire' crew. Ship was lost on 1 March 1942."

Officers

Name	Rank (Class)	Position
Nix, Joshua James	Lt. (USNA 1930)	Commanding Officer
Fairbanks, John Francis (Jr.)	Lt. (USNA 1932)	Executive Officer
Meyers, Richard W.	Lt. (USNA 1936)	Engineering Officer
Wild, Phil G. (Jr.)	Lt. (USNA 1936)	Gunnery Officer
Butler, Charles G.	Lt.DesDiv 57	Medical Officer
Snodgrass, Ray Arvel	Lt. (jg) (USNA 1937)	First Lieutenant
Gilmore, Morris D.	Lt. (jg) (USNA 1939)	Asst. Engineering Officer
Dell, Russell C.	Lt. (jg) (USNA 1939)	Torpedo Officer
Gustin, John Webster	Ensign, D-V (G)(USNR)	Communications Officer

Crew

Name	Rating	Service Number
Amory, Sidney Griffith*	F1c	256 32 84
Anderson, Clarence Bernhardt	SM3c	228 31 18
Andrus, Horace Wilbern*	MM1c	359 83 94
Balite, Gregorio Borbon	St3c	114 62 19
Baumgarten, Howard Fritz	TM3c	356 19 85
Berger, Leslie Leo	WT2c	375 88 03
Bonds, Woodrow Marshall	S1c	265 79 75
Borrego, Peter	WT1c	371 65 31
Brown, Howard Edwin	EM2c	279 43 58

Burgoyne, John Leo	Cox	234 13 96
Calpo, Feliciano	CBM(P)	420 52 75
Cameron, "J" "R" *	MM2c	287 11 75
Cantrall, Guy Nard	CMM(A)	299 68 89
Carrara, Marcola Anthony	SC1c	207 12 97
Casey, Virgil Edward	MM3c	360 07 18
Cassady, Sam Gilbert	RM3c	346 71 75
Christopher, Robert Levie	SC1c	267 90 28
Clemens, Lyman Edward	S2c	311 24 44
Cook, Howard James	S1c	274 36 69
Crosley, Verlin James	WT2c	368 18 84
Donaldson, Donald Gustav	MM3c	321 24 89
Duff, Elmore Earl	Cox	393 09 78
Faulkner, Willard Serge	Y3c	321 31 04
Floyd, Joseph Pettus	SF1c	272 00 31
Foster, Clarence Clinton	MM2c	342 14 08
Giese, Arthur John	CY(P)	305 14 82
Gilman, Wallace Bertram	RM2c	234 18 76
Halverson, Elmer Charles	S1c	328 70 37
Handy, David Dix	S1c	311 45 57
Hartpence, Earl Nixon	S2c	223 84 14
Haskins, Cecil William	S2c	266 19 87
Hayes, Carl "H"	SM3c	342 08 88
Hegerfeldt, Paul William	RM1c	214 75 35
Heintz, Jack	MM3c	375 94 66
Himmelmann, Leroy Rudolph	TM2c	336 80 06
Himmelmann, Otto Kenneth	S1c	337 46 19
Huntley, William Walter	S2c	291 31 16
Jackson, John Clifford	BM2c	259 31 16
Jennings, Lynn Logan	S2c	385 85 55
Jones, Kenneth Archie	RM2c	393 08 83
Jones, Robert Jackson	S1c	360 14 68
Jones, Thomas George	GM1c	368 14 59
Keeney, Leon Don	MM2c	355 90 31
Knowles, Walter Daniel	MM3c	272 23 07
Korsak, William Paul	S1c	223 54 80
Kraisser, Michael Jerome	FC3c	336 97 37
Kunold, Richard Louis	CEM(P)	380 63 66
Latham, Raymond Alpheus	GM2c	268 02 37
Lockhart, Ray Herman	S1c	342 15 00
Lopez, Pedro Aquino	ST1c	435 00 42
Loyd, Denver Wright	WT2c	287 10 01
Lyons, Alfred Gregory	GM3c	204 11 27
Mann, Harry Raymond	TM1c	381 02 57
Martin, Jack Eugene	S1c	276 66 98
Mathis, Claud Allan	F1c	356 16 25
Mauldin, Woodrow Wilson	S1c	372 18 20
Maynard, James Louis	MM1c	212 15 19
McClain, Robert Bruce	S2c	287 40 50
McGee, James Earl	QM2c	375 35 30
McKenzie, Norman Lawrence	S1c	291 64 99
Miles, Rodney Winfred	TM3c	337 26 78
Mills, Kenneth LeRoy	SC3c	316 60 20

Mittenholzer, William	Y2c	279 29 73
Moberly, James Grubbs	WT2c	287 11 44
Mohn, Ralph Clifford	S2c	328 60 33
Moore, Clayton Lloyd	MM2c	393 29 15
Morton, Robert George	S2c	382 14 80
Muir, Linwood Robert	QM1c	207 05 00
Myers, Loren Stanford*	S2c	337 25 37
Noe, Jack Grant	F1c	279 59 03
Norvellis, Albert Frank	S1c	300 05 37
Oed, John Joseph	MM2c	206 75 80
Olsen, James Lee Arthur	MM3c	360 07 13
Olson, Erret Blaine	MM3c	299 92 98
Olson, Oscar Albert	B1c	375 39 11
O'Neal, James Percy	GM3c	268 36 62
O'Neal, Robert Shilling	S1c	279 67 91
O'Neil, James LeRoy	MM1c	328 20 56
Parker, Louis Newman	CBM(P)	355 69 70
Parks, Harold George	CMM(P)	214 68 02
Parsons, Loys Aloysius	S2c	337 24 61
Paul, Robert Ross	S1c	337 20 14
Pickhardt, Thomas Vincent	GM3c	223 43 67
Pierce, Edward Ross	BM1c	153 21 55
Poffenberger, John Charles	F2c	328 55 77
Pool, Virgil William	MM3c	337 13 03
Prouty, Walter Raymond	CTM(P)	208 55 11
Ragan, Donald Robert	TM2c	291 52 45
Raney, Doc Bradford Jr.	S1c	359 85 99
Rawers, Paul	F1c	279 61 68
Rice, Harold Oren	RM3c	385 81 23
Riggio, Filippo	SM1c	214 88 11
Root, Lee Franklin	FC1c	316 26 04
Rosales, Sabas	Ck1c	501 25 24
Rossi, Daniel Armand	F1c	382 02 12
Rowland, Ralph Turner	S1c	356 38 80
Sanares, Ruperto	Ck2c	497 85 48
Sanderson, George Henry	CQM(P)	271 85 73
Saracina, Joseph John	B2c	201 59 48
Schmitt, Erwin Edward	CPhM(P)	336 05 01
Shelton, Girard David	CGM(P)	392 78 77
Slegt, William Jr.	MM2c	311 11 70
Smith, Charlie Culberth	CCS(P)	267 90 12
Smith, Elton Buck	CWT(A)	392 90 85
Snapp, Edward Nolan	[illegible]	368 27 67**
Snow, Irvine Crowell	SF2c	201 25 89
Steckenrider, Arnold Ray	CM1c	336 63 14
Steen, Elwood Howard	CMM(P)	259 23 64
Stewart, William Nielsen	TM1c	368 00 80
Stonecipher, Vernon Harold	SK3c	360 18 40
Stover, Lloyd Wayne	EM3c	295 54 91
Tate, John Abner Jr.	F1c	265 88 95
Taylor, John Henry	WT1c	267 88 40
Thaw, Henry Franklin	EM1c	295 14 98
Tsendeas, Elias	F1c	256 34 82

Vander Molen, Robert Jr.	F1c	311 51 06
Vandiver, Larry*	MM3c	283 39 00
Van Voorhis, Merrel Ellie	F1c	337 25 31
Vaughn, Charles William	MM2c	287 23 00
Vaughn, Noah David	MM1c	341 97 92
Ventura, Hilarion	Ck1c	497 61 30
Waltrip, Dennis Shaw	F2c	287 52 06
Watters, Donald Franklin*	F1c	328 71 49
Webber, Arthur	S1c	291 69 17
Weed, Arthur Goodwin	MM1c	406 09 83
Welch, Roscoe Wilber	S1c	311 64 13
West, Steve Charles	TM2c	393 22 27
Westwood, Dale Edwin	RM2c	342 12 01
Whipple, Walter Fred	S1c	382 21 20
White, Robert Frank	SK3c	328 70 02
Whitford, William Franklin	S1c	372 27 60
Williams, Harold	MM2c	337 10 37
Williams, John David	F1c	385 91 03
Williams, Robert Arthur	QM3c	250 52 44
Williams, Robert Eugene	S1c	337 47 00
Williamson, Waldo Ray	QM3c	265 85 47
Wilson, Allen Hardin	MM2c	258 20 73
Wilson, Noah Jacob A. Jr.	S2c	356 47 93
Wilson, Robert Frederick	S2c	376 22 97
Worley, Randolph Emerson	TM3c	268 33 88
Wren, Howard Richard	F1c	279 55 39
Yancy, Everett Preston	F2c	342 34 43
York, Clyde Ladelle	TM3c	356 24 75

* Crewmen whose remains were recovered after the end of the war.
** The number is largely illegible; this is my best guess.

USAAF Pilots

Name	Rank	Home State	File Number
Atkinson, Horace C.	2nd Lt.	Pennsylvania	0-428463
Augustine, Verne P.	2nd Lt.	North Dakota	0-427580
Bentley, John E.	2nd Lt.	Massachusetts	0-427696
Borden, William P.	2nd Lt.	Washington	0-424896
Boren, Lee M.	2nd Lt.	California	0-424897
Bridge, John E.	2nd Lt.	California	0-421622
Dierkens, Aime L.	2nd Lt.	New Jersey	0-428649
Eldridge, William H.	2nd Lt.	Oklahoma	0-421935
England, Arthur E.	2nd Lt.	Alabama	0-428483
Goodyear, Donovan G.	2nd Lt.	Iowa	0-427687
Gorman, Harrison A.	2nd Lt.	Massachusetts	0-427717
Green, Laurence H.	2nd Lt.	Massachusetts	0-427721
Handy, Oscar W. A.	2nd Lt.	California	0-425080
Holman, W.B.	2nd Lt.	unknown	0-421092
Hower, Justin J.	2nd Lt.	Pennsylvania	0-428503
Johnson, Bennett L.	2nd Lt.	Nebraska	0-424962
Keenan, Gerald M.	Capt.	Illinois	0-388608
Kennedy, William A. Jr.	2nd Lt.	Tennessee	0-424972
Koebel, Kenneth L.	2nd Lt.	Arkansas	0-421117

MacLean, Wallace B.	2nd Lt.	South Dakota	0-427601
Martin, Joe P.	2nd Lt.	Missouri	0-427557
McIntosh, Donald O.	2nd Lt.	Illinois	0-427451
McNutt, Charles C. Jr.	2nd Lt.	Texas	0-429965
Perine, William R.	2nd Lt.	Michigan	0-421303
Schmillen, Edward C.	2nd Lt.	Illinois	0-428570
Simpson, Clarence E., Jr.	2nd Lt.	Texas	0-394515
Skinner, Haley W.	2nd Lt.	Kansas	0-428537
Smith, James C.	2nd Lt.	Ohio	0-427668
Vann, John R.	2nd Lt.	Kansas	0-429998
Wallace, Robert W.	2nd Lt.	California	0-430003
Workman, Donald E.	2nd Lt.	Illinois	0-421371

Appendix II

Supplementary Material

There are other discrepancies in various Japanese accounts of the final action against *Edsall*. Although they are minor, some of these differences are included for the sake of completeness (and also because Mike Wenger went to the trouble of extracting this data, for which he deserves the credit and for which he has my thanks).

1. The detailed action report (DAR) of heavy cruiser *Chikuma* contains the following:
1727 sighted DD
1737 open fire/"All forces charge"
1752 DD makes smoke
1800 check-fire
1824 direct hit
1845 DD afire
1859 DD sinks
2. The *Senshi Sōsho* narrative was derived from two DARs (not war diaries, although these apparently also exist), of CruDiv 8 and BatDiv 3. The chart from which the *Senshi Sōsho* map is taken is from the BatDiv 3 report.
3. Evidently, Vice Admiral Nagumo did issue some type of "dispatch" regarding the air strikes on Tjilatjap (March 5), in lieu of an official report, but nothing at all re *Edsall*.
4. There is also a history for the carrier *Sōryu*, which Mike Wenger double-checked, but he found "nothing of a substantial nature for the Edsall action."

Concerning American primary source materials for the recovery of *Edsall*'s personnel, to say that the record is confused would be a very pronounced understatement: it is nothing if not baffling. There is agreement upon the number of bodies recovered and the identities of those remains found with identity tags. A consensus regarding the likely identity of the other, partial remains was reached suggesting the "strong" probability that these men were AAF personnel from USS *Langley* (AV-3). Beyond this are the indirect associations with the testimony of KNIL Pfc. Johan Tomasowa, a POW at Kendari, who evidently helped to dig the graves and bury the remains. (He is not mentioned by name in the Graves Registration papers, nor is *any* eyewitness.) I assume this was based upon Tomasowa's multiple statements to warcrimes investigators in 1945, 1946, and 1947, and his trial testimony in 1948. These are borne out by a brief paragraph in the November 30, 1946, American Graves Registration Service letter to the Office of the Quartermaster General:

Information gathered from our Search and Recovery Teams reveal that 8 Navy men were picked up by the Japanese during February [*sic*] 42 from the sea off the coast of Tjilatjap, Java, in a group of approximately 40 persons consisting of Americans and Chinese; that all were beheaded in mass slaughter at Kendari the next day and thrown into a pit. Pieces of U.S. Navy clothing was found on these remains and with the aid of Dutch Army Doctors, our Teams separated these 8 remains from other bodies. Identification tags . . . were found in this pit.

At the time of Tomasowa's two relevant 1947 statements, in January and June, the U.S. military and the Dutch knew of bodies recovered near Kendari's airfield and identified as *Edsall* crewmen. Both of these statements by Tomasowa tell of "thirty-six men" also identified as "white men" and "Americans" brought in to Kendari after their ship was sunk. Tomasowa repeatedly stated his belief that the captured sailors were from the nameless American warship he had seen in Kendari's harbor on January 24. Of course, they were not. But in all likelihood they *were* men from *Edsall* and from at least one other ship seized by the Japanese. According to the KNIL private, these men were "dressed only in a pair of drawers" with their hands bound behind their backs. After a brief period of detention and questioning, these men were lined up by Nakamura outside the Kendari prison—in the town itself, it appears—and a roll-call taken "from a piece of paper, which names apparently referred to those Americans, anyhow, I saw and heard that after each name called by Nakamura an American fell out and stood apart from the group." These seventeen were guarded by three Japanese, whose names (which I have quite serious doubts about) were given as "Fujimoto, Hamagami, and Kawamura." These men's ranks are said to be "*Go-cho*" (army corporals) in both statements, but in one warrant, Tomasowa says they carried out the killings themselves. In the other, he says the Americans were executed by "the Japanese *Sjoheiso*" (*Sui hei cho*, or "Leading Seaman", an Imperial Navy rank) and no names or names recorded. All of his accounts claim that three pits were dug for these killings, and each was "about two meters long, one and a half meter broad, and one meter deep."

The separate story recounted by Tomasowa concerning men who were *not* executed that day came from his June 1947 Statement (Jochems Warrant) given at Hollandia, New Guinea, where he was training as a paratrooper:

> After all seventeen Americans had been beheaded by Fudjomoto, Hamagani, and Kawamura, after which their bodies had been thrown into the three pits, we got order[s] from Nakamura to fill up the pits, which we did. Then we were taken back to prison. Why those seventeen Americans have been killed by the Japs, remained unknown to me and I do not know whether or not they have been condemned to death by a Japanese court. The surviving nineteen Americans remained locked up during about fourteen days in said prison after which they were all taken away by to me unknown Japs and, as I heard from rumors, were employed in the nickelmines at Pamala [*sic*] (Celebes). After that I never heard or saw anything of them.

This anecdote now strikes me as fantastic, but it could be explained by real events. In 1943, there were British prisoners sent from Makassar to Pomalaa to work as slave-laborers. Word of this may have spread to Kendari via regional merchants. Also, and similarly, another larger contingent of British and Dutch POWs was shipped from Java to Ambon in the Moluccas in 1943, where they too were used as slave laborers. Again, shipping between Kendari and Ambon was a regular occurrence and Tomasowa may well have picked up rumors from these sources and jumbled them in his memories.

Notes

Introduction
1. Roscoe, *United States Destroyer Operations*, 107.
2. Ibid.
3. Michael Schaller, "MacArthur's Japan" in Leary, *MacArthur and the American Century*, 298.
4. Ziegler, *Personal Diary of Admiral The Lord Louis Mountbatten*, 269.
5. Barenblatt, *A Plague upon Humanity*, 222.
6. *Index to the Correspondence of the Foreign Office for the Year 1946*, 590–91.
7. Finn, *Winners in Peace*, Chapter 18, "The Korean War."
8. Leutze, *A Different Kind of Victory*, 217–18.

Chapter One
1. Alden, *Flush Decks and Four Pipes*, 1.
2. Whitley, *Destroyers of World War Two*, 28.
3. Frost, *On a Destroyer's Bridge*, 112.
4. Pettitt, "They Were a Class Apart," 250.
5. Halsey and Bryan, *Admiral Halsey's Story*, 45.
6. Alden, *Flush Decks and Four Pipes*, 3.
7. Hague, *Destroyers For Great Britain*, 7, 8.
8. Reilly, *United States Destroyers of World War II*, 12.
9. Pettitt, "They Were a Class Apart," 241.
10. Senate Documents, Vol. 14: Navy Yearbook 1920–1921, 866.
11. Murray, *The Harding Era*, 349–50.
12. Beers, "U.S. Naval Detachment in Turkish Waters, 1919–1924," 5.
13. Roskill, *Naval Policy Between the Wars, Vol.1*, 197.
14. British Documents on Foreign Affairs (BDFA), Series B, Part II, Vol. 1, 133. Doc. 75 [151212], Sir Horace Rumbold, "Notes on the Nationalist Movement in the Samsoun Area." Undated.
15. *British Parliamentary Debates—House of Commons* (London: Hansard, 1919, 1920); Vol. 116 (May 19 to June 16, 1919): 1996.
16. Harbord, "Conditions in the Near East," 11.
17. British Documents on Foreign Affairs (BDFA), Series B, Part II, Vol. 29, 34, 35. Doc. 83 [E 9440/27/44], Sir Horace Rumbold to the Marquess Curzon of Kedleston, Constantinople, September 12, 1922.
18. Papers Relating to the Foreign Relations of the United States: 1922, Volume II, 418; Telegram: 767.68/297.
19. Papers Relating to the Foreign Relations of the United States: 1922, Volume II, 160. [867.512/86] The Consul General at Smyrna (Horton) to the Secretary of State, No. 292, March 2, 1921.
20. Ibid., 155. [667.003/102: Telegram] The High Commissioner of Constantinople (Bristol) to the Acting Secretary of State, January 24, 1921.

21. *Dictionary of American Navy Fighting Ships*, USS *Edsall* (DD-219).
22. Krasner, *Defending the National Interest*, 110.
23. Earle, *Turkey, The Great Powers, and the Bagdad Railway*, 346–47.
24. Allen, *Only Yesterday*. But of course that was then, and we *have* seen subsequent administrations of comparable venality.
25. La Botz and Doheny, *Petroleum, Power, and Politics*, 118.
26. Ibid., 118.
27. O'Connor, *The Oil Barons*, 235.
28. Quote from Schlumberger's "Les Isles des Princes" in Freely and Sumner-Boyd, *Strolling Through Istanbul*.
29. Ibid.
30. "Memorandum" from Bristol to Van H. Engert, dated 25 April 1920.
31. Dobkin, *Smyrna*, 173.
32. Hartunian, *Neither to Laugh*, 199.
33. "Humiliation for the Turk." Afterward even Admiral Bristol acknowledged in unofficial communications the responsibility he felt for the situation created at Smyrna. Later, however, such admissions were not to be found among his official reports.
34. Dobkin, *Smyrna*, 174.
35. Horton, *The Blight of Asia*, 178.
36. Ibid., 152–53. "Hepburn" was Capt. Arthur Japy Hepburn (1877–1964), Rear Admiral Bristol's chief of staff, and future commander in chief of the U.S. Fleet (CINCUS, 1936.)
37. "Smyrna and After, Part III," 165.
38. Dobkin, *Smyrna*, 190–94.
39. Papers Relating to the Foreign Relations of the United States: 1922, Vol. II, 422. The High Commissioner at Constantinople (Bristol) to the Acting Secretary of State [868.48/114: Telegram].
40. Dobkin, *Smyrna*, 175.
41. Ibid., 192–93.
42. Papers Relating to the Foreign Relations of the United States: 1922, Vol. II, 445–46. From the Acting High Commissioner at Constantinople (Dolbeare) to the Secretary of State; enclosure, from Powell to Bristol, dated 20 October 1922 [868.48/291].
43. Beers, "U.S. Naval Detachment in Turkish Waters," 11.
44. Pratt, "One Destroyer," 184.
45. British Documents on Foreign Affairs (BDFA), Part II, Series E, Vol. 29, 343. Palairet to Mr. Austen Chamberlain, Secretary of State for Foreign Affairs, July 20, 1925, "Shanghai Political Intelligence Report for June Quarter, 1925" [F 4135/351/10].
46. "The Upper Yangtze Patrol," 735.
47. Martin, *Over My Shoulder*, 164.
48. Jules James Papers.
49. Admiral M. M. Taylor to Pratt, 20 February 1932, NARA II, RG 45, Box 359.
50. Kidd and Winkel, *Twice Forgotten*, 21.
51. *The Treaty Ports of China and Japan*, 456–63.
52. Data courtesy of "Taki" (Akira Takizawa) at www.AxisHistoryForum; accessed August 19, 2007.
53. Deck log for USS *Edsall* (DD-219), May 1939.
54. Papers Relating to the Foreign Relations of the United States, 1939, Vol. IV, The Far East [893.102 Kulangsu/134: Telegram]. Consul MacVitty to Secretary of State Cordell Hull.

55. "Lots of Trouble."
56. British Foreign Office Confidential Papers [F/34/32/10] from Consul-General Fitzmaurice to Sir A. Clark Kerr in Shanghai on events at Amoy-Kulangsu contain a more realistic portrayal of this tense situation.
57. Frost, *On a Destroyer's Bridge,* 99.
58. Papers Relating to the Foreign Relations of the United States 1940, Vol. IV, The Far East [893.102 Kulangsu/283: Telegram] Consul MacVitty to Secretary of State Cordell Hull.
59. Dyer, *On the Treadmill to Pearl Harbor.*
60. Ibid., 425.
61. Ibid.
62. See Leutze, *A Different Kind of Victory,* 186–90, and Dyer, *The Amphibians Came to Conquer.*
63. Leutze, *A Different Kind of Victory,* 190–91.
64. Pearl Harbor Attack, Hearings Before the Joint Committee, Part 10, February 18, 1946, 4812.
65. ADB Conversations, 7.
66. Watson, *Chief of Staff,* 390.
67. Pearl Harbor Attack Hearings, Part 33, Proceedings of the Navy Court of Inquiry, 942–43.]
68. Tolley, "Divided We Fell."
69. Cook, "The Strange Case of Rainbow-5."
70. Hart, *Supplementary of Narrative,* 2–8.

Chapter Two
1. Cook, "The Strange Case of Rainbow-5," 67.

Chapter Three
1. *The Campaigns of the Pacific War,* 30–50.
2. *Netherlands East Indies Naval Operations.*
3. "Army Air Action in the Philippines and Netherlands East Indies—1941–1942," 119.
4. Nortier, *De Japanse aanval,* 63.
5. *Senshi Sōsho,* Vol. 26, map diagram 19, 214. This incident is also well recorded in Dwight R. Messimer's excellent *In the Hands of Fate,* 211–16.
6. "Army Air Action in the Philippines and Netherlands East Indies—1941–1942," 110.
7. Leutze, *A Different Kind of Victory,* 272.
8. Brereton, *Brereton Diaries,* 78.
9. FDR Presidential Library and Museum, Safe Files, Box 4, Navy Department, 1934–February 1942 Index. COMINCH to CINCPAC 092245 and CINCPAC to COMINCH 120307, 120459.
10. Ugaki, *Fading Victory,* 80.
11. Ibid., 87.
12. McEwan, *The Remorseless Road,* 116.
13. *Senshi Sōsho,* Vol. 26, Chap. 7, 494. Translation by Rear Adm. Edwin T. Layton, 1977.
14. Yokohama War Crimes Trials, Case #339, July 12, 1948, to December 28, 1948.
15. Pearl Harbor Attack Hearings, Part 28. *Proceedings of Army Pearl Harbor Board,* 1577–95.
16. McDougall, *Six Bells Off Java,* 94.
17. Multaluli, *Max Havelaar,* 214.
18. www.geocities.com/dutcheastindies/zantvoort.html
19. Indonesia, *A Travel Survival Kit,* 68.

20. E. A. Fricke, "The Unknown History of the Child Soldiers," 260–89 in Van Wijk, *Forced Labour*. Fricke ended up with his fellow teenaged recruits aboard the merchant vessel *Tjisaroea*, which was captured by Vice Admiral Kondō's units on March 4. With a guard force of twenty-six Japanese aboard, they were escorted back to Makassar and interned there on March 8. In late 1942, a number of these young men were shipped to Nagasaki, Japan.

21. Memoirs written in 2000 by Adriaan Willem Kik (b.1919), fourth (assistant) engineer on *Abbekerk*.

22. "War Diary of HMAS Bendigo," 7.

23. McDougall, *Six Bells off Java*, 112.

24. Ibid., 113.

25. McDougall, *By Eastern Windows*, 16.

26. Coox, "Recourse To Arms: The Sino-Japanese Conflict, 1937–1945," in Coox and Conroy, *China and Japan: A Search for Balance Since World War* I, 307.

Chapter Four

1. Francillon, *Japanese Navy Bombers of World War Two*, 51. However, the *Kanoya* group was a detachment from the 21st *Kōkūsentai* at Saigon.

2. Eccles' dictated narrative, "On the Battle of the Java Sea," from the Bates Papers of the Naval War College Library, is among the best documents to have been produced in the aftermath of the Java campaign's numerous debacles.

3. Abraham, *The Surgeon's Log*, 63.

4. *The Campaigns of the Pacific War*, 46.

5. Another source for some of these themes may be found in Capt. Charles O. Cook Jr.'s, articles, "The Strange Case of Rainbow-5" and "The Pacific Command Divided: The "Most Unexplainable" Decision."

6. Cook, "The Strange Case of Rainbow-5," 67.

7. Bell, *Condition Red*, 68.

8. Enright, *To Leave This Port*, 81.

9. Ibid., 85.

10. All excerpts from the Diary of Major Winthrop H. Rogers. Personal collection of the author.

11. "The Story of the U.S.S. *Houston*," a diary by Quentin C. Madson, Coxswain. Copy in the author's possession, courtesy of Otto C. Schwarz via Matt Johnson. Hereafter Madson Diary.

12. Bell, *Condition Red*, 69.

13. Hart, *Supplementary*, 3.

14. Reconstruction of the antisubmarine warfare (ASW) activities of *Edsall* off Port Darwin are taken from Declassified Confidential Action Reports of DD-219, dated January 22 and 31, 1942; a selection of RAN papers under the heading "Operations Against Enemy Submarines at Darwin" (March 30, 1942); the Report of Diving Operations by the C.O. of USS *Holland* (January 31, 1942); and a letter by Brian M. Viglietti and David Wright, in *Warship International* Vol. XXXVII, No. 2 (June 2000):, 201, 203.

15. Enclosure No. (v) to N.T. 0579/1 dated January 29, 1942, from C.O. HMAS *Deloraine* (Lt. Cmdr. D. A. Menlove, RANR) to the N.O.I.C. Northern Territory: "Attempted Torpedoing of HMAS Deloraine and Counter Attacks Carried Out."

16. Carpenter and Polmar, *Submarines of the Imperial Japanese Navy*.

17. Action Report Serial CF-01 of USS *Edsall* DD-219 "Activities of USS *Edsall* for January 20–21, Report Of. Covers Anti-Submarine Operations While Escorting TRINITY to Port Darwin, Australia," 1, and Confidential Report DD219/A16–3 (03), dated January 31, 1942, "Action taken against Submarines by USS *Edsall*," 3.

18. Australian Department of Navy Secret Message 1932/3/51 from N.O.I.C. Darwin, January 30, 1942.

19. Action Report of USS *Holland* (AS-3), "Diving Operations—report of." Dated January 31, 1942.
20. Ibid., 2.
21. Ibid., 3.
22. This occurred on January 29 and 30, 1943, off Kamimbo Bay, Sealark Channel, Guadalcanal, and is well covered in j-aircraft.com's tabular record of movement (TROM) for I-1, by Bob Hackett and Sander Kingsepp.
23. Lademan, "USS *Gold Star*—Flagship of the Guam Navy," 68–79.
24. Ibid.
25. Ibid.
26. See "Fueling for Battle, the SS *George G. Henry*," in Suman *Ships of the Esso Fleet in World War II*, and Messimer, *Pawns of War*, 22.
27. Glassford message NR 848 1845/22, Glassford files, NARA II.
28. There is a message in the Glassford files at NARA II, dated 0725 hours on the morning of February 27, which reads: "MOST IMMEDIATE/REQUEST BELITA BE SENT COCOS ISLAND FORTHWITH."
29. Commander R. P. McConnell, "Operations, action and sinking of the U.S.S. LANGLEY, period from February 22 to March 5, 1942," Serial C-01, Ap22/A16–3gjp. Dated March 9, 1942. Hereafter *McConnell Report*.
30. Messimer, *Pawns of War*, 44.
31. Hetherington, *Blamey, Controversial Soldier*.
32. *McConnell Report*, 65.
33. Ibid., 5.
34. Ibid., 6.
35. This final exchange between *Whipple* and *Edsall* is taken from Skip Wild Harrington's article "The Mystery of USS *Edsall*," 26–28.
36. From "Save Your Life!" An account by NAP 1/C Yamakawa Shinsaku, a *kanbaku* pilot aboard the carrier *Kaga*. Accessed on August 5, 2004, at www.geocities.com/dutcheastindies/pecos.html. This is another version of the same account recorded in Messimer's *Pawns of War* (1983), in which the pilot's name is given as Yamagawa, and the source identified as *Kokan Senshi No. 26*.
37. Dr. Haraguchi Shizuhiko (former assistant navigator on the cruiser *Chikuma*), "The Sea Battle off Tjilatjap."
38. Price, "Abandon Ship."
39. Abernethy, "The *Pecos* Died Hard," 79. Abernethy noted that he left Tjilatjap "with an augmented crew of 14 officers and 224 men."
40. Lowell Barty interview.
41. From a conversation with Paul Papish of Colorado Springs, CO, former SK3/C on *Houston,* in Dallas, Texas, summer 1994.
42. According to the postwar interrogation of Capt. Shibata, Bunzo, 21st Air Flotilla Staff officer, "While on a bombing mission to SOERABAJA one of our aircraft spotted the Allied ships and the attack resulted. We used all aircraft available."
43. From author's conversation in 2007 with Howard E. Brooks.
44. Weller, "Flight From Java."
45. The reminiscences of P. W. Wears are taken from a letter written in October 1992 to the American writer (and ex-POW) H. Robert Charles, a U.S. Marine Corps private from USS *Houston*. Bob Charles, a professional journalist, published a fine personal history entitled *Last Man Out*. All subsequent quotes are from this letter, which has never before been published. A copy is in the author's possession.
46. Declassified "Action Report," USS *Pecos*, March 7, 1942, written aboard USS *Mount Vernon* by Lt. Cmdr. E. Paul Abernethy. Hereafter: Pecos Action Report.
47. Abernethy, "The PECOS Died Hard," 80.
48. Messimer, *Pawns of War*, 155. The clumsy evolutions of the Japanese carrier's air groups should not be overlooked. It is open to question whether Rear Adm.

Yamaguchi Tamon's well-documented aggressiveness as the leader of CarDiv 2 may or may not have played a part in these problems.

49. Pecos Action Report, 5. The casualty figures reproduced in 1953 in Theodore Roscoe's book on destroyer operations seemed much too low. Roscoe neglected to mention the total number of men lost with *Pecos*: more than 450 in all.

50. Action Report, USS *Whipple* DD-217 Serial CF-015, March 4, 1942, "USS *WHIPPLE*—Activities Between 26 February and 4 March 1942," 4.

51. "*Kanbaku* War Notes," Part 3.

52. Abernethy, "The PECOS Died Hard," 81.

53. "*Kanbaku* War Notes," Part 3.

54. Quoted in Messimer, *Pawns of War*, 164. "NIFQ" was the call-sign for USS *Pecos* (AO-3).

55. Ibid., 80–82.

56. Tolley, *Cruise of the Lanikai*, 223.

57. Messimer, *Pawns of War*, 177.

58. Abernethy, "The PECOS Died Hard," 81. Moreover, Col. Gerald Dix, U.S. Air Force (Ret.), reconfirmed hearing explosions in a conversation with the author on March 1, 2006, sixty-four years later to the day.

Chapter Five

1. Robert H. Houle, CM2/c, SSMT1/c, The Mount Vernon (AP-22) Cruise Book, 1941–1946, 4.

2. Frost, *On a Destroyer's Bridge*, 60–65.

3. Quoted in K. W. L. Bezemer's *Geschiednis van de Nederlandse Koopvardij in de Tweelde Wereldoorlog*, (Amsterdam/Brussel: Elsevier , 1987), p.734. Bezemer's source is *Inventaris van het archief van Oorlogsonderscheidingen voor het Koopvardij-en Luchtvaartpersoneel, 1940–1975*, No. 361. The National Archives in The Hague. Translated for the author by Jan (Visje) Visser.

4. "Combined Fleet Doctrine: Battleship and Cruiser Doctrine, Imperial Japanese Navy," taken from primary sources by historian W. David Dickson. Mr. Dickson was kind enough to provide an edited copy of the revised December 1943–January 1944 booklets.

5. Haraguchi Memoir.

6. Ibid.

7. Ibid.

8. Action Report, USS *John D. Edwards*, March 4, 1942.

9. Haraguchi Memoir.

10. Michel, *Mr. Michel's War*, 77.

11. Falle, *My Lucky Life*, 36, 37.

12. Kik Memoirs, 4.

13. Kanbaku War Notes, and "Japanese Aerial Tactics Against Ship Targets," *JICPOA* Weekly Intelligence bulletin, Vol. I, No.15 (Oct. 20, 1944): 21. Access to this publication was provided by W. David Dickson.

14. Yamakawa, "Save Your Life!" and AAF Informational Intelligence Summary No. 43–24 (March 1943), 18.

15. From "Gunnery Training Memories" by Armed Guard veteran Lyle E. Dupra of Fairport, New York.

16. Scheck, "Prelude to Pearl Harbor," 24.

17. All details of the dive-bombing techniques of Aichi D3A1 pilots are taken from Kanbaku War Notes and AAF Informational Intelligence Summary No. 43–44, 18.

18. Motegi Meiji interview.

19. Price, "Abandon Ship." Also, Lowell Barty interview with the author, June 2008.

20. *Senshi Sōsho*, Vol. 26; the so-called Supplement/Appendix.

21. From *Senshi Sōsho*, translated by Cmdr. Seno, Sadao, JMSDF, Ret. Vol. 26, 498, date unknown, given to Capt. Walter Nix. Copy in the author's possession via Jim Nix.

22. Letter via e-mail from Mr. Motegi to the author, translated by Kan Sugahara, March to April 2006.

23. *Senshi Sōsho*, Vol. 26, 512. (Translation by Akio Oka, via Vincent P. O'Hara.)

24. Ibid., 512.

25. See USSBS Interrogations No. 67 and No. 395 of Captain Fujita Masamichi.

26. Letter of Mr. Motegi via e-mail to the author, translated by Kan Sugahara, March– April 2006.

27. This anecdote and the bulk of this section are indebted to the research and writings of Cmdr. Louis B. Dorny, U.S. Navy (Ret.), who has labored for three decades to write the definitive history of the Asiatic Fleet's Patrol Wing 10. Hereafter: Dorny, Asiatic Fleet Archives.

28. Abernethy, "The PECOS Died Hard," 82.

Chapter Six

1. Goethe to Friedrich von Muller, June 18, 1826. From Walter Kaufmann's *Goethe, Kant, and Hegel: Discovering the Mind; Volume One.*

2. *Senshi Sōsho*, Vol. 26, 211–12. Translations of the Kendari Operation by Akio Oka.

3. Velthoen, "Mapping Sulawesi in the 1950s," 9.

4. Brereton, *The Brereton Diaries*, 78; Womack, *The Dutch Naval Air Force Against Japan*, 89.

5. Nortier, *De Japanse aanval*, 61.

6. Ibid., 64.

7. Ibid., 65.

8. Ibid., 74.

9. Ibid., 64–66.

10. Ibid., 69.

11. "The United States v. (RADM) Tamotsu Furukawa et al."

12. Nortier, *De Japanse aanval*, 73.

13. *Senshi Sōsho*, Vol. 26, 210.

14. "Personal Accounts of Japanese Prisoners of War of the Three PW Camps on the Isle of Celebes (Sulawesi) January 1942–September 1945," from the Diary of C. F. Booy. Translated by Olly Van Driest-Young.

15. Hearn, *Sorties into Hell*, 30.

16. Defense Exhibit B, Case 307, U.S. v. Furukawa, et al., "Chain Of Command of the Naval Units at Kendari." NARA II, RG 331. The Base Force Dispatch Unit could be considered the Kendari Garrison, as it was also sometimes called, and would have included the Special Police, or *Tokkei Tai.*

17. See Chapter Six, note 14.

18. Interrogations of Japanese Officials, Vol. II (USGPO, 1946) USSBS No. 387, NAV No. 77. "Operations of 22nd Air Flotilla in Malaya." Interrogation of Captain Sonokawa, Kameo (AKA Takeo). Captain Sonokawa was later implicated in the murders of the nine PBY crewmen at Kendari, but was in the end acquitted.

19. "The Japanese Special Naval Police Force."

20. See Kaori Maekawa, "The Pontianak Incidents and the Ethnic Chinese in Wartime Western Borneo," in Kratoska, *Southeast Asian Minorities in the Wartime Japanese Empire*, 156–68.

21. Testimony of Johan Tomasawa under direct examination, 130. June 7, 1948, Yokohama, Japan. U.S. v. Tamotsu Furukawa, Vol. 1.

22. From an anonymous report circulated in Holland but believed to have been written by one of Coen's naval officers, Nicolas van Waert. In Hanna, *Indonesian Banda*, 56.

23. van der Post, *The Admirals' Baby*, 209.

24. Wilmott, *Grave of a Dozen Schemes*, 45.
25. Clifton, *Islands of Indonesia*, 262–63.
26. Gill, *Royal Australian Navy*, 1943–1945, 696–700.
27. Prosecution Exhibit No. 3, from "U.S. v. Tamotsu Furukawa, et al.," Case #307.
28. The sources for the disposition of the remains of *Edsall*'s survivors come from six letters written by the U.S. Navy and U.S. Army to the family of Loren Stanford Myers, supplied by RADM Rear Adm. Kenneth Riffey, USN (Ret.)—the nephew of Seaman Myers—and a two-page letter from the Quartermaster General dated March 10, 1949, which was supplied to me by historian William Bartsch.
29. Captain J. G. Godwin, investigating officer, 2nd Australian War Crimes Section, "Executions of Australian and Dutch POWs, Laha Airfield, Ambon Island, February, 1942," File 851–1.851,85K. (February 1950, SCAP, Tokyo, Japan).
30. Mullin, *Another Six Hundred*, 250–51.
31. E-mail communication in 2006 from Rear Adm. Robert B. Fulton II, U.S. Navy (Ret.).
32. Goodwin, *Shobun*. This small book, barely 140 pages long, examines in grisly detail the downing of a single PBY Black Cat over Kendari in early October 1944, and the murder of her nine survivors—including Lt. j.g. Bill Goodwin, the author's father; the book also examines the resulting war-crime trials.
33. United States of America vs. Tamotsu Furukawa, et al. Review of the Staff Judge Advocate, Yokohama, Japan, January 27, 1949, 4, NARA, Southeast Area, Atlanta.
34. Sworn Statement to J. R. S. Apontoweil, Hollandia, New Guinea, January 9, 1947
35. Warrant: Hearing of Evidence. 19095/R. Office of the Judge Advocate at Hollandia, G. G. Jochems, June 19, 1947. NARA II, RG 331, Stack 290, Box 945.
36. Werner Herzog, quote from a 2006 interview.
37. See Chapter 6, note 21. Earlier statements in 1947 by Tomasowa reported that he had been captured early in the morning of January 24, 1942—another of this individual's maddening contradictions.
38. Ibid., 132.
39. U.S. v. Tamotsu Furukawa, Interrogation of Johan Tomasowa, SCAP Legal Section, March 21, 1947, Manila, P. I. RG 331, Box 945, Folder 51, "NEI 151 Vol. 1, Johan Tomasowa Statements, etc." NARA II.
40. Barley, *Not a Hazardous Sport*, 48.
41. Van Der Post, *The Seed and the Sower*.
42. See Lt. Cmdr. Tom Donohue, U.S. Navy (Ret.), and his article "The *Houston* Survivors of Java," source N/A.
43. Bigalke, *Tana Toraja*, 187.
44. See Chapter Six, note 33.
45. See Chapter Six, note 21. Page 185.
46. From Rear Adm. Kent Riffey, U.S. Navy (Ret.), to the author.
47. Copy of original document from William Bartsch to the author, June 2006.
48. See Chapter Six, note 21. Page 113.
49. MacArthur Memorial, Norfolk, VA, RG-23: Papers of Major General Charles A. Willoughby, USA, 1947–1973.
50. This characterization of Willoughby is indebted to Takemae, *The Allied Occupation of Japan*.
51. Zenji, *The Emperor's Sea Eagle*, 81.
52. Jan Visser, "The Modjokerto Mystery," Netherlands Navy at War, http://www.netherlandsnavy.nl/special_modjokerto.htm.
53. Memorandum. 13 May 1942. Kpt-Lt H.M. Van Bemmelen, KMR. Gegevens MS "MODJOKERTO," in *Algemeen Rijksarchief, Tweede Afdeling. Oorlogsonderscheidingen Koopvardij-en Luchtvaart personeel*. 366-425. Nationaal Archief, den Haag.

54. Messimer, *Pawns of War*, 103–4.

55. Yamakawa, "Save Your Life!" See Chapter Four, note 36.

56. Haraguchi Memoir.

57. Additional information on *Modjokerto*'s victims comes from Johan Teeuwisse of the Netherlands War Graves Foundation (Oorlogs Gravenstichting, or O.G.S.) and Dr. A. P. Van Vliet of Nederlands Instituut voor Militaire Historie, Den Haag.

58. See Chapter Six, note 35. Page 3.

59. John Murphy, letter to G. Hernon Gill, Australia War Memorial.

60. Ibid.

61. Ibid.

62. John Murphy, *Smith's Weekly* account, Australia War Memorial.

63. Ibid.

64. Ibid.

65. Ibid.

66. IMTFE Exhibits 1804/1804A, 1805/1805A, and 1811/1811. All contain harrowing descriptions of Yoshida, Asauo's, cruelty and capriciousness. He was duly convicted as a class C war criminal.

67. McDougall, *By Eastern Windows*, 153.

68. See Tully, "Solving Some Mysteries of Leyte Gulf," 248–58.

Epilogue: Lest We Forget

1. Carlton, "Massacre as Tactical Exigency," in *Massacres* (1994.)

2. Quoted by J. Charles Schenking, *Making Waves*, 207.

3. Schenking, "The Imperial Japanese Navy and the Constructed Consciousness," 769–96.

4. Tanaka, "The Struggle for Guadalcanal," 72–73.

5. Todorov, *The Conquest of America*, 144.

6. Nornes and Fukushima, *The Japan/America Film Wars*.

7. Ibid., 144.

8. Okumiya, *Zero!*

9. Tolischus, *Through Japanese Eyes*, 153.

10. Brice, *The Royal Navy and the Sino-Japanese Incident 1937–41*, 130.

11. Hanser, "The Mystery of the Missing Destroyer."

12. "Tommy Hart Speaks Out."

13. Schultz, *The Last Battle Station*, 114.

14. Hanser, "Mystery of the Missing Destroyer."

15. British Documents on Foreign Affairs (BDFA), Part I, Series E, "Asia" Vol. 30, Pacific Islands, 267.

16. Ibid.

17. The account of the deaths of Lieutenant Freeman, Lieutenant Lansdale, Ensign Monaghan, Seaman *Edsall*, and others comes from several sources, including the *Dictionary of American Naval Fighting Ships [Is this the same as Ch. 1 note 21?]*; Hempenstall and Mochida, *The Lost Man*; Kriser, "Clash of the Would Be Titans"; British Documents on Foreign Affairs (BDFA), Part I, Series E, Vol. 30, "Pacific Islands," 1902, Document 137; Papers Relating to the Foreign Relations of the U.S., 1899. "The Massacre at Samoa," *New York Times*.

Postscript

1. Alden, *Flush Decks and Four Pipes*.

2. Secretary of the Navy Denby's report to President Calvin Coolidge on the Point Honda tragedy in 1923, when twenty-three sailors lost their lives after a navigational error caused seven destroyers to run aground at Point Honda, California.

Glossary

General
AAF Army Air Force, or USAAF (United States Army Air Force)

ABDA (American-British-Dutch-Australian) The joint Allied forces opposing the Japanese in Southeast Asia, including the Philippines, from January until late February 1942. Admiral Thomas Hart of the U.S. Asiatic Fleet was the naval commander in chief until February 12, at which point he was replaced by Vice Adm. Conrad Helfrich of the Royal Netherlands Navy. U.S. naval forces were then commanded by Rear Adm. William Glassford as Commander Southwest Pacific (COMSOUWESPAC).

ABDACOM Allied joint command in Southeast Asia; it opposed the Japanese in January and February 1942 (Supreme Commander Gen. Sir Archibald Wavell).

ABDAFLOAT Commander of ABDA (American-British-Dutch-Australian) naval forces (Adm. Thomas Hart, U.S. Navy, and later Vice Adm. C. E. L. Helfrich, Royal Netherlands Navy).

ABDAIR Commander of ABDA Air Forces (Air Chief Marshal Sir Richard Peirse, Royal Air Force)

ABDARM Commander of ABDA ground forces (Lt. Gen. Hein ter Poorten, Royal Netherlands Indies Army [KNIL])

ALUSNA United States naval attaché

CinC Commander in Chief

CINCAF Commander in Chief, Asiatic Fleet

CINCPAC Commander in Chief, Pacific Fleet

CINCUS (later COMINCH) Commander in Chief, U.S. Navy

CNO Chief of Naval Operations

CO commanding officer

COMSOWESPAC Commander Southwest Pacific (Naval Forces)

CZM (*Commandant Zeemacht Nederland*) Commander in Chief, Royal Netherlands Naval Forces

DAR detailed action report

IJN time (Tokyo time) 90 minutes ahead of USN time on March 1, 1942, south of Java; and 60 minutes ahead of Dutch time. For example: IJN = 12:00 noon; Dutch = 11:00 a.m.; USN = 10:30 a.m.

KNIL (*Koninklijk Nederlands-Indisch Leger*) Royal Netherlands Indies Army (RNIA)

NEI (Netherlands East Indies) Also known as the Dutch East Indies, today Indonesia.

RAAF Royal Australian Air Force

RAF Royal Air Force

RAN Royal Australian Navy

RN Royal Navy

RNN Royal Netherlands Navy

RNVR Royal Navy Volunteer Reserve

SCAP (Supreme Commander of the Allied Powers) Title of Gen. Douglas MacArthur's command as of August 15, 1945.

SEAC (South East Asia Command) An Anglo-American command and geographic theater, established in the second half of 1943, which included Burma, Ceylon, Sumatra, and Malaya. The Supreme Commander was Vice Adm. Lord Louis Mountbatten of the Royal Navy. SEAC was assigned the administration of the Netherlands East Indies at the end of the war, much to the relief of MacArthur and the exasperation of Mountbatten.

TROM Tabular record of movements; a general timeline and record of a ship's activities.

USAAF United States Army Air Force, or AAF (Army Air Force)

USN United States Navy

USNA United States Naval Academy

USNR United States Naval Reserve

WD war diary

U.S. Navy (may be used to describe Allied and Axis vessels as well)

AA antiaircraft

AD destroyer tender

AO oiler, or fuel oil tanker

AS submarine tender

ASW antisubmarine warfare

AV seaplane tender

AVD seaplane tender (high-speed)

BatDiv battleship division

BB battleship

CA heavy cruiser

CAP combat air patrol

CarDiv Carrier Division

CL light cruiser

CruDiv Cruiser Division

CV aircraft carrier

DD destroyer

DesDiv Destroyer Division

DesRon Destroyer Squadron (for example, DesRon 29, the Asiatic Fleet's destroyer squadron, which was made up of three DesDivs: 57, 58, and 59)

MB main battery (any warship's heaviest guns)

PatWing Patrol Wing

SS submarine

TF task force

TG task group

U.S. Navy Ranks and Ratings

Adm. admiral

AMM aviation machinist mate

Bkr. baker

BM boatswain's mate

Capt. captain

CK cook

CM carpenter's mate

Cmdr. commander

COX coxswain

DC-V (G) dental officer, general service

EM electrician's mate

Ensign ensign

F fireman

FC fire-control man
GM gunner's mate
Lt. lieutenant
Lt. Cmdr. lieutenant commander
Lt. j.g. lieutenant junior grade
MAtt mess attendant
MM machinist mate
Mus. musician
OS officer's steward
PhM pharmacist's mate
QM quartermaster
Rear Adm. rear admiral
RM radioman
S seaman: **S1c** (first class); **S2c** (second class); **S3c** (third class)
SF shipfitter
SK storekeeper
SM signalman
TM torpedoman
Vice Adm. vice admiral
WO warrant officer
WT watertender
Y yeoman

Japanese

Alf Kawanishi E7K2 (Type 94), an older floatplane used by warships and auxiliaries.
Betty Mitsubishi G4M (Type 1) land-based twin-engined attack bomber, capable of
    torpedo or level-bombing, also known as *Rikkō* (abbreviation of *Rikujō Kōgekiki*).
BKS Another abbreviation for the Japanese Defense Agency's (*Boeicho Bōeikenshūjo
    senshishitsu*) official War History Series, the gigantic *Senshi Sōsho* project: a history
    of the Pacific war published between 1966 and 1980. Each of its 102 volumes is
    500 to 600 pages in length. Although this extraordinary history is an indispensable
    resource for any serious student of the Pacific war, because of its vast scope,
    complexity, and arcane nomenclature, relatively little of it has yet been translated
    into English.
Chūtai Carrier air division, usually six to nine planes each.
CSNLF Combined Special Naval Landing Force (*Rengo Tokubetsu Rikusentai*; more
    than one SNLF unit operating together).
Dave Nakajima (Type 95) floatplane primarily used for scouting and gunfire spotting
    from heavy cruisers and battleships.
GF Grand Fleet or Combined Fleet (*Rengo Kantai*)
Hōmen kantai (several air fleets) Area, or regional, land-based air fleet.
IJA Imperial Japanese Army (*Nihon Rikugun*)
IJAAF Imperial Japanese Army Air Force (*Rikugun Kōkutai*)
IJN Imperial Japanese Navy (*Teikoku Kaigun*, or *Nihon Kaigun*)
JNAF Japanese Naval Air Force (*Kaigun Kōkūtai*)
Kate Nakajima B5N bomber, carrier borne, used in level bombing or torpedo attacks,
    also known as *Kankō* (abbreviation of *Kanjō Kōgekiki*).
Kidô Butai Mobile, or Striking Force. Although a generic term within IJN parlance,it
    usually refers to Japan's premier carrier group (First Air Fleet), the force that
    attacked Pearl Harbor on December 7, 1941; bombed Rabaul, Ambon, and
    Darwin; raided the Indian Ocean in April 1942; and was later destroyed at
    the battle of Midway in June 1942. It is often associated with its most famous
    commander, Vice Adm. Nagumo Chūichi.

Kōdōchōsho Aircraft unit combat operations report, a detailed summary of specific actions that gives units and unit number designations; pilots' names; take-off, attack, and landing times; et cetera.

Kōkū kantai (several carriers or air flotillas) Naval group of two or more carrriers, as the 1st *Kōkū kantai* under Vice Admiral Nagumo at Pearl Harbor, which consisted of the 1st, 2nd, and 5th *Kōkū sentai*. Also, a land-based naval air fleet, as later in the war during the Battle of the Philippine Sea, when the land-based air units under Rear Adm. Kakuda Kakuji were called 1st *Kōkū kantai*.

Kōkūsentai (several *Kōkūtai*) Carrier division; also a land-based naval air flotilla.

Kōkūtai (usually three or four *chūtai*) Carrier-borne naval air group, or a land-based naval air group.

Nell Mitsubishi G3M (Type 96) land-based twin-engined medium attack bomber, capable of torpedo or level bombing; also called *Chūko* (abbreviation of *Chūgata Kōgekiki*).

Sentai Squadron or division of ships; this does not correspond exactly to U.S. Navy nomenclature but is utilized in this work as "division" for clarity's sake (for example, *Dai hachi sentai*=8th Division or sometimes squadron, or Americanized as CruDiv 8).

Shōtai Smallest carrier air section (usually three or four planes in the early phase of the war); late in the war there were two-plane elements called *Kutai*, and two *Kutai* made up one *Shōtai*.

SNLF Special Naval Landing Force (*Kaigun Tokubetsu Rikusentai*), similar to marines.

Terms In Japan, officers would typically be identified by their Etajima (Imperial Japanese Naval Academy) graduating class number. The class number is counted annually beginning with 1872, e.g., the graduating class of 1930 would be "*Dai 58 ki.*" or "58th Term."

Tokkei May refer to *Tokubetsu Keibitai*, or Special Defense Unit, which was usually a land-based unit under Tokkon, or *Tokubetsu Konkyochitai*, a Special Garrison.

Tokkei Tai Special Naval Police Force (*Kaigun Tokubetsu Keisatsu Tai*). IJN security and intelligence force equivalent to the army's *Kempei tai*.

Val Aichi D3A1 (Type 99) carrier dive-bomber, also known as *Kanbaku* (an abbreviation of *Kanjō Bakugekiki*).

Acknowledgments

Research for *A Blue Sea of Blood* began with the assistance of Dr. Evelyn Cherpak of the Naval War College Library in Newport, Rhode Island, who provided materials from the papers of Rear Adm. Edwin Layton, including his translations from Japanese sources pertaining to *Edsall*'s last action. Dr. Cherpak's helpfulness and professionalism made a strong impression on me and gave me a positive feeling about my undertaking at the outset.

I must thank from the bottom of my heart the superb documentary filmmaker Niek Koppen, whose 1995 film *De Slag in de Javazee* contained the short Japanese film footage of *Edsall*'s violent end. From Holland, and after a gap of a decade, Niek could not have been more generous in helping me track down the source of this footage. In my estimate, no finer documentary on World War II has been produced since Niek's film, and very few before are its equal.

Within another six months, I made the acquaintance of the redoubtable J. Michael Wenger, military historian and Japanese Naval Air Force expert par excellence, who was as good as his word when he promised to "extract" the data on the KdB air strikes against *Pecos* and *Edsall* on March 1, 1942, from the official *kōdōchōsho*. This, too, was material of critical importance, and Mike Wenger has remained a staunch supporter and dependable fellow researcher who has never been anything but helpful and professional. Mike also shared pointers with me on the arcane, protocol-driven complexities of the National Archives II (NARA II) in College Park, Maryland. I feel profoundly indebted to Mike; I only hope that my work meets his high standards and that I will be given a chance to return the favor at some future point.

My friend and agent, James D. Hornfischer, gave me both private encouragement and professional suggestions, without which this project might never have found a publisher. He also gave useful advice on negotiating NARA II. There I was able to meet Patrick Osborne, a personification of crisp efficiency, who directed me to a wealth of material; I only wish I had possessed the unlimited time and resources it merited. But that might have resulted in a five-hundred-page tome.

Throughout the course of the project, many other individuals stepped up to help me with my investigations and provide the feedback necessary for a first-time author. I will name as many as I can but ask the forbearance of readers and collaborators if I have neglected or overlooked anyone. I first want to express my gratitude to naval historian Vincent P. O'Hara, author of *The German Fleet at War, 1939–1945* (2004), and *The U.S. Navy Against the Axis, Surface Combat, 1941–1945* (2007), who made a number of useful practical and structural suggestions at critical junctures during the writing of the book. Again, I hope to be able to repay his generosity and helpfulness at some future point. And my work benefited tremendously from my exchanges with William H. Bartsch, whose *Doomed at the Start* (1992) and *December 8, 1941: MacArthur's Pearl Harbor* (2003) are two of the finest studies ever produced on the Pacific war. Bill shared important source materials with me that proved of vital significance.

An international group of historians and archivists deserves special mention. The aid of Slovenia's Klemen Luzar has been inestimable; Lars Ahlberg of Sweden provided me with his expertise early in the project; in Holland, Jan Visser of the "Royal Netherlands Navy Warships of WWII" website and Bea Cramer at the Beeld en Geluid archives in Hilversum provided crucial NEI material; in the Antipodes, John Bradford of Australia contributed several documents that helped flesh out lacuna in *Edsall*'s mystery, and Jill Durney at the MacMillan Brown Library of

Canterbury University in Christchurch, New Zealand, located and copied rare International Military Tribunal for the Far East (IMTFE) records. Olly Van Driest-Young, born in the East Indies and chronicler of her own incarceration on Celebes by the Japanese during the war, made important last-minute translations of Nortier's NEI text, for which I am deeply grateful.

Jim Nix, the grandson of *Edsall*'s skipper (Lt. J. J. Nix), has been the embodiment of the "can-do" spirit of the Asiatic Fleet, and his friendship was absolutely central to the completion of this work. It was nothing short of extraordinary to meet Jim; he is the spitting image of his grandfather. When I first encountered him, it was like stepping back across time and space to come face to face with *Edsall*'s remarkable commander. That we are about the same age and of similar backgrounds made becoming friends—not always easy as one grows older—effortless.

Retired Rear Adm. Kenneth (Kent) Riffey, nephew of Loren Stanford Myers, has shared every shred of information he could lay his hands on from family members and acquaintances pertaining to the fate of his uncle and the history of DD-219. No other single individual has provided more invaluable material to me, and I have needed no more motivation than to tell the story properly for his sake and that of other *Edsall* family members and relatives. Similarly, I am indebted to Jo Gallagher and her mother, June Gallagher, niece and sister of Blackie and Smokie Parsons, the irrepressible Asiatic Fleet brothers who gave their lives on the same day aboard *Edsall* and *Houston*.

Several other friends in the USS *Houston* (CA-30) Survivors Association were instrumental in helping this non-sailor reconstruct the life and experiences of Asiatic Fleet personnel. Foremost among these have been Rear Adm. Robert Fulton, U.S. Navy (Ret.)—*Houston*'s junior engineering officer as a lieutenant—and Electrician's Mate 3rd Class Howard E. Brooks. But the number of *Houston* survivors I have known throughout the years is twenty to thirty times over again, and *all* to a man have been larger than life, and more vivid and worthy of admiration than I can begin to say. My "Ca30ng" (USS *Houston* Next Generation Organization) friend Vic Campbell, a documentary filmmaker (*Death Becomes the Ghost*) and author in his own right, has also been most helpful from the start. Commander Louis Dorny, U.S. Navy (Ret.), selflessly offered material from his thirty-plus years of research into the Asiatic Fleet and the valiant PBYs of Patrol Wing 10. My fellow IJN enthusiasts at the Combined Fleet's message board (combinedfleet's j-aircraft.org) also have my sincere thanks; Jim Lansdale, Tony Tully, Ed Low, and W. D. Dickson deserve special recognition.

My brother, David F. Kehn, was also supportive and generous throughout the project. My friend Taylor Trivi helped proof the manuscript and added helpful feedback laced with her usual droll humor.

Finally, another person who truly deserves special mention is my contact in Japan: the historian and translator Kan Sugahara. Without Kan, this book could not have appeared; it is just that simple. Kan spent almost a year looking for IJN personnel who might have been involved in those events so many decades ago. It was he who translated my English-language questions into Japanese for these veterans, and their answers back into English for me, and always with exemplary precision and fidelity. A member of the 77th Naval Academy term himself, he is that rarity today: a Japanese at home among the specialized language and nomenclature of Imperial-era documents from the Pacific war. His keen intelligence, good humor, and tact have made him a model of professionalism and a pleasure to work with for more than two years. Regarding our relationship, I offer the following line from Laurens van der Post's *The Seed and the Sower*. His words seem especially apt given the subject matter as well as the circumstances involved in the writing of this book, and I feel certain that Sugahara-san will grasp their sincerity and wisdom: "There is a way of winning by losing, a way of victory in defeat which we are going to discover."*

Although mistranslations or primary source errors may be beyond an author's control, the conception, tenor, and conclusions of the text are an author's alone, and for these I bear sole responsibility. Yet, this book is neither a debate nor an act of engineering, but rather a tribute to the lives of young men long since abandoned, lost, and forgotten. If it has shed some useful light for their family members and descendants on the sacrifices that their relatives made more than sixty-five years ago, it will have fulfilled the true purpose for which it was created.

* Laurens van der Post. *The Seed and the Sower*, page 35.

Bibliography

Primary Sources
Final Muster Roll
USS *Edsall* (DD-219) March 1942 Record Group 24, Box 121, Reel 1439. National Archives at College Park (NARA II)

Deck Logs, Records Group (RG) 24
excerpts from Deck Log for USS *Edsall* (DD-219), May 1939 (Washington, DC: National Archives [NWTC]).
excerpts from Deck Log for USS *Edsall* (DD-219) October 1941
excerpts from Deck Log for USS *Edsall* (DD-219) November 1941
excerpts from Deck Log for USS *Edsall* (DD-219) December 1941
excerpts from Deck Log for USS *Edsall* (DD-219) January 1942
excerpts from Deck Log for USS *Whipple* (DD-217) February 1942
excerpts from Deck Log for USS *Alden* (DD-211) February 1942
excerpts from Deck Log for USS *Houston* (CA-30) December 1941–January 1942
excerpts from Deck Log for USS *Houston* (CA-30) February 42 (reconstructed postwar)
excerpts from Deck Log for USS *Holland* (AS-3) January 1942
excerpts from Deck Log for USS *Tulsa* (PG-22) February 1942

Action Reports, RG 38, Office of CNO, NARA II<M
USS *Edsall* (DD-219) January 22, 1942 "Activities of USS *Edsall*"
USS *Edsall* (DD-219) January 31, 1942 "Action against Submarines"
USS *Alden* (DD-211) January 29, 1942 "Memorandum for Commanding Officer, USS *Trinity*" (by Lt. Ernest E. Evans, Executive Officer, USS *Alden*)
USS *Alden* (DD-211) March 7, 1942 "Engagement with the Enemy, Battle of the Java Sea, February 27, 1942"
USS *Whipple* (DD-217) March 4, 1942 "USS *Whipple*—Activities Between 26 February and 4 March 1942"
USS *John D. Edwards* (DD-216) March 4, 1942 "General Conclusions and Recommendations Based on War Operations To Date"
USS *John D. Edwards* (DD-216) March 4, 1942 "Reports of Action With Japanese on February 27, 1942, Events Before and After"
USS *Pope* (DD-225) January 25, 1942 "Night Destroyer Attack Off Balikpapan, January 24, 1942 [Netherlands East Indies Area]"
USS *Holland* (AS-3) January 31, 1942 "Report of Diving Operations"
USS *Pecos* (AO-6) March 7, 1942 "Action and Sinking of USS *Pecos*, 1 March 1942"
USS *Langley* (AV-3) March 9, 1942 "Operations, action and sinking of USS *Langley*, period from February 22 to March 5, 1942"

Archival Material and Interviews

AAF Informational Intelligence Summary No. 43–24 (March 1943), 18.

ADB Conversations, Pearl Harbor Hearings, Pt. 15. *Exhibits of the Joint Committee*. Washington DC: GPO, 1946. (pp. 1551–1584; p. 7 of ADB is p. 1558 in the text).

Allied Translator and Interpreter Section, Southwest Pacific Area (A.T.I.S. S.W.P. A.), Enemy Publications, August 11, 1943, No. 32: "Account of the Netherlands East Indies Operation, Feb–Mar '42."

"Army Air Action in the Philippines and Netherlands East Indies—1941–1942," U.S. Air Force. *Historical Study No. 111*.

Beers, Dr. Henry P. "U.S. Naval Detachment in Turkish Waters, 1919–1924." (Administrative Reference Service Report No. 2), Office of Records Administration, Navy Dept., June 1943.

Bristol, Rear Adm. M. L., U.S.N. "*Memorandum*" to Mr. C. Van H. Engert, Assistant High Commissioner, dated 25 April 1920. Van H. Engert Collection, Box 1, Folder 5, Georgetown Univ. Library, Special Collections Division, Washington, DC.

The Campaigns of the Pacific War, United States Strategic Bombing Survey (Pacific), Naval Analysis Division. Washington, DC: GPO, 1946.

Eccles, Cmdr. Henry E. "On the Java Sea Battle" (dictated August 30, 1942); Admiral Richard Bates Papers, Naval War College Library, Newport, R.I., Series II, Box 15, Folder 15.

Edwin Layton Papers, Naval War College Library, Newport, RI. MS Collection 69, Box 37.

Glassford, Rear Adm. William. COMSOWESPAC, March 12, 1942, "Operations of U.S. Naval Forces in Southwest Pacific."

Hart, Adm. Thomas C., U.S. Navy, CinC, Asiatic Fleet, Feb. 6, 1942. "Events and Circumstances Concerning the "Striking Force."

———. "Supplementary of Narrative," Op-29-B, Winter 1946–47.

Wiley, Cmdr. H. V., COMDESRON 29, March 4, 1942, "Makassar Straits Action— Comments and Recommendations Based on Action with Japanese Forces Off Balikpapan in a Night Destroyer Action."

Harbord, Major-General James G., U.S. Army. "Conditions in the Near East: A Report of the American Miltary Mission to Armenia." Washington, DC: GPO, 1920.

Haraguchi Memoir ("Sea Battle Off Tjilatjap") by Haraguchi, Dr. Shizuhiko. Kan Sugahara, trans.

"*The Japanese Special Naval Police Force,*" 14 pgs. Op-23F14, Translation No. 393, December 13, 1945. RG 125, Box 9, NARA II, College Park, MD.

"The Japanese Story of the Battle of Midway" (A Translation), OPNAV P32–1002, Office of Naval Intelligence, U.S. Navy, June 1947 (aka "The Nagumo Report").

Jules James Papers, Collection No. 223, East Carolina Manuscript Collection, J. Y. Joyner Library, East Carolina University, Greenville, NC.

"*Kanbaku* War Notes: A Narrative by Tokuji IIZUKA," Part 3, courtesy the Iizuka family via Dr. Minoru Kawamoto and James Lansdale.

Kik, Adriaan Willem. Memoirs written in 2000. Translated by Peter Kik, 2007. Copy in author's possession.

Lowell Barty Interview. By telephone with the author, June, 2008.

Motegi Meiji Interview. Conducted and translated by Kan Sugahara, March–April, 2006.

"Netherlands East Indies Naval Invasion Operations." Headquarters USAFFE, Military History Section, Japanese Research Division. (Japanese Monograph No. 101).

Pearl Harbor Attack Hearings, Part 28. *Proceedings of Army Pearl Harbor Board.*
    Washington, DC: GPO, 1946.
Pearl Harbor Attack Hearings, Part 33. *Proceedings of the Navy Court of Inquiry.*
    Washington, DC: GPO, 1946. 942–943.
Pearl Harbor Attack, Hearings Before the Joint Committee, Part 10. February 18, 1946.
    4812.
Sasaki Masao Interview. Conducted and translated by Kan Sugahara, December,
    2006–January, 2007.
Senate Documents, Vol. 14: Navy Yearbook 1920–1921. Compiled by Elwin A. Silsby.
    Washington, DC: U.S. GPO, 1922.
"Sumatra Invasion and Southwest Area Naval Mopping-Up Operations, Jan '42–May
    '42." Headquarters USAFFE, Military History Section, Japanese Research
    Division. (Japanese Monograph No. 79A).

War-Crimes Documents
NARA II, College Park, MD
"NEI 151 v01.1 Johan Tomasowa Statements, etc." January–June 1947.
RG 331 SCAP, Legal Section, Administrative Division, Area Case Files, Box 945, Folder
    51 (70 pages).
Sworn Statement to J. R. S. Apontoweil, Hollandia, New Guinea, January 9, 1947.
"The United States v. [RADM] Tamotsu Furukawa et al." May–July, 1948. RG 331, Box
    9592, Case #307. Prosecution Exhibit #3, "Information Obtained at Kendare [*sic*]
    19th October 1945" F/Lt. M. T. O'Shea, RAAF (3 pages).
———. RG 331. Defense Exhibit B: "Chain of Command of the Naval Units At
    Kendari."
———. RG 331, Box 1939, Folder 20. Two statements by Tamotsu Furukawa, February
    2/3, 1948, at Sugamo Prison (9 pages).
———. RG 331, Box 9592, Case #307. Direct and Cross Examination of Johan
    Tomasowa (80 pages).
"The United States v. [RADM] Tamotsu Furukawa et al." HQ 8th Army, Judge
    Advocate Section, War Crimes Defense APD 343. "Defense Motion for
    Disapproval of Findings and Sentences." RG 331, January 7, 1949 (4 pages).

Macmillan Brown Library, University of Canterbury, Christchurch, New Zealand.
International Military Tribunal for the Far East (IMTFE) documents:
Exhibit 1702 Capt. Charles Jongeneel (3 pages)
———. 1800/1800A Gōsuke Taniguchi (13 pages)
———. 1801/1801A Michinori Nakamura (6 pages)
———. 1803/1803A Yoshiyuki Nakamura (8 pages)
———. 1804/1804A George Tyndale Cooper (5 pages)
———. 1805/1805A Charles Jongeneel (9 pages)
———. 1810 Herman Dallinga (5 pages)
———. 1811/1811A Meindersma/Koerts (2 pages)
———. 1812 Ann Lilian Rolff (4 pages)
———. 1816 Johan Mairuhu (4 pages)
Warrant: Hearing of Evidence. 19095/R. Office of the Judge Advocate at Hollandia, G.
    G. Jochems, June 19, 1947. NARA II, RG 331, Stack 290, Box 945.

Secondary Sources

Books

Abe, Zenji, with Mike Wenger and Naomi Shin. *The Emperor's Sea Eagle*. Hawaii: Arizona Memorial, 2005.

Abeyasekese, Susan One Hand Clapping. *Indonesian Nationalists and the Dutch, 1939–1942*. Clayton, Australia: Centre of Southeast Asian Studies, 1976.

Abraham, J. Johnston. *The Surgeon's Log; Impressions of the Far East*. New York: E. P. Dutton & Co., 1929.

Alden, Cmdr. John D. *Flush Decks and Four Pipes*. Annapolis, MD: U.S. Naval Institute Press, 1965.

Alford, Lodwick H. *Playing For Time: War on an Asiatic Fleet Destroyer*. Bennington, VT: Merriam Press, 2006.

Allen, Frederick Lewis. *Only Yesterday: An Informal History of the Twenties*. New York: Harper & Row, 1931.

Andrews, Lewis Jr. *Tempest, Fire, and Foe; Destroyer Escorts in WWII and the Men Who Manned Them*. Charleston/Miami: Narwhal Press, 1999.

Baldwin, Hanson W. *Great Mistakes in the War*. New York: Harper, 1950.

Barenblatt, Daniel, *A Plague upon Humanity: The Secret Genocide of Axis Japan's Germ Warfare Operation*. New York: Harper Collins, 2004,

Barley, Nigel. *Not a Hazardous Sport*. New York: Henry Holt, 1988.

Bartsch, William. *December 8, 1941: MacArthur's Pearl Harbor*. College Station, TX: Texas A&M University Press, 2003.

Bell, Capt. Frederick J. *Condition Red: Destroyer Action in the South Pacific*. New York & Toronto: Longmans and Green, 1943.

Benda, Irikara, Kishi, eds. *Japanese Military Administration in Indonesia: Selected Documents*. New Haven, CT: Yale University Press, 1965.

Benedict, Ruth. *The Chrysanthemum and the Sword*. Boston: Houghton-Mifflin, 1946.

Bigalke, Terence W. *Tana Toraja: A Social History of an Indonesian People*. Singapore: Singapore University Press, 2005.

The Bluejackets' Manual 1943. Annapolis, MD: U.S. Naval Institute Press, 1943.

Brackman, Arnold C. *The Other Nuremburg: The Untold Story of the Tokyo War Crimes Trials*. New York: William Morrow, 1987.

Brereton, Lt. Gen. Lewis. *The Brereton Diaries*. New York: William Morrow, 1946.

Brice, Martin. *The Royal Navy and the Sino-Japanese Incident 1937–41*. Hersham, UK: Ian Allan, 1973.

British Documents on Foreign Affairs (BDFA). Numerous volumes 1919–40. Burke & Watt, ed. Frederick, MD: University Publications of America, 1994.

British Documents on Foreign Affairs (BDFA) Part I, Series E, Asia, Vol. 30, "Pacific Islands." Foreign Office, 1902. Frederick, MD: University Publications, 1995.

British Parliamentary Debates. House of Lords, Vols. 49, 51. London: Hansard, 1922.

———. House of Commons, Vols. 116, 130. London: Hansard, 1919, 1920.

Bruce, Ginny and Mary Covernton. *Indonesia: A Travel Survival Kit*. Melbourne, Australia: Lonely Planet, 1986.

Campbell, John. *Naval Weapons of World War II*. Annapolis, MD: U.S. Naval Institute Press, 1985.

Carlton, Eric. *Massacres: A Historical Perspective*. Atlanta, GA: Scholar Press, 1994.

Carpenter, Dorr and Norman Polmar. *Submarines of the Imperial Japanese Navy*. Annapolis, MD: U.S. Naval Institute Press, 1986.

Charles, H. Robert. *Last Man Out: Surviving the Burma-Thailand Death Railway; A Memoir*. St. Paul, MN: Zenith Press, 2006.

Chauvel, Richard. *The Rising Sun in the Spice Islands: A History of Ambon During the Japanese Occupation*. Ithaca, NY: Cornell University Press, 1985.

Churchill, Winston. *The World Crisis: The Aftermath*. New York: Charles Scribner's Sons, 1929

Clifton, Violet. *Islands of Indonesia*. London: Constable, 1927.

Connaughton, Richard. *MacArthur and Defeat in the Philippines*. New York: Overlook Press, 2001.

Conrad, Joseph. *An Outcast of the Islands*. New York: Doubleday & Co., 1964 reprint of 1896 original.

Coox, Alvin D. *The Unfought War: Japan 1941–1942*. San Diego, CA: San Diego State University Press, 1992.

Coox, Alvin D., and Hilary Conroy, eds. *China and Japan: A Search for Balance Since World War I*. Santa Barbara, CA: Clio Books, 1978.

Costello, John. *Days of Infamy*. New York: Pocket Books, 1997.

Cowman, Ian. *Dominion or Decline: Anglo-American Naval Relations in the Pacific, 1937–1941*. Oxford-Washington, DC: Berg, 1996.

Crawfurd, John. *A Descriptive Dictionary of the Indian Islands and Adjacent Countries*. London: Bradbury and Evans, 1856.

Cull, Brian. *Buffaloes Over Singapore*. London: Grub Street, 2003.

Cull, Brian, and Paul Sortehaug. *Hurricanes over Singapore*. London: Grub Sreet, 2004.

DeLeeuw, Hendrik. *Crossroads of the Java Sea*. New York: Garden City, 1931.

Dennis, Peter. *Troubled Days of Peace*. Manchester, England: Manchester University Press, 1987.

Dennys, N. B., ed. *The Treaty Ports of China and Japan*. London: Trubner & Co., 1867. Reprinted by Chinese Materials Center, Inc., San Francisco, CA, 1977.

Dictionary of American Navy Fighting Ships. Washington, DC: U.S. GPO, 1963.

Dobkin, Marjorie Housepian. *Smyrna: The Destruction of a City*. Kent, OH: Kent State University Press, 1988.

Dower, John W. *War Without Mercy*. New York: Pantheon Books, 1986.

———. *Embracing Defeat*. New York and London: The New Press, 1999.

Duus, Peters, Ramon H. Myers, and Mark R. Peattie, eds. *The Japanese Wartime Empire*. Princeton, NJ: Princeton University Press, 1996.

Dyer, Vice Adm. G. C. *The Amphibians Came to Conquer*. Washington, DC: U.S. GPO, 1971.

———. *On the Treadmill to Pearl Harbor: The Memoirs of Admiral James O. Richardson*. Washington, DC: Naval History Division, Department of the Navy, 1973.

Earle, Edward Mead. *Turkey: The Great Powers and the Bagdad Railway*. New York: Russell & Russell, 1966 reprint of 1923 original.

Edmonds, Walter D. *They Fought with What They Had*. Boston: Little, Brown & Co., 1951.

Enright, Francis James. *To Leave This Port*. Orick, CA: Enright Publishing Co., 1990.

Epton, Nina. *Magic and Mystics of Java*. London: Octagon Press, 1974.

Falle, Sam. *My Lucky Life*. Lewes, UK: The Book Guild, 1996.

Felton, Mark. *The Fujita Plan: Japanese Attacks on the United States and Australia during the Second World War*. Barnsley, UK: Pen and Sword, Military, 2006.

Finn, Richard B. *Winners in Peace: MacArthur, Yoshida, and Postwar Japan*. Berkeley, CA: University of California Press, 1992.

Francillon, Dr. René J. *Japanese Navy Bombers of World War Two*. New York: Doubleday and Co., 1969.

Freely, John and Hilary Sumner-Boyd. *Strolling Through Istanbul*. London: KPI, 1972.

Friend, Theodore. *The Blue-Eyed Enemy: Japan Against the West in Java and Luzon, 1942–1945*. Princeton, NJ: Princeton University Press, 1988.

Frost, Cdr. Holloway. *On a Destroyer's Bridge*. Annapolis: United States Naval Institute, 1930.

Fuller, Richard. *Shōkan*. London: Arms and Armour Press, 1992.

Gallagher, O'Dowd. *Action in the East*. New York: Doubleday, Doran, 1942.

Gidney, James B. *A Mandate for Armenia*. Kent, OH: Kent State University Press, 1967.

Gill, G. Hermon. *The Royal Australian Navy*. Vol. 1, 1939–1942. Canberra: Australian War Memorial, 1957.

———. *The Royal Australian Navy*. Vol. II, 1943–1945. Canberra: Australian War Memorial, 1957.

Ginn, John L. *Sugamo Prison, Tokyo*. Jefferson, NC: McFarland and Co., 1992.

Goffman, Daniel, Edhem Eldem, and Bruce Masters. *The Ottoman City Between East and West*. New York: Cambridge, 1999.

Golden Jubilee History of Nippon Yusen Kaisha, 1885–1935. Tokyo: Nippon Yusen Kaisha, 1936

Goldstein, Donald and Katherine V. Dillon, eds. *The Pacific War Papers*. Dulles, VA: Potomac Books, 2005.

Goodrich, Marcus. *Delilah*. New York: The Lyons Press, 2000 reprint of 1941 original.

Goodwin, Michael J. *Shobun: A Forgotten War Crime in the Pacific*. Mechanicsburg, PA: Stackpole Books, 1995.

Gunnison, Royal Arch. *So Sorry, No Peace*. New York: Viking Press, 1944.

Hague, Arnold. *Destroyers for Great Britain: A History of the 50 Town Class Ships Transferred from the United States to Great Britain in 1940*. Annapolis, MD: U.S. Naval Institute Press, 1990.

Halsey, Fleet Adm. William F., and Lt. Cmdr. J. Bryan III, *Admiral Halsey's Story*. New York: Whittesley House, 1947.

Hanna, Willard A. *Indonesian Banda*. Philadelphia, PA: Institute for the Study of Human Issues, 1978.

Harries, Meirion and Susie. *Sheathing the Sword*. London: Heinemann, 1987.

Hartunian, Abraham H. *Neither to Laugh Nor to Weep*. Boston: Beacon Press, 1968.

Hearn, Chester. *Sorties into Hell; The Hidden War on Chichi Jima*. Westport: Praeger, 2003.

Hempenstall, Peter, and Paula Mochida. *The Lost Man: Wilhelm Solf in German History*. Wiesbaden, Germany: Harrassowitz Verlag, 2005.

Hetherington, J. *Blamey, Controversial Soldier*. Canberra: Australian War Memorial, 1973.

Hornfischer, James D. *Ship of Ghosts: The Story of the USS Houston, FDR's Legendary Lost Cruiser, and the Epic Saga of Her Survivors*. New York: Bantam, 2006.

Horton, George. *The Blight of Asia*. Indianapolis: Bobbs-Merrill, 1926.

Hudson, W.J., and Wendy Way, eds. *Documents on Australian Foreign Policy, 1937–1949*, Volume VIII: 1945. Canberra: Australian Government Publishing Service, 1989.

Index to the Correspondence of the Foreign Office for the Year 1946, Part IV, S to Z. Millwood, NY: KTO Press, 1977.

Jones, F. C. *Japan's New Order in East Asia: Its Rise and Fall, 1937–45*. Oxford: Oxford University Press, 1954.

Kennan, George F. *American Diplomacy 1900–1950*. Chicago, Ill.: Univ. of Chicago Press, 1951.

Kidd, John F. and Erwin C. Winkel II, MD. *Twice Forgotten*. New York: Vantage Press, Inc., 2006.

Kodama Yoshiō. *Sugamo Diary*. Tokyo: Radiopress, 1950/1956.

Kojinsha Publishers Warships of the Imperial Japanese Navy, Heavy Cruisers: Mogami and Tone Class. Tokyo: Kojinsha, 1997.

Komatsu, Dr. Keiichiro. *Origins of the Pacific War and the Importance of "Magic."* New York: St. Martin's Press, 1999.

Krasner, Stephen D. *Defending the National Interest: Raw Materials Investments and U.S. Foreign Policy*. Princeton, NJ: Princeton University Press, 1978.

Kratoska, Paul H. *The Japanese Occupation of Malaya*. London: Hurst, 1998.

Kratoska, Paul, ed. *Southeast Asian Minorities in the Wartime Japanese Empire*. London: Routledge Curzon, 2002.

Krug, Hans-Joachim, Yōichi Hirama, Berthold J. Sander-Nagashima, and Axel Niestlé. *Reluctant Allies: German-Japanese Naval Relations in World War II*. Annapolis, MD: U.S. Naval Institute Press, 2001.

La Botz, Dan Edward L. Doheny. *Petroleum, Power, and Politics in the United States and Mexico*. NY/Westport, CT/London: Praeger, 1991.

Lacroix, Eric, and Lenton Wells. *Japanese Cruisers of the Pacific War*. Annapolis, MD: U.S. Naval Institute Press, 1997.

Leary, William M., ed. *MacArthur and the American Century, A Reader*. Lincoln and London: Univ. of Nebraska Press, 2001.

Lebra, Joyce C. *Japanese Trained Armies in Southeast Asia*. New York: Columbia University Press, 1977.

Leutze, James. *A Different Kind of Victory: A Biography of Admiral Thomas C. Hart*. Annapolis, MD: U.S. Naval Institute Press, 1991.

Lundstrom, John B. *The First Team: Pacific Naval Air Combat from Pearl Harbor to Midway*. Annapolis, MD: U.S. Naval Institute Press, 1984.

MacArthur, Gen. Douglas. *Reminiscences*. Annapolis, MD: U.S. Naval Institute Press, 2001 reprint of 1964 original.

Mack, Vice Adm. William P., U.S. Navy (Ret.), and William P. Mack Jr. *South to Java*. Annapolis, MD: Nautical and Aviation Publishing Company, 1988.

Manvell, Roger. *Films and the Second World War*. New York: Delta, 1974.

Marder, Arthur J., Mark Jacobsen, and John Horsfield. *Old Friends, New Enemies: The Royal Navy and the Imperial Japanese Navy*, Vol. II: *The Pacific War 1942–1945*. Oxford: Clarendon Press, 1981.

Martin, Bernard. *Over My Shoulder*. London: Duckworth, 1935.

Matsunaga, Ichiro, Gordon Van Wylen, and Kan Sugahara. *Encounter at Sea*. Troy, MI: Sabre Press, 1994.

McDougall, William H. Jr. *Six Bells off Java*. New York: Scribner's Sons, 1948.

———. *By Eastern Windows*. London: Arthur Barker, 1951.

———. *If I Get Out Alive; World War II Letters and Diaries of William H. McDougall Jr*. Ed. Gary Topping. Salt Lake City: Univ. Utah Press, 2007.

McEwan, James. *The Remorseless Road: Singapore to Nagasaki*. Shrewsbury, England: Airlife Publishing, Ltd., 1997.

McMillan, Richard. *The British Occupation of Indonesia, 1945–1946*. London: Routledge, 2005.

Mendenhall, C. *Submarine Diary: The Silent Stalking of Japan*. Chapel Hill, NC: Algonquin Books, 1991.

Mérimée, Prosper . *Letters To An Unknown*. Trans. Henri P. du Bois. New York: Brentano's, 1913.

Messimer, Dwight R. *Pawns of War*. Annapolis, MD: U.S. Naval Institute Press, 1983.

———. *In the Hands of Fate*. Annapolis, MD: U.S. Naval Institute Press, 1985.

Michel, Capt. John J. A. *Mr. Michel's War*. Novato, CA: Presidio Press, 1998.

Morehead, James B. *In My Sights; The Memoir of a P-40 Ace*. Novato, CA: Presidio, 1998.

Morison, Samuel Eliot. *History of U.S. Naval Operations in World War II*, Vol. 3, *The Rising Sun*. Boston: Little, Brown, 1953.

Morley, James, ed. *Japan Erupts*. New York: Columbia University Press, 1984.

Morton, Louis. *The Fall of the Philippines: U.S. Army in WWII*. Washington, DC: Center of Military History, U.S. Army, 1993.

Mullin, J. Daniel. *Another Six-Hundred*. Privately published, 1984.

"Multaluli" (Eduard D. Dekker). *Max Havelaar*. New York: Penguin Classics, 1975.

Murray, Robert K. *The Harding Era: Warren G. Harding and His Administration*. Minneapolis: University of Minnesota Press, 1969.

Newcomb, Richard. *U.S. Destroyers of the World Wars*. Paducah, KY: Turner Books, 1984.

Noda, Yosiyuki, ed., Anthony H. Angelo, trans. *Introduction to Japanese Law*. Tokyo: University of Tokyo Press, 1966/1976.

Nornes, Abé Mark, and Fukushima Yukio. *The Japan/America Film Wars: World War II Propaganda and Its Cultural* Context. London: Routledge, 1994.

Nortier, J. J. *De Japanse aanval op Nederlands-Indië*. Deel 1: *Celebes, Ambon, Timor*. Rotterdam: Ad. Donker, 1988. (Trans. for author by Olly Van Driest Young.)

O'Connor, Richard. *The Oil Barons, Men of Greed and Grandeur*. Boston and Toronto: Little Brown & Co., 1971.

Okada Fumihide. *A Lone Boat on the High Seas*. Tokyo: Privately published, 1974.

Okumiya Hirikoshi and Martin Caidin. *Zero!* New York: Simon and Schuster, 1956.

Papers Relating to the Foreign Relations of the United States, 1899. Washington, DC: U.S. GPO, 1901.

———, 1922, Vol. 2. Washington, DC: U.S. GPO, 1936.

———, 1939, Vol. 4, The Far East. Washington, DC: U.S. GPO, 1955.

———, 1940, Vol. 4, The Far East. Washington, DC: U.S. GPO, 1955.

Parshall, Jonathan, and Tony Tully. *Shattered Sword: The Untold Story of the Battle of Midway*. Washington, DC: Potomac Books, 2005.

The Pearl Harbor Attack Hearings, Part 10, Joint Committee. Washington, DC: U.S. GPO, 1946.

———. Part 38: the Hewitt Inquiry. Washington, DC: U.S. GPO, 1946.

Peattie, Mark, and Ramon Myers, eds. *The Japanese Colonial Empire, 1895–1945*. Princeton, NJ: Princeton University Press, 1984.

Pecci, Aurelio, and Daisuke Ikeda. *Before It Is Too Late*. Tokyo: Kodansha, 1984.

Petillo, Carol Morris. *Douglas MacArthur: The Philippine Years*. Bloomington, IN: University of Indiana Press, 1981.

Petsalis-Diomidis, N. *Greece at the Paris Peace Conference, 1919*. Thessaloniki, Greece: Institute for Balkan Studies, 1978.

Prange, Gordon, with Donald M. Goldstein and Katherine V. Dillon *God's Samurai*. Washington, DC: Brassey's, 1990.

Prins, Dr. J. *The Double Problem of the South Moluccan Minority*. Groningen, the Netherlands: Dutch-Melanesian Aid Foundation, undated.

Prising, Robin. *Manila, Goodbye*. Boston: Houghton-Mifflin, 1975.

Puleston, Capt. W. D. *The Armed Forces of the Pacific*. New Haven, CT: Yale University Press, 1941.

Ramsay, W. M. *The Historical Geography of Asia Minor*. London: John Murray, 1890.

Register of the Commissioned Officers, Cadets, Midshipmen, and Warrant Officers of the United States Naval Reserve July 1941. Washington, DC: U.S. GPO, 1941.

Reilly, John C. *United States Destroyers of World War II*. Poole, UK: Blandford Books, 1983.

Roscoe, Theodore. *United States Destroyer Operations in World War II*. Annapolis, MD: U.S. Naval Institute Press, 1953.

Roskill, Stephen. *Naval Policy Between the Wars*. Vol. I. New York: Walker and Co., 1968.

———. *The War at Sea, 1939–1945*. Vol. II. London: HMSO, 1956

Ross, Al. *The Destroyer Campbeltown; The Anatomy of the Ship*. London: Conway Maritime Press, 1990.

Ruhe, Capt. William J. *War in the Boats*. Washington, DC: Brassey's, 1997.

Schaller, Michael. *Douglas MacArthur: The Far Eastern General*. New York: Oxford University Press, 1989.

Schenking, J. Charles. *Making Waves.* Stanford, CA: Stanford University Press, 2005.

Schultz, Duane. *The Last Battle Station.* New York: St. Martin's Press, 1985.

Seagrave, Sterling and Peggy. *The Yamato Dynasty: The Secret History of Japan's Imperial Family.* New York: Broadway Books, 1999.

Seneca. *Oedipus.* Trans. E. F. Watling. New York: Penguin Classics, 1966.

Senshi Sōsho. Vol. 26: "Naval Operations in the East Indies and Bay of Bengal." Tokyo: BKS/Asagumo Shimbunsha, 1969.

Sherrod, Robert. *History of Marine Corps Aviation in World War II.* Washington, DC: Combat Forces Press, 1952.

Shimer, Barbara, and Gary Hobbs, trans. *The Kempeitai in Java and Sumatra.* Ithaca, NY: Cornell University Press, 1986.

Shores, Cull and Izawa. *Bloody Shambles.* Vols. 1 and 2. London: Grub Street, 1992–93.

Smith, Michael L. *Ionian Vision.* London: Allen Lane, 1973.

Smith, Peter C. *Fist from the Sky: Japan's Divebomber Ace of WWII.* Mechanicsburg, PA: Stackpole Books, 2005.

Stauffler, Alvin P. *The Quartermaster Corps: Operations in the War Against Japan.* Washington, DC: U.S. GPO, 1956.

Suman, John R. *Ships of the Esso Fleet in World War II.* NJ: Standard Oil Co., 1946.

Takemae, Eiji. *The Allied Occupation of Japan.* New York: Continuum, 2002.

Tanaka, Yuki. *Hidden Horrors: Japanese War Crimes in World War II.* Boulder, CO: Westview Press, 1996; first published in Japan as *Shiraezaru Senso Hanzai, Unknown War Crimes: What Japanese forces did to Australians.* Otsuki Shoten, 1993.

Thomas, David A. *Japan's War at Sea.* London: Andre Deutsch, 1978.

Thomas, David Y. *100 Years of the Monroe Doctrine, 1823–1923.* New York: The MacMillan Company, 1927.

Todorov, Tzvestan. *The Conquest of America: The Question of the Other.* New York: Harper & Row, 1984.

Toland, John. *The Gods of War.* New York: Doubleday, 1985.

Tolischus, Otto D. *Through Japanese Eyes.* New York: Reynal & Hitchcock, 1945.

Tolley, Rear Adm. Kemp. *The Cruise of the Lanikai.* Annapolis, MD: U.S. Naval Institute Press, 1973.

Ugaki, Vice Adm. Matome. *Fading Victory.* Eds. Donald Goldstein and Katherine V. Dillon. Trans. Masataka Chihaya. Pittsburgh, PA: University of Pittsburgh Press, 1991.

USSBS [Pacific]. Interrogations of Japanese Officials, Vols. 1 and 2. Washington, DC: U.S. GPO, 1946.

———. The Campaigns of the Pacific War. Washington, DC: U.S. GPO, 1946.

Van Der Post, Sir Laurens. *The Admiral's Baby.* New York: William Morrow, 1996.

———. *The Seed and the Sower.* London: Hogarth Press, 1963.

Van Wijk, J. M. *Forced Labour: In the Midst of Dangers.* Biggleswade, England: Providence Books, 2001.

Velthoen, Esther J. *Mapping Sulawesi in the 1950s.* In progress, ca. 2002.

Watson, Burton, trans., *The Tales of the Heike.* Haruo Shirane, ed. New York: Columbia Univ. Press, 2006.

Watson, Mark Skinner. *Chief of Staff: Prewar Plans and Preparations, U.S. Army in WWII.* Washington, DC: Historical Division, Department of the Army, 1950.

Weller, George. *Singapore Is Silent.* New York: Harcourt Brace and Co., 1943.

Whitley, M. J. *Destroyers of World War Two.* Annapolis, MD: U.S. Naval Institute Press, 1988.

Wilmott, H. P. *The Barrier and the Javelin.* Annapolis, MD: U.S. Naval Institute Press, 1984.

————. *Empires in the Balance.* Annapolis, MD: U.S. Naval Institute Press, 1982.

————. *Grave of a Dozen Schemes.* Annapolis, MD: U.S. Naval Institute Press, 1996.

Winslow, Capt. Walter G. *The Fleet the Gods Forgot.* Annapolis, MD: U.S. Naval Institute Press, 1982.

————. *The Ghost That Died at Sunda Strait.* Annapolis, MD: U.S. Naval Institute Press, 1984.

Womack, Tom. *The Dutch Naval Air Force Against Japan: The Defense of the Netherlands East Indies, 1941–1942.* Jefferson, NC: McFarland, 2005.

Yoshibumi, Wakamiya. *The Postwar Conservative View of Asia: How the Political Right Has Delayed Japan's Coming to Terms with Its History of Aggression in Asia.* Tokyo: LTCB International Library Foundation, 1999.

Yumeno, Kyūsaku. *Dogura Magura.* Vols. 1 and 2. Tokyo: Reprinted by Kadokawa-bunko, 1935.

Zenji, Abe. *The Emperor's Sea Eagle: A Memoir of the Attack on Pearl Harbor and the War in the Pacific.* Trans. Naomi Shin, Ed. J. Michael Wenger. Honolulu, HA: Arizona Memorial Museum Association, 2006.

Ziegler, Philip, ed. *Personal Diary of Admiral The Lord Louis Mountbatten, Supreme Allied Commander South-East Asia, 1943–1946.* London: Collins, 1988.

Articles

Abernethy, Adm. E. P. R., U.S. Navy (Ret.). "The Pecos Died Hard." *United States Naval Institute Proceedings* (December 1969): 74–83.

Cook, Charles O. Jr. Capt., USN (Ret.), "The Pacific Command Divided: The 'Most Unexplainable' Decision." *United States Naval Institute Proceedings* (September 1978): 56–61.

————. "The Strange Case of Rainbow-5." *United States Naval Insitute Proceedings* (August 1978): 67–75.

Costello, John E. "Remember Pearl Harbor." *United States Naval Institute Proceedings* (September 1983): 53–62.

"The Death of USS *Edsall*: A Gallant Fight Against Impossible Odds." *Shipmate* (April 1980).

Dorny, Cmdr. Louis B., U.S Naval Reserve. "Patrol Wing Ten's Raid on Jolo." *United States Naval Institute Proceedings* (Supplement, 1985): 72–77.

Hanser, Richard. "The Mystery of the Missing Destroyer." *Bluebook* (December 1952).

Harrington, Skip Wild. "The Mystery of USS *Edsall*". *Shipmate* (January–February 1980).

"Humiliation for the Turk." *New York Times* (March 4, 1920).

"Japanese Aerial Tactics Against Ship Targets." *JICPOA* Weekly Intelligence bulletin, Vol. I, No.15 (Oct. 20, 1944): 21. Access provided by David Dickson.

Lademan, Capt. J., U.S. Navy (Ret.). "USS Gold Star—Flagship of the Guam Navy." *United States Naval Institute Proceedings* (December 1973): 68–79.

"Lots of Trouble." *Time* magazine (June 26, 1939).

"The Massacre at Samoa." *New York Times* (April 13, 1899).

Meyer, Dr. Milton. "A World War II Vignette: The Darwin-Philippine Connection." *Bulletin of the American Historical Collection Foundation*, Vol. XXVI, No. 2, 103 (April–June 1998): 60–67.

Pettitt, Henry G. "They Were a Class Apart." *American Neptune*, Vol. XLVI, No. 4 (Fall 1986), 240–51.

Pratt, Fletcher. "One Destroyer." *Harper's Magazine* (January 1944).

Price, Mark J. "Abandon Ship: Akron man, 85, survived two naval disasters 48 hours apart in World War II." *Akron Beacon Journal* (February 26, 2007).

Roberts, Stephen S. "The Decline of the Overseas Station Fleets: The United States Asiatic Fleet and the Shanghai Crisis, 1932." *American Neptune*, Vol. XXXVIII, No. 3 (July 1977), 185–202.

Scheck, William. "Prelude to Pearl Harbor: The 60th Anniversary of the Sinking of the USS Panay." *Sea Classics*, Vol. 30, No. 4 (April 1997): 24.

Schenking, J. Charles. "The Imperial Japanese Navy and the Constructed Consciousness of a South Seas Destiny, 1972–1921." *Modern Asian Studies*, Vol. 33, Part 3 (July 1999): 769–96.

Sheldon, Charles D. "Japanese Aggression and the Emperor." *Modern Asian Studies*, Vol. 10, Part 1. Cambridge, England: University of Cambridge (February 1976).

"Smyrna and After, Part III" *The Naval Review*, Vol. XII, No. 1 (February 1924).

Tanaka Raizo, "The Struggle for Guadalcanal" *The Japanese Navy in World War II* (Annapolis: USNIP, 1969): 72–73.

Tolley, Rear Adm. Kemp, U.S. Navy (Ret.). "Divided We Fell." *United States Naval Institute Proceedings* (October 1966).

"Tommy Hart Speaks Out." *Time*magazine (October 12, 1942).

Tully, Anthony P. "Solving Some Mysteries of Leyte Gulf: Fate of the Chikuma and Chokai." *Warship International*Vol. XXXVII, No. 3 (2000): 248–58.

Unknown. "War Diary of HMAS Bendigo." Copy courtesy USS *Houston* Survivors Association via Matt Johnson.

"The Upper Yangtze Patrol." *The Naval Review*, Vol. XII, No. 4 (November 1924).

Weller, George. "Flight From Java." *Chicago Daily News* Foreign Service (March 14, 1942).

Online Sources

Kriser, L. "Clash of the Would Be Titans." www.geocities.com/cdferree/history/clash.htm.

"Taki" (Akira Takizawa). www.AxisHistoryForum. Accessed August 19, 2007.

Visser, Jan."The Modjokerto Mystery," Netherlands Navy at War. www.netherlandsnavy.nl/special_modjokerto.htm.

Yamakawa Shinsaku. "Save Your Life!" www.geocities.com/dutcheastindies/pecos.html. Accessed August 5, 2004.

Index